Ernst & Young's Personal Financial Planning Guide

Third Edition
Take Control of Your Future and
Unlock the Door to Financial Security

Ernst & Young's Personal Financial Planning Guide

Third Edition
Take Control of Your Future and Unlock the Door to Financial Security

Robert J. Garner

Robert B. Coplan

Martin Nissenbaum

Barbara J. Raasch

Charles L. Ratner

John Wiley & Sons, Inc.
New York • Chichester • Weinheim • Brisbane • Singapore • Toronto

In the preparation of this book, every effort has been made to offer the most current, correct, and clearly expressed information possible. Nonetheless, inadvertent errors can occur, and tax rules and regulations often change.

Further, the information in the text is intended to afford general guidelines on matters of interest to everyone. The application and impact of tax laws and financial matters can vary widely, however, from case to case, based on the specific or unique facts involved. Accordingly, the information in this book is not intended to serve as legal, accounting, or tax advice. Readers are encouraged to consult with professional advisors for advice concerning specific matters before making any decision, and the authors and publishers disclaim any responsibility for positions taken by taxpayers in their individual cases or for any misunderstanding on the part of readers.

Tables of the following: Comparing Three Portfolios—Investment Mix, Expected Return, Standard Deviation; Low-Medium-High Risk on Asset Allocation for Young, Midlife Individuals, Pre-Retired, and Retired Investors; Historical Average Returns; Value of $1 Invested in Various Assets; and Comparing Two Portfolios that appear in Chapter 4 of this book are © *Stocks, Bonds, Bills, and Inflation*™, Ibbotson Associates, Chicago (annually updates work by Roger G. Ibbotson and Rex A. Sinquefield). Used with permission. All rights reserved.

The text is printed on acid-free paper. ∞

Published by John Wiley & Sons, Inc.
Published simultaneously in Canada.

This publication is designed to provide accurate and authoritative information in regard to the subject matter covered. It is sold with the understanding that the publisher is not engaged in rendering professional services. If professional advice or other expert assistance is required, the services of a competent professional person should be sought.

Library of Congress Cataloging-in-Publication Data:
Ernst & Young's personal financial planning guide / Ernst & Young. —
   3rd ed.
      p.   cm.
    Includes index.
    ISBN 0-471-35232-2 (paper : alk. paper)
     1. Finance, Personal.   2. Investments.   I. Ernst & Young.
  II. Title: Ernst & Young's personal financial planning guide.
  III. Title: Personal financial planning guide.
  HG179.E73   1999
  332.024—dc21   99-23517

Printed in the United States of America

10 9 8 7 6 5 4 3 2 1

CONTENTS

■ v

ACKNOWLEDGMENTS

SPECIAL THANKS TO

Philip A. Laskawy, Chairman and C.E.O. of Ernst & Young LLP; Richard S. Bobrow, Senior Vice Chairman, Assurance & Advisory Business Services and Tax Practices; William J. Lipton, Vice Chairman, Tax Services; Beth A. Brooke, National Director, Tax Consulting Services; Deborah J. Kissire, National Director, Tax Sales, Marketing & Special Initiatives; David J. Kautter, National Director, Human Resources Services; Michael S. Kelly, National Director of Area Practices–Tax; William Arnone; Elda A. Di Re; David Gerson; Andrea S. Markezin; Marc J. Minker; Glenn Pape; Sylvia J. Pozarnsky; Bertram J. Schaeffer; Harvey B. Wishman.

OTHER ACKNOWLEDGMENTS

James Biles; Gary DuBoff; Diana Jenkins; Charles R. Kowal; Robert K. Samson; John R. Sanderson; Debra Englander and Janice Weisner of John Wiley & Sons, Inc.; and Jon H. Zonderman for his editorial assistance.

ABOUT THE AUTHORS

Robert J. Garner is the national director of Ernst & Young's Personal Financial Counseling practice. He served on the Executive Committee of the American Institute of Certified Public Accountants' Personal Financial Planning division and is a member of the Institute of Certified Financial Planners. Mr. Garner also serves as coeditor of the *Ernst & Young Financial Planning Reporter*. A frequent guest on television shows dealing with personal finance and taxation, Mr. Garner has appeared on CNN and has been quoted in *BusinessWeek, Newsday,* the *New York Times, Fortune,* Reuters, and several other regional and local media. He also serves on the editorial boards of *The Ernst & Young Tax Guide* and *The Ernst & Young Tax Saver's Guide* as well as the *Parent Care Advisor.* E-mail address: robert.garner@ey.com.

Robert B. Coplan is the national director of The Ernst & Young Center for Family Wealth Planning, which runs the Estate and Business Succession Planning section of Ernst & Young's Personal Financial Counseling practice. He has served as a branch chief in the Internal Revenue Service's Legislation and Regulations Division with responsibility for regulations in the areas of estate, gift, and trust taxation. Mr. Coplan lectures frequently on estate planning topics and has authored articles for *Estate Planning, Trusts & Estates, The Tax Advisor,* and other publications. He also serves as coeditor of the *Ernst & Young Financial Planning Reporter* and is a member of the American Bar Asscociation Tax Section's Estate and Gift Tax Committee, the D.C. Bar's Estate and Death-Related Taxes Committee, and the Washington, D.C., Estate Planning Council. E-mail address: robert.coplan@ey.com.

Martin Nissenbaum is Ernst & Young's national director of personal income tax planning. He is a member of the AICPA Committee on Taxation of Individuals. He is an attorney and CPA and holds an LL.M. in tax; he is a certified financial planner and holds the Personal Financial Specialist accreditation from the American Institute of Certified Public Accountants. Mr. Nissenbaum is a speaker on compensation and personal, financial, and tax planning to professional organizations, including the New York State Society of CPAs, the NYU Tax Society, and the Tax Executives Institute. He has been quoted in the *Wall Street Journal,* the *New York Times, Money* magazine, and many other publications, and has been named by *PRWeek* as one of the top quoted spokespeople in the business press. He is an author of *Ernst & Young's Retirement Planning Guide.* E-mail address: martin.nissenbaum@ey.com.

Barbara J. Raasch, formerly the national director of Investment Counseling at Ernst & Young's Personal Financial Counseling Practice, is now the partner in charge of Investment Advisory Services in Ernst & Young's New York office. She also serves as a national instructor for Ernst & Young in the area of investment counseling. Ms. Raasch, a Personal Financial

Specialist, is a member of the editorial board of *The Ernst & Young Tax Guide* and authored a weekly personal financial planning column for the Sunday *Dallas Times Herald*. She is a member of the American Institute of Certified Public Accountants, the Texas Society of CPAs, and the Institute of Certified Financial Planners. E-mail address: barbara.raasch@ey.com.

Charles L. Ratner is the national director of the Personal Insurance Counseling section of Ernst & Young's Personal Financial Counseling practice and a managing director of the Ernst & Young Center for Family Wealth Planning. Mr. Ratner has authored articles published by the American Bar Association, Commerce Clearing House, and Best's Review. He is contributing editor to *Ernst & Young's Financial Planning Reporter* and a contributing editor on the American Bar Association's Insurance Counselor Series. He has presented insurance topics to a wide range of audiences including the American Bar Association, the American Institute of Certified Public Accountants, and numerous estate planning councils and professional societies across the nation. He has been quoted on insurance in the *Wall Street Journal, BusinessWeek,* and other financial press. He is an author of *Ernst & Young's Retirement Planning Guide.* E-mail address: charles.ratner@ey.com.

INTRODUCTION

For most people financial planning is a challenge. Resources are limited and needs can seem endless. As with most challenges, achieving financial security is very much a matter of understanding information, organization, and developing a workable process.

At Ernst & Young, we approach financial planning as preparing for a series of life events. Rather than thinking about financial planning as a one-time activity, we think of financial planning as a series of steps you take at certain times in your life to make various life events more financially manageable.

WHY DO FINANCIAL PLANNING?

Many people struggle with a sense of vague anxiety about their personal financial circumstances. Life is always uncertain, and in many ways you can't control its hazards and opportunities. What you can do, however, is anticipate problems and take advantage of opportunities. You can save money and invest wisely. You can purchase appropriate insurance. You can plan to ensure your family's long-term well-being. Financial planning can help you strengthen your control over these situations.

Consider retirement planning. Like most people, you probably look forward to your retirement years. However, you may be unsure about how and when you'll accomplish that goal. How much money will you need each year? What happens if you outlive your resources? To what degree will Social Security supplement your own retirement savings? These are difficult questions. But, careful financial planning can help you size up your individual situation, calculate what you need for retirement, analyze sources of income and means of investment, and design a plan to meet your short- and long-term goals.

Divorce is another example. No one would deny that it's an emotional event of the most powerful sort; however, it's also a financial event. Many people acknowledge the financial issues, but few see financial planning as part of their response to an impending divorce. This is an uncomfortable time for confronting financial issues. Even so, that pre-divorce period is critical for starting financial planning. The financial picture is about to change, perhaps dramatically. Unfortunately, ignoring the situation can have far reaching, significant effects, while good financial planning can help secure the future.

In short, financial planning *gives you options for dealing with the future.* There are many ways to approach financial planning. Some people feel more comfortable receiving their information from books. Some like to navigate their own way using computer software programs. Others prefer watching financial planning videos, attending seminars, or seeking help from a personal financial planner. What matters most is that you do financial planning.

THE ERNST & YOUNG APPROACH: LIFE EVENT FINANCIAL PLANNING

Ernst & Young's Personal Financial Planning Guide is unique in two important respects. One is Ernst & Young's long-standing expertise in the field of financial planning. For many decades, our specialists have counseled a wide range of clients—from individuals and couples to small businesses to employee groups of some of the biggest corporations in America—about retirement, investments, insurance, estate taxes, and all other financial planning disciplines. This book reflects our collective knowledge and expertise.

The other unique aspect of *Ernst & Young's Personal Financial Planning Guide* is our emphasis on the relationship between life events and financial planning. Most books approach financial planning as one all-inclusive topic. This type of comprehensive planning is useful, but we believe it's only the starting point. Depending on your stage of life, you may find certain aspects of financial planning more applicable. If you're in your 20s, for instance, saving for a home may be more important to you than retirement planning. Similarly, if you have young children, you may be more concerned about education funding than about other issues. You should, of course, recognize the need to look—and *plan*—ahead for future events. But, a general—and potentially superficial—approach to financial planning may detract from zeroing in on what concerns you most right now.

For this reason, we at Ernst & Young have written this book to focus on the *events* that are significant at specific stages of your life. The advantage of this life-event approach is that you can pick and choose among the topics; discussions aren't grouped into a single, massive treatment. Among these events are:

- Dealing with your job
- Getting married
- Buying or selling a home
- Raising a family
- Starting a business
- Coping with divorce
- Funding your children's education
- Retiring

All of these events have tremendous personal financial significance. They can be stressful, even disruptive, if not approached with care and forethought. With careful planning, you can maintain control of these events. For this reason, *Ernst & Young's Personal Financial Planning Guide* recommends a targeted approach to financial planning, one in which you:

- Assess where you are in life
- Decide what events are likely to affect you
- Plan in ways that help you control your financial future
  (If your focus is on retirement, you should get a copy of *Ernst & Young's Retirement Planning Guide*.)

A Two-Part, Flexible Structure

To help you put this approach into action, we've created this unique book. The book is organized into two parts. In Part I you can learn about the fundamentals of financial planning. One or more chapters focus on each of the traditional financial planning disciplines: the planning process, investments, insurance, and estate planning. This overview gives you the basic information you need to understand what follows.

In Part II you can explore the financial aspects of major life events. What life events are affecting you now? What upcoming financial transitions will influence your decisions? What other issues should you take into account? This half of the book is essentially a financial planning resource "shelf": a broad selection of data, recommendations, tips, and resources from which you can choose those suited to your own individual circumstances. As your situation changes, you can read up on another life event and how it affects you financially. And, reading the whole book will give you an excellent overview of financial planning throughout the entire life cycle.

REVISIONS IN THIS EDITION

The Taxpayer Relief Act of 1997 became law in August 1997. As part of this Act, changes were made in the Tax Law that impact not only how you file your taxes but also how you conduct financial planning throughout your life. Significant revisions were made to the laws governing paying for college, the tax impact of selling a home, and Individual Retirement Accounts (IRAs).

Incorporated into this text are explanations of these new provisions and what you need to know in order to make sound financial decisions. Among the highlights of the Act:

- **Creation of New Education IRAs.** The Act permits taxpayers to contribute up to $500 per beneficiary into an "education IRA," which is created exclusively for the purpose of paying qualified higher education expenses. The education IRA is effective for taxable years beginning after December 31, 1997.
- **Deductible IRAs.** The Act increases the deductible IRA income phaseout limits gradually beginning in 1998. A spouse who is not covered by a retirement plan can make a deductible contribution even if the other spouse is a plan participant, at higher income levels.
- **Roth IRAs.** The Act creates a new IRA, called the Roth IRA, which provides for nondeductible contributions, but qualified distributions from a Roth IRA are not includible in income.
- **Long-Term Capital Gains.** The Act reduces the top tax rate on capital gains for individuals from 28% to 20% or 10% for taxpayers in the lowest tax bracket.
- **Treatment of Home Sales.** The Act also replaces the rollover and age 55 rules related to gains on the sale of a personal residence with a $500,000 exclusion for joint filers ($250,000 for single filers) and is effective generally

for sales after May 6, 1997, as long as you owned and lived in the house for two out of five years before the sale.

- **Child Credit.** The Act provides for a credit against tax of $500 for each child under the age of 17.
- **Education Credits.** The Act provides for two new tax credits—the "Hope Scholarship Credit" and the "Lifetime Learning Credit" for certain education expenses.

The IRS Restructuring and Reform Act of 1998 made a number of clarifications to the 1997 tax law. It also eliminated the required 18-month holding period for the maximum rate of 20% on long-term capital gains. This text incorporates those changes as well. The text also incorporates changes made by the Tax and Trade Relief Extension Act of 1998, which affect self-employed individuals and charitable donors.

REGAINING CONTROL, PROVIDING FOR THE FUTURE

Financial planning is, first and foremost, a way to build for a secure financial future and deal effectively with ongoing financial needs. It's not a cure-all. It's not a way to "get rich quick." Rather, it's a disciplined way of achieving control and providing for yourself and your family in an organized manner.

Our hope is that *Ernst & Young's Personal Financial Planning Guide* will serve you well in meeting your financial goals throughout *all* of your life's events.

PART I

THE FUNDAMENTALS OF FINANCIAL PLANNING

Taking Charge of the Financial Planning Process

If you're concerned with keeping control of your financial future, you have lots of company. Investments, inflation, taxes, and other money matters concern nearly everyone. Yet even if you recognize the importance of financial planning, you may have trouble taking action, sizing up your situation, and putting all the pieces of a plan together. You may find the planning process itself difficult. You may have trouble following the plan you've created. Or you may feel unsure even where to begin.

Ernst & Young's Personal Financial Planning Guide will help you take control of your finances, determine which financial goals best suit your purposes, and plan to meet those goals for your own well-being and your family's as well. If you're completely new to financial planning, we'll give you a method for getting started. If you have some ideas but no clear sense of how to coordinate them, we'll suggest ways to develop those ideas into a consistent, comprehensive financial plan. And even if you've already designed a plan, we'll explain how you can make it better.

In later chapters of the book we explain how to control your finances for specific purposes. First, however, you should take stock of your situation, determine your financial strengths and weaknesses, and start to decide what you want from financial planning. Chapter 1 is a starting point for everything else in this book—a sequence of steps for taking charge of the financial planning process.

These are the steps:

- *Step 1*: Determine where you are financially.
- *Step 2*: Set goals.
- *Step 3*: Develop a plan.
- *Step 4*: Keep simple records.
- *Step 5*: Make an informal budget.
- *Step 6*: Deal with shortfalls, credit, and debt.
- *Step 7*: Review your progress.

STEP 1 DETERMINE WHERE YOU ARE FINANCIALLY

Your current financial position is the starting point from which you should measure progress toward your financial goals. To understand your financial position, however, you need a practical means for taking stock of the situation. A standard device for this purpose is the *net worth worksheet*. This worksheet allows you to estimate your assets and liabilities as a first step to financial planning.

> **Net worth:** *what's left after you subtract your liabilities from your assets.*

Calculating Your Net Worth

Take a few moments to complete the net worth worksheet below. As you fill it in, make sure that you indicate your assets in terms of their current fair market value, not in terms of what you paid for them. For example, let's say that 5 years ago you bought some shares of stock for $1,000. That stock is now worth $2,000 (i.e., its current fair market value is $2,000). Put $2,000 rather than $1,000 on the worksheet. Similarly, you should assess the value of any real estate you own as accurately as possible. One way of doing so is to check with local realtors for the recent sale prices of properties similar to yours.

One final consideration before you fill in the worksheet: This is *not* a financial "report card." There are no right or wrong answers. Don't be judgmental of yourself as you assess your situation. What you discover as you calculate your net worth may or may not please you; you may come away from the exercise either reassured about your financial situation or concerned about it. *But only by assessing your financial picture in an open-minded fashion can you see where you stand and take control of the situation.*

Note: Be sure to list all assets at their current value without reducing them to reflect any indebtedness. For example, if your home is currently worth $100,000 and you have a $70,000 mortgage, list the house at $100,000 in the asset section; show the $70,000 mortgage in the liability section that follows.

YOUR NET WORTH AS OF _____

ASSETS

Cash equivalents

Checking accounts	$_____
Savings accounts	_____
Money market accounts	_____
Money market fund accounts	_____
Certificates of deposit	_____
U.S. Treasury bills	_____
Cash value of life insurance	_____
Total	$_____

Investments

Stocks	_____
Bonds	_____
Mutual fund investments	_____
Partnership interests	_____
Other investments	_____
Total	$_____

Retirement funds

Pension (present lump-sum value)	_____
IRAs and Keogh accounts	_____
Employee savings plans (e.g., 401(k), SEP, ESOP)	_____
Total	$_____

Personal assets

Principal residence	_____
Second residence	_____
Collectibles/art/antiques	_____
Automobiles	_____
Home furnishings	_____
Furs and jewelry	_____
Other assets	_____
Total	$_____
Total assets	$_____

LIABILITIES

Charge account balances	_____
Personal loans	_____
Student loans	_____
Auto loans	_____
401(k) loans	_____
Investment loans (margin, real estate, etc.)	_____
Home mortgages	_____
Home equity loans	_____
Alimony	_____
Child support	_____
Life insurance policy loans	_____
Projected income tax liability	_____
Other liabilities	_____
Total liabilities	$(_____)
Net worth	$_____

Later in the book we'll look at the various categories of assets; we'll separate them into long-, medium-, and short-term categories; and we'll consider which of these assets appreciate the most reliably. For now, let's focus solely on the issue of net worth.

The net worth worksheet has three possible outcomes:

- Assets equal liabilities
- Assets exceed liabilities
- Liabilities exceed assets

The hope, of course, is that your assets exceed your liabilities. This means that you have a net worth. If your assets equal your liabilities, or if your liabilities exceed your assets, your financial position is obviously weaker than it should be. Whatever the outcome, though, it's crucial for you to face it straight on. There's no advantage in denial. Refusing to acknowledge a less than ideal net worth will limit your ability to overcome the obstacles before you.

Analyzing Your Cash Flow

In addition to preparing a statement of assets and liabilities, you also need to look at your expenses and sources of income. This is your *cash flow analysis*. In financial planning, determining your cash flow is extremely important. There are four reasons why. Assessing your income and expenses will:

- Indicate your ability to save
- Let you size up your standard of living
- Indicate if you're living within or beyond your means
- Highlight problem areas

All of these issues affect your ability to do financial planning, but they're especially significant as you proceed to plan for retirement.

Here's an example of why cash flow is so important. Let's say that you're 45 years old. You intend to retire at age 60, and you feel you're ready to start planning for retirement. To start the planning process, however, you should ask yourself a series of questions that identify your options.

- What do I want my retirement to be like?
- What will my sources of income be during retirement?
- What standard of living would I like to enjoy at that time?
- Will I work?
- Do I intend to move, or will I stay in my current residence?
- How will I cover health care expenses?
- What kinds of insurance coverage should I maintain?

- What is my likely life expectancy, and will my resources suffice if I reach or exceed that expected age?

These are among the many questions that will determine how much retirement income you'll need and what assets you'll have to accumulate to provide that income. By implication, you need to look at how your *current* standard of living will influence your *future* standard of living.

One measure of your current standard of living—perhaps the most important measure, too—is the living expenses you now incur and your ability to pay for them. Performing a cash flow analysis will help you with this assessment. To do this cash flow analysis, you must set forth all the various expenditures you incur on a regular or erratic basis, compare those with your income, and by this means define your current standard of living.

In assessing your current expenses, here are three rules to follow:

- Set forth your expenses in categories.
- Be complete.
- Don't guess too low.

Many people approach this exercise simply by recording the numbers more or less off the top of their heads. However, you may prefer to proceed in a more systematic way. You may actually need to track the figures, either historically (perhaps for the past 6 months) or prospectively (perhaps for the next 3 months), to create a good, detailed record of what the expenses really are. Regardless of your method, you can use the following cash flow worksheet to help you organize your data.

CASH FLOW WORKSHEET

Income	Monthly	Annual
Salary		
Bonuses		
Self-employment income		
Dividends		
Capital gains		
Interest		
Net rents and royalties		
Social Security		
Pension distributions from trusts or partnerships		
Other income		
Total cash available		$

CASH FLOW WORKSHEET (continued)

Expenses	Monthly	Annual
Uses of cash		
Home mortgage (or apartment rent)	_____	
Utility payments	_____	
Gas/oil	_____	
Electricity	_____	
Water	_____	
Sewer	_____	
Home maintenance	_____	
Property taxes	_____	
Car payments	_____	
Car/commuting expenses	_____	
Maintenance and repairs	_____	
Gas	_____	
Commuting fees/tolls	_____	
Credit card/loan payments	_____	
Insurance premiums	_____	
Life	_____	
Health	_____	
Disability	_____	
Car	_____	
Home	_____	
Liability	_____	
Other	_____	
Income taxes	_____	
Employment taxes	_____	
Clothing	_____	
Child care	_____	
Food	_____	
Medical expenses	_____	
Education	_____	
Vacations	_____	
Entertainment	_____	
Alimony	_____	

CASH FLOW WORKSHEET *(continued)*

Expenses	Monthly	Annual
Charitable contributions		
Gifts		
Personal items		
Savings/investments		
Vacation fund		
Emergency fund		
Investment fund		
Other		
Other payments		
Total expenses		$(_____)
Net cash inflow/(outflow)		$_____

You may, of course, need to adapt this cash flow record to reflect your particular situation. The main goal here is to note everything that's a regular expense. In addition, however, you should note erratic expenses as well, such as capital expenditures or purely discretionary items such as gifts and vacations. These include spending for:

- A new car
- Other vehicles (boats, campers, etc.)
- Electronic equipment (computer, satellite dish, etc.)
- Home improvements
- A second home

You should factor in these expenses, too, as you analyze your income and expenditures.

In later chapters of the book we'll explore how to refine your understanding of your assets. For now, your main task is to gain a general sense of where your money comes from and where you're spending it.

STEP 2 | SET GOALS

Financial planning is by definition a prospective exercise. Since we can't foresee the future, we have to make certain assumptions about what may occur, then plan for contingencies. Here are some of the questions that influence these assumptions:

- How long will you continue to work?
- What will happen with your income—will it remain the same, rise, or fall?
- What will happen with tax rates?
- What investment rates can you reasonably expect?
- What about the rate of inflation?
- How much involvement do you wish to have in managing your investments?

Your answers to these questions will determine how you must respond to plan for your financial future. In later chapters of *Ernst & Young's Personal Financial Planning Guide*, we'll examine each of the issues implicit here, and we'll sort through your options for responding to them. Before we do so, however, we should deal with a more immediate, personal issue: What are your financial goals?

The Importance of Setting Goals

Many people find goal-setting a difficult exercise. Here's an exchange similar to what many financial planners have with some of their clients:

> *Financial Planner*: "What are your financial goals for the next 5 to 15 years?"
> *Client*: "Well—I don't really have any."
> *Financial Planner*: "Do you plan to retire?"
> *Client*: "Of course. I'm just not sure when."
> *Financial Planner*: "Do you intend to make any major purchases?"
> *Client*: "Probably."
> *Financial Planner*: "A new car? Maybe a second home?"
> At this point, the client may become more specific.
> *Client*: "Now that you mention it, I want to have a second home when I'm 55." And as the planner asks more questions, the client's financial goals begin to clarify. "My wife and I purchased a parcel of land in New Mexico, and we plan to build a house on the land and retire there."

Here are some goals typical of what people indicate to financial planners:

- "I'll need to fund my son's postgraduate education."
- "I want to become financially independent by the time I'm 55."
- "I'd like to buy a bass boat next year."
- "I love to travel, so I'd like to take a major trip each year once I've retired."
- "I'd like to quit my present employer and go into business on my own."

- "I want to have a large estate for my children."
- "I want to make significant gifts to charity."

This client's response—and any other response—implies a financial goal. And to meet any financial goal, you have to take action. First, however, you must take steps to determine what your own goals are and—just as important—what your priorities are in achieving them.

How to Identify Your Financial Goals

Most people never take time to identify their financial goals. They either just don't get sufficiently organized, or else they feel safe "winging it" and making financial decisions as each new situation arises. Yet a realistic framework is vital to the process of fulfilling your goals—not just the goals you're aware of, but also those you may not even have identified. To develop a framework of this sort, you should therefore try to define where you want to be, financially speaking, in the future. The worksheet on financial concerns that follows will help to clarify your thinking.

Let's look first at relatively general financial concerns. Given your present economic position, rank the items on the financial concerns chart at the bottom of this page in order of personal concern, with 1 = most important and 9 = least important.

By answering these questions, you have begun to get a sense of which financial goals are most important to you. Now let's take the goal-setting process a step further. Having clarified some general concerns, you should identify your specific financial objectives.

FINANCIAL CONCERNS

_____ To have adequate funds to cover both routine living expenses and foreseeable future needs, including education expenses for my children.

_____ To minimize income taxes.

_____ To be able to retire comfortably.

_____ To increase the assets going to my heirs by utilizing various estate planning techniques.

_____ To accumulate sufficient assets to enable me to increase my standard of living, acquire a business, purchase a vacation home, etc.

_____ To have sufficient funds and insurance coverage in the event of serious illness.

_____ To develop an investment program that will provide a hedge against inflation.

_____ To accumulate a sizable estate to pass on to my heirs.

_____ To enable my family to maintain their standard of living in the event of my death.

Using the worksheet on specific financial goals that follows, designate your most important financial objectives. Use 1 for the most important, 2 for the second in importance, and so forth, for each time frame indicated. An important consideration: The ranking for each objective will probably change from one time period to another as your lifestyle and stage of life continue to change.

SPECIFIC FINANCIAL GOALS

Goals	Short Term (0–1 yr.)	Medium Term (1–5 yrs.)	Long Term (5–10 yrs.)	Longest Term (>10 yrs.)
Education expenses				
Debt reduction				
Buy a house				
Make home improvements				
Buy a car				
Any other large purchases (e.g., boat, plane, art)				
Take a dream vacation				
Income tax minimization				
Change of employment				
Buy a vacation home				
Financial independence				
Adequate retirement income				
Have children				
Increase level of charitable giving				
Buy a retirement home				
Adequate disability income				
Provide for survivor in event of my death				
Be protected against inflation				
Take early retirement				
Start a business				
Fund a buy–sell agreement				
Other				
Other				
Other				

Comprehensive or Specific Planning?

At this point, you need to decide what you want from the financial planning process. Do you want a comprehensive view of your financial future? Or are you interested only in specific suggestions on specific financial issues? Either alternative is fine; the deciding issue is simply *what best suits your individual needs*. For example, you may be interested only in retirement planning, in assessing your insurance position, in planning to pay for your children's education, or in estate planning. If so, fine. Your strategies and planning should concentrate primarily on these issues. On the other hand, you may want a full financial "checkup" and a prescription that covers all aspects of your financial life. If so, that suggests a different kind of planning process—one that starts with a general assessment of your current position, then proceeds to a more detailed identification of your goals, which leads in turn to creating a comprehensive plan.

There are many ways to achieve both the specific and the more comprehensive kinds of financial planning. Either way, subsequent chapters of this book will be useful as you undertake the process.

The Advantages of Event-by-Event Planning

Precisely because individuals' needs differ so widely throughout the life cycle, *Ernst & Young's Personal Financial Planning Guide* takes a life event view of financial planning. The various financial planning issues tend to be lumped together in most comprehensive plans. You may, in fact, need to address many of these issues at once. (Someone in middle age may well be concerned with income tax issues *and* investment issues *and* insurance issues *and* college-funding issues *and* estate planning issues *and* retirement planning issues.) In any case, you can use this book to focus on the issues that, given your stage in life, are most important to you. In short, you should focus not so much on your *age* but, rather, on the *events* that have financial significance to your life.

Here are some of the life events likely to have a major impact on your finances:

- Getting married
- Raising a family
- Buying or selling a home
- Funding children's education
- Pursuing a career
- Starting a business

- Getting divorced
- Dealing with aging parents
- Retiring (You might want to review *Ernst & Young's Retirement Planning Guide,* which discusses this goal in much greater detail.)

Given the variety of issues involved in these different life events, you'll find a targeted approach to financial planning more useful than a scatter-shot approach. By using a specific, focused process, you can assess where you are in life, what the big events are in the near term, and what financial planning issues you can expect at the time of these events.

What each major life event requires you to do is size up its financial impact and then do what's possible to prepare for the consequences. When you start a family, for instance, your biggest concern is probably protecting your spouse and children financially and building in the appropriate safeguards. Regarding your career, the big concern is maximizing your earned income and your participation in retirement plans. With divorce, the big issue is lessening the emotional and financial devastation that can ensue. With retirement, the issues revolve around establishing stable sources of income and sensible estate planning.

The final stage of setting goals, then, is to prioritize the goals that you've identified. Obviously, the short-term goals may well require the most immediate attention. On the other hand, delaying action on long-term goals (such as retirement) may cause you significant problems down the line. And putting off certain goals is potentially catastrophic. (Neglecting to obtain adequate life insurance and disability insurance is a particularly hazardous temptation.) A list of personal financial goals might look something like this:

E
X
A
M
P
L
E

Short-Term Goals

- Pay off credit card and consumer debt
- Start savings plan
- Set aside cash for a contingency fund equaling 3 months' expenses
- Acquire additional term life insurance
- Acquire individual disability insurance

Medium-Term Goals

- Start college savings plan
- Diversify investment portfolio
- Convert term life insurance policy to cash-value policy
- Contribute maximum to 401(k) plan and IRA

Long-Term Goals

- Purchase retirement property
- Retire at age 62
- Maintain preretirement standard of living during retirement

STEP 3   DEVELOP A PLAN

You're now ready to take your goals and develop a plan for achieving them.

Primary Concerns

When developing a plan, keep three primary concerns in mind: *flexibility, liquidity,* and *minimization of taxes.*

Flexibility. It's important to remember that as you develop your plan, the decisions you make aren't carved in stone. Your personal and financial goals can (and often do) change; you need a plan that's flexible enough to change with your circumstances throughout the major and minor life events you experience.

For example, events such as births, deaths, illnesses, and marriage can affect your goals profoundly. Employment changes, inflation, unusually good or bad investment results, and inheritances will also affect your financial circumstances. For these reasons, you should avoid making plans that are rigid or unresponsive to change.

Liquidity. Similar to the need for flexibility (and closely related to it) is the need to provide for adequate liquidity. Liquidity is, of course, especially important so that you can deal with financial emergencies. Most financial advisors recommend that you have funds available that are equivalent to 3 to 6 months of your expenses. Appropriate locations for these funds are checking, savings, and money market accounts. Other advisors suggest having a standby line of credit to accomplish this same result. The important factor either way is to have sufficient reserves set aside so that you can deal with emergencies.

> **Liquidity:** *the characteristic of an asset that can be converted readily to cash without loss of principal.*

Minimization of Taxes. The third primary concern is minimizing taxes. Minimizing taxes must serve as a means to meet your objectives; it isn't an end in itself. (Or, as some advisors put it, Don't let the tax "tail" wag the financial "dog.") An effective plan will minimize both income taxes and estate taxes. (Tax strategies aren't noted separately throughout this book, but are interwoven through discussions of other financial planning topics.)

CREATING A PLAN

As for the plan itself, you can proceed in one of several different ways. One is to use a financial planning program on your computer. Software of this sort can streamline the process in the long run, although you'll have to invest some time initially to enter the relevant data. Another way to set up your plan is less high-tech but still reliable: Sketch it out on paper. The most important thing is to determine how to meet your goals, then follow through. A simple plan for the short-term goals mentioned above might look as shown below.

SHORT-TERM GOALS	
Goal	**Action Steps**
1. Pay off credit card debt	Postpone vacation
	Reduce entertainment expenses
	Delay purchase of new car
	Consolidate debt into home equity loan (interest is generally tax-deductible thereby usually making the debt cheaper)
2. Start savings plan	Fund with savings from goal 1
	Reduce discretionary spending
	Arrange for payroll deduction for savings
3. Start contingency fund	Obtain home equity loan fund from curtailed expenses equivalent to 6 months' expenses (ideally) or unsecured line of credit
4. Acquire $100,000 term insurance	Pay for in cash
5. Acquire supplemental disability insurance	Pay for in cash

You should also create a plan for your intermediate- and long-term goals. Here, again, try to stay flexible. If anything, the need for flexibility increases as your time horizon recedes; you'll have less control over distant events. Remember, too, that the most carefully constructed plan will be worthless unless you actually go ahead and implement it. Keep a record of each action step, including when and how it was accomplished. Be patient—implementing your plan can be a time-consuming process. Your personal situation will dictate whether you decide to proceed with or without professional help. Most people will benefit from assistance at some point, at least in implementing their plan. (See the final section of this chapter for guidelines and suggestions on choosing a financial planner.)

STEP 4   KEEP RECORDS SIMPLE

Keeping accurate, detailed records is important for two main reasons. First, keeping records in a regular, orderly fashion simplifies a task that most people dislike but that almost everyone must do: tracking expenses for tax purposes. If you categorize and note your living and business expenses on a regular basis, the burden of longer-term recordkeeping is easier and less frustrating.

Second, keeping good records has the obvious advantage of letting you know how, where, and how fast you're spending your money. You can track cash flow by category and note when you're spending too much or too little on a particular need. Accurate records allow you to notice "red flags" and alert you to pending financial problems.

Both of these aspects of recordkeeping dovetail conveniently with the process of keeping a budget; they provide a system not just for recording your expenditures and income but also for comparing expenditures against what you've actually budgeted. (We'll get to budgets in a moment.) Ideally, this comparison occurs on an ongoing basis, which allows you to make adjustments proactively rather than on an occasional, reactive basis.

Options for Keeping Records

Is there any best way to keep your financial records? Certainly, some ways are fancier or more elaborate than others, but the "best" way is simply the one that you yourself can maintain most consistently and accurately. The range of possible methods is enormous. The simplest method is to keep track of cash receipts, checkbook entries, and credit card statements. At the other extreme, you can use any of the current fairly sophisticated computer programs for personal financial management. The middle ground involves preparing an annual month-by-month budget (based on checks written and charges made), which you then compare to your actual income and expenditures.

None of these methods is difficult to maintain. The computer programs are the easiest to use in the long run, but they require a fair amount of attention to set up. The various manual methods require ongoing effort but are the quickest and simplest at the beginning. In all instances, the task is simplified by keeping track of your expenses through checks and credit cards. Frequent use of automated teller machines (ATMs) may be counterproductive in this situation; it's simply more difficult to recall what you spent in cash than it is to look at a checkbook record or an itemized credit card statement. (However, using credit cards for this purpose does *not* mean racking up big credit card balances. Instead, you should charge your expenditures but pay them off at the month's end, thus avoiding interest charges. Alternatively, you could use a charge card that requires you to pay off the charges each month, such as American Express.)

Using the Information

As noted earlier, one of the great benefits of keeping accurate records is that you can be more realistic about how you spend your money. It's harder to kid yourself about your spending habits when the evidence is right before you in black and white. To analyze what you're spending, you should accumulate your data, record them by whatever means you've chosen, then categorize your expenses. (The categories you've already used for your cash flow analysis are appropriate here, too.)

Something you should check at this point is whether your expenditures seem appropriate given your goals and overall financial situation. There are two ways to consider this issue.

Expenditures in Relation to Objective Norms. There are individual differences in how people spend their money; however, normal limits exist for each category of expense. Financial planners use certain objective norms to identify expenditures that may be problematic. These norms are generally expressed as ratios or percentages. If you found, for instance, that rent accounts for 55% of your overall expenditures, something is probably amiss. Similarly, entertainment costs that take up 25% of your budget could also signal a problem.

Expenditures in Relation to Your Goals and Values. Even if your spending patterns fall within normal limits, are you using your money in ways that seem right to *you*? Perhaps you feel that you're spending too much on vacations—even if the percentage of your income isn't out of line compared to what others spend. Perhaps postponing the purchase of a new car will allow you to save money you'll need for your children's education. Do you feel that you're spending too much money *in general*?

On the other hand, you may sense that you're overly stringent with your spending. One example is maintaining an older automobile whose frequent breakdowns inconvenience you or even put you in physical danger; buying a new, more reliable car may serve you well in this instance.

One way or the other, it's quite possible that you should pay more attention to what your hunches are telling you—either to curtail or to increase expenditures. The crux of the matter is that this is your money; you should feel comfortable with how you're using it.

STEP 5   MAKE AN INFORMAL BUDGET

By now you've assessed your financial situation. You've set some goals. You've started keeping detailed records to track your expenses. Now what?

The answer to that question depends largely on what your recordkeeping reveals. You may find yourself in a position where your expenditures clearly exceed your income. You can't realistically do any long-term financial planning until you get out of debt. In this situation, you may decide that more of your income should go toward debt liquidation until you've eliminated most or all of your outstanding debts.

On the other hand, you may find that your income exceeds your expenditures and that your expenditures themselves are within normal limits. In this case, it makes sense for you to invest the excess rather than just park your funds in a low-interest checking account. You can now proceed to start analyzing your risk tolerance and other aspects of the investment process. (We discuss investment planning in detail in upcoming chapters.)

Either way, the whole idea is to gain control over your finances. You want to know what you're spending and why you're spending it, and you want to maintain this knowledge on a continuous basis. The means to this end is making (and following) a budget—a step that goes to the heart of the financial planning process.

The Foundation to Your Budget

It's important to note, however, that several bedrock assumptions should underlie your budget. These assumptions are essentially the foundation that your budget is built upon, and most of them have to do with income:

- Is your job secure?
- Are your other sources of income secure?
- What degree of financial risk are you assuming?

If your job isn't secure, for instance, you may need to set aside more abundant savings and spend less, just in case you end up unemployed. This will give you some funds to tide you over until you find another job. Similarly, your tolerance to financial risk will influence how you budget funds for investments. However, it's important for you to assess these issues as carefully as possible. Wishful thinking has doomed more than a few budgets at the outset.

Setting Up and Following a Budget

Initially, your budget bears a close resemblance to the cash flow analysis you performed earlier. The difference is that the budget isn't a historical record of *what you've spent* but a benchmark for *what you plan to spend*. And in this sense, the budget is a changeable, relatively fluid document. Finding realistic guidelines may require several months' effort before you "get it right."

If you're just starting to keep a budget, you should work at it consistently and you should be conservative in the assumptions you make and in the actions you take. Don't assume more income or fewer expenses just because an optimistic scenario seems likely. Defer whatever gratification you can until you have your guidelines established and can predict accurately what you're bringing in and what you're spending. Don't make big financial commitments at first—these expenditures could be disastrous if your income doesn't reach certain levels. (Commitments of this sort include buying a home or making major investments.) Perhaps you should live more modestly at the beginning. As you establish yourself, however, you can take greater risks.

How should you implement your budget? Generally speaking, you should work from what you've already accomplished—your records of income and expenses—using the method you've already employed. We've already discussed both the high-tech computer method and the low-tech paper-and-pencil method. Both work well. What you must do either way is to use your budget as a way of shaping (and generally that means *limiting*) present and future expenditures. This means having the budget influence your decisions on an ongoing basis.

Using the computer method means inputting your expenditures frequently and in detail—perhaps even day by day—so that you can sense the drift of your overall or specific expenditures. Most financial planning software programs will generate reports about any expense criteria you select. Keeping tabs on your expenditures creates an awareness of how much money remains within a given budget category for that particular month.

The low-tech budget method is predictably more basic but can serve the same end. You post a copy of your budget somewhere you find convenient—next to your kitchen calendar, perhaps, or in your study. You then note your day-by-day expenditures on blank spaces provided next to each expense category. The figures you note serve to remind you of how much remains for each month's expenditures.

Either way, the keys to success for keeping close to budget are:

- Accuracy of recordkeeping
- Consistency of effort
- Discipline in curtailing expenditures

Even the best-designed budget is worthless if you ignore it.

STEP 6 DEAL WITH SHORTFALLS, CREDIT, AND DEBT

If you find that your expenditures exceed your income—or even if the situation seems headed in that direction—you must take immediate action. Otherwise, you're headed for trouble.

The Various Categories of Debt

It's important to look not only at the level of debt you have, but also at the *categories* of debt. Lumping all your debts into one category isn't a useful practice. For instance, lumping home mortgage debt with investment-related debt and personal debt doesn't give you an accurate picture. The interest on home mortgage debt is generally tax-deductible; the interest on investment debt may be partially or entirely tax-deductible; the interest on personal debt isn't tax-deductible at all (except for student loan interest, in certain circumstances). The overall implications are fairly straightforward: Home mortgage debt costs less than personal debt. So you should put your debt into those three categories:

- Home mortgage debt
- Investment debt
- Personal debt

If you have personal debt, you should determine why you have it and the degree to which it's necessary. An example: Let's say that you have a car loan following the purchase of a second car. What purpose does this car serve? If you've purchased the car because it's necessary for your work, the debt is probably appropriate. If, however, you've purchased the car simply on whim—and if your overall financial situation doesn't really have room for such a luxury—you should reconsider the wisdom of carrying that debt. It's also probably safe to say that student loans are generally worthwhile because education is a worthwhile "investment." It's also important to look at these aspects of debt:

- The level of debt
- The interest rate you're paying
- Whether you can liquidate it in the near future

Problematic Debt

Next we look at some of the most common sources of debt that cause frequent problems.

Credit Cards. Many people get into debt because they overuse their credit cards. Paying with plastic is so easy that one thing leads to another, and soon you've racked up a huge balance. Even with interest rates at "only" 13%, 14%, or 15%, you're paying exorbitantly for what you've purchased.

A habit of paying no more than the minimum monthly payment for your credit card debt compounds the problem. You may feel that you're digging your way out bit by bit, but you're mistaken. In fact, paying only the minimum monthly payment will leave you in debt seemingly forever.

Car Purchases. Like credit cards, car loans are easy to obtain but costly to pay off. Car loan rates may seem reasonable, yet the long-term costs can add up alarmingly. The low rates that many car dealers advertise—2%, even 0%—are often simply a ruse; dealers absorb the costs of offering low interest rates by raising sticker prices.

Impulsive or Compulsive Spending. Of course, one of the main reasons for high levels of debt is simply spending too much. We're all bombarded by incessant advertisements to buy this, that, and whatever. Small wonder that we often succumb to impulse. The sad truth remains: A series of relatively insignificant impulse purchases can add up to enough that you must forgo the funding of more critical financial objectives.

Compulsive spending is even more problematic—an emotional disorder akin to compulsive gambling that warrants professional help.

■ **Tip:** Have a problem with unmanageable debt or compulsive spending? Lots of people do—and many of them are people who may outwardly seem financially high and dry. An organization founded to help people with debt or spending problems is Debtors Anonymous. Modeled after the 12-step Alcoholics Anonymous program, Debtors Anonymous works with people from all backgrounds and socioeconomic levels. For information, check your local phone listings, or write to DA's national headquarters at Debtors Anonymous, P.O. Box 400, Grand Central Station, New York, NY 10163-0400. (www.debtorsanonymous.org) ■

"Keeping Up with the Joneses." Similarly, social pressures to maintain appearances can seem harmless in the short term yet do real damage to your financial health. Whether it's a question of redecorating an already attractive house, dressing in all the latest fashions, or generally living beyond your means, you may well have to resist the external pressures of consumer society to achieve your long-term financial goals.

Ignoring Your Own Financial Goals. And that brings us back to the central issue. What, exactly, are your financial goals? If you've defined them, focusing on them will make the task of avoiding and reducing debt much easier. If you have yet to define them, it's harder to see individual expenditures in the wider context. Ignoring your financial goals can easily result in accumulating unneeded debt.

How to Reduce Debt

Let's say you've concluded that you have too much debt, and you've resolved to reduce it. What are your options? Here are some suggestions.

Reduce Expenditures

This may seem self-evident, but many people avoid facing reality and refuse to cut their level of expenditures. Do you really need to maintain as high a standard of living as you currently have? Is it possible that some of your "needs" are really "wants" instead? Can you find places to trim expenditures even on items that are necessities? Would moving into less expensive housing, for example, ease the financial pressures in other areas of your life? Are there other changes that might cut costs as well or better? Typical categories that warrant scrutiny (or that can tolerate reductions in what you spend) are:

- Entertainment
- Travel
- Clothes
- Gifts
- New cars
- Home improvements

Curtailing credit card expenditures is especially important given the high cost of this kind of debt

Pay Off Credit Card Debt

The next step is to pay off your credit card debt. Eliminating this kind of debt does more than just take a heavy burden off your finances; it's actually equivalent to earning a significant investment return. For instance, if you pay off a credit card balance that racks up interest at a 15% rate, liquidating that debt is like earning 15% on an investment.

(Paying off that debt would, of course, be an important step to take before investing your money in ways that offer lower yields. If you invest money at 7% while paying 15% to service debt, you're still losing the 8% difference between your debt and the investment. Tolerating that level of loss doesn't make sense. Pay off the debt first.)

If you're able to pay off your credit card debt only over the long haul, consider doubling up payments to diminish the monthly service charges. The faster you pay off the debt, the lower your overall cost.

Consolidate or Transfer Debt

If you can't eliminate the debt altogether, you might consolidate your debts or transfer some or all of them to another creditor. This course of action won't eliminate debt, but it can make it cheaper. Here are some alternatives:

Find a cheaper credit card. Obtain credit with a company offering a lower-rate card, then pay off the expensive debt with the cheaper debt. For a current list of low-interest credit cards, contact Bankcard Holders of America, 560 Herndon Parkway, Suite 120, Herndon, VA 22070. This nonprofit organization charges a $4.00 fee for the information.

Obtain a home equity loan. This arrangement allows you to pay off the high-rate credit card debt, then service the lower-rate, tax-deductible loan at a considerable savings. One risk here: Home equity loans have specific, rigid contractual terms that, if violated, can put your home ownership in jeopardy.

Get help from a nonprofit agency. Many cities and some states have agencies that will help you analyze your debt problems, consolidate debt, and negotiate with creditors to arrange a repayment schedule.

Switch to Debit Cards

Since credit cards often lead to excessive and expensive debt, you might try debit cards as an alternative. Debit cards work much like an ATM card: Every debit you make is deducted from your checking account. The difference—and convenience—is that you can use a debit card not only at automated teller machines but at a growing variety of retailers.

The advantages are obvious. Although a debit card won't stop you from spending, it will certainly prevent you from spending money that isn't in your account. The awareness of your balance can serve as a restraint. Unfortunately, your own bank may not offer debit card services; you may need to switch banks to obtain one.

Use Savings to Pay Off Debt

You can also tap your savings to liquidate debt. The disadvantage of this course of action is obviously that it diminishes your savings; the advantage, however, is that you will get out from under the burden of long-term debt. Take care, of course, that using your savings doesn't leave you vulnerable to unanticipated expenses or a temporary loss of income.

Borrow from Your Family

Hitting up your relatives for a loan may sound simplistic, but it's worth considering. It's certainly a time-honored method for temporarily easing a debt crunch. Although not without risks—chiefly in the potential strain on relationships—this method can be an important alternative.

Borrowing from your family doesn't necessarily mean that you borrow interest-free. You might, for instance, offer to pay interest at a level that splits the difference between an interest-free loan and the loan you're trying to liquidate. (If you were paying off a credit card balance calculated at a 14% rate, the interest rate on the loan from your relative would be 7%.) This would offer advantages to all parties involved. You'd cut the cost of debt in half, and your relative would earn an interest rate considerably higher than that in most current liquid accounts. No matter what terms you arrange, however, you should put the agreement in writing and make sure that everyone understands the terms.

File for Bankruptcy. As a last resort, you can declare bankruptcy. *This is a major calculated gamble.* Bankruptcy is not to be taken lightly. You should seek legal and financial counseling before taking this step. On the one hand, declaring bankruptcy eliminates some of your current debts; on the other hand, bankruptcy inflicts 7 years of damage to your credit rating. It's important to note, as well, that *declaring bankruptcy absolves you only from certain debts*, among them:

• Credit card debt
• Medical bills

- Auto loans
- Utility bills
- Rent

It does not allow you to cancel other debts, including:

- Child support
- Alimony payments
- Student loans
- Taxes (some very old tax liabilities may be discharged)
- Court-ordered damages

If you're on the verge of bankruptcy, you can take a series of steps to protect yourself, to deal with your creditors, and to set forth a clear, rational plan for liquidating the debt.

The Income Side

On the other hand, perhaps the credit and debt problems you face aren't limited to spending too much; perhaps you're simply not earning what you need to maintain the standard of living you desire. Under these circumstances, what can you do to increase your income? Here are two possibilities that may make a difference in this regard.

First, if you're working 9 to 5, you might consider other employment in addition to your regular job—a temporary arrangement, perhaps, that will get you through your current hard times. Such an arrangement might allow you to pay off your debt, thus putting you in a more favorable position.

A second possibility is to lower your standard of living temporarily to finance the costs of reeducating yourself or your spouse. Perhaps further education will allow you to pursue a career conducive to the living standard you want. Education is expensive; however, it's one of the best investments that you can make—both financially and in many nonfinancial ways.

STEP 7 | REVIEW YOUR PROGRESS

How often you review your financial plan depends on how old you are, what kind of planning you've decided to do, and what life event you're planning for. In most cases, an annual review of your financial plan is adequate. If you've just begun the process, however, or if you have some significant financial problems, a more frequent review is probably appropriate. Many people find a monthly review helpful. When problems are severe, even a weekly review may be advisable. But in most cases, an annual update will serve your purposes.

Here are the general questions to ask:

- Have your financial goals stayed the same?
- Are you meeting your budget?
- Are you earning the investment rates of return you anticipated?
- To what degree is inflation affecting your finances?
- Has your tax situation changed?

By answering these questions, you can decide whether your financial assumptions have been correct and whether your overall situation has changed.

Do You Need a Financial Planner?

Although this book and other resources may serve you well in planning your financial future, no single source of printed information can answer all readers' questions. Even computer programs and other interactive media are subject to inherent constraints in providing data and advice. For this reason, you may end up choosing to consult a financial planner at some point for specific, personalized counsel on one or more aspects of your individual situation.

When, exactly, should you seek help from a financial planner? That question has no single answer. One determining factor is your level of income. If you're making $30,000 a year, for example, you probably won't need a financial planner under most circumstances. If, however, you've earned $30,000 a year and now find yourself on the verge of bankruptcy, you may well benefit from a professional planner's financial advice. (Unfortunately, one complicating factor is that a financial planner's fees may aggravate your money problems still further.) In addition to income level, though, the issues that prompt many people to seek help from a financial planner are issues of complexity. This is particularly true when you get into such areas as estate planning, tax planning, and retirement planning.

When to Seek Help

Next we outline the three main reasons for you to consult a financial planner.

Confirmation. Let's say that you're capable of setting your own financial course, and you do a good job of it. However, you want the sense of confirmation that a professional can provide. A financial planner can check your numbers, review your goals, suggest alternative courses for attaining them, and provide a "second opinion" on your plan's fundamental soundness.

More Detailed Guidance. On the other hand, perhaps you find financial planning difficult even when you have an overall sense of direction. You may feel intimidated by quantitative analyses or overwhelmed by the numerous investment options available. Despite having the books and software programs to help you do your own planning, you don't feel confident of how to proceed. Or else you've taken the initial steps for do-it-yourself planning, but you now need advice on investment strategies, sophisticated insurance planning, or estate planning. Here, too, a financial planner can provide more detailed guidance.

Financial Planning from the Ground Up. Finally, you may feel sufficiently overwhelmed by the tasks of good financial planning that you decide to seek professional help for comprehensive advice. In such cases you clearly need a financial planner from the start. One caveat, however: *Seeking help on these issues, even on a broad basis, doesn't absolve you from having to make decisions*. It's your money; it's your future. Just as expert legal or medical advice doesn't eliminate the need for you to choose a course of action, expert financial advice leaves you with the fundamental responsibility to chart your course.

If one of these reasons matches your situation, you should consider the possibility of consulting a financial planner. In all three situations, a financial planner can offer some or all of the following kinds of help:

- Identifying problems and goals
- Identifying strategies for reaching your goals
- Setting priorities
- Providing advice on tax issues
- Saving you time on research
- Purchasing commission-free financial products
- Providing objectivity
- Helping you with specific finance-related tasks

Options for Financial Planning

There are two main categories of financial planners: commission-based and fee-based. (A third category of planners—those who charge you both a fee and some commission as well—are somewhat less common than the other two.)

Commission-Based Planner. Commission-based planners provide financial advice; then, in the late stages of the planning process, they sell you products to meet the needs you've identified—needs for insurance, investment products, and so forth. You pay for these services through commissions on whatever products you purchase. The chief advantage of this arrangement is that it provides one-stop shopping. The chief disadvantage is that basing the planner's fee on commissions may prompt questions about his or her objectivity and independence. In some instances, you may have to look elsewhere to obtain products unavailable through the commission-based planner. You can find commission-based financial planners at brokerage houses, insurance companies, and financial planning boutiques.

Fee-Based Planner. By contrast, fee-based financial planners provide advice but not the actual products themselves. The arrangement is strictly fee for service. There are no commissions. The advantage of this arrangement is a more predictable degree of objectivity and independence, since the fee-based planners have no vested interest in one product over another. The disadvantage is that you pay the fee outright, regardless of whether you act on the advice or not; the cost of any commissions on investments, insurance, and so forth, is in addition to the advisory fee. The biggest players of this sort are accounting firms, accompanied by some fee-only boutique planning firms.

Sizing Up Financial Planners

How do you know if the financial planner you've selected is qualified and responsive to your individual needs? Unfortunately, it's sometimes hard to know in advance; choosing carefully in the first place is your best safeguard. One way to hedge your bets is to start by considering planners who are accredited by one or more of the standard professional organizations. The most common credentials are described below.

Personal Financial Specialist (PFS). These planners are CPAs who have taken the additional steps of preparing for and passing a rigorous, comprehensive financial planning exam administered by the American Institute of Certified Public Accountants. They must also receive recommendations from their clients and from other financial advisors, and have a minimum of 3 years' financial planning experience, including a minimum of 500 hours per year in financial planning.

Certified Financial Planner (CFP). Planners with the CFP credential may have taken courses and have passed six exams administered by the Institute of Certified Financial Planners. They have at least 3 years of work experience, and have a continuing education requirement each year.

Chartered Financial Consultant (ChFC). The ChFC credential results from a 10-course sequence during a 2- to 4-year period of study; 2-hour exams are required at the conclusion of each course.

Masters of Science in Financial Services (MSFS). The MSFS credential follows 40 hours of coursework and a 2-week residency at the American College in Bryn Mawr, Pennsylvania (which also grants the Chartered Financial Consultant credential).

Registered Financial Planner (RFP). The International Association of Registered Financial Planners grants the RFP credential following completion of academic and practical requirements.

In addition to selecting someone with proper credentials, you should also consider the following aspects of financial planners' backgrounds.

Experience. How long has the planner worked for clients with your needs? Even the most heavily credentialed planner should have at least a few years' experience in the field pertinent to your questions. Some planners specialize. Is your planner's specialty in keeping with your needs? A specialist in investments may not serve you best if your concern is estate planning.

Access to Experts. In a complex and fast-changing field, no one can maintain complete knowledge of all aspects of personal finance. A planner should therefore be willing and able to consult with colleagues on matters affecting your financial future.

Fees and Commissions. As in other fields, fees for financial planning vary. You should clarify in advance what services you will receive and what fees or commissions will be charged. Consider the possibility of shopping around; although the time involved may seem burdensome at first, you may find considerable disparity among several planners.

Here are some situations that might warrant concern as you select and work with a financial planner:

- Does the financial plan you receive have a "canned" feel to it?
- Do all the planner's recommendations involve buying products that the planner's own company sponsors?
- Has the planner been in business for just a short while?

Finally, keep in mind that even if you end up hiring a helpful, thoughtful, experienced financial planner, the arrangement doesn't absolve you from responsibility. You still have to do your homework. You still end up making the ultimate decisions. The financial planner will offer recommendations and advice, not a free ride to painless or anxiety-free wealth.

BUILDING WEALTH TO MEET YOUR GOALS

Now that you've gained an overview of the financial planning process, let's turn to the first of its three main disciplines: building wealth. For no matter what your goals—funding your children's education, raising your standard of living, saving for retirement—building wealth is one of the fundamental ways that will help you reach your financial destination.

In this chapter and the four that follow we explain the many ways in which you can build wealth. Most of these chapters concern investment planning. Before we delve into the complexities of that subject, however, let's consider the importance of retirement plans and savings.

BUILDING WEALTH THROUGH RETIREMENT PLANS

One of the best ways to build wealth is by participating in retirement plans. These plans encourage you to save both because they provide a disciplined approach to saving and because they all provide tax advantages. Among the tax advantages: The contributions and investment returns are not taxed until they are distributed to you.

Company Plans

Most company retirement plans are *qualified plans*.

> **Qualified plan:** *a plan that meets certain requirements that enable it to offer tax advantages to both the company and the employees.*

The most common kinds of qualified plans are:

- Pension plans
- Profit-sharing plans
- Employee stock ownership plans (ESOPs)
- 401(k) and 403(b) plans

Pension Plans. Pension plans have been the most traditional form of corporate retirement plans: In recent years, however, some companies have been moving away from retirement planning arrangements of this type.

For the most part, employer pension plans (also called *defined benefit plans*) are a relatively painless way to build wealth for retirement. Under a pension plan, when you retire you receive a monthly pension benefit determined by the plan's formula. Pension plans provide the greatest benefit for you when you work for a particular company over the long haul—for 25 or 30 years, for example.

If you're working for a company that provides a pension benefit, you should consider the benefit that you will forgo before changing jobs. The salary and benefits you would accrue from a new job must be high enough to compensate you for the additional pension benefits you would earn if you stayed put.

Here's an example. Assume that you work 10 years at Company A, then switch to Company B and work there 10 years also. Assume as well that both companies have the same pension plan and that your salary is $30,000 and growing at 5% per year. Look at how large the difference in your annual retirement benefit could be if you stayed with Company A for 20 years compared to switching to Company B.

	YEARS WORKED	PENSION BENEFIT
Company A	10	$7,053
Company B	10	11,490
		$18,543
Company A	20	$22,980
Company B	0	0
		$22,980

The difference of $4,437 per year occurs because the benefit is computed according to your salary level prior to termination and your years of service with the employer.

Profit-Sharing Plans. Rather than providing a pension plan, some companies have adopted a profit-sharing plan (also called a *defined contribution plan*). Your company determines its total contribution. One variable here is how well your company does during a particular year. A rise or drop in profits can create a pro-portional increase or decrease in the amount contributed to the plan. Another variable is how well the investments of the plan perform. At retirement, you receive payments that are equal to your allocable share of the plan investments.

Employee Stock Ownership Plans (ESOPs). ESOPs also allow you to share in your company's success. An ESOP is a qualified plan that invests pri-marily in the securities of the employer. Contributions to the plan are not primarily dependent on the employer's profits. Like a profit-sharing plan, an ESOP provides a formula for allocating the contributions among the partici-pants. You have the potential of gaining from such an investment in your company if the company stock value increases over time. If the plan invests only in your own company's stock, however, changes in the value of that stock will affect your account value.

401(k) and 403(b) Plans. Increasingly popular during the past few years, 401(k) plans are tax-deferred retirement plans that provide unusual flexibility. These plans allow you to set aside a portion of your salary on a before-tax basis and then have these funds invested in the plan for your retirement; however, cer-tain restrictions apply to your before-tax contributions. (See *The Ernst & Young Tax Guide* and the *Ernst & Young Retirement Planning Guide*, both published by John Wiley & Sons, Inc., for more details.)

An added benefit is that your employer may match your contribution to some degree. In situations that include your employer's contribution, you have especially strong reasons to save for retirement by this means. Your employer's contribution is essentially a kind of raise—one you can't spend until retirement—but your only option for receiving it is by contributing to the plan. Then, when you retire, you receive the combined contributions, plus whatever the investment has earned.

Often, 401(k)s have specific advantageous features, including:

- *Loan provisions*
- *Flexible investment options*
- *Employer matching contributions*

E X A M P L E

■ Mary Lou needed to buy a new car. Instead of taking out a standard auto loan from a bank, however, she borrowed the money from her 401(k) plan. The rules stipulated that she take out a 5-year loan; the length of this term suited her purposes as well as meeting the requirements. Mary Lou then paid off the loan in monthly installments, just as she would have paid off a bank loan—except that she was essentially paying the interest to herself instead. ■

A 401(k) plan encourages you to save for three main reasons:

- Automatic payroll deductions make saving easy.
- Company contributions, if any, apply only if you contribute to the plan.
- Tax law and plan distribution provisions encourage you to keep your money invested.

A 403(b) plan is a type of retirement plan sponsored by certain religious, charitable, and public educational organizations. Like a 401(k) plan, it allows employees of these organizations to set aside part of their compensation and have the funds invested for their retirement.

If you're eligible to contribute to a 401(k) or 403(b) plan, doing so is a definite "must" because of their distinct tax advantages. The only common disadvantage is that the asset isn't easily available for you to spend until after your retirement. However, this may prove an advantage, since it encourages you to save for retirement. Normally 401(k) and 403(b) plans are considered very good savings options due to their ability to defer taxes on some of your salary and investment income.

Other Retirement Plans

In addition to the plans we've discussed, here are other kinds of retirement plans to consider:

- Individual Retirement Accounts
- Keoghs, SEPs, and SIMPLEs

Individual Retirement Accounts (IRAs)

IRAs allow you a maximum annual contribution of $2,000 as long as you have earned income or received alimony of up to that amount. Married couples in which one spouse does not have any earnings are permitted to make contributions of $4,000 per year, $2,000 allocated to each spouse's IRA. A single limit applies to all IRA contributions for the year. Your IRA investments then grow tax deferred until you withdraw the money. You can contribute to a regular IRA until the year you reach age 70½, at which age you must start taking money out of the IRA. Withdrawing the money before age 59½ generally results in a 10% penalty. There are a few exceptions to this rule. Two newer exceptions are withdrawals of $10,000 from any IRA account to pay for a first home purchase or unlimited amounts for higher education neither of which will be subject to the 10% penalty.

A new kind of IRA is also available—the Roth IRA. Contributions to a Roth IRA are nondeductible, but if you meet certain requirements the income you earn in the Roth IRA will be tax *free* when you withdraw it. You can contribute to a Roth IRA even if you're over 70½ and you can convert a regular IRA into a Roth IRA.

Deductible and Nondeductible IRAs. Since 1986, only people who aren't participating in a company retirement plan or whose adjusted gross income (AGI) falls below certain limits can deduct their contributions. (See the IRA deduction table below.)

If neither you nor your spouse participates in a company retirement plan you can make a deductible IRA contribution regardless of your income. If either of you is participating, you can make a deductible contribution based on your adjusted gross income as follows:

IRA DEDUCTIONS: ADJUSTED GROSS INCOME (IN $) ALLOWABLE DEDUCTION

Married Filing Jointly[a]	Single	Not an Active Participant	Active Participant
0–50,999	0–30,999	2,000	2,000
51,000–59,999	31,000–39,999	2,000	200–2,000[b]
60,000–60,999	40,000–40,999	2,000	200[c]
61,000 and over	41,000 and over	2,000	0

[a] A married couple filing separately is subject to a special limitation.
[b] The $2,000 amount is reduced by a percentage equal to your adjusted gross income in excess of the lower adjusted gross income limits divided by $10,000. For example, a single person with an adjusted gross income of $32,000 is allowed an IRA deduction of $1,800.
[c] The IRA deduction will not be reduced below $200 until it is reduced to $0 at $61,000 (married filing jointly) and $41,000 (single) of adjusted gross income.

The deductible IRA income limits will increase gradually through 2007. The following table illustrates the gradual increase in the limits:

GRADUAL INCREASE IN DEDUCTIBLE IRA INCOME LIMITS

Tax Years Beginning in	Limit Range for Joint Filers	Limit Range for Single Filers
2000	$52,000–$62,000	$32,000–$42,000
2001	$53,000–$63,000	$33,000–$43,000
2002	$54,000–$64,000	$34,000–$44,000
2003	$60,000–$70,000	$40,000–$50,000
2004	$65,000–$75,000	$45,000–$55,000
2005	$70,000–$80,000	$50,000–$60,000
2006	$75,000–$85,000	$50,000–$60,000
2007 and after	$80,000–$100,000	$50,000–$60,000

Even if your IRA contributions are nondeductible, contributing to an IRA account may make good sense. But if your IRA contribution is nondeductible it usually makes sense to make it a Roth IRA contribution.

You should start contributing to an IRA at as early an age as possible. This gives your IRA more time to build up tax-deferred income.

**E
X
A
M
P
L
E**

■ Compare the value of IRAs at age 65 under two scenarios: Suppose that Becky and Alida are the same age. Becky contributed $2,000 per year to her IRA starting at age 35. Alida also contributed $2,000 per year, but she started when she was 45. Both women earned 8% interest on their IRAs. At the time that they both turned 65, however, Becky's IRA was worth $244,692, while Alida's was valued at $98,846. ■

Setting up an IRA is simple if you follow these suggestions:

First, decide on the investment vehicle you prefer. There are rules regarding what you can and cannot invest in, but you have considerable leeway to choose from most of the available vehicles. (A sample exception: You can't invest in life insurance inside an IRA.)

Second, establish your IRA through a bank, insurance company, brokerage firm, or mutual fund company that offers numerous appropriate investment choices.

Third, make your IRA contribution as early as possible each year and no later than April 15 of the following year.

Spouse of Active Participant

A special rule applies if only one spouse is covered by an employer retirement plan. In that case the other spouse will be entitled to a deductible IRA even if their joint AGI exceeds the regular limits shown on page 43. This IRA deduction is phased out for the nonparticipant spouse between $150,000 and $160,000 of AGI.

Roth IRA

Similar to the nondeductible IRA, contributions to a Roth IRA are not tax deductible. In addition, the maximum annual contribution of $2,000 is reduced for singles whose adjusted gross income falls between $95,000 and $110,000 ($150,000 and $160,000 for couples filing jointly). However, the Roth IRA offers the potential for significant tax savings on investment earnings. As long as your Roth IRA has been open for 5 years, money withdrawn could completely escape income taxes provided you meet one of the following requirements:

1. You are age 59½ or older.
2. You are applying the distribution to the cost of a first-time home purchase (cannot exceed a lifetime cap of $10,000).
3. You are disabled.
4. You died and payment is made to your beneficiary.

Contributions can be made to both a Roth IRA and a regular IRA; however, the combined amount of the contributions cannot exceed the annual $2,000 contribution limit. Also, unlike the regular IRA, contributions may continue to be made to the Roth IRA after the individual reaches age 70½ and distributions from the Roth IRA are not required to begin at age 70½. If your adjusted gross income is $100,000 or less, you may roll over an existing IRA to a Roth IRA. If you decide to convert your IRA account, income taxes will be imposed on the amounts converted, but the 10% penalty tax will not apply. A conversion may make sense if you plan on leaving the money in a Roth IRA for a long period of time. Run the numbers before you decide to convert. Check out the conversion calculator at www.ey.com/pfc.

Keoghs, SEPs, and SIMPLEs

A Keogh plan is a retirement plan that is available to anyone who has self-employment income. This is generally income from any unincorporated business that you conduct.

A simplified employee pension (SEP) is a plan that allows an employer to make contributions toward an employee's retirement without becoming involved in more complex retirement plans. If you are self-employed, you can contribute to your own SEP. A SIMPLE is a simplified IRA or 401(k) established by your small employer which may allow higher contributions without complex discrimination tests; it is also available to the self employed.

Even if your employer makes contributions to a SEP or SIMPLE for your account, you can make contributions to your own IRA. The IRA deduction rules discussed previously apply to any amounts you contribute to your IRA.

For more information on these ways of saving for retirement see Chapters 24 and 25.

10 Big Mistakes in Investing—#1
Buying tax-favored investments (e.g., municipal bonds, Series EE bonds) inside tax-advantaged vehicles (i.e., IRAs, Keoghs)

For instance, on municipal bonds you pay no federal or state income tax if the bonds are issued by the state in which you live or by a municipality in that state. If, however, you put such a financial instrument into your tax-deferred retirement account, the income earned becomes taxable when you receive the money from the plan. In effect, you have converted a tax-free investment into a low earning, taxable one. Series EE U.S. Savings Bonds are taxed at the federal level, but generally only when you redeem them so there is no benefit from putting them into the plan. Also, the income is not subject to state income tax. Again, by putting them into a tax-deferred retirement account, you subject them to tax at the time you take disbursements from your fund.

Education IRAs

Education IRAs are savings accounts specially geared toward funding higher education expenses. People can make a nondeductible contribution of $500 per year per child into an education IRA up until the time the child reaches age 18. The $500 annual contribution limit is reduced for singles with income between $95,000 and $110,000 and for couples with joint income between $150,000 and $160,000. Multiple education IRAs may be created for one child, as long as the combined contributions in any one tax year do not exceed $500. (*Note:* No contribution may be made by any person to an education IRA during any year in which any contributions are made by anyone to a qualified state tuition program on behalf of the same beneficiary.)

The money you invest in an education IRA can be withdrawn tax free as long as it is used to pay for expenses such as tuition, fees, books, supplies, and equipment. Room and board is also eligible for students enrolled on at least a half-time basis. Any balance remaining in an education IRA at the time the beneficiary reaches age 30 will be subject to income taxes as well as a 10% penalty tax. However, the unused money can be transferred to another family member of the same generation for higher education funding use.

BUILDING WEALTH THROUGH SAVINGS

Saving money is one of those things that almost everyone considers a good idea but too few people actually do to a large enough degree. We all have our reasons: not enough income, too many bills, no time to check out the available savings plans. Unfortunately, the need to save will haunt you even if you stall for time. Unless you inherit a fortune, win the lottery, or simply earn so much money that you have all you'll ever need, you simply won't succeed at building wealth unless you save.

One rule of thumb is that you should save at least 10% of your annual gross income toward your retirement goal. If you're past 50 and still haven't started saving toward retirement, the figure for necessary savings will rise to 20%.

Most people find this "savings bite" painful. It *is* painful. Still, it's generally less painful than the alternatives, most of which involve eventually running short of the money you need in order to do important things—whether that means retiring comfortably, educating your kids, starting a business, or having a contingency fund sufficient to protect you during unemployment or other setbacks.

What compensates for the pain of saving is the payoff from *compounding*. This is a relatively straightforward mathematical process by which your money increases in value, slowly at first, then with much more dramatic speed. The following table illustrates the power of compounding for a saver depositing $300 a month.

COMPOUNDING TABLE FOR SAVER DEPOSITING $300 A MONTH

After-Tax Return	Year 5	Year 10	Year 15	Year 20	Year 25
4%	$19,890	$44,175	$ 73,827	$110,032	$154,239
5%	20,402	46,585	80,187	123,310	178,653
6%	20,931	49,164	87,246	138,612	207,898
7%	21,478	51,925	95,089	156,278	243,022
8%	22,043	54,884	103,811	176,706	285,308
9%	22,627	58,054	113,522	200,366	336,337

Saving well means saving regularly enough—and, ideally, *early* enough—so that your money has plenty of time to compound. For most people, this means having more than just the *desire* to save.

Setting Up a Savings Plan

The key to building wealth successfully through savings is to have a plan. There are many ways to accomplish this goal, but here's a method that many people find useful.

STEP 1

START AS SOON AS POSSIBLE

Don't wait until some ideal time to start your savings plan. No time will seem ideal; you'll always find excuses to delay another month. At some point you simply have to take the plunge. The earlier you start, the better "grip" you'll have on your finances.

STEP 2

FORECAST YOUR CASH FLOW

You should forecast your anticipated cash flow for various increments of the year. Usually, this means forecasting the year on a monthly basis. Once you determine your income and expenses, how much is left over?

STEP 3

PROJECT MONTHLY SAVINGS

Start with anticipated monthly savings; then project for the entire year. This may involve averaging. For instance, if you can save $330 in February and $270 in March, you might decide to save $300 a month.

STEP 4

PAY YOURSELF FIRST

What this means is that on receiving your monthly salary, the very first check you write is the $300 payment for your savings. Alternatively, you may be able to arrange for an automatic payroll deduction at your workplace, or arrange for automatic monthly or weekly transfers from your checking account to your investment account.

STEP 5

CONTRIBUTE MORE WHENEVER POSSIBLE

The $300 monthly savings amount shouldn't be where you stop; it's just the start. If, for instance, you receive bonuses as part of your compensation (or if you receive some sort of windfall, such as an inheritance), you should consider contributing part or all of it to your savings plan. The extra money may seem an opportunity to enhance your current lifestyle; on the other hand, it's also a great opportunity to enhance your future lifestyle.

STEP 6

REVIEW YOUR PLAN AT THE SAME TIME EACH YEAR

Consistent annual review is important to maintaining an effective savings plan. Any time you choose can serve the purpose; however, you might pick the time of year during which you find out what your annual raise will be.

Undertaking your review at that time will help you plan how to use your increased cash flow most productively.

Don't be surprised if you wind up unable to save the amount that your savings plan specifies. Most people's actual expenses exceed what they've anticipated—there are always unexpected costs!

Here are some do's and don'ts to help you save:

Don't *just sit down at the kitchen table with pen and paper and try to guess your expenses.* Pull out the check register from your checkbook and gather your credit card receipts for the last 12 months. Total your *actual* expenses. Study them. See what the patterns are. You'll probably find that your living expenses are a lot higher than you thought.

Do *write your check to your savings before you write any other check that month.* However, make sure to deposit that check in an investment that's liquid—just in case you need to pull some money back out by month's end.

Don't *get frustrated if your savings plan specifies $300 per month but you've only saved $100 monthly during the last 6 months.* You may need a year or so to determine how much you can really save each month.

Do *start now—even if you can only save $10.* Ten dollars per month growing at 8% per year equals $35,143 in 40 years.

Finding the Right Balance

A successful savings plan obviously depends on more than just setting up a plan. It's no secret that success over the long haul requires both the discipline to save and a positive view of saving. Discipline should be self-evident: The more consistently you save, the more reliably the money will add up. A positive view of saving means that you feel fundamentally right about setting aside money rather than spending it. However, part of the task of saving goes beyond either factor; it's a question of finding the right balance.

E X A M P L E

■ Samantha and Pete agreed that they ought to start a savings plan. They both felt committed to the task and aware that a degree of belt-tightening would result. After crunching the numbers, Samantha concluded that she and her husband should set aside $300 per month; Pete however, worried that the amount his wife advocated would end up feeling burdensome. He argued that a monthly contribution of $150 or $175 made more sense. The young couple discussed the issue for several months. Then, seeing their opportunity slip away, they decided to take a more flexible approach. They compromised and chose an initial savings payment of $250 per month. Saving $250 consistently made more sense than saving $300 sporadically. As it turned out, Pete and Samantha managed to reach their goal of saving $300 per month in less than a year's time. ■

You may find the startup phase of saving more difficult than later stages. Once you have a savings mechanism in place, however, it will force you to start looking at your expenses and seeing more clearly what's crucial and what isn't. You may find, too, that saving money is easier than you thought. Saving $300 a month may seem easy enough that $350 is an acceptable next step. Soon you'll be saving more than you thought possible.

Other Aspects of Saving

In addition to the steps discussed above, here are three other aspects of saving you may need to consider:

- Setting up a contingency fund
- Saving if you're self-employed
- Saving by paying extra principal on a mortgage

Contingency fund: a source of liquid assets (usually at least 3 to 6 months' expenses) intended to cover some or all of your expenses during a period of diminished cash flow, unemployment, or personal emergency. *Synonyms:* emergency reserve or rainy-day fund.

Setting Up a Contingency Fund

Everyone should have a contingency fund. Regardless of whether you're self-employed or on a payroll, you should have sufficient liquid assets available to meet your financial needs during an emergency or disruption of your income. The rule of thumb is that your contingency fund should equal at least 3 months of your expenses. The size of your contingency fund will depend on the nature of your work and the variability of your income. If you're self-employed, you may be more vulnerable to inconsistent cash flow. Even if you have a salaried position, however, the financial ground underfoot may be less solid than you imagine.

Some financial advisors recommend not only a liquid savings account but a second source of emergency funds as well. This source can take the form of credit cards or a line of credit. (Note, however, that you must arrange for a line of credit *before* a personal or professional emergency occurs, since most institutions are unlikely to extend credit if your situation has become precarious.)

> **Fixed expenses:** *personal or business expenses (generally paid monthly or annually) over which you have little or no control. Compare to variable expenses—those costs over which you have some degree of control.*

Saving If You're Self-Employed

If you're self-employed, you'll have fixed and variable expenses that affect your ability to save. Your savings plan under these circumstances will be somewhat more complex than for salaried employees. Everyone has certain expenses that must be covered before he or she can save. For the self-employed person, however, these are generally higher. For this reason, you'll have to do a lot more planning to see what income is coming in and what expenses you must pay. You should also consider accumulating a larger contingency fund than you'd have otherwise, since you have no employer whose benefits—sick days, leave of absence, etc.—serve as a safety net.

Self-employed persons should set up a business contingency fund as well as one for personal needs. The amount should typically equal 6 months of fixed business expenses. The precise amount will depend on the nature of your work and the variability of your income.

10 Big Mistakes in Investing—#2
Failing to maintain a sufficient contingency fund

You may be required to sell a long-term investment (a stock or stock mutual fund, for example) in a down market in order to raise cash.

Saving by Paying Extra Principal on a Mortgage

Some people feel that paying extra principal on their mortgage is a logical and convenient use of funds. However, choosing to make these payments is an investment decision that you should consider carefully.

Generally speaking, you probably don't want to start paying down your mortgage until you have a contingency fund set up, plus ideally some other investments as well. The reason is *liquidity*. During good economic times, paying extra principal may seem to make good sense; during an economic downturn, however, you could end up unemployed and thus need access to liquid assets. A shortage of assets that you can easily turn into cash at such a time could be disastrous. Whatever extra payments you've made on your mortgage contribute to your equity, but that equity isn't readily accessible. By paying down the mortgage quickly you're making a decision not to diversify your investment portfolio. For these reasons, extra payments of principal should generally fall low on a list of savings options. You should build other assets—assets that you can draw on and use to diversify your portfolio—before paying down the mortgage. (See the discussion of diversification in Chapter 4.) Also, remember that paying extra principal reduces the interest you will pay over time, which generally would be tax deductible. If you have a low-interest mortgage, and an opportunity to invest the extra principal payment in an investment with a higher return than the tax-effective rate of your mortgage interest, you should probably do that.

> **Liquidity:** *the characteristic of an asset that can be converted readily to cash without loss of principal.*

Savings Options

Now that you've decided to start saving money, where should you put it? There are all sorts of options—some of which we'll discuss now, some in forthcoming chapters. One consideration you should start to address, however, is tax benefits. Tax-deferred compounding can do wonders for your savings plan. (Note, however, that *for tax reasons, there are strong reasons **not** to withdraw funds from these plans too early*.)

Here are a few tax-advantaged savings vehicles:

401(k) Plans. If available through your employer, your 401(k) plan clearly represents your most attractive savings vehicle. The tax advantages and plan flexibility (such as multiple investment options and loan privileges) are unmatched by any other type of savings vehicle.

If your 401(k) plan includes an employer matching contribution, unless you have cash flow or liquidity problems, you should contribute at least the maximum amount that will be matched by your employer. For example, your company makes a contribution of $1 for every $2 of your salary that you contribute, with a maximum company contribution of 3% of your salary. In this case, you should contribute at least 6% and receive the matching contribution of 3%. The employer's matching contribution is the equivalent of an immediate 50% return on your investment!

Next, and again, unless you have cash flow problems, you should contribute at least the maximum amount that the law allows on a pretax or tax-deferred basis. (The law sets limits as to the total amount that can be contributed to a 401(k) plan.) You will have more dollars working for you than if you had chosen not to make the contribution. You might also consider maximizing your contribution to a Roth IRA if available and appropriate.

Finally, and again, absent cash flow problems, you should also make the maximum allowable after-tax contributions to the plan. After-tax contributions to a 401(k) plan are like nondeductible contributions to an IRA. In both cases, you do not get a deduction for the contributions. However, unlike nondeductible IRA contributions, your after-tax 401(k) contributions may be available to you currently (albeit with limitations) through the loan provisions of the plan. You can't borrow from an IRA.

IRAs. Before 1986, you could make tax-deductible contributions to an IRA even if you were a participant in an employer retirement plan and regardless of your income level. As discussed above, deductible IRA contributions are now limited if you are a participant in an employer plan and your income is above certain levels, although nondeductible contributions may be allowed.

Since 1986, many people have simply stopped making IRA contributions, knowing that their contributions would be nondeductible. Though there is no tax benefit on the contribution, nondeductible IRAs offer people a way to take advantage of tax-deferred or, with the Roth IRA and Education IRA, tax-free investment growth. Whether your goal is retirement, first home purchase, or higher education, consider making maximum annual contributions to an IRA.

Keoghs, SEPs, or SIMPLEs. As discussed above, these plans are available to you if you have any type of self-employment income. You may be surprised to learn the types of income that are considered self-employment income. For example, director's fees are self-employment income, as are executor fees if you are a professional executor. And commission income is self-employment income if you are not considered an employee.

Other Investments and Investment Vehicles. A 401(k) plan, an IRA, and a Keogh are all tax-advantaged retirement plans through which you can invest in a wide variety of investments. There are also certain investments which themselves offer tax advantages, including municipal bonds and tax-deferred annuities. Such investments may or may not be appropriate for you. We discuss municipal bonds in detail in Chapter 3 and annuities in Chapter 5.

In Chapter 4 we discuss the most fundamental investment decision that you must make—how much of your capital should you invest or allocate among the major investment categories such as cash, stocks, and bonds? This process is known as asset allocation.

INHERITANCE AND OTHER UNEXPECTED WINDFALLS

If you receive an inheritance, win the lottery, or gain some other windfall, you will obviously find that your financial options have expanded. You may feel that an unexpected gain should allow you some unexpected pleasures. But you could save the extra money. Consider investing the after-tax proceeds so that you can retire early and live better in the future. Alternatively, you could help out some of your family members or give something back to your community. If you make a donation to charity, you may not only contribute to a worthy cause but also benefit from a tax standpoint, given the possibility of a charitable deduction. The important thing is to consider your alternatives and plan carefully. It's nice to get a reward or windfall, but it's also useful to consider how the extra cash can pay off in the long run.

Regarding inheritance: To the degree possible, you should try to coordinate your estate plan with your parents' (or with anyone from whom you know you will be inheriting money). Many options exist that can save your family money and heartache as each generation considers what it will provide for the next generation. See Chapters 9 to 13 on estate planning to explore these issues in detail.

Finally, *remember that many windfalls—a gambling win or a contest (but not most inheritances)—are subject to income tax.* All too many people have delighted in their great good luck until they had to pay the tax bill. How much of this money is really yours, and how much belongs to Uncle Sam? This can be particularly difficult if what you've won isn't a liquid asset. The $30,000 car you've won at a local contest can become a heavy millstone indeed when you realize that you owe federal, state, and possibly local taxes. (See *The Ernst & Young Tax Guide*, published annually by John Wiley & Sons, Inc., under "Prizes and Awards" for more details.)

3

BUILDING WEALTH THROUGH INVESTMENT PLANNING

- ■ **Set Your Financial Goals**
- ■ **Understand Investment Vehicles**

Investments play a significant role in your ability to accumulate and pre-serve wealth. However, it's crucial to realize from the start that *no single investment is right for everyone*. You have unique financial needs, goals, and personal circumstances that determine which specific investments are appropriate for your individual situation. To accumulate wealth effectively, selecting appropriate investment vehicles is a must. Thus the most impor-tant financial planning question isn't, "What's the best investment?" but rather, "How do I determine which investments are best for *me*?"

Here's a six-step process to assist you in answering that question.

- *Step 1*: Set your financial goals.
- *Step 2*: Understand investment vehicles.
- *Step 3*: Understand financial markets and concepts.
- *Step 4*: Develop an investment strategy.
- *Step 5*: Implement your strategy.
- *Step 6*: Monitor your investments.

In this chapter and the next two, we'll walk through all six steps of the investment process. In this chapter we address Steps 1 and 2; in Chapter 4 we explain Steps 3 and 4; and in Chapter 5 we discuss Steps 5 and 6.

STEP 1 | SET YOUR FINANCIAL GOALS

The first step of the investment planning process is to determine where you're coming from, financially speaking, before you commit yourself to specific investments. This determination is necessary before you decide what investment choices suit your purposes.

10 Big Mistakes in Investing—#3
Jumping on the bandwagon
The investment that all your friends are excited about may not be right for *you*.

Your financial goals will determine what investments you should make. The more specific your financial goals, the more easily you can select investments that will help you meet those goals. Imagine, for instance, that you state one of your financial goals as follows: "I want to be able to retire some day." A more specific goal would be: "I want to retire at age 55 and be able to spend $50,000 in today's dollars annually for the rest of my life." From a financial planning standpoint, these two statements are worlds apart. Merely setting the goal of eventual retirement doesn't indicate what you need to do to achieve your goal. The second statement, however, lets you begin to project how much money you'll need for retiring in the manner you desire. From there you can determine the level of annual savings and the mix of investments that can help you accumulate funds for retirement.

Here are four factors that determine how you should set your financial goals:

- Your investment time horizon
- Your priorities
- Quantification
- Your personal investment profile

Your Investment Time Horizon

The length of time that you have to reach your goal is considered by many advisors as the most important factor in determining which type of investment is best suited to meet that goal. Investments that are appropriate for funding a long-term goal (e.g., retirement in 15 years) would generally not be appropriate for a shorter-term goal (e.g., saving money to buy a vacation home in 3 years). The reverse is true as well. We talk more about time horizon when we discuss the types of investments later.

Your Priorities

You must also prioritize your financial goals and decide which are necessary and which are merely desirable. Depending on the time frame, you may need to invest for your highest-priority goals first, then wait until you feel confident you'll attain them before investing to meet lower-priority goals.

Quantification

After determining your financial priorities, you should develop financial projections and calculate different alternative scenarios to quantify your goals. From these calculations, you can then establish the amount you can save and what rate of return is necessary from your investments to assure that you'll achieve your goals.

Quantifying your goals involves projecting income and expenses, for both the short and long terms. Using these projections, you can establish parameters for funding multiple goals; lacking these parameters, however, you simply won't have enough information to allow for informed decision-making.

What are your options for quantifying goals? The most common means are:

- Seeking assistance from financial advisors
- Using financial planning software

The first of these options is the more traditional; the second has become increasingly common in recent years. Whichever method you use, however, you must know where you stand and where you want to go in specific terms.

Your Personal Investment Profile

Your investment profile is the key to determining which types of investments are right for you. Your investment profile is shaped by:

- Your age and the stage in your career
- Your need for liquidity
- The size of your portfolio
- Your cash flow needs
- Your income tax bracket
- Your required rate of return
- Your risk tolerance

Your Age and the Stage in Your Career. Your age and the stage in your career are important elements in determining which investments are right for you. Generally, if you are young and in the early stages of your career, you have time on your side. You may be able to experience a loss and recover through years of additional savings. Your peak earnings lie years ahead of you. If you are older, investment loss can be devastating. You may be retiring in a couple of years and have little time to replace your losses with additional savings.

Remember, however, that the time horizon to the goal is the critical factor regardless of your age. If the time horizon to the goal is 3 years, the appropriate investment can be the same for the 30-year-old investor as for the 60-year-old investor, based on their risk tolerance.

E X A M P L E

■ Marilyn, Joshua, and Ted represent three generations in a family with a long history of personal investing. Marilyn is 26 and just a few years into her business career. She enjoys the challenges of investing and feels confident that time is on her side, so she tolerates investment risks that Joshua, her 53-year-old father, once took as well but now avoids. While Marilyn invests 10% in cash, 20% in bonds, and 70% in stocks, Joshua feels more comfortable with 10% in cash, 40% in bonds, and 50% in stocks, which provide a lower expected return but have lower risk as well. As for Ted—74 now and reliant on his investments for a significant portion of his income—he restructured his portfolio to 10% cash, 60% bonds, and 30% stocks before retiring. This asset allocation helps provide stable cash flow. ■

Your Need for Liquidity. As noted earlier, a liquid asset is one that can be converted to cash in a short period of time without loss of principal. You can tell whether an investment is liquid or not depending on how certain and how fast you'll get all your money back. (For example, money market funds are highly liquid.) You may require higher investment liquidity to cover large near-term expenditures (such as tuition for a son or daughter about to enter college) or to fund your contingency fund.

The Size of Your Portfolio. By the size of your portfolio, we mean the total value of your investments. The size of your portfolio is both an absolute and a relative number. Most of us would agree that a $400,000 portfolio is large in absolute terms. However, if you are retired, have no pension benefit, and require $40,000 a year to live in your current lifestyle, your $400,000 portfolio is small relative to your living expense requirements.

Your portfolio's size will dictate the manner in which to invest. For example, if you have $50,000 to invest in stocks, buying the stocks of only a few individual companies may not be appropriate. You simply cannot achieve sufficient market diversification. Mutual funds that invest in stocks would be a better investment choice.

The size of your portfolio will also indicate the types of investments to include in your portfolio. A large portfolio may give you the ability to purchase certain investments that, because of their risk, minimum purchase requirement, or liquidity characteristics, are inappropriate for a smaller portfolio. Investing 20% of your investments in illiquid assets such as real estate may be all right if you have a large portfolio to invest but may not be appropriate if you have only $50,000.

But, again, remember that everything is relative. The retired person discussed above who requires $40,000 a year to live probably cannot afford illiquidity despite his $400,000 portfolio. That's why it is important to sketch out your entire personal investment profile before you invest.

Your Cash Flow Needs. If you need to supplement your cash flow, investments providing current income (such as dividends or interest payments) may be preferable to those whose return comes largely from capital appreciation. Significant excess cash flow decreases the need for liquidity; shortages increase the need.

Cash flow may not be your primary concern right now, but you should always keep it in mind. When you restructure your portfolio just before retirement, for example, cash flow may be your main consideration as you will no longer receive a check to meet your expenses. Another consideration: If you have real estate in your portfolio, cash flow will be more important to you than to someone whose portfolio contains only stocks and bonds, since there's always the possibility of negative cash flow when you own real estate. (See Chapter 6 for discussions of real estate and investing for retirement.)

Your Income Tax Bracket. Your income tax bracket determines how much of your taxable investment income you can keep. Being in a high tax bracket may lead you to invest in more tax-favored investments; being in a low tax bracket allows you to realize a greater after-tax return from investments that are fully taxable.

Keeping taxes in mind when making your investments can really pay off. Assume, for instance, that you have $10,000 to invest and have two alternatives that differ only in their taxation:

1. 6% tax-exempt interest income
2. 7% taxable interest income

If your combined tax bracket (federal, state, and local) is 30%, your $10,000 investment would grow to $32,071 in 20 years with alternative 1, compared to $26,032 with alternative 2 (net of tax). This calculation assumes that your investment earnings are reinvested each year. You'd be over $6,000 better off by taking advantage of the tax-favored investment.

The table below shows the yield you would have to earn on a taxable bond in order to generate the same after-tax earnings that a tax-exempt bond would provide at a correspondingly lower yield.

Equivalent Yield Needed from a Taxable Bond

Tax-Exempt Yield	Your Combined Federal, State & Local Marginal Tax Bracket						
	28%	31%	33%	36%	39.6%	42%	46%
4.00	5.56	5.80	5.97	6.25	6.62	6.90	7.41
4.50	6.25	6.52	6.72	7.03	7.45	7.76	8.33
5.00	6.94	7.25	7.46	7.81	8.28	8.62	9.26
5.50	7.64	7.97	8.21	8.59	9.11	9.48	10.19
6.00	8.33	8.70	8.96	9.38	9.93	10.34	11.11
6.50	9.03	9.42	9.70	10.16	10.76	11.21	12.04
7.00	9.72	10.14	10.45	10.94	11.59	12.07	12.96

Your Required Rate of Return. This is the amount of total return you need from your investments to meet your financial goals. For example, you may determine that to retire as planned, you need an average annual return of 8% per year, assuming that inflation is 5% per year or less. This required return will help you determine the types of investments you need to meet your financial goals.

Your Risk Tolerance. This factor relates to the degree that risk influences your choice of investments. If you're like most investors, you're risk-averse: You don't want to take any more risk than is absolutely necessary. However, the phrase "No risk, no reward" applies here just as in other situations. The degree of risk you'll accept will affect your potential return. If you have a low risk tolerance, you may tend to avoid investments you perceive as risky; however, you'll pay a price in the return you will achieve.

Identify Your Investment Objectives

As you develop your investment profile, you should also identify your specific investment objectives. (*Note:* Investment objectives differ from financial goals.) Investment objectives relate to the attributes you decide you need in your investments. The following checklist on investment objectives will help you decide which are most important to you, and in what priority.

Investment Objectives. What are your investment objectives? Rank the following objectives numerically to find out.

- Liquidity (*instant cash with no loss of principal*)   _____
- Current income (*maximize income today*)   _____
- Future income (*maximize income in future periods*)   _____
- Inflation protection (*protection against loss of purchasing power*)   _____
- Capital growth (*real increase in value of assets*)   _____
- Safety of principal (*minimal risk of losing principal*)   _____
- Diversification (*minimize risk by investing in a variety of assets*)   _____
- Marketability (*convertible quickly to cash, but could have loss of principal*)   _____
- Ease of management (*relief from day-to-day decisions*)   _____

However, keep in mind that *no single investment can satisfy all these objectives*. While many investments can help you achieve one or more investment objectives, meeting all at once means investing in a variety of investment vehicles. Each investor's investment objectives are different. For this reason, you should select the mix of investments that's most appropriate for you.

STEP 2 UNDERSTAND INVESTMENT VEHICLES

The next step is to review and understand the major investment vehicles:

- Cash
- Bonds
- Stocks

In later chapters we also review other investment types, such as gold, real estate, and foreign securities.

Category 1: Cash Investments

You may think you know what cash is—that crinkly green stuff in your wallet—but in fact, *cash* refers to investments with a high level of liquidity and little or no risk to principal.

> **Principal:** the sum of money you invest.

In general, cash investments are short-term interest-bearing securities and deposit accounts that offer liquidity, safety of principal, and current interest. The cash investments that individual investors use most frequently include savings accounts, certificates of deposit (CDs), money market funds, and Series EE bonds. In addition, many employees elect to invest some of their 401(k) plan investments in the guaranteed investment contracts (GIC) option. This is also a cash type of investment.

The FDIC generally insures passbook accounts, money market deposit accounts, and CDs issued by member banks and savings and loans. There is federal deposit insurance for credit unions that differs slightly from that provided by the FDIC. You should inquire about this protection when you open an account at a new institution to confirm your balances will be covered. Because the maximum protection of $100,000 is determined by how the account is titled on the institution's records, you should also consider the name (or names) placed on new accounts to avoid losing deposit insurance protection.

The following is a rundown of frequently used cash investments:

- Passbook accounts
- Money market deposit accounts
- U.S. Government Series EE bonds
- Certificates of deposit (CDs)
- Money market mutual funds
- U.S. Treasury bills
- Guaranteed investment contracts (GICs)

Here are some of the kinds of cash investments you can obtain from specific sources:

Cash Investments Available Through Banks and Thrift Institutions

- Passbook accounts
- Money market deposit accounts
- Series EE bonds
- CDs

Cash Investments Available Through Brokerage Firms

- Brokered CDs
- Money market funds
- U.S. Treasury bills

Cash Investments Available Elsewhere

- Money market funds—from mutual fund companies
- Guaranteed investment contracts—through participation in many 401(k) plans

Now let's consider each of these cash investments.

Passbook Accounts. You can obtain passbook accounts through most banks, savings and loan institutions, and credit unions. Typically, they pay a relatively low rate of interest. Passbook accounts are liquid, but they generally do not include check-writing privileges.

Money Market Deposit Accounts. Generally paying a higher rate of interest than passbook accounts, money market deposit accounts typically require a minimum deposit, and they may charge fees if your balance falls below a minimum requirement. Money market deposit accounts, unlike money market mutual funds (discussed later), are federally insured. Because of their high degree of liquidity, however, money market deposit accounts generally return a yield somewhat lower than other less liquid, longer-term cash investments, such as certificates of deposit.

U.S. Government Series EE Bonds. Also referred to as savings bonds, these are cash investments that can provide relatively high interest rates and tax advantages. Series EE bonds:

- Are purchased at 50% of the face amount
- Range in face value from $50 to $10,000
- Are limited to $30,000 face value per year total purchase for any one person
- Increase in value, based on a floating interest rate equal to 85% of the average return on 5-year Treasury securities, if held for at least 5 years
- Cannot be redeemed any time before the first 6 months
- Do not require federal taxes to be paid on the accrued income until the bonds are redeemed, unless the owner elects otherwise
- May result in no tax on the interest income if the bond proceeds are used to pay qualified education expenses, provided that the taxpayer's adjusted gross income doesn't exceed certain levels

The interest on Series EE bonds—which is already exempt from state and local income taxes—may be exempt from federal income tax as well if you pay tuition at colleges, universities, and qualified technical schools during the year you redeem the bonds. The exemption applies not only to your children's education but also to your own higher education.

This educational benefit is straightforward, but there are restrictions. To qualify, the bonds:

- Must have been issued after December 31, 1989, to persons who are at least 24 years old
- Must be issued in either one or both parents' names (who are at least 24 years old) if the bonds are to benefit dependent children

- Must be redeemed in a year that the bond owner pays qualified educational expenses, which are tuition and fees, to an eligible educational institution

In addition, the bonds will be fully exempt from federal income tax only if your income is below certain limits, *and* the exemption applies only to the extent of the qualified amount of tuition and fees you've paid during the year. See Chapter 19 for more details.

For more information on Series EE bonds, contact: Office of Public Affairs, U.S. Savings Bonds Division, Washington, DC 20226 (www.publicdebt.treas.gov).

Certificates of Deposit (CDs). CDs are deposits made with a bank or savings and loan for a specified period of time, usually a minimum of 3 or 6 months. The institution generally pays a fixed rate of interest for the term of the certificate, with rates generally increasing with the amount and term of the deposit. You may also be able to purchase CDs with variable interest rates. Early withdrawal may result in a significant penalty.

Because they aren't as liquid as money market deposit accounts, new CDs should pay interest at a rate higher than money market accounts at the same institution. Shop around for the best rates—banks and other institutions aren't uniform in the rates they offer. Also, don't limit your search to these institutions alone. Most stock brokerage houses sell CDs issued by banks and savings and loans. Such CDs are also federally insured. Brokered CDs provide several additional advantages:

- A *secondary market*, which allows you to sell your CD before maturity without incurring any early withdrawal penalty.
- *Potentially higher interest rates* than are available at your local bank.
- *Geographic diversification.* Brokerage houses offer CDs issued by banks and thrifts located throughout the country; this provides you with another sort of diversification.

Money Market Mutual Funds. One of the most popular cash investments, money market mutual funds are funds that invest in U.S. Treasury bills, commercial paper, jumbo CDs, and other short-term interest-bearing securities. Securities held by money market funds normally have an average term to maturity of approximately 30 to 90 days. The interest earned on money market mutual funds is often higher than that earned on passbook savings accounts and money market deposit accounts.

Money market mutual funds don't have federal insurance protection; however, they lack the risk of uninsured bank accounts. One advantage of money market mutual funds is that you may be able to increase your after-tax rate of return for the cash portion of your portfolio by investing in tax-exempt money market mutual funds that invest only in short-term municipal securities. Both tax-exempt and taxable money market funds frequently offer services such as check-writing privileges and/or the ability to telephone-transfer funds from your money market mutual fund to another mutual fund in the same family of funds. Consider these conveniences when selecting your money market fund, as they can be more important than a slightly greater rate of return.

U.S. Treasury Bills. Investors who have large cash balances and who are interested in maximum safety and interest income that is free of state and local taxes should consider U.S. Treasury bills. U.S. Treasury bills are sold on a discount basis. The difference between the discount price and the maturity value is considered the interest income. U.S. Treasury bills are purchased through weekly Federal Reserve Board auctions in minimum denominations of $10,000. They have 3-, 6-, or 12-month stated maturities. U.S. Treasury bills are also traded on the secondary market. Interest on U.S. Treasury bills is taxable for federal income tax purposes at the time of sale or maturity, but interest is not taxed at the state level. Treasury securities can be purchased directly from the U.S. Treasury through the "Treasury Direct" Program. For information, go to www.publicdebt.treas.gov.

Guaranteed Investment Contracts (GICs). GICs are fixed-interest-bearing contracts typically issued by insurance companies and purchased by 401(k) plans. The interest rates paid on GICs often dramatically exceed those paid on other cash investments. They tend to have 3- to 5-year maturities, but the value of a GIC fund doesn't fluctuate with changes in interest rates. GICs are backed by the issuing company. That's not as safe as federal insurance protection; however, barring default, your principal will remain safe even when interest rates increase.

Commercial Paper. Commercial paper constitutes high-grade, unsecured notes issued by major corporations. Maturities range from 30 to 270 days. Commercial paper can be purchased through broker/dealers and commercial banks. Interest is fully taxable.

Comparison of Cash Investments

Investment	Possible Check Writing	Interest	Possible Tax Advantages	Liquidity
Passbook accounts	No	Low	No	High
Money market deposit accounts	Yes	Low	No	High
Series EE bonds	No	High	Yes	Low
Certificates of deposit	No	Medium	No	Low
Money market mutual funds	Yes	Medium	Yes	High
U.S. Treasury bills	No	Medium	Yes	Medium
Guaranteed investment contracts	No	High	NA	NA
Commercial paper	No	Medium	No	Medium

Category 2: Bonds

Bonds are debt instruments, typically issued by a government or a corporation. When you purchase a bond, you (the investor) are granting a loan to the issuer. You put up current cash in exchange for regular interest payments (except in the case of zero-coupon bonds) and the return of the principal at maturity. A *zero-coupon bond* doesn't have regular interest payments; instead, it's purchased at a discount and matures at a higher face value, similar to a U.S. Series EE bond.

Given these characteristics, bonds are typically appropriate in two situations:

- If you are seeking steady cash flow
- If you don't have an immediate need for the principal invested

Moreover, bonds can be used to diversify your portfolio and can be excellent vehicles for funding short- to intermediate-term goals, since you can match the bond's maturity to the date you need funds for the goal. An example: Your retirement is 5 years away. You want to purchase a second home at that time. Under these circumstances, a 5-year bond ensures that the principal amount will be available when you retire (assuming that the issuing institution does not default).

Generally speaking, the longer the maturity of a bond, the higher the interest rate. That's because enticing you to commit money for a longer period requires the issuers to pay a comparatively higher rate. Before selecting a bond, you should therefore consider whether the issuer is offering sufficient additional interest for the length of time you're investing your money.

Who has issued the bond is also important, since this will determine the extent to which the interest paid by the bond is taxable. For example, interest paid by state or local governments (i.e., for municipal bonds) is

BOND RATINGS

Moody's	Standard & Poor's	Meaning of Rating
Aaa	AAA	Best quality
Aa	AA	High quality
A	A	Upper-medium quality
Baa	BBB	Medium quality
Ba	BB	Below investment grade
B	B	Low grade
Caa	CCC	Very risky
Ca	CC	Highly speculative
C	C	Lowest grade
D	D	In default

exempt from federal taxes. Another factor: Different issuers may have higher or lower credit ratings, which means that the possibility of default varies from one issuer to the next.

Two organizations—Moody's and Standard & Poor's—rate the ability of issuers to repay principal and make interest payments, using bond ratings shown in the table below. These organizations employ financial analysts to review the issuers' creditworthiness at the time of the investment's initial sale as well as at periodic intervals. The rating assigned is an independent indication of the offering's investment quality: You should review it before you invest in bonds.

In addition to default risk, bonds are subject to possible loss of value if interest rates rise. As interest rates rise, the value of bonds falls: Conversely, if interest rates fall, the value of bonds rises. The closer the bond is to maturity, the less price fluctuation you can expect because (barring default) you will receive full face value at the date of maturity. Consequently the longer the bond's term to maturity, the greater the risk to its interest rate and the greater the risk of default.

> **Maturity:** *the date on which a loan or bond comes due and is to be paid off.*
> **Default risk:** *the possibility that a company or other bond issuer will fail to make payment on its debts.*
> **Interest rate risk:** *the risk that interest rates will rise, thus lowering the market value of bonds issued earlier.*

The bonds we'll consider are:

- Corporate bonds
- U.S. government securities
- Municipal bonds
- Mortgage-backed securities

Corporate Bonds. Corporate bonds can be issued in many different forms. They can be secured by assets, or they can be an unsecured promise to repay an amount borrowed. Debentures are unsecured promissory notes supported by the corporation's general creditworthiness. In the case of default or bankruptcy, this unsecured debt is redeemed only after the secured creditors' claims are satisfied. Debentures that are *subordinated* have more risk of default because they are paid off after regular unsecured debt.

 Q: What are junk bonds?

 A: Junk bonds are corporate bonds characterized by low quality ratings and consequently higher-than-average interest rates.

Typically, corporate bonds pay their holders interest semiannually. The interest earned on the bonds is subject to federal tax and to the investor's resident state and local income tax, if any. These bonds nearly always pay higher interest rates than government bonds, since there is a higher risk of default. The interest rates offered vary widely depending on the issuing corporation's financial strength. The weaker the company, the greater the risk and the higher the interest rate.

 Q: What's the best way to reduce the risk of the bonds I buy?

 A: Purchase high-quality bonds—A- to triple A–rated bonds—and make sure that they mature in no more than 5 years. Then your bonds are less likely to be subject to interest rate risk or default risk.

The term to maturity of the bond will also influence its interest rate. The longer the term, the greater the risk of default and interest rate risk. Consequently, longer-term bonds typically pay higher interest than do shorter-term bonds. This general rule does not apply in times where interest rates are expected to decline. The following table shows the effect of a one percentage point change in interest rates on the value of bonds with varying maturities and interest rates.

WHAT IF INTEREST RATES CHANGE BY 1%?

Current Interest Rate	Maturity: Bond's Percentage Price Change					
	3 months	1 yr	5 yr	10 yr	20 yr	30 yr
12%	0.25	1.0	3.7	5.7	7.5	8.1
11%	0.25	1.0	3.8	6.0	8.0	8.7
10%	0.25	1.0	3.9	6.2	8.6	9.5
9%	0.25	1.0	4.0	6.5	9.2	10.3
8%	0.25	1.0	4.1	6.8	9.9	11.3

Note: *The table estimates the percentage price change of a bond paying interest semiannually. It assumes that the bond's coupon is roughly the same as the current interest rate and that the bond is priced to maturity rather than to a call date.*

Keep in mind, too, that many corporate bonds have a call feature that enables the corporation to redeem them prior to maturity. You should consider this feature when selecting bonds to meet your desired average term to maturity. This call feature may cause the bond to be redeemed at an amount other than its par value on a date other than its date of maturity.

U.S. Government Securities. Federal government securities are similar to corporate securities in many respects. However, some important differences exist as well. U.S. government securities are generally considered the safest form of investing (from a standpoint of risk of nonpayment of principal or interest) because of the government's taxing authority. This safety means that the yields are lower than those of comparable-term corporate securities.

U.S. Treasury notes and Treasury bonds are government debts distinguished primarily by their terms to maturity. U.S. Treasury notes are intermediate-term obligations that mature in 2 to 10 years. You can purchase 2- and 3-year notes for a minimum of $5,000, while longer-term notes have a $1,000 minimum investment requirement. Treasury bonds are long-term debt maturing in 10 to 30 years. The minimum available investment in long-term Treasury bonds is $1,000. Interest on U.S. Treasury notes and bonds is paid semiannually and is subject to federal income taxation, but exempt from state and local tax.

Among the most popular forms of government securities are *inflation indexed securities, zero-coupon Treasury securities,* and *agency bonds.*

Inflation Indexed Securities. These U.S. Treasury bonds have semiannual interest payments that fluctuate based on the inflation-adjusted principal at the time of the payment. The principal is adjusted for inflation (based on the consumer price index for all urban consumers (CPI-U)), but the interest rate remains fixed. The interest rates on the inflation indexed bonds will be lower than those on comparable U.S. Treasury bonds.

At maturity, the securities are redeemed at the greater of their inflation-adjusted principal value or their par amount at original issue. These securities provide additional protection against loss of value in high-inflation times.

Zero-Coupon Treasury Securities. Zero-coupon Treasury securities are sold by the U.S. Treasury Department under its STRIPs program and by major brokerage houses under such names as CATs, LIONs, and TIGRs. The semiannual interest coupons are "stripped off." Consequently, these bonds do not pay interest currently; however, a lump-sum amount is paid at maturity equal to the bond's face value. These bonds are sold at a deep discount to face value. For example, you might pay only $5,000 for a bond that will pay you $10,000 in 10 years. The discounted purchase price makes up for the fact that the bond pays no current interest. However, since interest income is taxed as it accrues over the term of the bond, "zeros" produce taxable income without current cash payments of interest. The new "inflation-indexed" Treasury Securities have the same tax treatment. The principal increase due to inflation is subject to current taxation.

A new type of zero-coupon Treasury bond, known as the "I-Bond" is available as of September 1, 1998. I-Bonds are sold at face value and grow with inflation-indexed earnings for up to 30 years. You can invest from $50 to $30,000 a year. But like Series EE bonds, the interest is not taxable until you cash them in.

Agency Bonds. Similar to U.S. Treasury obligations, agency bonds are issued by government agencies other than the Treasury itself. They resemble Treasury bonds in having maturities ranging from short-term to long-term, paying interest subject to federal taxation semiannually, and having an active secondary market. Agency bonds often provide investors with slightly higher interest income than that of comparable U.S. Treasuries. For example, a 5-year note issued by the Federal Farm Credit Bank may pay 5.55% in interest, at the same time a 5-year U.S. Treasury note pays 5.4%. While the Federal Farm Credit Bank debt is not backed by the full faith and credit of the U.S. government (as U.S. Treasury obligations are), the federal government is unlikely to permit the Federal Farm Credit Bank to default on its debt in 5 years.

Municipal Bonds. State and local governments issue municipal bonds, usually to finance long-term projects. Municipal notes such as "tax anticipation" notes are for short-term needs. Similar to federal securities, municipal

10 Big Mistakes in Investing—#4
Misunderstanding the meaning of "high yield"
This doesn't mean more interest income without any additional risk. Usually, it applies to a junk bond or a mutual fund investing in lower quality bonds.

bonds are usually not secured by a tangible asset; rather, they are debts payable from the state or local government's general tax revenue. These bonds are known as "general obligation" bonds. In some instances, revenue from a specific source may be used for servicing the indebtedness. Such bonds are appropriately named "revenue" bonds.

Municipal obligations differ from federal government issues in that they are subject to the risk of default. Like corporate debt securities, municipal obligations are rated according to their creditworthiness. A triple-A rating indicates the lowest risk of default. The lower the risk of default, the lower the required interest rate.

Next we look at some other features of municipal bonds that influence their levels of risk and return.

Insurance Features. Some issues of municipal bonds are insured against failure to repay principal by an independent insurance company. Bonds with this insurance feature usually pay lower interest than do similar uninsured bonds because the insurance reduces their risk of default.

Pre-Refunding. Municipal bonds that are "pre-refunded" are also considered to be subject to low default risk. The reason is that the municipality issuing your municipal bond has purchased U.S. government securities with the same term to maturity as your bond. Held in a special account, these U.S. government bonds essentially provide collateral for the bond you hold, thus providing security against default.

Call Features. Many municipal bonds have call features enabling the municipality to redeem them prior to maturity. This may result in prepayment risk, since the issuer may return your principal to you when interest rates are lower.

Interest Rate Risk. All municipal obligations are subject to interest rate risk similar to that of other bonds. The longer the term to maturity, the higher the interest rate risk and consequently the higher the interest rate.

Municipal bonds and mutual funds that invest in municipal bonds traditionally have been an important part of the high-bracket taxpayers' investment portfolio. One of the main reasons is their tax-favored status. Here are some of the relevant issues:

Federal Income Tax Status. The semiannual interest payments of bonds issued by state and local governments are generally free from federal income tax. This provides a potentially greater after-tax rate of return than for comparable taxable investments.

Alternative Minimum Tax. The interest on some state and local "private activity" bonds is subject to the alternative minimum tax (AMT). Bonds issued for normal governmental purposes (running the government) remain tax-exempt for regular tax as well as for AMT purposes. If you aren't subject to the AMT, consider buying private activity municipal bonds that aren't AMT exempt, because they typically have a higher interest rate. (See both *The Ernst & Young Tax Guide* and *Tax Saver's Guide*, published annually by John Wiley & Sons, Inc., for more information on the AMT.)

Resident State Income Tax. The interest earned on municipal bonds and funds is frequently subject to the investor's resident state income tax. However, most states don't levy a tax on the interest income paid on their own governmental entities' issues.

Mortgage-Backed Securities. Mortgage-backed securities are debt issues secured by pools of home mortgages. Mortgage loans made by banks and savings and loan associations are "pooled" together; units in the pool are then sold to investors, who receive distributions (payments of interest and principal) as the loans are paid off. Mortgage-backed securities can be issued by federal as well as private institutions. "Pass-through" is the generic name given to any pool of mortgages that provides periodic payments of interest and principal to investors. It generally refers to mortgage pools established by the following agencies.

- *GNMA:* the Government National Mortgage Association ("Ginnie Mae")
- *FHLMC:* the Federal Home Loan Mortgage Corporation ("Freddie Mac")
- *FNMA:* the Federal National Mortgage Association ("Fannie Mae")

Two other mortgage-backed securities are *collateralized mortgage obligations* (CMOs) and *real estate mortgage investment conduits* (REMICs). Before investing in these securities, or mutual funds that invest in mortgage-backed securities, it is important to understand their risks as well as return potential. CMOs separate the mortgages held in the pool into different groups (called tranches) based on maturity dates. The tranche selected by the investor dictates whether the principal payments will be accelerated or postponed. (Sophisticated investment knowledge is required to understand the risk and return characteristics of the various tranches.)

Mortgage-backed securities are not without risk. Although the risk of default is minimal, the risk of prepayment (particularly in periods of falling mortgage rates) can be substantial. This causes larger amounts of principal to be returned to you when interest rates drop and lowers the expected return.

Category 3: Stocks

Stocks represent an ownership interest in a company. As an owner, you'll realize a positive return from the investment only to the extent that the company's earnings are more than sufficient to satisfy the claims of the company's creditors.

After a company has paid all of its bills each year (including any payments to bondholders), the remaining cash flow belongs to the shareholders. For this reason, a stock investment is considered a residual interest in the company. This residual interest may be paid to shareholders each year in the form of dividends, or it may be reinvested in the continuing operations of the company, thereby increasing the value of the stockholder's shares over time (resulting in growth and capital gains). Dividends generally are fully taxable when you, the shareholder, receive them: Capital gains are generally not taxed until the stock is sold. At that time, the gain may be taxed at favorable rates, depending on the tax law in effect at the time. The most common form of stock is *common stock*. However, preferred stocks offer investors another option that is typically less risky than common stocks.

Where can I find information about stocks?

Here are some good sources, in both print and electronic media:

In Print

Financial newspapers. The *Wall Street Journal, Barron's,* and *Investor's Business Daily,* in addition to the **stock listings in most daily newspapers.**

Company annual reports. Information about a company, usually including audited financial data.

Analysts' reports. Information about specific companies, often with recommendations to buy, hold, or sell specific stocks.

Moody's Investors Services. Specific publications include *Moody's Manuals* (compendiums of current and historical data on several thousand companies), *The Handbook of Common Stocks* (data on roughly 1,000 stocks), and *Annual Dividend Report* (a record of publicly traded companies' current dividend payments). Available from brokers or directly from Moody's, 99 Church Street, New York, NY 10007-2701. Phone: (800) 342-5647.

Standard & Poor's Corporation. Various publications, including S&P *Stock Reports* (current and historical analytical data pertaining to domestic stocks) and *Stock Guide* (a compendium of data on more than 5,000 stocks). Available from libraries, brokers, or directly from S&P, 65 Broadway, 8th floor, New York, NY 10006. Phone: (800) 221-5277.

Value Line Investment Survey. Information on approximately 1,700 stocks and closed-end funds, plus analysis and recommendations. Available from libraries or directly from Value Line Publishing, 220 E. 42nd Street, New York, NY 10011. Phone: (800) 633-2252.

Online Investment Information

America Online, Inc. Stock and mutual fund quotes and other current investment data. Produced by America Online, Inc., www.aol.com

CompuServe. Stock and mutual fund quotes and historical data. Produced by CompuServe, Inc., www.compuserve.com

Dow Jones Market Monitor. Market quotes, investment news, data bases, investment information security snapshots, and abstracts of analysts' research reports. Produced by Dow Jones & Co., Inc., www.dowjones.com

Microsoft Network. Stock quotes and investment news and information. Produced by Microsoft, www.msn.com

Prodigy. Stock quotes and investment news and information. Produced by Prodigy Information Services, www.prodigy.com

Reuters Money Network. CD, stock, mutual fund quotes, and investment news and information. Produced by Reuters Limited, www.reuters.com

Value Line. Current data on market prices. Produced by Value Line Publishing, www.valueline.com

Yahoo! Finance. Market quotes, investment news and research, analysts' research reports, company profiles, and historical data. Produced by Yahoo! Inc., www.quote.yahoo.com

---

Common Stocks. Common stocks can help accumulate wealth in two ways:

- They can provide income through dividends, which are distributions to shareholders of corporate earnings.
- They can appreciate in value, generally as a result of successful company operations or the prospect of successful future operations.

Keep in mind that the possibility of capital appreciation is mirrored by the possibility of a decline in the value of your investment. Risk varies from stock to stock and from industry to industry. See Chapter 4 for a discussion of these factors.

Publicly traded stocks (i.e., stocks listed on the NYSE, AMEX, and NASDAQ) are considered readily marketable investments because they can be converted into cash quickly. Since they are subject to potential loss of principal, however, they aren't considered liquid. Nonpublicly traded stocks are generally regarded as nonmarketable because they are difficult to sell and the selling price is uncertain.

> **NYSE** *(the New York Stock Exchange—known as "the Big Board"): the largest securities exchange in the United States.*
> **AMEX** *(the American Stock Exchange): the second-largest exchange, also located in New York City.*
> **NASDAQ** *(the National Association of Securities Dealers and Automated Quotations): an automated information network that provides brokers and dealers with price quotations on OTC (over-the-counter) stocks.*

Publicly traded common stock can be segregated into several broad categories based upon the type of return offered (i.e., dividends vs. capital appreciation), financial stability of the company, industry of the company, and susceptibility to changes in stock value resulting from changes in market and economic conditions. In some cases, a stock will fit into more than one category. The following categories are one way to segregate stocks:

- Income stocks
- Growth stocks
- Value stocks
- Cyclical stocks
- Defensive stocks
- Blue chip stocks

> **Market capitalization:** *the per share price of a company multiplied by the number of shares outstanding.*
> **Large capitalization stocks:** *the stock of companies with market capitalizations of more than $5 billion.*
> **Midcapitalization stocks:** *the stock of companies with market capitalizations between $1 billion and $5 billion.*
> **Small capitalization stocks:** *the stock of companies with market capitalizations of less than $1 billion.*

Let's consider briefly the characteristics of each category.

Income Stocks. Income stocks are those with a long and sustained record of paying high dividends. Generally, a company whose common stock falls into this category is in a fairly stable and mature industry (e.g., an electric utility company). These companies normally pay out a relatively high percentage of corporate earnings as dividends to common stockholders. Because these companies distribute (rather than reinvest) their earnings, their stocks are less likely to experience substantial capital appreciation. They are also more likely to be sensitive to interest rate fluctuations. Income stocks are particularly popular with people who need current cash flow from their stock investments.

Growth Stocks. Growth stocks are stocks that are expected to experience high rates of growth in operations and/or earnings. These growth rates are usually substantially higher than the market averages. To support their high growth rates, these companies generally reinvest their earnings instead of distributing them as dividends. Growth stocks are generally much riskier than income stocks. The price of growth stocks tends to rise faster than that of other stocks, and their total return tends to be greater than that of income stocks. On the other hand, growth stocks are also more likely to suffer a price decline in a bear market. Stocks of companies in new and rapidly expanding industries—computers, engineering, and other high-technology industries—are frequently considered growth stocks.

Growth stocks don't fit especially well with an investment strategy calling for high current cash flow from investments and a high degree of investment principal stability. If your objectives include holding investments for long-term capital appreciation, and if you're willing to assume the risk of a stock performing poorly, investing a portion of your available funds in growth stocks may be appropriate.

Value Stocks. These are stocks of companies which are considered undervalued because they may be in an industry that is out of favor, they may be experiencing management turmoil, or they may be restructuring their business operations. These stocks tend to have lower price/earnings and price to book ratios than growth stocks do. Therefore, their prices are cheap compared to the prices required to be paid for growth stocks.

Frequently a company's stock may be considered a value stock in one year and, following a fundamental change, may be considered a growth stock the next year. Studies have been performed to compare the returns of investors who purchase value stocks versus those who purchase growth stocks. While in certain years, growth stocks' returns dramatically exceed the returns of value stocks, over time the average annual return of value stocks has exceeded that of growth stocks.

Cyclical Stocks. Typically, cyclical stocks are stocks of companies whose earnings tend to follow the business cycle. Highly cyclical industries include oil and other natural resources, steel, and housing. Cyclical stocks are often more risky than stocks in companies less subject to changes in the business cycle. If you choose to invest in cyclical stocks, your objective is to purchase these stocks when you envision an economic upturn and sell them before an economic downturn.

Defensive Stocks. Defensive stocks are stocks that are, in a sense, counter-cyclical. Prices of these stocks tend to remain stable or perhaps rise during periods of economic downturn, while showing poorer results (in comparison to other stocks) during periods of economic upturn. Investors frequently use defensive stocks to balance their investment portfolio. Defensive stocks are well-established companies producing goods that are generally still in demand during an economic downturn, such as food, beverages, and pharmaceuticals.

10 Big Mistakes in Investing—#5
Refusing to let go
Some securities will never "come back." Even if they do, the rate of return you receive in the meantime may not rival what you would have gotten on an alternative investment.

Blue Chip Stocks. The stocks of the companies with the highest overall quality are those considered to be "blue chips." The companies with blue chip common stocks are financially stable companies with steady dividend-paying records during both good and bad years. They are usually the leaders within their industry or industry segment. Blue chip stocks include all of the Dow Jones 30 industrial companies, some utilities, and the stocks of other large and successful companies. Because of the blue chips' high level of quality and relative stability, many investors find them attractive long-term investments.

Preferred Stocks. Like the various kinds of common stock, preferred stocks also represent an ownership interest in a corporation. The reason preferred stocks are "preferred" is that the ownership of this type of stock allows the investor a right or preference not found in common stocks. Preferred stocks are in many ways a cross between common stocks and bonds. Preferred stocks represent an equity interest in a company, similar to common stocks, but they generally pay a fixed dividend, much as bonds pay interest. Prices of preferred stocks are particularly affected by interest rate changes.

The standard preferences inherent in preferred stocks include:

- *Dividend*: the right to be paid dividends before the common stockholders
- *Liquidation*: the right to receive the par value of the preferred stock on liquidation of the company prior to any distributions to common stockholders

Other features may include:

- *Voting*: the right to have more votes than those held by common stock-holders or to elect more directors
- *Convertibility*: the right to exchange preferred shares for a fixed number of common shares
- *Cumulation of dividends*: if preferred dividends are ever omitted, all prior and current preferred dividends must be paid before common shareholders can be paid dividends
- *Participation*: the right to receive more than the stated amount of dividends under certain circumstances

In addition, preferred stocks may be subject to a "call" feature. This allows a corporation to "call in" or redeem the preferred shares at a fixed price.

Preferred stock almost always has a dividend yield in excess of the company's common stock. The higher current yield is required because most preferred stocks, unlike common stocks, do not participate in the earnings growth of companies. Thus the price of preferred stocks tends to be more stable than the price of common stocks. However, since preferred stocks are generally considered less risky than common stocks, they have commensurately lower total return expectations (dividends plus capital appreciation) and do not serve as an inflation hedge as do common stocks, except in the case of convertibles. Convertible preferred stock can serve as an inflation hedge because the value of the preferred stock will increase once the value of the underlying common stock exceeds a certain level.

4

BUILDING WEALTH THROUGH INVESTMENT PLANNING

- ■ **Understand Financial Markets and Concepts**
- ■ **Develop an Investment Strategy**

In addition to investment vehicles, several other concepts are important to your overview of the investment planning process. Understanding these concepts is Step 3 of the investment planning process; developing a strategy is Step 4.

STEP 3 UNDERSTAND FINANCIAL MARKETS AND CONCEPTS

Before you match your investment profile and objectives to assets whose attributes suit your purposes, you'll need to understand certain financial concepts. The most important concepts for our purposes are:

- Concept 1: Investment return
- Concept 2: Investment risk
- Concept 3: Portfolio structure

Concept 1: Investment Return

The return on investments comes in the form of income, capital appreciation, or both. The *total return* on an investment refers to the sum of these components. For example, let's suppose that you purchase a common stock for $100. After one year it produces $5 of dividends. The income return on the investment is $5/$100, or 5%—the current *yield*. If at the end of the year, the stock is also now worth $107, it has appreciated by 7% ($7/$100); this is its *growth rate*. The sum of these figures—in this example, 12%—is the stock's *total return*.

Depending on the type of investment you own, however, some or all of this return may be subject to federal and/or state income taxes. The amount you keep after paying taxes is called the *after-tax return*. The tax rate is the combined federal and state tax percentage (stated as a decimal) that you pay on the return component on which you are focusing (i.e., interest, dividends, and capital gains). (*Note:* Your tax on long-term capital gains, which applies to assets held for more than one year, may be lower due to maximum federal tax rates ranging from 8% to 20%, depending on your regular tax bracket, applicable to such income. Also, the tax on the growth part of the return is deferred until the growth is recognized by selling the stock.)

Generating capital gains could be one of your big opportunities to save on taxes. With the new tax law changes, the tax benefit of long-term capital gains has again become substantial. The new law creates a 20% tax rate (10% for gains in the 15% bracket) on capital gains on investment assets held more than 12 months.

Additionally, the capital gains tax rate on the sale of assets held over 5 years and which are purchased after 2000 will be reduced to 18% (or 8% for gains in the lowest tax bracket regardless of when purchased).

If you incur losses from the sale of a capital asset, you can deduct those losses to the extent they equal capital gains from the sale of other assets. If your losses exceed your gains, you can only deduct $3,000 ($1,500 if you are married and filing separately) of capital losses in a tax year against other income on Form 1040. You can carry losses forward and continue to deduct $3,000 ($1,500 if filing separately) annually against other income until your losses are used up.

After-tax return is an effective way of comparing two investments that are taxed differently. Here's a quick way to calculate after-tax return:

after-tax return = taxable return × (1 − tax rate) + nontaxable income

Let's say that you're comparing a U.S. Treasury bond paying 7% to a municipal bond paying 5%. To make a realistic comparison, you need to look beyond the coupon rate to see which bond offers you the highest after-tax return. The U.S. Treasury bond's interest is taxable at the federal level but not at the state level, whereas the municipal bond is tax-free at the federal level but could be taxable at the state level. Which investment provides the higher return depends on your individual income tax bracket and the tax laws of your state.

E
X
A
M
P
L
E

■ Tom is considering two different options for his $10,000 contingency fund. The first option—a taxable money market fund—currently pays 5% interest. The second option—a tax-exempt money market fund—currently pays 4% interest. If Tom's federal income tax rate is 28% and if he lives in a state that does not impose tax on investment income, Tom should compare his two investment options as follows:

taxable money market fund return after-tax income =
$$5\% \times (1 - 28\%) = 3.6\%$$
tax-exempt money market fund return after-tax income = 4%

The after-tax return for the tax-exempt fund is higher, therefore a better choice for Tom. ■

For a comparison of equivalent yields needed from a taxable bond, see Chapter 3.

When calculating after-tax return, you should compare only bonds that are similar to each other in maturity and risk. You wouldn't compare a U.S. Treasury bond to a tax-exempt money market fund, for instance, because their maturities are different. Similarly, you can't compare an A-rated municipal bond to a U.S. Treasury bond; their default risks differ too substantially to allow the comparison.

Expected Return for the Future. Although it is relatively simple to calculate an investment's return over the *past* year, it's entirely different to try determining what an investment will return over the *next* year—or over the next 5 years or more. For most investments, the return in the previous year will be of little or no help in predicting the next year's return. Nevertheless, while past performance is no guarantee of future performance, longer-term historical data may at least provide an estimate (within an acceptable range) of an investment's (or portfolio's) future expected return.

10 Big Mistakes in Investing—#6
Focusing only on return
Here, as in so many other ways, there's no such thing as a free lunch.

Investment professionals sometimes estimate future return by using the average return an asset has produced over a 10-year, 20-year, or longer period. To determine an asset's average return we simply add the annual returns for each of the years we are reviewing and divide the result by the number of years. Based on history this return is what we expect to receive on average if we were to invest in that asset. The table below shows the historical average returns for various asset types from 1926, 1978, and 1988 (the longest period over which data are available) until the end of 1998. As a comparison we have included the average inflation rate over these periods as well. Subtracting the inflation rate produces the *real return* (which we discuss in a moment). We have used certain market indices as proxies for the historical performance of the asset type. For example, we have used the S&P 500 Index as a proxy for the historical performance of large capitalization domestic stocks.

HISTORICAL AVERAGE RETURNS

	1926–1998	1978–1998	1988–1998
Treasury Bills	3.76%	6.99%	5.45%
Long-Term Government Bonds	5.33%	10.27%	11.26%
S&P 500	11.22%	16.29%	17.81%
Small Stocks	12.41%	18.30%	11.51%
International Stocks	NA	14.36%	12.87%
Inflation	3.08%	4.82%	3.17%

You can see that an investment in Treasury bills produced an average annual return of 3.76% since 1926. Since the average rate of return is just that—*an average*—you wouldn't necessarily receive a return of 3.76% every year from Treasury bills. In some years you would receive a higher return, and in other years you would receive a lower return. The next table shows how much you would have accumulated (before taxes) at the end of 1998 if you had invested $1 (with earnings reinvested) in each asset type in 1926, in 1978, or in 1988.

VALUE OF $1 INVESTED IN VARIOUS ASSETS

	1926–1998	1978–1998	1988–1998
Treasury Bills	$14.94	$4.73	$1.99
Long-Term Government Bonds	$44.18	$9.47	$4.00
S&P 500	$2,351.04	$32.14	$8.42
Small Stocks	$5,117.12	$47.74	$4.12
International Stocks	NA	$21.91	$4.82

Because one of the primary goals of investing is to maintain the purchasing power of your capital, it's useful when estimating future returns to consider only the return in excess of inflation. This return is called the *real rate of return*. The third table shows the real rates of return for various asset classes over the same time periods as the two earlier tables.

REAL RATES OF RETURN			
	1926–1998	1978–1998	1988–1998
Treasury Bills	0.68%	2.07%	2.21%
Long-Term Government Bonds	2.18%	5.20%	7.84%
S&P 500	7.90%	10.94%	14.20%
Small Stocks	9.05%	12.86%	8.09%
International Stocks	NA	9.09%	9.38%

Concept 2: Investment Risk

Although return is an important aspect of determining whether an investment is appropriate, it's equally important to consider the risk associated with an investment. Each type of investment offers a different level or type of return; similarly, each investment has different associated risks.

When we say that an investment is risky, we generally mean that it may not return the average return that we expect each and every year. Although it may return more than we expect in some years, we are more concerned that it may return less than we expect in other years—and may even have a negative return (i.e., a loss of principal). A riskless security provides a rate of return that is predictable and has no chance of principal loss. Even if the total return were guaranteed, however, changing inflation rates would cause the real rate of return to vary, thus creating risk. Therefore a truly riskless investment, in addition to having a guaranteed rate of return, would need to exist in a state of unchanging financial conditions. Based on this definition, *there can be no truly riskless investment.*

Although we can't eliminate risk altogether, we *can* minimize risk by using an appropriate investment strategy. And minimizing risk means understanding it and knowing how to measure it.

Quantifying Risk. Generally, we measure risk by the *volatility* of total return. The most risky assets are the most volatile—those whose annual returns fluctuate the most from what we expect to receive on average. These fluctuations are measured statistically using *standard deviation of return.* Standard deviation describes how far from the expected return (in either direction) we must go to capture most of the *possible* returns that an investment might produce. One standard deviation in either direction of the average captures about two-thirds of all possible returns, with the remaining third split equally outside this range. Two standard deviations in either direction of the average captures about 95% of all possible returns.

> **Volatility:** *a state of being characterized by rapid change, in this case change of returns.*

The longer you hold any asset, the smaller its standard deviation. The implication is that returns become more predictable over longer periods of time. Thus, while the range of returns from the S&P 500 in any one year might be from 27.9% to 33% (one standard deviation), the range over 20 years is significantly smaller—from 6.34% to 15.26% (based on historical returns). This occurs because the greater-than-expected returns in "good" years counteract the worse-than-expected returns in "bad" years. An asset whose risk is unacceptable based on its one-year risk level may have acceptable risk if held 20 years. Therefore, your *investment horizon*—the length of time your funds will be invested—should play an important role in your choice of investments.

Types of Risk. Understanding investment risk allows you to select appropriate investments based on the amount and type of risk you're willing to tolerate. The degree of investment risk you'll accept is your *risk tolerance level*. Every investment is subject to some degree of risk. However, your risk tolerance level is an important aspect of identifying investments consistent with achieving your financial goals. The risk pyramid (shown below) is one way of illustrating the concept of risk.

Different kinds of investments are subject to different kinds of risk. The three major investment classes are cash, bonds, and stocks. The risks that typically affect each of them are:

Cash. The chief risk is *purchasing power risk*—the risk that the return on the investment or value of investment principal, as measured by purchasing power, will decrease due to inflation. Here's an example: If you invest in a cash investment that pays you 4% while the inflation rate is 3.75%, you'll actually lose purchasing power if your 4% income is subject to tax.

Bonds. Here you're betting on two outcomes:

- The interest rate will beat inflation.
- The interest will be paid *and* you'll get your money back.

Consequently, the relevant risks here are *interest rate risk* (i.e., will interest rates rise, thereby reducing your bonds' value?) and *default risk* (will the bonds' issuer *pay you back?*).

E X A M P L E

■ What happens if you take on a lot of risk and win or lose? Here are some typical outcomes:

Action	Risk	If you win	If you lose
You buy 30-year bonds	Interest rate	Capital gain	Capital loss
You buy junk bonds	Default	High interest	Loss of principal ■

THE RISK PYRAMID

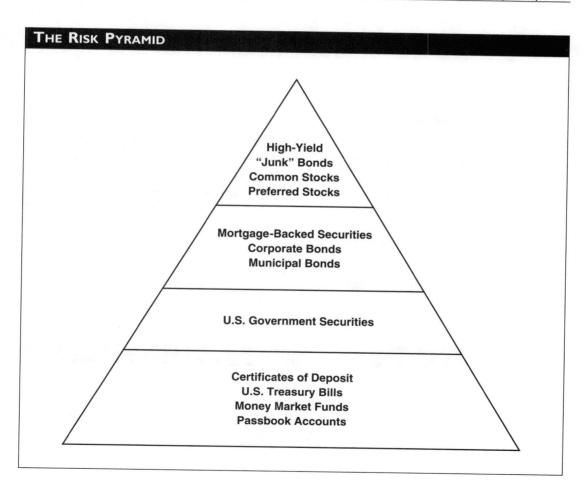

High-Yield "Junk" Bonds
Common Stocks
Preferred Stocks

Mortgage-Backed Securities
Corporate Bonds
Municipal Bonds

U.S. Government Securities

Certificates of Deposit
U.S. Treasury Bills
Money Market Funds
Passbook Accounts

Stocks. You're betting on the payoff—what the issuing company's perform-ance will be over time. The stock's price can be valued in today's dollars by what the market expects the company to pay each shareholder in the future. That value is based on the company's expected profits. If the profits turn out to be lower or higher than expected, you bought the stock for the wrong price.

In addition, the stock price may be affected by any economic considera-tion affecting the company, the industry, the region, or the entire stock mar-ket. This is referred to as *market risk*. Certain indicators can help you assess to what extent companies will be subject to market risk. One useful concept for this purpose is *beta*. Analysts determine a stock's beta by comparing the stock's historical price changes to that of the market. A stock's beta measures the volatility of its price changes in relation to the stock market's volatility, as represented by the Standard and Poor's 500 Stock Composite Index. A secu-rity possessing a beta of 1.0 experiences changes in returns that are approxi-mately equal in proportion and direction to that of the S&P 500. A beta below 1 indicates market risk less than that of the S&P 500, while a beta of greater than 1 indicates market risk above that of the S&P 500.

Concept 3: Portfolio Structure

We have all heard of the adage "don't put all of your eggs in one basket." What this means for asset allocation purposes is that portfolio risk can be reduced by adding asset classes that behave differently from one another. This is commonly known as diversifying your portfolio.

You can use your knowledge of investments and your understanding of risk and return to structure an investment portfolio. The table below com-pares three portfolios.

- Portfolio A contains only large capitalization U.S. common stocks.
- Portfolio B contains only U.S. Treasury bills.
- Portfolio C contains one-half large capitalization U.S. common stocks and one-half U.S. Treasury bills.

COMPARING THREE PORTFOLIOS			
	INVESTMENT MIX	EXPECTED RETURN	STANDARD DEVIATION
Portfolio A	100% U.S. Stocks	11.22%	20.26%
Portfolio B	100% Treasury Bills	3.77%	3.22%
Portfolio C	50% U.S. Stocks 50% Treasury Bills	7.95%	10.01%

As you might expect—given performance data since 1926—the portfolio containing one-half stock and one-half Treasury bills has an expected return approximately halfway between the two assets' individual expected returns. However, the risk, 10.64%, is lower than halfway between the two assets' individual standard deviations because of the diversification theory described above.

Diversification theory is based on the premise that market values of some assets tend to rise and fall together, whereas the market values of other assets move in opposite directions. Factors independent of the financial characteristics of a particular investment, such as economic, political, and social events, can affect its value. While portfolio risk cannot be totally eliminated, it can be reduced by constructing a diversified portfolio that contains a mix of asset types whose values have historically moved in opposite directions or in the same direction but to a greater or lesser magnitude.

If you're searching for a particular rate of return, you could combine various assets together to generate this expected return. Many portfolios might provide the same expected return (based on the assets' historical average return), but these portfolios would have different risks. If you're shrewd, you would therefore select the portfolio that meets your return goal but has the lowest possible risk. This is the objective of what is often called *asset allocation*. Asset allocation simply means investing in different types of assets so as to have a diversified portfolio with the highest expected return at a given level of risk. Computer software asset allocation models can help you identify the asset allocation with the highest expected return for a given level of risk.

The following table compares two portfolios with different asset mixes but with the same level of risk (standard deviation). Based on historical data, however, Portfolio B has a higher expected return than Portfolio A. Therefore, if you had a choice of Portfolio A or Portfolio B, you should choose Portfolio B.

COMPARING TWO PORTFOLIOS		
	PORTFOLIO A	PORTFOLIO B
Treasury Bills	5%	40%
U.S. Stocks	15%	19%
Long-Term Government Bonds	75%	31%
Small Stocks	5%	10%
Portfolio Expected Return	6.48%	6.73%
Portfolio Standard Deviation	8.42%	8.42%

The range of risks and returns achievable (based on historical risk and return relationships) are limited by the assets considered in making up the portfolio. Since different assets can have different risk and return characteristics, and since they can behave differently in different economic scenarios, portfolios with higher returns and identical risks may be possible by adding asset classes. For instance, adding international stocks to a portfolio comprised of only U.S. stocks and bonds will reduce risk and increase expected return. This happens because international stocks have historically behaved differently from domestic securities. The diversification effect of international stocks decreases a portfolio's risk (even though international stocks alone can be risky investments). (For a more detailed discussion of international investments, see Chapter 6.)

10 Big Mistakes in Investing—#7
Having too many eggs in one basket
It's important to diversify *among* different investment types (stocks, bonds, cash, international stocks, gold) as well as *within* those asset classes.

STEP 4 | # DEVELOP AN INVESTMENT STRATEGY

Once you understand the investment concepts we've discussed, Step 4 is to develop an investment strategy that meets your specific needs. Developing this strategy involves five tasks:

- *Task 1:* Select an asset allocation.
- *Task 2:* Formulate a goal-funding plan.
- *Task 3:* Consider all special opportunities.
- *Task 4:* Understand transaction costs.
- *Task 5:* Weigh the pros and cons of implementation alternatives.

Task 1: Select an Asset Allocation

What asset classes do you want in your portfolio, and in what combination? The asset classes should be as many as possible based on your investment profile. The proportion of your portfolio to allocate to each asset class is ideally determined based on historical data. One way to do this is to use computer software to select a portfolio that meets your target return goal while minimizing your risk. The tables on the following pages show sample asset allocations for young, midlife, pre-retired, and retired investors.

Task 2: Formulate a Goal-Funding Plan

Before you make actual investments, you must identify the specific goals that you want to fund. Then you can purchase the appropriate investments based on when the item being funded will be paid. Therefore, your first task in developing an investment strategy is to formulate a goal-funding plan.

Here are some typical investments suitable for three sample goals:

- *Contingency fund:* money market fund
- *College funding for a 16-year-old:* bonds maturing in 2-6 years
- *College funding for a 2-year-old:* common stock portfolio

Frequently—especially when you're just getting started—your desired long-term asset allocation, based on your risk tolerance and rate of return objectives, won't be possible if you first designate assets to fund your specific goals (e.g., contingency fund, children's college educations, etc.). When this occurs, you may want to focus on funding your short-term goals first; after you've funded those goals, invest in the assets needed to achieve your desired long-term allocation.

Task 3: Consider All Special Opportunities

Part of developing a strategy is to consider the pros and cons of all special opportunities that present themselves. What follows is a brief rundown of some of these opportunities.

Disciplined Savings Opportunities

- Payroll deductions, including deductions for:
  - Credit union
  - U.S. Series EE bonds
  - Employee stock purchase plan (discussed in Chapter 20)

- Automatic transfers from checking account to:
  - Other bank accounts
  - Mutual funds

Tax-Advantaged Vehicles (discussed in Chapter 2)

- 401(k)/403(b) plans
- IRAs
- Keoghs/SEPs
- SIMPLE

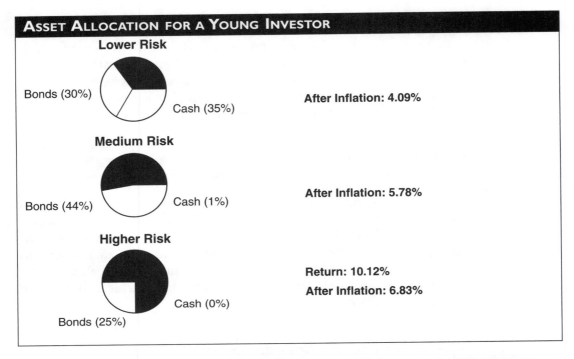

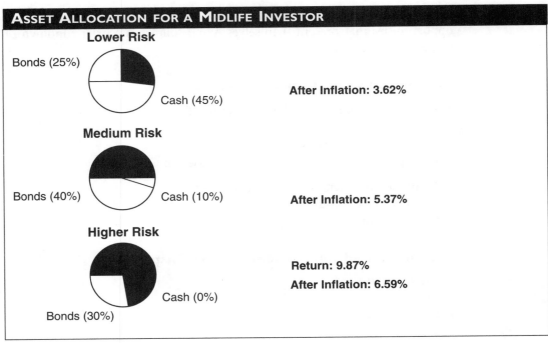

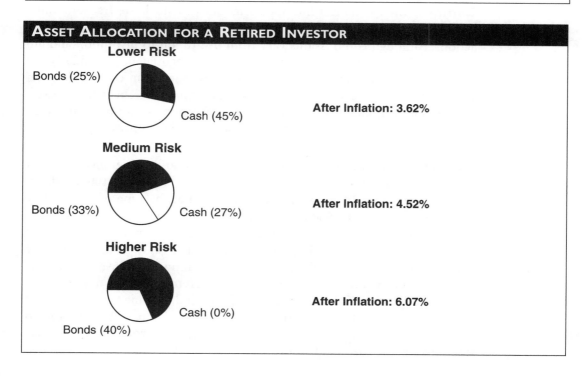

ASSET ALLOCATION FOR A PRE-RETIRED INVESTOR

Lower Risk

Bonds (21%)

Cash (54%)

After Inflation: 3.16%

Medium Risk

Bonds (36%)

Cash (19%)

After Inflation: 4.94%

Higher Risk

Cash (0%)

Bonds (35%)

Return: 9.6%

After Inflation: 6.33%

ASSET ALLOCATION FOR A RETIRED INVESTOR

Lower Risk

Bonds (25%)

Cash (45%)

After Inflation: 3.62%

Medium Risk

Bonds (33%)

Cash (27%)

After Inflation: 4.52%

Higher Risk

Cash (0%)

Bonds (40%)

After Inflation: 6.07%

Other Investment Incentives

- Waive service fees if account exceeds particular sums (checking accounts, mutual funds).
- Receive frequent flyer miles for investing in a particular mutual fund.

10 Big Mistakes in Investing—#8
Failing to implement your strategy in hard times
If your investment strategy calls for investing in a stock fund every month, do it even if you believe the stock market may decline next month.

Task 4: Understand Transaction Costs

You must also consider the transaction costs involved in investments. Generally, these costs are *commissions* and *income taxes.*

Commissions. Financial intermediaries such as stockbrokers, some mutual funds companies, and banks charge commissions to execute your transactions. Although commissions vary from institution to institution and are based on the type of transaction, they can be negotiated, particularly for large transactions. Commissions on purchases differ from commissions on sales, and the commission percentage will differ for different types of assets as well as for transactions of different sizes. By shopping around, you will be able to compare rates and services that the institutions provide.

Income Taxes. The taxes on investments may also be a significant cost. If you buy a stock for $40 per share and sell it 2 years later for $100 per share, there will generally be a tax on the capital gain at the time of sale. In this case, the gain would be $60 per share, and the federal tax at 20% (the maximum federal capital gains rate on assets held over 12 months) will be $12 per share. Most states also impose a tax on capital gains. Thus, in this case you have at most 88% of the asset's value remaining to reinvest. The reinvestment choice must outperform your current stock by a significant amount to make up for the tax cost. Keep in mind, income taxes should *not* be the primary factor in making investment decisions: The decision to retain or sell a particular asset should rest largely on your personal situation, investment goals, and so forth.

Task 5: Weigh the Pros and Cons of Implementation Alternatives

Because you have several different alternatives for implementing your investment strategy, you should carefully weigh the pros and cons of each before proceeding. Perhaps the most significant aspect of your decision is determining what's important to *you* regarding implementation.

Here are some issues that you'll have to face in implementing your strategy. Each involves some trade-offs.

- *Time versus money.* Do you want to hire someone to look after your investments, or can you do it yourself?
- *Recordkeeping.* Do you want all your investment data on one statement, or are you comfortable with receiving lots of paper documentation? It's easy to underestimate the paperwork involved in tracking individual investments yourself.
- *Income tax planning.* Are you willing to complicate your life to save taxes? For example, an IRA would be yet another account you'd need to keep track of. Are the tax benefits worth the additional paperwork and annual service fees?

5

BUILDING WEALTH THROUGH INVESTMENT PLANNING

- **Implement Your Strategy**
- **Monitor Your Investments**

In Chapter 4 we explored Steps 3 and 4 of the investment planning process. Let's now continue with the remaining two steps, in which you:

- Implement your strategy
- Monitor your investments and progress toward reaching your goals

STEP 5   IMPLEMENT YOUR STRATEGY

Once you've decided on an investment portfolio and an appropriate investment strategy, the next step is to implement your investment plan. This involves two fundamental issues: *how to buy* and *when to buy*.

Implementing Your Strategy: *How to Buy*

There are several ways that you can buy investments. Determining the right way for you can be just as important as choosing the investments themselves. In general, you have four options for implementing your plan:

- Through a broker (either full-service or discount)
- Through a professional money manager

- Through a mutual fund
- Through an insurance company

Independent Investment Advisors. Many individuals hire an independent investment advisor to help them design their investment strategy, identify mutual funds and/or professional money managers to implement the strategy, and monitor the performance of their overall portfolio. These professionals usually manage/supervise investment portfolios for a fee based on a percentage of assets. These advisors often come from a general financial planning background. Therefore they are able to incorporate appropriate estate planning and income tax strategies into the investment plan.

Full-Service Brokers. If you don't have the time, knowledge, experience, or inclination to select securities and manage your portfolio, you should consider a full-service brokerage firm. Full-service brokerage firms provide their customers with a wide variety of services and financial products. If you invest through a full-service brokerage firm, you will receive the firm's research on the economy and particular securities, and periodic newsletters and advice on financial, retirement, and business planning. These firms also offer accounts with check-writing privileges and access to credit cards and other credit facilities. More important, you will receive professional assistance in selecting and managing the securities that are compatible with your investment objectives and goals. Of course, you generally pay for these services and the professional assistance in the form of higher commissions than you would pay if you bought and sold securities yourself through a discount broker.

If you decide to use a full-service firm, make sure that you share your entire financial picture with your broker and articulate your goals and objectives clearly. It is important that your broker understands both what you need and what you expect from him or her.

Discount Brokers. As the name implies, the transaction costs or commissions of a discount broker will generally be lower than the transaction costs at a full-service firm. It is important to remember, however, that although discount brokerage firms can offer a wide array of services, you shouldn't expect to receive personal assistance in the selection and management of the securities in your portfolio. You aren't paying for personal advice— you must decide which investments to purchase or sell. Therefore, using a discount broker is appropriate if you have sufficient time, knowledge, experience, and the inclination to manage your own portfolio.

If you decide that the potential cost savings outweigh the disadvantages, you may want to shop around for your discount broker, since the commission costs and service capabilities of discount brokers can vary dramatically.

Many discount brokers now allow you to invest directly over the Internet with substantial commission savings. Some of these brokers are:

- Brown & Co. (www.brownco. com)
- Charles Schwab (www.schwab.com)
- Datek (www.datek.com)
- DLJdirect (www.dljdirect.com)
- E*Trade (www.etrade.com)
- Fidelity Web Xpress (www.fidelity.com)

Professional Money Managers. If you have a large sum to invest, you should consider using a professional money manager. Professional money managers have typically distinguished themselves in their profession by way of education, training, and experience in the field of investments.

All money management firms require that you maintain an account at the firm of some minimum size. The minimum size varies from firm to firm. Most firms require an account size of at least $500,000 to $1 million. However, it is possible to access professional money managers through brokerage firms once your account size is at least $100,000.

Professional money managers charge an annual fee for their services based on a percentage of the assets under their management. A typical annual fee is 1% on the first $1 million under management. In addition, they may also receive the commissions on the buy and sell of securities, depending on whether their firm has the ability to execute the trades.

The advantages of professional asset management are several. First, your portfolio will be individually tailored to meet your personal needs and objectives. You will also receive a high level of personalized services. Most management firms will submit quarterly reports to you that indicate what you own, the activity of your account during the quarter, and most important, how well your portfolio has performed over that quarter and other time periods compared to relevant market indices. Most managers will also meet with you each quarter to discuss your portfolio and their rationale for purchasing or selling specific securities, and to hear from you first-hand any changes in your personal and financial circumstances, and your tax situation.

One important aspect to remember is that the interests of you and the manager are closely aligned. The manager charges a fee based on the value of your portfolio. You want the value of your portfolio to increase and so does the manager. The higher the value of your portfolio, the higher the fee paid to the manager. Because the manager's fee is determined primarily by the value of your portfolio, there is no apparent incentive for the manger to trade the securities in your portfolio excessively in order to earn commissions.

Owning Mutual Funds. One alternative to purchasing individual securities outright is owning mutual funds. A mutual fund is an investment company that invests in cash, bonds, stocks, or other investments. The purchasers of the fund's shares essentially each own a portion of each investment owned by the fund.

For diversification purposes, mutual funds can be an appropriate investment vehicle for small to medium-sized portfolios. If you can't afford to purchase 100 shares of 30 different stocks, you may be able to afford 100 shares of a mutual fund that invests in those same 30 stocks. Your funds are pooled with many other investors, thereby enabling the pool to invest in more securities than might otherwise be feasible.

An additional advantage: The firms that manage the mutual fund, as well as the person who is responsible for investing the money, are professionals. Although you, your stockbroker, or your financial planner must research the mutual fund, you do not have to research every asset it holds.

Because mutual funds are important investments, we explore this subject in more detail in the next chapter.

Investing in Annuities. An annuity is a contract between you—the annuitant—and an insurance company. You invest in the contract and receive a promise from the insurance company to pay a series of payments for a fixed number of years or over your lifetime. The payments can begin immediately or can be delayed to a future date.

The primary advantage of a tax-deferred annuity is that the investment earnings remain tax-deferred until the funds are withdrawn. With certain exceptions, any earnings withdrawn prior to age 59½ are generally subject to a 10% penalty for early withdrawal in addition to ordinary income taxes. (See both *The Ernst & Young Tax Guide* and *The Ernst & Young Tax Saver's Guide*, published annually by John Wiley & Sons, Inc., for details of these early withdrawal penalties.) In this regard, annuities operate similarly to IRAs. However, unlike IRAs, you aren't limited in the amount of money you can place in a tax-deferred annuity.

There are two kinds of annuities: *immediate* and *deferred*.

- *Immediate annuities.* With an immediate annuity you invest in the annuity and your payments start immediately.
- *Deferred annuities.* With a deferred annuity you pay your premium and payments don't start until more than a year later. Deferred annuities constitute the bigger segment of the market by far. The reason for their popularity is that the annuity's buildup, like that of an IRA, is tax-deferred until withdrawn.

Deferred annuities themselves come in two types. One is the *fixed annuity*, which functions like a CD in a tax-sheltered wrapper. Your account is credited with a fixed interest rate that the company can change at fixed intervals (usually once a year). By contrast, the *variable annuity* has mutual fund clones within it—separate funds in which you can put your money. You can then transfer to different mutual funds within the annuity. Variable annuities are quite popular because they allow both free deferral of investment income and the ability to diversify among several types of funds. With current high tax rates, the attraction is obvious.

If you're considering a fixed annuity, you need to investigate these issues for each product:

- The company's financial strength, and thus its ability to invest and safeguard your money
- The product's specific features, including:
  - Its surrender charges
  - The conditions under which you can withdraw money without a surrender charge
  - The conditions under which you can bail out of the policy penalty-free if it doesn't meet certain criteria
- The company's crediting history (i.e., have they consistently paid reasonable rates to annuity holders over the years?)

For a variable annuity, you should consider these issues:

- How good are the investment choices?
- What are the track records for those funds?
- What are the features of that particular annuity?
  - Are you able to move money around easily?
  - Is there an 800 number to call, or do you have to make changes through your broker?
- How high are the annual charges?

What makes one annuity better than another? It depends on whether your primary desire is a pre-determined rate of return (fixed) or tax-advantaged investments (variable).

Is an annuity right for you? Perhaps—if you can wait long enough for the annuity's compounding to offset the additional charges as well as phase out the back-end load. People who have sufficient liquidity and investable assets outside their retirement plan are good candidates for annuities. Other candidates are people who feel sure they will be in the same or a lower bracket at the time of retirement. Under those circumstances, an annuity can be a useful vehicle. However, you should have enough liquidity outside the annuity so that you can leave your money in the annuity for the required timespan, at least to avoid a back-end load.

Implementing Your Strategy: *When to Buy*

We've explored the various means to investing; now for the issue of timing your investments. Frequently, investors will try to time their investment decisions according to whether they believe a particular market is over- or undervalued. For example, if you think the stock market is overvalued, you may decide to wait until it declines before making additional stock market investments. You may even reduce your current stock market holdings, reasoning that you'll increase them again once the market has bottomed out after its "inevitable" decline.

The flaw in this strategy is that it's very difficult for individual investors to forecast accurately when financial markets will rise or fall. Any information that an individual investor has is almost certainly already known by investment professionals and is therefore already reflected in the market's value. The most experienced investment analysts who track financial markets daily cannot predict market swings with much accuracy—are you likely to outdo them?

Based on historical market data, it appears that an asset allocation should be strategic and long-term rather than one that you change frequently depending on your forecast of the markets. Most investment advisors agree that you have a much better chance of reaching your goals if you have a long-term investment perspective.

10 Big Mistakes in Investing—#9
Timing the market
It doesn't work—the opportunity cost of investing in cash investments tends to exceed market losses over time.

Since it's impossible to predict consistently whether the market is high or low, the problem is to invest at the right time without resorting to market timing techniques. For example, if you invested $20,000 in the stock market on one day and the next day the market lost 20% of its value, you will wish that you had waited an extra day before you invested.

One method of investing that addresses this concern is *dollar cost averaging*. Here's an example. Let's say that you have $2,500 to invest. Using dollar

DOLLAR COST AVERAGING			
Month	Price per Share	Dollars Invested	Number of Shares
1	$ 5.00	$ 500	100
2	4.00	500	125
3	2.50	500	200
4	4.00	500	125
5	5.00	500	100
Total	$20.50	$2,500	650

cost averaging, as shown in the table above, you'd not invest all your money at once; instead, you'd invest (for example) $500 per month for 5 months. When the stock's price is low, this $500 purchases more shares; when the price is high, it purchases fewer shares. While the average price of the asset over the 5 months is $4.10 ($20.50/5), the average cost you've paid is only $3.85 ($2,500/650). By being disciplined and not investing more money when the price *seems* low or less money when the price *seems* high, you've managed to get neither the best price nor the worst price. But what you have achieved is an average cost that is lower than the average price. Note that the time period over which you invest the money can span several months (as shown here), several quarters, or even several years, depending on how much money you have available to invest and what your preferences are. Moreover, committing your savings to the market at predetermined intervals enables you to take advantage of dollar cost averaging continuously.

STEP 6

MONITOR YOUR INVESTMENTS AND PROGRESS TOWARD REACHING YOUR GOALS

Once you implemented your investment strategy, it's important that you monitor your investments from time to time to ensure that they remain appropriate for your financial goals. While you should generally try to avoid frequent changes to your investments, you should periodically assess each investment's performance to see that it meets your expectations. A long-term investor generally shouldn't make new investment decisions based on a one-year return, but it's important for you to understand why a particular investment outperformed or underperformed expectations.

When evaluating your investments' performance, you should consider the financial environment in which the performance occurred. One cause for underperformance of an investment or a money manager may be the financial markets in general. You should always consider your investments' performance in relation to the appropriate benchmarks. For example, you might want to compare your U.S. stock portfolio's returns to the S&P 500, and your international stock portfolio's performance to the EAFE (Europe/Australia/Far East) index.

Just as you must consider risk as well as return when selecting investments, you must also consider risk when evaluating your investments' performance. If your money manager or mutual fund takes on more risk than the market itself does, the return should also exceed that of the market over the long term.

E X A M P L E

■ Let's suppose that the S&P 500's return was 10% and your U.S. stock mutual fund's return was 10.5%. Should you be pleased? The answer: It depends. Comparing these returns without making an adjustment for risk prevents you from comparing apples to apples. ■

To understand how your investment performed, given its risk, you need to adjust the return to account for the risk difference. *Beta*—described in Chapter 4—is often used to make this adjustment. If your mutual fund's beta is 1.10, your mutual fund manager may have taken on 10% more risk than the market. Therefore if the return is not 10% greater than the market's return, the performance may be lower than the market's on a risk-adjusted basis, even though its nominal return is higher.

The measurement that compares returns on a risk-adjusted basis is *alpha*. If alpha is a positive number, it means that the investment portfolio performed better than expected, given the risk of the portfolio. The higher the alpha, the better the risk-adjusted performance has been. A negative alpha indicates underperformance, given the portfolio's presumed risk.

Another important factor: In reevaluating your investment plan, you should consider whether your investment objectives have changed due to a change in your personal or financial circumstances. Changes in your income tax rate, portfolio size, or risk tolerance may affect your investment strategy as well. Finally, because financial markets are continually evolving, the spectrum of investment vehicles available may expand over time, offering you new choices that may fit your investment goals more precisely.

SUMMARY

It takes careful planning, discipline, and diligence to achieve your financial goals. The wide variety of investment products available, the increasing complexity and globalization of financial markets, and the changing income tax laws mean that you should make use of all available resources to succeed in today's investment environment.

To begin your investment planning process, you must ask yourself the following questions:

- Specifically, what are my financial goals?
- Considering my existing investments, future savings, and time horizon, what investment return must I achieve to meet these goals?

These questions will prompt you to evaluate your current financial situation and use financial projections to determine how you can achieve your goals.

Once you have answered the questions posed above, you should ask:

- What characteristics am I looking for in an investment to help me meet my goals?
- Considering the array of investment products available to me, which classes of investments match my investment objectives?

After studying financial markets and researching investments, your next steps are to:

- Determine what mix of asset classes might allow you to achieve the return you need while taking the minimum risk.
- Consider whether you have sufficient cash to meet your short-term needs and unexpected emergencies.
- Decide which assets are appropriate inside your retirement plans and which to invest elsewhere. (See Chapter 6 for further information.)

To implement your investment plan, you must then decide whether to purchase individual securities through a broker, use mutual funds or tax-deferred annuities, or employ a professional money manger. Once your investment plan is in place, you should periodically:

- Monitor the performance of your investments.
- Reevaluate your financial goals and investment objectives.
- Reassess financial markets and the investments available to you.
- Make changes in your investment plan as necessary.

6

BUILDING WEALTH (CONCLUDED)

Through the preceding four chapters, we've worked our way systematically through the investment planning process. Here, now, are discussions of five issues that overlap with one or more aspects of investing:

- Mutual funds
- Foreign investments
- Real estate
- Gold
- Investing for retirement

MUTUAL FUNDS

In Chapter 5 we briefly mentioned mutual funds as a method for investment. Mutual funds are, in fact, one of the most appropriate means of investing for many people.

Successful investing requires time, effort, and knowledge. You have to spend time identifying your objectives and designing an investment strategy to meet them. However, you don't necessarily need to spend the considerable amount of time and energy required to search for investment opportunities and to monitor the investments you select. Instead, you can have a professional investment manager assist you in implementing your investment strategy. As we noted earlier, however, a personal investment manager can be inaccessible unless you have at least $500,000 to invest—and many managers won't even consider a client with investments of less than $1 million.

Does this mean that you're entirely on your own? Not at all. You can receive professional investment management through *regulated investment companies* such as mutual funds or unit investment trusts. These investment companies don't provide you with a portfolio designed for you individually. Instead, you own an interest in the entire pool of investments managed by the professional investment manager.

Regulated investment companies are firms that receive funds from many investors, pool the funds, and use them to purchase investments that the companies' professional investment managers select. Since the investor owns shares in the investment company, he or she owns a share of its portfolio of investments. Regulated investment companies are commonly referred to as *mutual funds*.

The advantages that investment companies can offer you are numerous, including:

- Professional investment management of assets at a relatively low cost
- Ownership in a diversified portfolio
- Potentially lower commissions, since the investment company buys and sells in large blocks
- Prospectuses and reports of various periodicals to assist people in readily accessing information needed to perform fund comparisons
- Other special services, such as dividend reinvestment plans, periodic withdrawal and investment plans, telephone switching, and in some cases, check writing

---

Q: Where can I find information about mutual funds?

A: Try these sources:

Morningstar Mutual Funds. An exhaustive compendium of mutual fund data on over 1,300 funds. Updated every other week. Price: about $400 per year or $5 per page on individual funds. Source: Morningstar, Inc., 225 West Wacker Drive, Suite 400, Chicago, IL 60606. Phone: (800) 876-5005.

Directory of Mutual Funds. Data on approximately 3,000 funds. No performance information. Updated annually. Price: about $10. Source: Investment Company Institute, 1401 H Street, NW, Suite 1200, Washington, DC 20005. Phone: (202) 326-5800.

Investor's Guide to Low-Cost Mutual Funds. Detailed information about 750 no-load and low-load funds; updated twice annually. Price: $5.00. Source: Mutual Fund Education Alliance, 1900 Erie Street, Suite 120, Kansas City, MO 64116. Phone: (816) 471-1454.

Individual Investor's Guide to Low-Load Mutual Funds. In-depth analysis of over 800 funds; updated annually. Price: about $25. Source: American Association of Individual Investors, 625 North Michigan Avenue, Suite 1900, Chicago, IL 60611. Phone: (312) 280-0170.

The Value Line Mutual Fund Survey. Data on approximately 1,500 established funds and 500 newer funds. Updated three times per year. Price: about $300 per year. Source: The Value Line Mutual Fund Survey, Dept. 6708, 220 East 42nd Street, New York, NY 10017. Phone: (800) 284-7607, ext. 6708.

Standard & Poor's/Lipper Mutual Fund Profiles. Data on approximately 750 funds; updated quarterly. Price: about $150 per year. Source: Standard & Poor's, 25 Broadway, Suite 1900, New York, NY 10004. Phone: (800) 221-5277.

And these online sources:

- www.mfea.com/educidx.html
- www.fundfinder.com
- www.fundfocus.com
- www.quicken.com/investments/mutualfunds/finder

Investment Objectives

Mutual funds are classified according to their investment objectives. Following is a summary of the various types of funds categorized by their investment objective.

Aggressive Growth Funds. These funds are characterized by high risk and high return: They typically seek capital appreciation and do not produce significant interest income or dividends.

Growth Funds. Growth funds aim to achieve an increase in the value of their investments over the long term (capital gains) rather than paying dividends.

Growth and Income Funds. Also called "equity-income" and "total return" funds, these funds aim to balance the objectives of long-term growth and current income.

Balanced Funds. These funds have three objectives: to conserve investors' initial principal, to pay high current income through dividends and interest, and to promote long-term growth of both principal and income. Balanced funds invest in both bonds and stocks.

Bond Funds. Bond mutual funds invest primarily in bonds. Some funds may concentrate on short-term bonds, others on intermediate-term bonds, and still others on long-term bonds.

Sector Funds. Sector funds invest in one industry, such as biotechnology or retail, and therefore do not offer the diversity you generally receive from a growth mutual fund, for example.

Index Funds. Index mutual funds recreate a particular market index (e.g., the S&P 500). The holdings and the return should mirror that of the index.

Types of Regulated Investment Companies

In addition to categorizing investment companies by their investment objectives, investment companies are classified according to their capital structure. The three types are:

- Closed-end funds
- Unit investment trusts
- Open-end funds

Closed-End Funds. Closed-end investment companies have a set capital structure with a specified number of shares. For this reason, investors must generally purchase existing shares of closed-end funds from current stockholders. Investors who wish to liquidate their position in closed-end investment companies must sell their shares to other investors. Shares in closed-end funds are therefore traded on the open market just like the stock of publicly held corporations. As a result, closed-end funds have an additional risk that isn't present in open-end funds—their price does not necessarily equal their net asset value. Closed-end funds that are sold at a discount from the value of the underlying investments can produce an opportunity for greater return.

 What happens if my mutual fund company goes broke? Do I lose my investment?

 No. The mutual fund company only *manages* the investments held by the fund.

Unit Investment Trusts. Unit investment trusts are a variation of closed-end funds. Unit trusts typically invest in a fixed portfolio of bonds that are held until maturity rather than managed and traded, as is the case with bond mutual funds. As an investor you purchase units that represent an ownership in the trust assets. Because the bonds are not traded, the annual fees charged for unit trusts may be lower than those charged by bond mutual funds. The unit trust collects the interest income and repayment of principal of the bonds held in the portfolio and distributes these funds to the unit holders. Unit investment trusts can provide you with a portfolio of bonds that have different maturity dates and an average holding period that meets your objectives. Cash flow is relatively predictable, since the intention is to hold the bonds until maturity.

Open-End Funds. Commonly referred to as mutual funds, open-end funds differ from closed-end funds in that they do not have a fixed number of shares to issue. Instead, the number of shares outstanding varies as investors purchase and redeem them directly from the open-end investment company. An investor who wants a position in a particular mutual fund purchases the shares from the fund either through a stockbroker or by contacting the fund directly. Conversely, mutual fund shareholders who want to liquidate their position sell their shares back to the company. The value of a share in a mutual fund is determined by the net asset value (NAV). Funds compute NAV by dividing the value of the fund's total net assets by the number of shares outstanding.

Mutual Funds Fees

The costs associated with open-end fund shares resemble those for closed-end funds. Like closed-end funds, open-end funds bear the trading costs and investment management fees of the investment company. However, mutual fund investors may or may not be subject to a sales charge referred to as a "load."

Depending on the type of load charged (if any), open-end mutual funds are classified as:

- No-load funds
- 12b-1 funds
- Load funds

No-Load Funds. No-load funds don't impose a sales charge on their investors. Purchases and sales of shares in a no-load fund are made at the fund's NAV per share. Consequently, every dollar invested gets allocated to the fund for investment rather than having a portion permanently kept back to cover sales charges.

12b-1 Funds. 12b-1 funds are a variation on no-load funds. While every dollar paid into the fund is committed to investment, the 12b-1 fund shareholders indirectly pay an annual fee to cover the fund's sales and marketing costs. This 12b-1 fee typically ranges from 0.1% to the maximum 1% of total fund assets. [*Note:* The 12b-1 fee is assessed every year (instead of only once); thus the longer you hold your 12b-1 fund shares, the greater the sales charge you will bear.]

Load Funds. By contrast, load funds charge the shareholder a direct commission at the time of purchase and/or when the shares are redeemed. "Front-end loads" are charged to the investor at the time of purchase and can be as high as 8.5% of the gross amount invested. On the other hand, some load funds charge their shareholders the load at the time their shares are redeemed. This cost will be either a "back-end load" or a "redemption fee." A back-end load is based on the lesser of the initial cost or final value of the shares redeemed and may disappear after a few years. A redemption fee is similar to a back-end load, but is based on the value of the shares you choose to redeem rather than your initial investment. It typically applies if the investor sells within a very short period of time (usually 30 to 60 days). The purpose of such fees is to discourage shareholders from short-term trading of fund shares.

Investors can choose when to pay the load based on the "class" of mutual fund shares they purchase.

A Class Shares. These are traditional load funds with the sales charge due at the time of purchase. These funds have ongoing annual expense charges and may have 12b-1 fees annually.

B Class Shares. These funds have a deferred or "back-end" load assessed at the time the fund is sold. These funds have ongoing annual expense charges and may have 12b-1 fees annually.

C Class Shares. These funds do not have a front-end or back-end load; however, the annual expense may be much higher than a class A or B share.

All fees, loads, and charges reduce your investment return. Therefore, you should consider not only a fund's return, but also all of the expenses that affect this return.

Mutual Fund Literature

Fund literature produced by the mutual fund company managing the fund is generally readily available. It will provide you with important information, such as what expenses a fund assesses. The Securities and Exchange Commission (SEC) has imposed minimum uniform reporting requirements on these companies to facilitate consumer comparison of funds.

Prospectus. The prospectus is the most important document that the fund provides. In fact, you are required to sign a statement stating that you've read this document and that you're familiar with its contents before you can purchase fund shares. The SEC has standardized the content and format of mutual fund prospectuses. All prospectuses now include a fee table listing all its expenses. The table also gives the fund's return, net of these expenses, for 1, 2, 3, 5, and 10 years, assuming a $1,000 initial investment and a 5% annual growth rate. This lets you compare apples to apples.

Prospectuses also include condensed financial information providing statistics of income and capital changes per share in the fund. Among the most useful data are the following:

- *The net investment income line* enables you to determine the level and stability of net income over the time period analyzed.
- *The annual net asset value amounts* help you trace the change in value per share from year to year.
- *The ratio of expenses to average net assets* helps you compare the funds' expense ratio.
- *The portfolio turnover rate* indicates how many times the value of all holdings have been sold, allowing you to assess trading costs.

The prospectus also gives you the fund's investment objectives and policies. The fund's objectives and attitudes toward risk should coincide with your objectives and risk tolerance.

Statement of Additional Information. Another SEC-required document is the "Statement of Additional Information." Sometimes included in the prospectus, this statement elaborates on the fund's investment objectives, restrictions, board of directors, and tax consequences of fund distributions.

Portfolio Manager. One important item that you usually *don't* find in the prospectus or other literature provided by the mutual fund company is the portfolio manager's name and tenure. The portfolio manager works for the fund and is responsible for the fund's daily investment activities. For some funds more than others, it may be important to make sure that the person who achieved the returns you initially found impressive is still employed by the fund. You can typically call the fund and request this person's name and experience.

Account Statements. Account statements track your reinvested dividend and capital gains distributions, purchases, redemptions, and fees. You should save these statements for tax purposes. You are taxed on dividends and capital gains as you earn them, even if you reinvest them. Therefore, you will also receive a Form 1099-DIV in January of each year for the prior year's distributions. The amount of any reinvested distributions is added to the cost basis of your mutual fund shares.

10 Big Mistakes in Investing—#10
Paying income tax on someone else's capital gain
Most mutual funds charge their shareholders of record on a particular date in December with their proportionate share of all the capital gains that the funds have realized from selling assets all year. The result: You gain immediate taxable income without increasing your shares' value. To avoid this problem, find out when the fund posts its gains for the year; then buy your shares after that date.

Mutual Fund Application Form

When completing a mutual fund application form, you have the opportunity to make elections that will facilitate managing the account. For example, you will be asked whether you want to receive your distributions in cash or have them reinvested in your account. Electing the reinvestment option prevents your having to reinvest the funds, since they are reinvested for you automatically. Reinvestment is similar to dollar cost averaging, since your distributions will buy shares each payment date.

Other elections include:

- *Wire transfer of distributions* to your regular bank account
- *Transfer of funds* directly from your checking account to your mutual fund account
- *Telephone redemption of shares*

All of these services can facilitate fund transfers and reduce your time commitment and paperwork.

FOREIGN INVESTMENTS

Investment professionals in this country are of two minds about foreign investments. Some argue that foreign investing can result in greater overall portfolio returns, given the advantages of diversifying among investments and taking advantage of differing economic scenarios worldwide. (See the diversification discussion in Chapter 4.) Other successful investment managers advocate investing only in domestic enterprises: They believe that given American companies' foreign operations or foreign sales, domestic stocks provide the needed foreign exposure. Certainly, the incremental return on any foreign investment must be large enough to compensate for the applicable foreign exchange risk. Note also that you will probably be subject to foreign taxes on your foreign investments. In most cases, these taxes can be directly credited against your federal tax liability.

> **Foreign exchange risk:** the risk that a foreign currency will depreciate in relation to the U.S. dollar, thus diminishing the dollar value of the foreign investment.

If you decide to diversify your portfolio internationally, you have several ways to implement your choices.

- Direct foreign stock purchases
- American depository receipts (ADRs)
- Stock mutual funds
- Foreign stock mutual funds
- Foreign bond mutual funds
- Foreign currency accounts
- U.S. bonds denominated in foreign currencies

Direct Foreign Stock Purchases

If you have timely access to foreign information, a desire to keep abreast of the international market, and lots of time, you might consider investing directly in foreign stocks. A caveat, however: This course of action requires a relatively large amount of investment capital, may be complicated, and can be expensive.

American Depository Receipts (ADRs)

ADRs are dollar-denominated negotiable receipts that represent the stock of a foreign company. This stock is held by foreign branches of U.S. banks. These receipts are listed on one of the major U.S. stock exchanges and represent an alternative to direct investing. As with direct foreign stock purchases, be sure you have adequate information to evaluate the foreign company and the market in which it operates.

Stock Mutual Funds

Many stock mutual funds invest in foreign stocks. In 1994, for instance, Fidelity Magellan had approximately 10% invested in foreign stocks. Thus you may get foreign exposure even in a mutual fund that isn't technically a foreign mutual fund.

Foreign Stock Mutual Funds

Hundreds of mutual funds exist that allow American investors to share in a piece of the international investing pie. Fund managers handle the investment research and selection process for their investors. They trade securities daily, seeking potentially favorable opportunities while hedging against unfavorable movements in interest rates and currency exchange rates. Mutual funds in this market go by many names but can be divided into the following categories:

- *Global or world funds*. These funds invest anywhere in the world, including the United States.
- *International or foreign funds*. Such funds invest anywhere in the world except the United States.
- *Regional funds*. These invest in specific geographic areas, such as Europe, Latin America, or the Pacific Rim.
- *Country funds*. Funds of this sort invest entirely in a specific country. For the most part, single country funds are closed-end mutual funds that typically trade on either the New York Stock Exchange or the American Stock Exchange.
- *International index funds*. These are mutual funds that parallel the concept of a domestic equity index fund. They are designed and operated so that their portfolios mirror the composition of the market index after which the funds are named.

Foreign Bond Mutual Funds

In addition to foreign stock funds, numerous foreign bond funds are available for investment. Since economic conditions differ from country to country, interest rates vary as well. At any given time, you can usually find several countries with interest rates higher than those in the United States. There is a downside to consider, though. Overseas interest rates may be more attractive, but language barriers, differing regulations, and illiquid markets all increase the challenge of foreign investments. Fluctuating currency values, although a potential advantage, can work against you if the currency of your foreign investment loses value relative to the U.S. dollar.

The emphasis on stable share prices is strongest with short-term global income funds. Short maturities help lessen the effect of interest rate fluctuations on asset values. This helps keep share-price volatility low, thereby allowing you to take advantage of worldwide, short-term interest rates with relatively low risk to principal. If you prefer a more aggressive approach, consider global income funds that invest in longer-term debt securities. The interest rate risk increases with longer maturities, but opportunities for higher returns increase as well.

Foreign Currency Accounts

Larger U.S. banking institutions offer deposit accounts through which you may invest in foreign currencies. The types of accounts, minimum investments, and currency selections vary. Foreign currency accounts let you take advantage of foreign interest rates at times when they are superior to domestic money market and CD rates, and they allow you to benefit from currency rate fluctuations. Furthermore, your deposits are insured by the Federal Deposit Insurance Corporation (FDIC) for up to $100,000. A caveat, however: The FDIC doesn't insure against loss of principal due to unfavorable exchange rates.

U.S. Bonds Denominated in Foreign Currencies

These investments offer the familiarity and safety of a U.S. issuer coupled with the opportunity to benefit from foreign currency fluctuations. During the 1980s, U.S. government agencies (such as the Student Loan Marketing Association and the Federal Home Loan Bank) offered several foreign currency issues that are traded in U.S. markets. In addition, several major domestic corporations offer bonds denominated in foreign currencies. They are available in varying maturities, yields, and currency assignments. Upon maturity, the face value will be paid in the listed currency, such as the Japanese yen or the British pound. Depending on the currency exchange rate at maturity, you may realize gain or loss on the currency transaction.

REAL ESTATE

Real estate has long been popular, for more reasons than investment alone. Fully 60% of Americans own their own homes, and many do so for reasons that go beyond considerations of financial planning. There's an intrinsic satisfaction in owning your own property. Small wonder that many people regard home ownership as part of their concept of the American Dream. (See Chapter 18 of this book for a detailed description of buying and selling a home.)

Direct Ownership	Indirect Ownership
You can pick the property	Someone else picks the property
Ability to find a good deal	Greater diversification opportunities (geographic and type of real estate)
Possible tax advantages	Reduced tax advantages (but still able to offset net rental income with deferral)
Complicates tax return (you must learn depreciation and other rules about tax deductions)	Complicates tax return (you must wait to receive the K-1 to be able to prepare your return and learn complicated tax rules)
Control	Professional management
Greater cash requirements and cash flow risk	Lower cash commitment and limited liability

Ownership

You can own real estate either directly or indirectly. Direct ownership involves purchasing particular properties (e.g., your home or a duplex). Indirect ownership involves investing money in a partnership or trust that owns one or more pieces of real estate. The pros and cons of the direct versus indirect ownership of real estate are shown in the table above.

Kinds of Real Estate Investment

Direct ownership is the most common method of investing in real estate, dominated by ownership of primary residences. Ownership of vacation homes or rental properties are the second-most-common arrangements. Indirect ownership is accomplished primarily through limited partnerships and real estate investment trusts (REITs).

Home Ownership. Many people have found that home ownership has provided an investment return as well as a physical shelter. The investment return comes from your home's increase in value while you own it. This so-called investment return, however, cannot be realized in the form of cash until the homeowner is ready to "trade down." The main drawbacks of direct ownership are the amount of time spent in managing the property, and possible uninsured risks.

Have you considered buying a vacation home as an investment? Sometimes it works out well—but look before you leap. It's not always the care-free haven you imagine. First, consider the costs you'd never have to think about regarding non-real estate investments, including:

- Furniture and decorating
- Home maintenance
- Landscaping or upkeep of the yard
- Utilities
- Security

There are also other, nonfinancial demands the property will make on you. Once you buy the place, you'll feel you have to spend all your vacations there. You want to get your money's worth, right? Perhaps you like the area so much you're always happy to be there. On the other hand, many people find a vacation home more work than they thought. What are the odds, for instance, that you'll spend most of your "off time" doing household projects?

Another possibility is that you bought the vacation home as a future retirement home. This may well suit your purposes. The leverage benefits of real estate can make buying this sort of property in advance advantageous. However, consider these other issues as well:

- Are you sure that the home is located where you want to retire?
- How near will your friends and family be to the home?
- Will owning the home limit your options for travel elsewhere?

Rental Property. Rental property can be a source of a current income stream—and due to available depreciation deductions, often a tax-deferred income stream at that. In addition, rental property (as is also true for personal residences) has historically provided investors with an inflation hedge and potential for capital appreciation. You should consider the potential disadvantages of rental arrangements, however:

- The tax rules for deducting out-of-pocket expenses and depreciation are complicated. (See *The Ernst & Young Tax Guide*, published annually by John Wiley & Sons, Inc., for more details.)
- Demands on your time for upkeep and paperwork may be burdensome.
- Ownership may limit your mobility under some circumstances.

> **Depreciation deduction:** *a tax deduction or write-off of the cost of an asset over its estimated useful life.*

Limited Partnership Interests. A limited partnership interest can provide passive participation in real estate in two characteristic situations: (1) for larger properties, and (2) where direct investor management isn't desired or practical. Unlike a corporation, a partnership itself is not subject to tax. Instead, the partnership's items of income and deduction flow through to and are reported on the tax returns of the individual partners. This will complicate your preparation of tax returns, since you must wait to receive a Schedule K-1 from the partnership before you can finish your return. (Even when you finally receive it, you may find it so confusing that you'll have to hire an accountant to help you make sense of it.) Limited partners do not have a voice in the management of the partnership but have liability limited to their investment in the partnership.

> **Limited partnership interest:** *an interest in an investment in which the investor's liability is solely the investment and the limited partner is not involved in the administration of the partnership.*

Real Estate Investment Trusts (REITs). REITs are publicly traded entities that invest in real estate. Their operations are similar to those of mutual funds. REITs generally invest in income-producing properties and/or mortgages and pass the income and capital gains through to investors. Advantages of REITs include professional and centralized management, greater liquidity, and diversification. However, REITs (unlike limited partnerships) cannot pass through losses.

The Ups and Downs of Real Estate

When evaluating property for investment, you need to look at its real growth potential, not just its ability to act as an inflation hedge. During the 1970s, making money in real estate was easy, but a great deal of the increase in property values resulted from inflation and not necessarily from real growth. Although real estate is often an excellent hedge against inflation, there are risks associated with any real estate investment. The *location and age of the property* and the *general economic conditions* may affect both its income and appreciation potential. *Triple net leases*—in which the tenant is responsible for the costs of maintenance, insurance, and taxes—may offer less risk than leases in which the lessor is responsible for these costs. Also, the extent to which *debt or leverage* is used can magnify the potential upside and downside of a real estate investment.

Due to these many risks, a diversified portfolio of real estate is a safer investment vehicle than an investment in a single piece of property. Some limited partnerships and REITs own many properties in different locations, thus allowing for diversification.

Another attribute of real estate is *illiquidity*. Unlike a U.S. Treasury note or common stock, real estate cannot quickly be turned into cash at its fair market value. It takes time for a transaction to close. Also, if you hold the real estate in a limited partnership, your limited partnership interests aren't readily salable.

Tax Issues and Real Estate

In the past, many people relied on depreciation expenses and the deductibility of tax losses to improve the rate of return on their real estate investments. Now, not only have depreciation deductions been reduced; if operating expenses exceed operating income, the net cash loss may no longer be offset by tax savings. Losses from rental real estate are generally considered passive losses. For this reason, they can be used only to reduce passive income, not income from other sources (such as compensation, interest, or dividends). There is an exception if you actively participate in the real estate activity under which a maximum of $25,000 in losses may be currently deductible if your adjusted gross income is under $100,000. You may be able to deduct even more if you are a real estate professional.

> ***Active participation:*** *participating in ways that include management decisions or arranging for others to provide services.*

Before you invest in real estate, you should therefore consider the possibility that any operating or tax losses incurred may not be deductible currently, although unused "suspended" losses can generally be used when you sell the property. A thorough reading of the pertinent sections of *The Ernst & Young Tax Guide* and *The Ernst & Young Tax Saver's Guide* should be your first step.

In addition to potential tax benefits and diversification advantages, real estate can provide you with leverage.

Leverage. Leverage means that you can purchase an asset with debt as well as some cash. The greater the debt, the higher the leverage. High leverage results in an ability to magnify your investment returns as well as your risk.

Here's an example of leverage at work in a real estate investment. Let's say that you've invested $10,000 cash and borrowed $40,000 and now own a $50,000 real estate investment. If the value of the property increases 10% or $5,000, the return on your cash investment is 50%, not 10%.

Although you can leverage with stocks, you can leverage even more with real estate. The most you can leverage stocks is generally 50%; by contrast, you can put down only 20% on a real estate investment resulting in much greater leverage.

GOLD

To protect against inflation and to diversify your portfolio, some investment professionals would recommend allocating a small percentage of your funds to gold and other precious metals. Historically, gold has provided a hedge against falling stock prices, since it tends to behave in a manner opposite to that of stocks in most economic scenarios. Gold and other precious metals are therefore significant investments from a diversification standpoint.

 The value of gold has risen dramatically during past global crises. Is this likely to happen at such times in the future?

 Historically, gold has behaved in a manner opposite to stocks' performance. When there's a financial or political crisis, some investors abandon stocks for a tangible asset which they feel will always have value. Whether this will happen in the future remains uncertain.

A final consideration: Owning gold involves costs atypical of other investments. These costs include:

- Assaying
- Storage
- Illiquidity
- Insurance

> **Assaying:** examination and determination as to certain characteristics, such as weight, measure, or quality.

An alternative to owning gold outright is investing in companies in that industry. You could do so by purchasing individual stocks or by purchasing shares in a mutual fund that invests in gold stocks or precious metals.

INVESTING FOR RETIREMENT

Finally, let's touch on another topic that overlaps with the general discussions so far but also involves its own specific issues. This topic is investing for retirement.

There are two schools of thought regarding which investments to select with the money inside your retirement plans. One school says that you should invest in stocks; the other bonds.

The Case for Stocks

In setting up a retirement plan, you're putting in assets today that you don't intend to use until you reach your 60s and beyond. Consequently, the assets being invested to meet your retirement goals probably have the longest *investment horizon* relative to the other assets in your portfolio. The longer your time horizon, the more risk you can tolerate. Therefore, the argument goes, your retirement plan assets should be invested in the riskiest types of investments in your portfolio. This generally means stocks.

The Case for Bonds

The primary investment advantage of funds placed in an IRA or other retirement plan is their tax-deferred compounding of earnings. For this reason, the counterargument goes that it is generally appropriate to invest in assets that ordinarily produce a lot of current income each year—that is, bonds.

Stocks or Bonds?

Capital losses are generally allowed up to $3,000 annually, although those realized inside an IRA or other retirement plan are not deductible. In addition, net capital gains are taxed at lower rates if realized outside an IRA, and that tax is deferred until the time of sale for assets held outside an IRA. All distributions from IRAs and other retirement plans are taxed at the higher ordinary income tax rates (except for certain Roth IRA distributions), albeit with the tax deferred until the funds are distributed. Thus you may be better off holding lower-yielding, growth-oriented investments such as stocks outside IRAs and retirement plans to take advantage of their benefits, while investing in higher-yielding investments such as bonds inside retirement plans. If you invest in a Roth IRA, however, these investment principles may differ since the income from a Roth IRA is tax free.

Whichever approach you select, remember to make sure that you're achieving your overall asset allocation when you're investing your retirement plan assets. Let's look at investment strategies specific to 401(k) plans and IRAs.

401(k) Plans. Often, 401(k) plans offer several investment choices. Many people choose to invest their 401(k) plan assets in some or all of the investment choices, based on their desired asset allocation. Some employers assist employees in selecting this mix by providing them with sample asset allocations, based on the historical risk and return of the available investment choices.

Most 401(k) plans also offer a guaranteed investment contract (GIC) as an investment. The reason? GICs often provide a higher rate of return than other cash-type investments. GICs are not risk-free. However, they may have a valid role to play in the retirement planning portion of a diversified portfolio. There are situations in which GICs make sense, since they are generally more predictable than stocks, and they generally offer interest comparable to that of a long-term bond. For example, you may need to focus on preserving capital if you're nearing retirement. GICs can provide a reasonably secure investment, making them attractive in these cases. GICs may also be useful as a safe haven of extreme volatility in the stock or bond markets. GICs may not be the answer to all your investment needs, but they contribute to a diversified investment plan's overall stability.

IRAs. In addition to the tax advantages of retirement plan assets' tax-deferred or tax-free compounding, you should note that withdrawals from most retirement plans other than qualified distributions are typically disadvantageous. Withdrawing from IRAs before you absolutely have to will terminate the opportunity to receive tax-deferred or tax-free compounding on the amount withdrawn; it may also result in the imposition of ordinary income tax as well as penalty tax on the amount withdrawn. For this reason, your most liquid investments should generally be held outside your retirement plans except to the extent of any retirement plan withdrawals you anticipate in the near term.

You should delay distributions from Roth IRAs for as long as possible since the income that builds up is tax free. Unlike with regular IRAs, you are not required to take any money out of your Roth IRA even after you reach age 70½.

7

Protecting Your Family and Assets Through Life Insurance

Insurance takes the shape of an unusual form of investment: You pay for something you hope you never have occasion to use. Because of the irony inherent in this arrangement, some people hesitate to invest adequately in insurance coverage. This view, however, is a form of risky wishful thinking. Terrible events can befall even the most wonderful people. And even if you're single and have no obligations to anyone else, certain forms of insurance can save you from financial catastrophe. If you have a spouse and children, insurance is all the more crucial as a way for you to meet your obligations.

Risk Management and Insurance Choices

Choices about insurance are, in fact, a subset of risk management, so let's start by considering how to identify and assess the risks you face. One way to undertake this process is to make a list of the fundamental risks:

- Death
- Disability
- Accidents or illness

- Property loss or damage
- Litigation for real or imagined negligence

Risk management: *the discipline of determining how likely certain events will be, then deciding what steps will limit or transfer the consequences.*

Any of these events can cause you not just a severe personal crisis, but also a potential loss of income or liquidity affecting you, your family, or both. Risk management therefore serves as a way of limiting the negative consequences of such events.

Once you've identified at least the general kinds of risk you face, how can you limit them? You can limit some risks by decisions about how you live your life. Many of these decisions are obvious (although their obviousness doesn't seem to stop some people from ignoring them). Don't drive while drunk. Don't eat a high-fat diet. Don't take up hang gliding, ice climbing, or amateur bull fighting. In short, sensible choices about personal behavior can limit or even eliminate certain risks. However, given the inescapable nature of some risks—death being the most obvious—risk management sometimes functions more to reduce rather than to eliminate the effects of harmful events on your life. And one common way of reducing risk is to purchase insurance.

10 Big Mistakes in Insurance—#1
Knowingly underinsuring any major risk that you could cover inexpensively

Insurance is essentially a means of transferring risk. Rather than risk all the consequences of physical disability, for instance, you pay a premium and transfer some of the risk to an insurance company. How much risk should you retain, and how much should you transfer? Those are essentially personal decisions, but here are some influencing factors:

- The degree of risk you're willing to tolerate
- The degree to which the risk can be transferred
- The likelihood of the risk affecting you
- The cost of transferring the risk

■ Mary Lou K. has an intense fear of earthquakes. Having lived through several recent quakes in California, she chose to leave that state rather than risk being there for the Big One. She's now living in Maine. She still worries about earthquakes, although she knows that quakes are unlikely in that part of the country. She's also aware that she could buy earthquake insurance to protect her against losses from property damage. Living in Maine, however, Mary Lou has only a slight risk of suffering death or property loss from an earthquake. Besides, coverage is expensive. Why bother? Under these conditions, it's reasonable for Mary Lou to retain the risk of earthquake damage rather than to transfer it. ■

■ Rick L. tends to dismiss the notion that he could suffer a disabling illness or accident. He's young, healthy, and careful; he can't image getting decked out from a medical problem. What Rick doesn't realize is that during youth, everyone has a much greater chance of being disabled than of dying. Disability insurance is quite expensive; still, the odds make it much more sensible to transfer this risk than to retain it. Despite Rick's confidence in his physical well-being, he should definitely obtain disability insurance. ■

In this chapter and the next, we explore the many ways in which insurance can transfer risk and, in so doing, provide financial and emotional well-being: financial well-being, because insurance can serve as a series of safety nets for you and your family; personal well-being, because the presence of these safety nets can significantly lower your level of worry.

Before considering the kinds of insurance you need, however, let's have a quick look at some kinds you probably don't need.

Inadvisable Insurance Products

Certain insurance products generally aren't worth the trouble or cost. Some of these products are useless; others respond to a legitimate purpose but cost too much; still others distract you from focusing on more urgent insurance needs. Here's a partial list of inadvisable insurance products:

Dread Disease Insurance. Dread disease policies generally duplicate coverage that's included under comprehensive health insurance programs—or ought to be.

Health Insurance on Pets. A pet's illness is unlikely to have severe financial consequences. Moreover, most health insurance policies for pets include many restrictions and are not automatically renewable.

Hospital Indemnity Insurance. Hospital indemnity policies pay you a predetermined amount for each day you are hospitalized. Although premiums are cheap—generally just a few hundred dollars per year—hospital indemnity insurance has minimal benefits: often as little as $100 per day. Their chief risk is distracting you from careful analysis of your comprehensive medical coverage, which should be increased if it's inadequate.

Credit Insurance. Many kinds of lenders—banks, credit card companies, auto dealers, retailers, and mortgage lenders—offer policies designed to pay your remaining balance in the event of your death or disability. Coverage of this sort may be a good idea; however, the coverage offered through these programs may not be as cost-effective as obtaining an individual term policy. (Note, however, that a term policy would cover your expenses only in the event of your death, not your disability.)

As for the kinds of insurance you do need, life insurance is the first and certainly one of the most important.

LIFE INSURANCE

First of all, everything you do about life insurance will be meaningless if you don't accept your own mortality and your family's needs in the aftermath of your death. This may sound self-evident; however, a remarkable number of people speak of their own death in terms of *if*, not *when*.

So the starting point for a discussion of life insurance is literally to imagine that you're going to die tomorrow. Then sit down and figure out what you want to happen afterward. Obviously, the answer will depend on the specifics of your own particular circumstances—whether you're single or married, whether you have children or not, and so forth. Family structures have enormous impact on the discussion. For the moment, however, let's assume the "traditional" family of husband, wife, and 2.3 kids. What are the things you want taken care of following your death?

There are two main branches to the discussion and analysis: (1) needs for immediate and intermediate-term cash, and (2) long-term income continuation.

Needs for Immediate and Intermediate-Term Cash

First, your dependents will need cash for the first few weeks and months after you die. Typical expenses usually fall into two categories:

I. Needs for Immediate Cash

- Emergency fund
- Funeral costs
- Medical bills
- Other bills

2. Cash to Be Used for the Intermediate Term or Set Aside for the Longer Term

- Federal or state taxes
- Mortgage payoff (if advisable)
- Spouse's education or retraining costs
- Children's education costs (present or future)

When you consider this list, it's not hard to see why a significant amount of money may be needed in both the short and intermediate term.

Income Continuation

There are also the issues of how much income your family needs after you die, and how long that income should continue. This is the second main branch of the analysis.

The relatively easy part of analyzing income continuation is toting up the expenses you anticipate. Here are the typical categories of expenses for income continuation:

- Mortgage payments (if the mortgage hasn't been paid off)
- Rent
- Taxes (other than those withheld)
- Food
- Child care
- Utilities and fuel
- Insurance premiums
- Household maintenance
- Auto and other transportation expenses
- Loan payments
- Medical bills (other than those covered by insurance)
- Clothing expenses
- Savings and investments
- Charity
- Recreation and entertainment
- Miscellaneous

Estimating your expenditures based on this list should give you a rough sense of your projected expenses. (The job will be easier and the results more precise, of course, if you have already established a budget. See Chapter 1 to review this subject.) Let's say that your spouse will need $4,000 per month. Where is the money going to come from? How long will that monthly sum be necessary—for the rest of his or her life, perhaps, or until your children leave for college? Meanwhile, don't forget the consequences of inflation, which will render $4,000 considerably less valuable in the long run.

Common sources of income for supporting a family following the income provider's death are:

- The survivor's salary
- Interest and dividends
- Rents received
- Social Security benefits
- Veterans' benefits
- Existing life insurance
- Income from decedent's employee benefits

Consider two important aspects of this situation:

Be realistic about your spouse's likely income. This is especially relevant in situations where the spouse hasn't worked outside the home in some years. Here are some crucial questions to ask:

- What is the current job market in her or his field now?
- What after-tax income is likely, given current economic conditions?
- How emotionally stressful will she or he find returning to outside employment?
- What are the likely costs of preemployment education or training?
- What are the additional costs of returning to work (attire, child care, etc.)?

Once you calculate the total income from these sources, you should ask *what are the influences that can diminish their real value?* You may value your 401(k) plan at $100,000, for instance, yet you should also factor in the tax bite to determine its actual worth. Still another consideration is the "blackout" period for Social Security benefits. (Payments to the surviving parent stop when the child reaches 16; payments to the child stop when the child reaches 18. Payments to your spouse resume when he or she reaches age 60.) During this time, your spouse won't receive any Social Security benefits. In short, you should subject your analysis to as stringent a set of reality checks as possible.

When you've assessed the complete sources of income, put the sources up against the needs. The difference (and the difference is almost always a shortfall) is your *capital gap*. If you're like most people, looking at your capital gap for the first time will be a huge shock. The gap is much bigger than you probably expected. The reason? What you'll need to provide $4,000 a month at 4% inflation rate for a spouse who is, say, 35 years old—a spouse who may have a life expectancy of 80—is an enormous sum of money. And remember, you're calculating the money you need *after* having taken many thousands of dollars off the top to pay off the mortgage, educate the kids, and pay some taxes.

Capital gap: *the difference between the amount of money you have (or will have) and the amount of money you need to provide for the objectives you've identified.*

Many people question the validity of these figures when they first see them. However, blaming the analysis that reveals your capital gap is like blaming the x-rays that reveal a medical problem. Throwing out a set of alarming x-rays won't make you healthy.

Facing the Situation

How, then, should you deal with your capital gap?

The first step, as when facing other worrisome situations, is not to panic. Denial and alarmism will only complicate your task.

The second step is to reach an agreement with your spouse on *the current value of your assets* and on *your financial objectives for the future, including the level of financial support that your family will need in the event of your death.* Among the issues you need to explore when considering the aftermath of your death are:

- Does your spouse intend to work outside the home?
- Is this realistic, given his or her background and/or the job market?
- Does a return to work suit his or her own preferences?
- Is this eventuality preferable to the alternative of buying additional insurance *now?*

How you answer these questions is a personal matter, of course, though a financial advisor can assist in the process. Once you've reached an agreement, however, you can lock into a number that indicates your insurance need. And that is your true starting point in making decisions about life insurance.

Q: I've heard that I can determine my life insurance needs simply by quadrupling or quintupling my annual income. Is this true?

A: Sometimes this method works. Unfortunately, it often results in overkill or underkill—sometimes gross underkill. Like most rules of thumb, this one isn't terribly accurate. It certainly isn't a method that takes individual needs and circumstances into account. A more rigorous, personalized analysis can spare your family much worry and heartache—not to mention expense.

As you deal with the issue of your capital gap, there are two main questions to ask:

- What are your insurance needs now?
- What will your insurance needs be 15, 20, or 30 years from today?

If you were to die tomorrow, your family's needs would resemble what we discussed earlier: paying off the mortgage, funding education, providing income for your spouse. If you were to die 15 to 20 years from now, however, you might imagine that your insurance needs would diminish considerably. "My kids will have been educated and my mortgage will be pretty much paid off," you say, "so my spouse will need a lot less income."

Rather, the *complexion* of their needs will have changed, although the *amount* of the capital gap may not have changed.

EXAMPLE

■ At 35, Arthur N. had one set of life insurance needs, most of which focused on making sure that his family would have sufficient income and educational funds if he were to die. Twenty years later Arthur's needs have changed but haven't disappeared. He has paid off his mortgage and provided for his children's education, but he and his wife now have retirement on their minds. Arthur has also done sufficiently well financially that he has the beginnings of an estate tax problem to address. He has significant amounts of money locked into retirement plans. If he were to die tomorrow, he'd want his wife to let that money sit and compound rather than having her take it out as ordinary income now, and he'd want the estate to be able to pay his estate taxes. In short, Arthur's need for insurance hasn't magically changed all that much *in quantity,* although the specific *purposes* for insurance coverage have changed remarkably. ■

There's another reason for making specific, detailed plans in addressing your capital gap. As you begin to plan for retirement, you should pay closer attention to the tax and investment characteristics of insurance.

Some policies may prove beneficial to your long-range retirement and investment plans. The reason is that certain life insurance products actually provide specific tax advantages that aren't related to capital needs analysis alone. (We'll address these issues shortly in discussions of insurance products.)

10 Big Mistakes in Insurance—#2
Naming minor children as beneficiaries of a life insurance policy

Term vs. Cash Value Insurance

Your most fundamental decision about insurance is whether to buy *term* or *cash value* (also called *permanent*) products. Both of these categories of insurance can have a legitimate place in your financial and estate planning. We'll consider each of the specific kinds shortly. First, however, let's consider the general issues involved.

As with other aspects of financial planning, rules of thumb concerning life insurance are common. One of the most common is "Buy term and invest the rest." (That is, since a term policy will be cheaper than a cash value policy for the same face amount, you should buy the term policy, then invest the difference between the annual term and the cash value premiums.) Another rule of thumb is "Buy term insurance for 'term' needs and cash value insurance for 'permanent' needs." As with other kinds of folk wisdom, there's some validity to these bits of advice; at the same time, they tend to oversimplify the situation, often to a risky degree.

Term Insurance in a Nutshell. Term insurance is simply that—insurance that covers a specific term. You pay your premiums; the insurance company pays a benefit if you die. The relatively low expense of term insurance is its chief advantage over cash value products. Unlike cash value insurance, however, term products have no savings or investment features. There are several kinds of term insurance (discussed later).

Cash Value Insurance in a Nutshell. By contrast, cash value insurance is initially more expensive than term but offers a wide variety of savings, investment, and payment options. A common comparison used to describe term and cash value products is that term insurance is analogous to renting a house, while cash value resembles purchasing a house with a mortgage.

How can you know whether to purchase term or cash value insurance? We'll examine in detail the various advantages and disadvantages of both kinds in a moment. First, here are some other issues that can influence your decisions.

Discretionary Income. As noted earlier, term policies are initially cheaper than an equivalent face amount of cash value insurance. If you can afford only term insurance, you have no sensible choice but to buy term. However, if you have enough discretionary income to purchase whatever type of insurance you want (or at least enough to buy some cash value insurance in addition to term), you should examine your particular needs and consider their duration.

Duration of Needs. Depending on your age, the type of policy, and other factors, a cash value policy may require at least 15 years to develop enough after-tax cash surrender value to beat a buy-term-and-invest-the-rest approach. (This assumes a reasonable after-tax return on the difference between the two premiums.) For this reason, term insurance is probably appropriate for needs you expect to exist for about 15 years, and perhaps up to 20. (Typical needs to consider: paying off a mortgage, funding a child's education, and funding a spouse's financial requirements.) Needs likely to exist for more than 15 to 20 years should probably be covered by some form of cash value insurance.

Long-Term Economics. Locking into a cash value policy may look more expensive in the short run, but it is, after all, *permanent* insurance; once covered, you may have the ability to maintain a level premium for the life of the coverage or even to stop your premiums but still retain the coverage. By contrast, term insurance premiums increase at regular intervals (determined by the specific policy) and may become prohibitively expensive past middle age.

Investment Discipline. The rule of thumb urging you to "buy term and invest the rest" assumes that you have enough investment discipline to follow through and really invest the extra money, let alone invest it well. Some people do; some don't. Unfortunately, even the best intentions don't guarantee that "the rest" will end up invested well—or invested anywhere at all.

10 Big Mistakes in Insurance—#3
Using term insurance for permanent insurance needs

Term Insurance in Detail

Most buyers of term insurance purchase one of two kinds:

- Annually renewable term
- Level premium term

Annually Renewable Term. With annually renewable term insurance, you pay the premium and your policy remains in force. The benefit stays level; your premium goes up every year. Many policies distinguish between the "current premium" and "maximum guaranteed premium," which the company will specify in the policy. Annually renewable term is the most common form of term insurance.

> **Current premium:** what the insurance company is now charging and expects to charge for the coverage.
>
> **Maximum guaranteed premium:** what the insurance company is contractually able to charge for the coverage, if they so choose.

 Are there computer programs for analyzing my insurance needs?

 Good programs are available. However, even the best programs currently in use may not address all the relevant issues or personalize the solutions sufficiently.

Level Premium Term. Level premium term insurance costs more per year initially than the annually renewable kind, but the premiums stay level for a period of 5, 10, 15, or even 30 years. There is no issue of a "current premium" vs. a "maximum guaranteed premium" during that period in which you've locked into a rate that continues for the term specified. You'll take a physical exam after the guarantee period, after which (assuming you pass) you are covered for another period of equal duration at excellent rates. If you fail to pass the exam, however, continuing coverage is much more expensive.

Other Issues Regarding Term Insurance. Next we note a few other factors to contemplate as you sort through decisions about term insurance.

Convertibility. Many policies allow you to convert from term to cash value insurance without evidence of insurability. The chief advantage here is that a temporary policy becomes permanent—an option particularly useful to policyholders whose health may have deteriorated at some point while holding term insurance. Converting a term policy may be the cheapest, the easiest, and sometimes the only way for such people to obtain life insurance given their state of health at that time. But note how long you'll have to make the conversion after you purchase the term policy.

Features Included in Some Term Policies. Insurance companies routinely offer several other features that can affect any of the basic kinds of term policies. The most common of these are *declining, decreasing,* or *reducing coverage,* which diminish the death benefit over time; and the *disability waiver,* which provides for automatic payment of the premium if you become disabled.

Advantages of Guaranteed Level Term Policies. The most popular term policies nowadays are those that guarantee a 10-, 15-, 20-, or 30-year lock on a given premium. Many people like the certainty that the multiyear lock provides; in addition, the premiums on such policies are much cheaper after a few years than the normal renewable premiums would be. The risk here, however, is that you may not be able to continue at the attractive rates once the term ends. A crisis can occur if you end up 13 or 14 years into a 15-year policy at a time when your health has deteriorated. You may now not qualify for the next round of attractive rates. (Bear in mind, however, that you may be able to convert the policy at the standard risk classification you were when you purchased it.) A related issue: Insurance regulators are currently concerned that 15-year fixed premium policies will strain some insurance companies' surpluses and reserves. As a result, the regulating authorities may move to reduce the attractiveness of this product option.

Advantages of Convertible, Annually Renewable Policies. By contrast, the annually renewable term policy may be ideal for you *as long as it's convertible to a cash value policy.* The reason for this opinion is that on a present-value basis, the annual renewable term insurance *may* be cheaper for the term during which you need the coverage. The big uncertainty here is that, lacking a crystal ball or divine guidance, you can't realistically know how long you're going to need the coverage.

When to Convert a Term Policy to Cash Value Insurance. Most term policies are convertible, although some convert more cheaply than others. When should you convert? In addition to converting when your health changes for the worse, you should consider conversion at any time when you've decided that you may as well purchase cash value insurance. One reason for doing so is strictly financial. If you see that you have more than a 15- to 20-year need for insurance, the cash buildup and tax advantages from a cash value policy will work to your advantage by enabling you to keep your premium level.

Cash Value Insurance in Detail

There are three basic kinds of cash value policies:

- Whole life
- Universal life
- Variable life

One feature that whole life, universal life, and variable life insurance policies all have in common is that their cash value grows on a tax-deferred basis, much like an IRA.

Whole Life. This is the traditional cash value insurance product. Whole life insurance is just that: a product designed to cover you for your whole life, with the premiums to be paid for your *whole life*. Whole life insurance offers distinct advantages and disadvantages over term.

First, the advantages:

- Fixed premium for the life of the policy
- Automatic savings program for the policyholder
- Cash values build on a tax-deferred basis
- Option to borrow from the cash value
- Option to use your cash value or dividends to pay the policy's premiums
- Option to convert cash value to an annuity at your retirement

The disadvantages are:

- Higher initial premiums
- A long-term commitment that may reduce your flexibility by locking you into a stream of payments

 What is "ordinary life" insurance?

 It's whole life insurance under another name.

Whole life insurance is available in a variety of formats. The most common are:

- *Participating,* for which the company pays dividends to the policyholder. More accurately, the company *may* pay dividends. The dividends are, in fact, not guaranteed—either in terms of their amount or in terms of there being any dividends at all.
- *Interest-sensitive.* These policies may look and work the same as the participating kind; the so-called returns above the guarantees are called excess credits.
- *Indeterminate premium.* These have lower premiums than other kinds of whole life, but the insurance company retains the right to increase premiums up to a guaranteed level. There are no dividends and no excess credits.

Premium structures for either participating or nonparticipating policies can make use of various approaches to premiums. The most common is the *level premium* concept. Another is the *modified premium,* in which the premium might be $5,000 per year for the first 15 years; then, at year 16, it might double. Or there might be a *graded premium*—one that would increase for a certain number of years. There are also policies that are paid up after 10 or 20 years, or when you reach age 65. At such points, the policy has contractually received all the money needed to provide you with your insurance coverage.

Universal Life. During the late 1970s and early 1980s, partly as a result of the high interest rates at that time, the insurance companies began to develop a new kind of policy. This is universal life. The premise with universal life is essentially to "buy term and invest the rest," but inside a single account designed with open architecture—one in which you are able to see your actual cost of insurance, the rate of interest credited on your cash value, and the amount of expenses against your cash value. (Note that with whole life insurance the consumer can't determine any of these factors. Compared to universal life, whole life is essentially a "black box.")

Some additional features and benefits of universal life insurance are:

- Flexibility in determining the policy's face amount
- Flexibility in determining premium payments
- Annual reports indicating present and projected insurance, cash value, fees, and so forth

As this list suggests, the most persuasive feature of universal life insurance is flexibility. Universal life even allows you (within certain limits) to determine your own premium. For instance, you can ask your insurance agent to calculate (given a reasonable rate of interest and the current cost of insurance) a level annual premium that will keep your policy in force indefinitely. Or you can ask the agent to show you the premium that, assuming you pay for 10 years and then stop, will also keep the policy in force. In short, you can have many of the advantages of whole life but considerably more flexibility.

Are there disadvantages to universal life policies? Predictably, there are. The main issue is that the flexibility can work against you. When you buy a universal life policy, it enables you to have a lower initial premium than for a comparable whole life policy. The lower initial premium, however, is predicated on the company's keeping its cost of insurance and interest rates at the level projected. Yet if the company eventually reduces its interest crediting or increases its cost of insurance, and if you fund your universal policy with too low a premium, your payments won't be sufficient to carry the policy over the long term. These policies therefore call for your eternal vigilance.

Bear in mind as well that the decision to use the lower premium is also a decision to pay that premium much longer than you'd otherwise need to pay an equivalent whole life premium. With most whole life policies, you'll be able to put away your checkbook sooner or later.

Variable Life. The third general kind of cash value insurance, variable life, differs from regular whole life and universal life products chiefly in allowing you more leeway in your investment choices. Unlike whole and universal life policies (for which insurance companies manage the underlying investments), variable life policies allow you to invest in various combinations of stock, bond, and money market funds. You can't select any investment you want; you have to work within the separate accounts that the company makes available to you for your particular product. Some companies use only their own funds, while others have assembled six, seven, 10, or even more separate outside funds to choose from. This may allow you to take advantage of the equities' returns over those from fixed income investments.

Variable life can take the form of *variable whole life* or *variable universal life*. Some advisors regard variable universal as the best of all possible insurance worlds, for it provides all the flexibility of universal life while giving you investment flexibility as well. Many people find that flexibility attractive. It means essentially that within certain limits, you can put more or less premium money into the policy in a given payment period; and you have a much higher degree of input over where the investment share of your premium will go.

What about disadvantages? These are the typical drawbacks:

- Fees for variable life policies are somewhat higher than for other types of insurance because of their administrative complexity.
- The investment flexibility that variable life products offer may "provide you with enough rope to hang yourself" because:
  - Unrealistic expectations for investment returns may cause you to underfund your policy.
  - Your investment decisions may not pan out, leaving you with more premiums to pay than you anticipated.

These products—whether variable whole life or variable universal—are significantly more complicated than the regular insurance products. You need to work a lot harder to come to grips with the variable products than with other kinds. If you aren't prepared to spend some time and energy monitoring your investments, you may be better off in a traditional product with steady growth and lower internal charges.

Whether you choose to purchase term insurance, cash value insurance, or a combination, here are some factors you should consider regarding any policy.

Nonforfeiture Options

You have certain legal rights when you purchase insurance. Nonforfeiture options assure you that you will have some value at a given moment in time. Any cash value product must offer the consumer or policy owner certain nonforfeiture options that you can take your cash value and apply it in certain ways.

Dividend Options

In a participating policy (one that pays dividends) you have several options for applying the dividends. The usual options are:

- You can take them in cash.
- You can ask the company to apply the dividends to reduce the premium.
- You can ask the company to reinvest the dividends within the policy to buy paid-up additional insurance.
- You can ask the company to use the additions to buy term insurance.

- Paid-up additions are small, single-premium policies purchased at net rates (i.e., without commission) that have their own cash value and death benefits. Paid-up additions in turn pay their own dividends.

Settlement Options

When you die, your beneficiaries can take the insurance benefits as a lump-sum payment. However, other options exist for receiving insurance benefits. The most common are:

- Taking them in installments
- Leaving them invested to compound at interest
- Taking them as an annuity

Disability Waiver

A disability waiver means that if you become disabled, the life insurance company will take over the premium payments and relieve you of the obligation to pay any further premiums while you are disabled. For some policies, the waiver is for the entire premium; other policies simply waive the cost of insurance to enable you to maintain the coverage.

Final Considerations on Term vs. Cash Value Policies

Every life insurance policy is, at bottom, a term policy. Every policy provides a death benefit in exchange for premiums, and every policy factors in the company's administrative expenses. Beyond that, your decision is whether you want to buy basic term insurance or instead to buy a product with features allowing you to pre-fund future premiums with cash value. The virtue of cash value policies, however, is that they are constructed to allow a level premium and even (under some circumstances) for you to cease paying premiums at all without loss of coverage. This is simply not possible with straight term insurance.

Here are some final considerations about term versus cash value insurance.

The Tax Advantages of Cash Value

Another factor affects primarily people with high incomes. Let's say that you're an executive whose deferred compensation includes both qualified and nonqualified plans. All of that income will come to you at retirement. However, let's also suppose that you still have some insurance needs today for survivor income: Your kids aren't quite grown yet. You can fund cash value policies that cover your insurance needs but also provide a means for building tax-deferred sums you may be able to take out in various tax-free ways. This is a marvelous tax diversification strategy *while* you're covering your life insurance needs. Theoretically, you could buy term insurance to cover the remainder of your capital gap. But the cash value insurance can provide some retirement and investment planning flexibility that you wouldn't have later on without that insurance.

For Others, the Option for Greater Control Through Term

If, on the other hand, you feel confident that you really will "buy term and invest the rest," term may ultimately be your best product. The big issue here is control over your cash value. There are numerous shades of gray in this regard. If you invest in a whole life policy, you have no control over what the insurance company does with your money in its portfolio. A variable policy offers you considerably more flexibility for investment, plus the tax advantages of traditional insurance. Without question, however, "investing the rest" allows you the greatest leeway as to how you proceed. If you're convinced you have the knowledge and discipline to invest "the rest," go with term.

Life Insurance for Children

Finally, a difficult issue that can pertain equally to term or cash value insurance: The question of life insurance for children. Some people regard life insurance policies for children as inadvisable. They argue that your money would be far better spent on adding coverage for you and your spouse, whose death is statistically far more likely and would devastate your children's financial future. To some extent, there's a grain of truth in this attitude. However, the overall situation is more complex. There are, in fact, good reasons to take out life insurance on a child.

The Financial Impact of an Illness or Accident. If your child were to suffer a debilitating illness or accident and die, the resulting medical expenses could ruin you financially. Life insurance may serve to protect your family's well-being overall.

A Child's Policy as the "Ground Floor" for Later Coverage. Purchasing cash value insurance on a child may provide a relatively inexpensive "ground floor" for coverage that could last your son or daughter all the way through a long, healthy life. Alternatively, the coverage might end up even more important if your child ends up having difficulty obtaining life insurance later, given some sort of health problem.

The Hazards of Modern Life. The world is sufficiently hazardous that life insurance for a child isn't farfetched anyway.

Any or all of these considerations might justify purchasing life insurance for a child. At the same time, it's important to note that obtaining life insurance for children is, in fact, inappropriate *until the parents are adequately covered.*

Ways of Obtaining Life Insurance

Once you determine the amount and kind of life insurance you need, you should consider the options for obtaining a policy.

Purchase Through an Agent. This is the "traditional" way to obtain life insurance. The reasons for buying from an agent are that the agent:

- May represent a good company whose products are unavailable through other means of purchase
- May offer assistance in educating you about life insurance
- May have tools for determining your insurance needs

Part of your task in deciding whether or not to buy insurance from an agent, then, is to determine how much help you need, what sorts of companies you wish to purchase from, and who the agent represents. You want a qualified, credentialed insurance professional willing and able to "shop around" to find the product best suited to your needs. You want an agent who will assess the marketplace to a reasonable degree, attempting to match products to your specific situation. The insurance marketplace is filled with thousands of products; you can't expect an agent to check out every one. At the same time, given current technology for inputting specifications to define various policies' terms, you aren't asking too much of an agent to have him or her "run the numbers."

Direct Purchase. You can also buy insurance by telephoning any of several companies that are direct marketers or by surfing the Internet. These are companies that sell various insurance products on a no-load basis with no sales commission. By purchasing from these companies, you are not dealing with an agent. You'll be dealing with the company's salaried representative, who will provide information about the products, including examples and quotes. Some of these representatives will be knowledgeable and helpful; however, others may not offer a high level of expertise.

Fee-for-Service Providers. A third route is to work with a fee-for-service (or fee-based) insurance provider. Such providers will charge you a fee for their time and effort to select a product that is either no load/no sales commission, or carries only a small commission. Fee-for-service providers earn their money through your fee. These, too, represent just a handful of companies. At the moment, there aren't many companies offering insurance by this means, but their number is growing.

Group Insurance. Finally, you can obtain insurance through your work. Many companies offer inexpensive term insurance policies. In addition, a fast-growing segment of the marketplace is group universal life insurance. If you're self-employed, you may be able to obtain insurance through professional associations—the bar association, accountants' associations, consultants' associations, and so forth.

Which of these means for obtaining insurance is best? This is a difficult question to answer. The most significant questions to ask about sources of coverage are:

- How much assistance do you need in selecting insurance products?
- What kind of value do you put on the professional relationship you have with the agent?
- To what degree does the counsel from a fee-for-service arrangement counterbalance the service provider's fee?
- Does the company you intend to buy from in fact provide its products only through agents?

Remember: *The bottom line is finding the right product.* With or without a commissioned agent, you want to buy the best policy you can afford from the best company you can find.

10 Big Mistakes in Insurance — #4
Calculating life insurance needs by rules of thumb rather than by assessing your actual circumstances

Rating Insurance Companies

Whatever source you choose for purchasing insurance, which companies warrant your trust? Generally speaking, consumers can obtain information about insurors from several independent firms that rate insurance companies' financial stability. These firms include A.M. Best, Duff & Phelps, Moody's Investors Service, Standard & Poor's (S&P) Corporation, and Weiss Research. Libraries, insurance agents, and the rating firms themselves are all convenient sources of the rating firms' data. You can obtain these ratings from your library, from your insurance agents, and sometimes from the rating firms themselves.

Once you have the data, however, a more difficult task begins: interpreting them. As so happens, the five firms noted above aren't consistent in how they present their ratings. Each has its own system, and the ratings don't necessarily correlate with one another. For example, A+ is A.M. Best's second-highest grade, but it's fifth from the top for S&P's and Duff & Phelps's, while Weiss Research grants an A+ rating to very few insurance companies at all. Trying to find a perfect correlation among the ratings for a particular company will be an exercise in frustration. On the other hand, if you take the various ratings and line them up, you will begin to see some patterns in how insurance companies stack up against one another. All the raters are examining the same features: the companies' financial strengths and weaknesses, momentum, and quality of management. However, even if you scrutinize insurance companies carefully, you run the risk of missing an important point.

Recent events within the insurance industry have created a "flight to quality" among insurance consumers. In and of itself, this emphasis on the carrier's quality isn't a bad thing; however, it's potentially problematic because *the strength of the company doesn't necessarily guarantee well-designed, competitively priced products.* It also doesn't necessarily follow that the companies with the highest ratings have provided the best values to their policyholders—or, for that matter, the products that best suit your needs. The rating firms rate companies, not products. You may have purchased a weak product from a strong company. Or you may have purchased a good product that's unnecessarily expensive.

Given this complex situation, what should you do?

First, your agent or financial counselor should establish the parameters for what you need in a policy. Perhaps what you need is, in fact, term insurance—or perhaps that's all you can afford. Perhaps you have the discretionary cash flow and long-term goals that make a cash value policy appropriate. Whether you choose term or cash value, the parameters you set indicate the kind of policy that the agent should obtain for you.

Second, your agent or counselor should size up the policy for its fundamental soundness. Checking the insurance company's ratings is a step in the right direction. However, the agent should also determine how the policy is constructed. What are its performance characteristics? What are its inherent risks? How does it compare with similar policies offered by other firms? By answering these questions, you can determine that the product from Company A is in fact built better and priced more competitively than the products from Companies B and C. In short, you should avoid the knee-jerk reaction to buy from the highest-rated company you can find. Set some minimum standards for your ratings, but spend as much time as possible on the competitiveness and credibility of the individual *product.*

8

PROTECTING YOUR FAMILY AND ASSETS THROUGH HEALTH, DISABILITY, PROPERTY/CASUALTY, AND AUTO INSURANCE

Life insurance is only the first of several kinds of insurance you need to protect yourself and your family from life's uncertainties. You need to protect your health as well—and your family's health. You need to protect yourself from the loss of income that a debilitating illness or accident might cause. Your home and car, too, must be insured. In this chapter, therefore, we delve into each of the kinds of insurance that provide protection against these risks.

HEALTH INSURANCE

Like life insurance, health insurance is a crucial component of risk management. Unlike life insurance, however, health insurance may be on the verge of major changes throughout the United States; reform proposals may alter how (and at what cost) many Americans receive health care coverage.

The fact that most Americans acquire health insurance through their workplace simplifies the situation to some extent; group coverage is typically cheaper, and often more complete, than what you can obtain as an individual. Yet even the work-related nature of health insurance in this country won't make all your decisions easy. Options abound, with more and more different programs to choose from. In addition to fee-for-service arrangements, you may have to consider choosing among health maintenance organizations (HMOs) or preferred provider organizations (PPOs). Losing your job throws the entire situation into a tailspin. Among the questions you'd have to ask at such a time are:

- What are your health insurance options while unemployed?
- How long can you retain your former coverage under the federal law called COBRA?
- What happens when that coverage expires?

And even if you remain happily employed until retirement, what happens after that? How will you close the many gaps in your Medicare coverage? It's no wonder that many Americans find the subject of health care profoundly worrisome.

10 Big Mistakes in Insurance—#5
Generally overestimating coverage under Medicare

How Much Health Care Insurance Is Enough?

Unless you're independently wealthy, you simply must have health care coverage. Even a relatively "minor" hospitalization—a hernia operation, for instance, or a few days' medical observation following a car accident—can cost you thousands of dollars. A major illness or accident requiring multiple surgeries, expensive drugs, physical therapy, and a protracted hospital stay can easily leave you bankrupt. Responding to the question, "How much is enough?" the glib answer is clearly "As much as possible." The reality is that you probably don't have a whole lot of choice in the matter; health care plans come to you as precisely that—*plans*. You may have some latitude regarding which plan you choose or regarding how much of that particular plan you select, but it's hard to customize your own health insurance the way that you might customize your life insurance policies. Specific limitations may apply because of the nature of your family, your health, any preexisting conditions, and so forth. In addition, the appropriateness of coverage isn't simply a matter of the total coverage you can receive. Other crucial factors include deductibles, co-payments, and stop-loss provisions. Before we consider how these specific issues add up, however, let's look at the general forms that health insurance currently takes.

Kinds of Health Care Coverage

Most Americans pay for their health care coverage through one of the following methods:

- Fee-for-service policies
- Health maintenance organizations (HMOs)
- Preferred provider organizations (PPOs)

At the moment, fee-for-service arrangements predominate, but HMOs and PPOs are increasing in number and popularity. Future health care reforms may tip the balance further.

Fee-for-Service Policies. This form of coverage allows you the greatest leeway in selecting physicians and other health care providers. You receive treatment; the insurance company then pays some or all of your medical bills. The level of coverage depends on the specific plan you have joined. Here are the most common forms of coverage:

- *Basic:* includes hospitalization, inpatient nursing services, supplies, x-rays, lab tests, and medications; surgical procedures and anesthesia; and doctors' fees for both in- and outpatient consultations.
- *Supplemental Major Medical:* augments the basic plan with backup coverage that covers most health care costs up to a predetermined limit.
- *Comprehensive Major Medical:* covers most medical costs up to a lifetime maximum.

 Q: Are dental bills covered under my health care insurance?

 A: Probably not. However, some policies include dental care as a rider to the main policy. You may also be able to obtain individual dental coverage.

Even within each of these three forms of coverage, however, many differences exist from one policy to another. Some of the differences focus on what conditions or treatments will or won't be covered; just as significant are differences between how (and how much) the company will pay of your expenses. The three big issues in this regard are deductibles, co-payments, and stop-loss provisions.

Deductibles are the amount you pay out-of-pocket before the insurance company starts to pay its contribution to your bill. Typical deductibles range from $100 to $1,000. Deductibles can differ as to amounts, when they apply, to whom they apply, and so forth. Generally, the higher your deductible, the lower your insurance premiums.

Co-payments are the portion (expressed as a percentage) of your bill that you pay over and above the deductible; the insurance company pays the rest. A typical co-payment is 20%.

Stop-loss provisions are the cutoff point after which you pay nothing more. Typical stop-loss provisions are about $2,000 to $2,500 per year.

Maximum benefit amount is the aggregate amount that the insurer will pay under the policy.

Combined, your deductible, co-payment, and stop-loss provision determine how much you will pay of your medical expenses.

Selecting your deductible is an important consideration. How high a deductible should you choose for your policy? This is a difficult question to answer—one influenced heavily by individual circumstances.

If you're young and healthy, you can afford to have the higher deductible; you're treating your health care policy essentially as a catastrophic plan. Your risks tend to lie at one end of the extreme or the other: You either have a few minor colds and other minor illnesses, or you get hit by a truck. On the other hand, if you're older, if you have a family member who's sick a lot, or if you have a lot of kids, the higher deductible will cause you significant out-of-pocket expenses over the course of a year. There's no simple, certain way to predict what will be the right deductible. What you choose is partly just a factor of how much risk you're willing to tolerate and (just as important) how high a premium you're able to afford.

For all policies, you should carefully check the following factors:

- What expenses are covered by the policy? What expenses are *not* covered?
- What are the deductibles, co-payments, and stop-loss provisions?
- What conditions or treatments are covered by the deductible?
- What is the company's maximum for payments?
- Are there interior limits within the policy—conditions and services that aren't covered?
- Is the plan guaranteed renewable and noncancelable?

Health Maintenance Organizations. With HMOs, you join the organization, pay your monthly fee, and receive your medical care, all under the umbrella of a single provider. The advantages for you are lower payments, significantly reduced paperwork, and potentially "one-stop shopping" for your health care needs. The disadvantage is chiefly the greater limitations as to which physicians and other providers you can choose. People enrolled in HMOs report widely varied levels of satisfaction with the arrangement; it's difficult to generalize about whether HMOs are "better" than fee-for-service arrangements in this sense. Statistically, however, HMOs are becoming more and more common in this country.

Should you consider joining a health maintenance organization? As we noted earlier, there are significant advantages but also genuine disadvantages to these programs. You should consider a whole range of issues before you decide. Increasingly, you may not have a choice in the matter of whether or not to join an HMO, since many companies that pay most or all of the health insurance costs for their employees are switching to only HMO coverage. If you work for other companies, you may have to pay for more of your health insurance premium if you choose a fee-for-service plan over an HMO.

Current Relationships with Physicians. Membership in an HMO means that you'll be using the organization's own doctors. If you have close patient–physician relationships with any doctors who aren't affiliated with the HMO you may find the switch disruptive.

Level of Medical Needs. The more numerous and chronic your medical needs, the more likely an HMO will pay off economically. However, you should check carefully to make sure that the HMO covers the specific conditions for which you and your family need treatment.

Travel Issues. Since most HMOs are located in urban or suburban areas, your location may affect the convenience of travel to the organization's clinic and hospital. You should also consider whether the HMO offers reimbursement for medical care you receive while traveling outside the area. (Most HMOs reimburse for emergency care elsewhere, but not all will pay for nonemergencies.)

Quality of Care. To the degree possible, try to assess the HMO's quality of care. Some organizations offer open-house tours and get-acquainted sessions during which you can see the facilities and ask questions about the program.

Costs. In addition to membership fees, what are the HMO's out-of-pocket expenses? HMOs often charge lower co-payments than fee-for-service programs do, but you should ask in detail what they are. Even if lower than for fee-for-service, they will add up quickly during an extended illness.

Preferred Provider Organizations. PPOs offer a compromise between the traditional fee-for-service programs, in which you have almost complete freedom to choose medical providers, and HMOs, in which you are essentially locked into one group of providers for your health care needs. Under a PPO arrangement, a carrier (your employer or professional association) has arranged discounts or other financial incentives with a certain group of health care providers. Such arrangements stipulate that the carrier will encourage its employees or members to seek service among the health care providers in exchange for lower fees. The employees receive less expensive medical care; the medical providers benefit from lower administrative costs.

Theoretically, you can be a member of a PPO and still receive care from any physician you choose. In practice, however, the situation is more complicated. You may receive care from any physician—even those who aren't on the preferred provider list—but the PPO won't pay for those other physicians at the reduced rates. You save money only if you stay with the approved list. In this sense, membership in a PPO could complicate your choices if you felt a need, for instance, to receive care from a noncovered specialist.

 Does my employer provide health care insurance?

 You'll have to check with your personnel or employee benefits department to determine the answer. Most large and midsized companies currently offer their employees some form of health care coverage.

Other Health Care Insurance Issues

In addition to group or individual health care insurance, you should explore your options for other kinds of coverage. These are:

- Medicare
- Medigap
- Long-term care
- COBRA

Medicare, Medigap, and long-term care are all issues that affect you chiefly after retirement, so we discuss them in Chapters 24 and 25. COBRA, however, is something that can enter the picture at any point in your adult life.

The Consolidated Omnibus Budget Reconciliation Act (COBRA) is a law that allows you to continue your group health insurance coverage if you lose or leave your job under a variety of circumstances. COBRA's advantage is obvious: interim health care coverage at times of life transition. To obtain benefits, you must fill out the required forms at your employer's benefits office. Once the period of COBRA coverage expires, you may have the option of converting your old policy to individual coverage through the same carrier. Coverage of this sort will probably be more expensive and with more limited benefits than what you had formerly, but the policy may still be cheaper than what you could obtain on your own.

You are not entitled to coverage under COBRA if you lose your job for cause or because of misconduct; however, it applies under the following circumstances:

- If your hours are cut so that you no longer qualify for health insurance coverage under your company's current plan
- If you lose your job for reasons other than misconduct
- If you leave a company to become self-employed
- If you leave a company because you became disabled
- If you are covered under your spouse's group plan and your spouse dies or becomes eligible for Medicare, or if you get divorced
- If you are too old to retain coverage under your parents' group plan
- If your spouse and dependents have group coverage through your retirement plan but the company files for Chapter 11 bankruptcy
- If your new policy has a waiting period for coverage

Coverage under these conditions varies. The final condition on this list offers coverage only for the waiting period. Quitting your job allows 18 months of coverage. Disability allows 29 months. Widowhood, a spouse's eligibility for Medicare, divorce, a company's bankruptcy, or disqualification from group coverage because of your age all allow 36 months.

An important warning: Coordinating COBRA benefits at the time of retirement is potentially tricky. Suppose that you retire at age 65. At that point you will be eligible for Medicare. As regards your individual situation, you're home free. Suppose, however, that your spouse is only 60 when you retire. Your spouse will receive health care coverage through COBRA until age 63. The problem is that your spouse will then have a gap of two years between the end of COBRA-mandated coverage and the onset of Medicare coverage—a gap that will occur at a time when many people experience a significantly increased need for medical services. If your spouse should suffer a major health problem during that gap in coverage, the financial consequences for both of you may be devastating. For this reason, we discuss COBRA again in Chapter 25, this time with special reference to retirement issues.

10 Big Mistakes in Insurance—#6
Expecting Medicare to cover a sustained need for long-term care

DISABILITY INSURANCE

Many people who make thoughtful decisions about life insurance and health care coverage take little or no action to obtain disability insurance. The reasons are fairly simple. It's somehow easier to imagine getting sick or dying than being disabled. Or else the idea of disability is more alarming even than death. As a result, there's a temptation to put the whole thought out of mind.

The fact remains: If you're in your 30s or 40s, you have a much greater chance of being disabled than dying. (Or as someone put it, you're much more likely to be "laid up" than "laid out.") The risk of disability doesn't drop markedly until you reach your mid 50s. So the difficult question you should ask yourself is, "What would happen to my family finances if I had a heart attack or got hit by a car and couldn't work?" Once you recognize disability as a real possibility, you try to transfer the risk through insurance.

 How much disability coverage is enough?

 Once again, as much as you can get. However, insurance providers are extremely cautious about how much coverage they allow; the amount you can get will be based in part on a straightforward percentage of your income. The rule of thumb is that you should try to have at least 60% of your income covered.

Group Disability Coverage

Your workplace may allow you access to the cheapest kind of disability coverage available, which is group or association disability. Coverage of this sort is basic, bread-and-butter disability insurance. It's cheap and fairly limited, but it has its advantages. Group coverage tends to be liberal in its definitions of disability for the first 2 years; many companies will define disability as your inability to perform *your own job*. After those two years, however, the companies become much more restrictive. Definitions of disability tend to be limited at that point to your inability to do *a* job. If you can be gainfully employed in some sense—even if the employment isn't your usual work—the insurance company probably won't consider you disabled at all.

An important tax consideration, however: If you pay your own disability premium and subsequently become disabled, the benefits you receive aren't taxable. However, if your employer pays your disability premiums, you will be taxed on the benefits.

Group disability policies have some other problems as well. They have limited features compared with individual policies. More significantly, they "cap out" at a specific amount per month that may not meet your expenses. Let's say you make $120,000 per year. Your group disability payments, however, are limited to $5,000 per month, or $60,000 per year. Assuming that you have fixed expenses of about $70,000 to $80,000 per year, how are you going to cover the gap between those expenses and your disability income? One possibility (depending on your employer) is to "wrap" an individual policy around your group coverage to close your capital gap. Another possibility is to find another carrier to sell you an individual policy that would provide the full disability income you need. In either case, the important thing is to compute your projected expenses realistically, then to find the best coverage you can afford.

Individual Disability Coverage

Once you've decided to obtain an individual policy and you've determined how much you want, you have many choices. You should check the following aspects of disability coverage, however, no matter what plan you're considering.

Definition of Disability. Do you feel that you must be insured for your own specific occupation? Are you disabled *if you can't continue your usual work?* Or are you disabled *only if you can't work at all?* The definition of *disability* will affect what you pay for coverage, with a more specific definition costing more than a more general one.

Waiting Period. How long must you wait before disability benefits begin? Typical waiting periods are 30, 60, 90, 120, and 180 days. The longer the wait, the lower your premiums. The price difference between a 30-day wait and a 180-day wait is significant; between 180 and 360 days, the difference is less dramatic. (The gap between the onset of disability and the onset of benefits will be more or less tolerable, depending on your company's sick-leave policies and short-term disability policies.)

 Is pregnancy covered under my disability insurance policy?

 Most policies do not cover normal pregnancies. However, they may cover disabilities that result from pregnancy.

Benefit Period. This is the duration of the disability benefits. A longer benefit period means higher premiums.

Renewability and Noncancelability. Your contract should be guaranteed renewable and noncancelable. A guaranteed-renewable, noncancelable policy means that the company can't cancel it if you continue paying the premiums. However, most companies will cancel the policy once you turn 65.

Cost-of-Living Escalator. Suppose that you buy $1,000 worth of benefits. Ten years from now, when you become disabled, you start getting your $1,000 monthly benefit, but every month the benefit goes up by 5%. This cost-of-living escalator covers for inflation.

Waiver of Premium. This means that if you become disabled, you won't have to pay any premiums during the period of disability—a significant feature, considering the probable financial strains on you at the time.

 10 Big Mistakes in Insurance—#7
Ignoring the need for disability insurance

Two final considerations. First, the most important aspect of disability insurance is simply that you *understand the need itself*. Few people can afford as much disability insurance as they ought to have. (The wealthier you are, the less probable it is that an insurance company will sell you enough to cover your expenses.) Being unable to close your capital gap completely, however, is no excuse for not trying to close it as much as possible.

Second, don't presume to rely on Social Security Disability Income (SSDI). SSDI does offer benefits in some instances, but only for severe, long-term disability. Most claims for SSDI are at least initially rejected. SSDI can become part of your disability income under certain circumstances, but it's not something you should count on.

PROPERTY/CASUALTY INSURANCE

We now move on to another category of insurance: policies that protect you and your family against economic losses from property damage and injury to other people. If you're like most people, you find the possibility of damage to your home or financial losses resulting from lawsuits almost as unpleasant as the notion of being disabled. And casualty and liability insurance is a subject you'd just as soon ignore altogether. Unfortunately, casualty/liability insurance resembles disability insurance in more ways than one. You are, in fact, at high risk of damage to your residence. Legal action against you is less likely, but almost anything is possible in our litigious society. And although you probably have some casualty/liability insurance, you may be inadequately or improperly insured. You may feel confident that you have sufficient coverage, yet the aftermath of a fire, flood, or accident may reveal that your policy is full of gaps, caps, and exclusions.

Determining Your Level of Need

As with other kinds of insurance, determining your need for casualty and liability insurance starts with careful risk analysis. Some risks, such as fire, theft, and water damage, can affect all homeowners. Other risks—snow and ice damage, flooding, or earthquakes—are far more likely to threaten your property in some geographic areas than in others. The number of teenage drivers in your family, the kinds of cars you drive, the profession or trade you practice, and other factors all influence your risks for suffering an accident or being sued. So the first step in deciding on the level of casualty/liability insurance you need is realistically to take stock of the risks you face.

You can't determine need on a general basis, however, so your risk analysis should include a thorough inventory of your home and its contents. This step of the process is a good opportunity to begin accurate recordkeeping of what you own. At a minimum, you should photograph your household possessions; an increasing number of homeowners are using camcorders instead to obtain a more detailed record. Either method is fine, although camcorders probably allow you to gather a quicker, more detailed information about your possessions. Whether you photograph or videotape, however, you should also make a list of the possessions themselves, noting model and serial numbers, approximate purchase cost, and estimated replacement cost. (Your insurer may require an appraiser to estimate replacement costs for big-ticket items, including jewelry, silverware, art objects, and antiques.) Once you've finished making your list and visual record, keep both in a place *other* than your house.

10 Big Mistakes in Insurance—#8
Carrying unrealistically low limits under your liability policies

The purpose of homeowners' insurance is to enable you to rebuild your home if it's damaged or destroyed and to replace belongings that end up stolen, destroyed, or damaged. For this reason, your goal in obtaining a policy is *to buy enough to replace most or all of your possessions that are at risk.* It's easy to underestimate your need. Many homeowners calculate their need for insurance on what they paid for their property or belongings years earlier; however, replacement or reconstruction usually costs far more now than before.

As always with insurance, the key issues for homeowners' insurance are:

- *The right policy.* Are the specific features of this insurance right for you?
- *Adequate breadth of coverage.* Are you covering what you need to cover?
- *Adequate limits.* Given your status in life, the value of your property, and the risks you're covering, is the amount of insurance truly adequate?
- *Competitive pricing.* Is this policy priced appropriately for what it offers?

The Two Aspects of Homeowners' Insurance

Homeowners' insurance includes two separate aspects: *property coverage* and *liability and medical payments.*

Property Coverage. Property coverage breaks down into three general categories.

Coverage A: House and Grounds. Your coverage must be at least 80% of the replacement cost to get the full benefit of the policy; otherwise, the benefits are limited to the actual cash value—which is replacement cost minus depreciation. What you want for Coverage A, however, is 100% guaranteed replacement coverage, 100% of replacement cost. That is, the insurer will replace the property *no matter what it costs to do so.* Older homes, especially, may cost vastly more to repair or replace than you would estimate. However, you may find that guaranteed replacement coverage for older homes is difficult to obtain.

Coverage B: Other Structures. Amounting to 10% of Coverage A, this insures your unattached garage, tool shed, or other outbuildings on your property.

Coverage C: Contents. This coverage insures everything inside your home excepting whatever may be specifically excluded; typical exclusions are gold, silver, and jewelry, which require separate riders. Coverage is generally 50% of Coverage A; however, there are specific limitations on certain items, such as watches, jewelry, and gold coins. Companies pay actual cash value—replacement less depreciation. You can pay a higher premium and obtain replacement cost as well as coverage for specific items. Some people, for instance, insist on 70% coverage to insure the contents of their dwelling.

 Q: Does my homeowners' insurance cover loss of or damage to jewelry I've loaned to my children?

 A: You are generally covered if you loan jewelry to your children on an occasional basis.

Coverage D: Loss of Use. This coverage allows you living expenses during the time required to repair or rebuild your house. The amount is 20% of Coverage A.

Note: Using specific riders, you can obtain more insurance for Coverages B, C, and D.

 Although these terms are common, you should shop around to find an insurer who offers a complete and competitively priced policy. Some companies sell package deals that may offer favorable terms, including:

- Higher internal limits
- Fewer exclusions
- More specific kinds of coverage

In addition, you should determine whether your insurance company offers discounts for certain precautions you may have taken. Typical discounts apply for safety measures such as:

- Smoke detectors
- Fire extinguishers
- Deadbolts
- Alarm systems

A good insurance agent can help you choose among the available possibilities and obtain the greatest number of discounts. Talk to your insurance agent about what's available. There may be some flexibility in determining what's the most cost-effective policy with the most reasonable deductible. Specific homeowners' policies take the following forms.

HO1—the basic policy—covers the following risks:

- Fire or lightning
- Windstorm or hail
- Explosion
- Riot or civil disturbance
- Damage from an aircraft
- Damage from a vehicle
- Smoke damage
- Vandalism or malicious mischief
- Theft
- Breakage of glass that is part of a building
- Volcanic eruption

10 Big Mistakes in Insurance—#9
Carrying inadequate deductibles on property/casualty insurance

HO2—broad coverage—covers all risks specified under HO1, as well as:

- Burglary
- Falling objects
- Weight of ice, snow, or sleet

- Freezing of plumbing, heating, or air-conditioning system, of an automatic fire protective sprinkler system, or of a household appliance
- Accidental discharge or overflow of water or steam from a plumbing, heating, or air-conditioning system
- Sudden and accidental discharge from an artificially generated electric current
- Sudden and accidental tearing apart, cracking, burning, or bulging of a heating, air-conditioning, or protective sprinkler system or of an appliance for heating water

HO3—special homeowners' coverage—covers all perils except those explicitly excluded from the contract, usually:

- Flood
- Earthquake
- War
- Nuclear accident

HO5—provides even broader coverage than HO3. This policy extends the all-risk coverage to your contents, as well as to your home, unattached property, and loss of use.

HO4 and *HO6*—provide coverage for renters and condo owners, respectively. (*Note:* HO4 and HO6 coverage apply only to the contents of an apartment or condo, not to its structure—property that the renter or condo dweller doesn't own.)

HO8—equivalent to HO1, but for older homes.

Personal Liability. Within personal liability insurance there are two subcategories: Coverage E (Personal Liability) and Coverage F (Medical Payments to Others).

Coverage E covers certain risks whether you are at home or away from home. The typical coverage is $100,000 per occurrence for your liability for bodily injury or property damage; however, the recommended amount is at least $300,000.

Coverage F pays up to $1,000 per person for medical bills if someone is injured on your property. You might want to increase this coverage to $5,000.

Keeping Your Policy Current

Once you've selected the appropriate policy, you shouldn't neglect to keep it current. Changes that may require more extensive coverage include remodeling a kitchen or other rooms, building an addition, and acquiring valuable possessions (artwork, antiques, computers, etc.).

Filing a Claim

In the event of property damage, loss, or theft, the obvious first step is reporting to your insurance agent. However, you should also photograph any damage and obtain your records (photographs, videotapes, and lists of property) to provide the insurance adjuster. It goes without saying that you should notify the police if a theft has occurred.

Here are some questions to ask your agent during your initial conversation:

- Does my policy cover the damage or loss?
- Does my claim exceed my deductible?
- How long will processing my claim take?
- What is the procedure for getting estimates on repairs or replacement?

No matter how congenial this exchange may go, you should follow up the initial conversation with a letter detailing the damage or loss. Include evidence for your claim: photographs, model and serial numbers of appliances, and descriptions of items affected.

In cases of damage to residences, you should also take action to prevent further damage (i.e., weather damage to leaky roof). Save all receipts for repairs. If the property damage requires you to seek temporary lodging, save all receipts for hotel and restaurant expenses.

The sequence of events after filing usually goes more or less as follows:

- The insurance agent and adjuster receive your information.
- They either accept or reject your claim.
- If they accept it, they offer you a settlement.
- You can accept this settlement or reject it.
- If you reject it, you can ask your agent for an explanation of its terms.
- If this explanation is unacceptable, you can negotiate a settlement until you're satisfied.
- If you remain dissatisfied or if your claim is rejected, you can appeal the settlement through the following steps (each of which you should explore fully before proceeding to the next).

  - Send your documentation to the insurance company's chief claims officer and explain the dispute.
  - Call the National Insurance Consumer Helpline at (800)942-4242 for advice and assistance on your claim.
  - Complain to your state insurance department.
  - Have an independent arbiter decide if the settlement is fair.
  - As a last resort, hire a lawyer and sue the insurance company to collect a fair settlement.

AUTOMOBILE INSURANCE

Personal auto policies are designed to cover your legal liabilities, injury to you and your family, and property damage. The coverage is broken down into Coverage A, B, C, and D.

 What if I have more than one car to insure?

 You can insure several cars under one policy. In fact, you may well receive discounted rates on the second and subsequent cars.

Coverage A: Liability Coverage. Bodily injury, pain and suffering, medical bills, funerals, lost income, and property damage to the other car. Recommended limits: $250,000 per individual; $500,000 per accident. Or: $500,000 as a single limit, with no reference to per-person maximums.

Coverage B: Medical Payment Coverage. Bills to the doctor if you're hurt in the car; it protects you (the insured), your family, and others. The standard coverage is $1,000, but $10,000 is recommended.

Coverage C: Protection from Uninsured or Underinsured Drivers. This coverage protects you if you're hit by a car whose driver is uninsured or underinsured, or if you're hit while a pedestrian. The recommended limits are $250,000–$500,000.

 Does my auto insurance cover me if I'm traveling overseas?

 No, you must obtain insurance from the rental company.

Coverage D: Physical Damage. This takes shape either as *collision* or *comprehensive*. Collision is coverage for getting hit and goes up to the actual cash value of the vehicle. Comprehensive is all risks other than collision—fire, theft, and so forth. Recommendation: Take the highest affordable deductible.

 10 Big Mistakes in Insurance—#10
Carrying collision coverage on an inexpensive automobile

UMBRELLA POLICIES

Finally, let's have a quick look at a form of insurance coverage that can protect you from financial losses exceeding what your typical property/casualty policies provide: umbrella liability insurance.

Umbrella policies are essentially extended personal liability coverage. Imagine, for instance, that someone suffers an accident on your property. Your liability coverage stops at $500,000. But the accident victim sues you for negligence and demands $1 million in damages. Under these circumstances, an umbrella policy will protect you for whatever amount you've chosen. Typical face amounts range from $1 to $5 million. Policies of this sort include coverage of your home, automobiles, other vehicles (boats, snowmobiles, etc.), and other property. In most cases, they also cover you against suits for slander, defamation, libel, and plagiarism. (The exceptions apply to professional writers.)

Surprisingly, umbrella policies are fairly cheap. The main reason for their affordability is that their payout occurs only on an excess basis. Their nature limits the number of claims that insurance companies actually receive, since they are statistically far less frequent than other types of claims. Don't let the slim chances of having to file deter you from owning this kind of coverage: Not having an umbrella policy is one of the biggest insurance mistakes you can make.

> ***Excess basis***: *claims that exceed what your other policies have already covered.*

This image of the umbrella is potentially useful in perceiving how all insurance coverage works. An umbrella protects you from misfortunes that might rain down on you and your family. A better image, however, might be that of the safety net: something that catches you if you slip and, precisely by catching you, prevents a mishap from being catastrophic. Obviously, any number of images serve the purpose. What matters is that you perceive the need for insurance, you analyze your insurance needs, and you select your specific policies carefully.

Insurance doesn't simply catch you when you fall; it also eases your anxieties about the risks inherent in being human, thus allowing you to focus on life itself rather than worrying about threats to your well-being.

9

PROVIDING FOR YOUR FAMILY THROUGH ESTATE PLANNING

Like insurance, estate planning is one of those subjects you'd probably prefer to avoid altogether. Benjamin Franklin said long ago that "Nothing is certain except death and taxes," and estate planning strikes many people as unpleasant in part because it requires thinking about *both* of these topics simultaneously. The fact remains: Estate planning is crucial as a means of providing for your family over the long term. Failing to plan for the legal and financial aftermath of your death won't spare your loved ones from the consequences; on the contrary, they'll simply have less control (and more bureaucratic hassle) than they would have otherwise. The possible results of failure to plan range from inconvenience to catastrophe.

In planning your estate, it's usually later than you think, but it's never *too* late. The big hurdle is simply getting started. The best way to begin the process is to follow six steps:

- *Step 1:* Calculate your estate's size.
- *Step 2:* Decide on your objectives.
- *Step 3:* Keep your plan flexible.
- *Step 4:* Provide for liquidity.
- *Step 5:* Aim to minimize taxes.
- *Step 6:* Schedule periodic reviews.

STEP 1 | CALCULATE YOUR ESTATE

Calculating your estate's size is crucial for at least three reasons:

- You simply should have an overview of the assets you hold and what they're worth.
- Your estate—and therefore your potential tax liability—may turn out to be larger than you imagine. This is true for many people, including most who purchased a house or other real property before the 1980s boom.
- What you own and how much the assets are worth will determine many of your estate planning strategies.

If you've filled out the net worth (assets and liabilities) worksheet in Chapter 1, you've already done what you need for this exercise. If not, you should use it now. Below (modified slightly to account for assets receivable at death) is the assets and liabilities worksheet once again.

ASSETS AND LIABILITIES WORKSHEET

ASSETS*

Cash Equivalents

Checking accounts	$_____
Savings accounts	_____
Money market accounts	_____
Money market fund accounts	_____
Certificates of deposit	_____
U.S. Treasury bills	_____
Death benefits of life insurance (with cash value of life insurance)	_____
Total	$_____

Investments

Stocks	_____
Bonds	_____
Mutual fund investments	_____
Partnership interests	_____
Other investments	_____
Total	$_____

Retirement Funds

Pension (present lump-sum value)	_____
Joint and survivor annuities (present value)	_____
IRAs and Keogh accounts	_____
Employee savings plans [e.g., 401(k)]	_____
Total	$_____

Personal Assets

Principal residence	_____
Second residence	_____
Collectibles/art/antiques	_____
Automobiles	_____
Home furnishings	_____
Furs and jewelry	_____
Other assets	_____
Total	$_____
Total assets	$(_____)

*Your estate includes one-half of the value of assets you hold with your spouse as joint tenants with right of survivorship. Other jointly held assets are included in proportion to the amount you contributed to the asset's purchase.

ASSETS AND LIABILITIES WORKSHEET *(continued)*

LIABILITIES

Charge account balances	_____
Personal loans	_____
Investment loans (margin, real estate, etc.)	_____
Home mortgages	_____
Home equity loans	_____
Life insurance policy loans	_____

Projected income tax liability	_____
Estate settlement costs	_____
Final medical costs	_____
Funeral expenses	_____
Other liabilities	_____
Total liabilities	$(_____)
Assets minus liabilities	$_____

By subtracting your total liabilities from your total assets, you'll have an idea of your estate's taxable value. This will enable you to have a clearer picture of where you stand regarding your assets and liabilities; from there you can start to determine estate planning objectives. Two important considerations, however:

First, when indicating an asset's worth, *be sure to specify its current fair market value*. What you paid at the time of purchase doesn't count. Thus, the purchase price for your home in 1973 isn't the issue; rather, it's what you could sell the house for *now*. Similarly, you should calculate the value of stocks, bonds, and other investments as accurately as possible.

Second, *beware of hidden assets*. You may neglect to consider certain items that are, in fact, part of your estate. For instance, many people don't realize that the proceeds from an insurance policy are included in the taxable estate—even though they aren't subject to the court-administered probate process. Be sure to include your share of any jointly owned property you hold with your spouse or someone else (see Chapter 10).

Here are some other items you should be sure to factor in as you calculate your estate:

- Automobiles
- Other vehicles (boats, etc.)
- Collectibles and art objects
- Antiques, including furniture
- Jewelry
- Intellectual property (patents, copyrights, etc.)
- Assets owned overseas

Here again, the governing principle is fair market value.

10 Big Mistakes in Estate Planning—#1
Omitting foreign-owned assets from your estate plan
If you're a U.S. citizen or reside in the U.S. and own any asset overseas, the assets are still subject to U.S. estate tax. Depending on the type of asset, the laws of the other country and whether the U.S. has a treaty with that country, tax may be owed to that country with the U.S. allowing a credit.

STEP 2 | DECIDE ON YOUR OBJECTIVES

Any personal estate plan must meet your objectives and the objectives of your family. If it fails in this fundamental way, the plan isn't worth the time you invest in creating it. Your first step in making an estate plan is therefore to determine what you want to accomplish. Keep in mind that your objectives will almost certainly change over time; however, later steps in the estate planning process will accommodate these changes.

The Range of Possible Objectives

Deciding on objectives in an estate plan involves far more than just answering the question, "Who gets what when I die?" That issue isn't a minor detail, but it's not the only thing you should decide. Your decisions should also address these issues in the following order of priority:

Your Own Personal Needs and Wishes. Although estate planning serves essentially to look out for others' needs, you have every right to honor your own preferences.

Your Spouse's Needs and Wishes. If you're married, one of your primary goals is probably to place your surviving spouse in a financial position that lets him or her maintain the same standard of living that the two of you enjoyed during your time together. You may well want to provide enough money for special needs, such as educating children and providing for medical expenses and emergencies.

Tax Considerations. These are important but secondary to other issues. If you neglect to achieve your personal goals, you can't consider your financial plan successful no matter how much money you save in taxes.

In addition to meeting your own needs and your family's needs, you may wish to provide funds for your heirs to:

- Supplement your children's income for normal living costs
- Buy a home
- Enter into a business venture
- Fund other appropriate endeavors

Estates and the Younger Generation

You should consider three important aspects of how estate planning can affect the younger generation.

First, *a plan that leaves too much money to children or young adults can have negative rather than positive consequences.* The ready availability of money may diminish or end the incentive to work; in addition, children may lose the joy and sense of reward from individual accomplishment.

Second, *some parents question their children's ability to manage significant sums of money prudently.* They may worry that their inheritance will be dissipated without proper supervision. In light of these considerations, you must decide how much property to leave to your family, to charity, or to others.

Third, *you must decide how much control over property each of your heirs should have,* and on what dates or at what ages to confer such control.

Estates and Closely Held Businesses

If you have an interest in a closely held business, you should consider to whom and in what manner you will dispose of the interest. You may wish to retain your interest in the business within your family, or eventually sell out to the other owners. In either case, you must plan now to achieve your objectives.

Q: **What's the urgency about estate planning?**

A: If you don't address the often perplexing and even unpleasant dilemmas involved in deciding who gets what, *someone else will eventually make those decisions for you.* Do you really want state law or an outsider to determine what happens? If not, you should clarify your goals and write them down. You can always rewrite them—and you should, in fact, probably do so from time to time.

STEP 3 KEEP YOUR PLAN FLEXIBLE

There are several fundamental ways to establish control over and yet maintain the flexibility of your estate. The two most important ways are *wills* and *revocable trusts*.

The Will

Your will is the primary means of controlling the disposition of your assets after you die. While the operation of law determines the disposition of certain property (such as jointly held property), your will generally determines who inherits property that is held in your name without beneficiary designations. It's hard to overstate the importance of having a valid, up-to-date will. If you don't have a will, you should have one written soon. If you do have a will, you should review it on a regular basis with your advisor.

If you die without a will—that is, *intestate*—your assets will be distributed according to state law regardless of your wishes. For example, state laws typically divide an intestate husband's property among his widow and children, even though he might have preferred that his wife have use of the entire estate during her life. In addition, a will enables you to designate a guardian for your minor children in the event that you and your spouse die simultaneously. In the absence of a designated guardian, a governmental agency will be responsible for selecting the person to raise your children. The choice may very well be someone that you yourself would never have chosen.

Where's the best place to keep a will?

Many people instinctively place the original of their will in their safe deposit box. However, this can be a mistake in those states, such as New York, where the box is sealed upon the death of the renter. That's because the original must be filed with the Register of Wills following your death to formally name your executor and to begin the probate process. In states where the box is sealed at death, this process can be delayed and additional costs may be incurred in order to open the box before an executor is named. It may be best to leave the original with the attorney who drafted the will. You should also keep copies of the will in your safe deposit box and in a safe place in your home so that it's quickly available when needed.

The Revocable Trust

Having an attorney write a current will for you (and your spouse) is the best way to ensure implementation of your plan. However, revocable trusts may be used along with a will to control the disposition of certain assets. (For a discussion of revocable trusts, see Chapter 12.)

> **Revocable trust:** *a living trust that can be amended, modified, or canceled at any time.*

Other Means of Maintaining Flexibility

Revocable trusts and wills are exceptionally flexible tools that can help you meet your present objectives. Generally, you may execute a will and a revocable trust and still be able to revise your estate plan at any time. These arrangements allow you to retain complete control over any property that will pass under the provisions of your will or that is included in your revocable trust. The catch is that assets disposed of either by a will or by a revocable trust will be included in your gross estate for estate tax purposes. (See Chapter 10 for a detailed discussion of estate tax.)

In addition to maintaining flexibility by means of the documentary form you choose (i.e., a will, a revocable trust, etc.), you can attain flexibility by other means. Two of the most common are a *power of appointment* and *careful management of your own affairs during life.*

Power of Appointment. Including a *power of appointment* in a trust instrument preserves a degree of flexibility. It gives the possessor the power to direct distribution of the trust property to satisfy the changing needs of your beneficiaries. By this means, trust assets can be distributed when the holder of the power—someone you trust—believes that the beneficiaries need them most at the time the power is exercised.

Managing Your Affairs During Disability. Providing flexibility in managing your affairs during life is also important. An effective durable power of attorney for both you and your spouse can ensure that someone you trust will have the authority to manage your assets in case of disability. To be durable (i.e., effective even in the event of physical or mental disability), the power of attorney must be drafted in accordance with the law of the state in which you intend to use it. (See Chapter 13 for a discussion of durable powers of attorney.)

Situations That Reduce Flexibility

Finally, here are three situations that can reduce flexibility:

- Joint ownership of property
- Gifts
- Irrevocable trusts

Joint Ownership of Property

Jointly owned property (i.e., property you hold with someone as *joint tenants with right of survivorship* or as *tenants by the entirety*) passes under local law to the survivor upon the death of the first joint owner. Thus the first decedent's will (or trust instrument) will have no effect on the disposition of such assets. Also, joint ownership can sometimes create tax problems. It's therefore preferable in most estates of around $650,000 to $1,500,000 to maintain joint ownership with right of survivorship *only for your residence and a working bank account.* (Ownership as tenants in common allows you to state to whom your interest should pass.) Furthermore, many states require that both joint tenants must act to make desired changes in ownership. This restriction can sometimes curtail freedom to sell assets, make gifts, transfer property into trusts, corporations or partnerships, and make other desirable arrangements.

10 Big Mistakes in Estate Planning—#2
Holding all assets jointly

If you hold all assets jointly, these assets pass by law to the survivor when one holder dies, which can render ineffective otherwise carefully constructed estate plans. For example, joint accounts set up for convenience with only one child can upset an equal distribution pattern in your will. Also, overuse of joint tenancy with a spouse can frustrate the intended use of both spouses' unified credits. (See Chapter 10.)

Gifts

To make a gift that's effective for tax purposes, you must part with control of the property. Consequently, gift giving is a highly inflexible arrangement and doesn't allow for changing circumstances. However, a gift program can often produce large tax savings; you should therefore consider it when gifts are otherwise appropriate. (See Chapter 11 for a detailed description of gifts, gift taxes, and gift programs.)

Irrevocable Trusts

Under the proper conditions, *irrevocable trusts* are useful and can provide the tax savings afforded by gifts. Although they are somewhat inflexible, they provide a greater degree of continued control over the property than do outright gifts. You should limit their use to situations where you can retain enough assets to allow you the flexibility to cope with unexpected changes in your objectives. (See Chapter 12 for a detailed discussion of irrevocable trusts.)

STEP 4   PROVIDE FOR LIQUIDITY

Depending on the size of your estate, a large portion of it may be needed to pay estate and inheritance taxes. Your family may require cash for various administrative and other expenses associated with your death. Typical expenses immediately following death include:

- Funeral expenses
- Executor's fees
- Legal fees
- Accounting fees
- Appraisal fees
- Medical expenses incurred during a final illness

Your estate must generally pay all debts outstanding at the time of your death; the exceptions are those that provide for a specified term of payment, such as a mortgage on your home. Your family will also need income to cover readjustment and living expenses. All of these expenses underscore the need for liquidity.

> **Liquidity:** *in this context, your estate's ability to meet cash requirements arising at the time of your death.*

Sources of Liquidity

Sources of cash under these circumstances include:

- Social Security benefits payable to your survivors
- Separate income-producing property
- Cash in the bank
- Certificates of deposit
- Life insurance proceeds

- Marketable securities
- Payouts from an employee benefit plan

In Chapter 13 we discuss some specific liquidity issues.

Closely Held Business Interests

If your estate includes closely held business interests, you may wish to consider a *buy-sell agreement* (either with your co-owner or with the business entity) to ensure that these interests can be converted into cash or notes receivable following your death. Such agreements serve several purposes: to create cash at the time of death, to shift control of the entity, to secure continuity of management, to fix a value for the interests, and to accomplish other business and personal objectives.

Nonliquid Assets and Their Consequences

Assets not readily convertible into cash may be of substantial value. Their value can increase estate taxes and other administration costs, however, since costs associated with insurance, appraisal, and management of such large holdings rise as the value rises. To complicate matters, these assets may not generate ready cash to meet expenses.

Nonliquid assets include:

- Real estate
- Closely held corporate stock
- Partnership interests
- Notes and mortgages
- Jewelry
- Art objects
- Antiques

If your estate contains a disproportionate amount of such nonliquid assets, you and your advisors can find several solutions to the problem.

EXAMPLE

■ You may choose to write a definite plan for disposing of at least some of these assets during your lifetime, or you may make arrangements for an orderly sale at the time of your death. If you choose the latter, you'll have to work closely during your lifetime with the people you've selected to handle your estate after death. Even if you fail to prepare for sale, your executor may still be able to dispose of some of the nonliquid assets in an orderly way. ■

Remember this point when deciding which assets to sell during life and which to keep: Appreciated assets will trigger a capital gains tax if sold during life, but will have their basis stepped up to fair market value if held at death. This step up avoids tax on any gain which arises before death. And when naming your executors in your will, consider selecting someone who has expertise in dealing with the types of assets that comprise your estate.

Special Tax Rules Can Help Relieve Liquidity Problems

If your estate meets certain technical requirements, special redemption provisions are available for closely held stock. Your estate may also be eligible for *paying estate taxes in installments* if an appropriate portion of it consists of an active trade or business. (For a discussion of these techniques, see Chapter 13.)

You may also qualify for (1) tax deferrals based on demonstrating "reasonable cause" or hardship, and (2) special valuations for certain real property.

STEP 5   AIM TO MINIMIZE TAXES

Assuming that your basic goal is to conserve as many of your assets as possible to benefit your heirs, minimizing taxes is a major consideration. Federal estate taxes and state inheritance taxes in some estates can erode your assets if you don't plan carefully. Next we look at some of the tools for trimming death taxes.

Marital Deduction. The *marital deduction* is a key tax-saver or tax-deferror designed for married couples. This subject is so important that we cover it in detail in Chapter 10.

Gifts and Charitable Contributions. Here are two more important ways to save taxes. However, these are sufficiently complex topics that we discuss them separately in Chapter 11.

Trusts. Here again, this is a topic of tax-saving programs that warrants a detailed discussion (see Chapter 12).

STEP 6   SCHEDULE PERIODIC REVIEWS

As noted earlier, your planning objectives are sure to change with new circumstances and needs. Certain life events can knock even the best-made estate plan out of kilter, and others can make fine-tuning necessary:

- Birth or adoption of children
- Death of a spouse or other heir
- Marriage
- Divorce
- Illness
- Educational needs
- Maturity of family members
- Employment change
- Receipt of a gift or inheritance
- Conversion of property to cash
- Changes in property values
- Changes in federal or state tax laws
- Changes in state property or probate laws
- Court decisions and government rulings

Keeping your plan flexible will enable you to make changes to meet altered circumstances; even so, obviously you must review the plan to determine where and when you need revisions. The only realistic way to do so is to establish a date when you and your spouse will review your plan. In fact, you should perform such a review at regular intervals—every September, for example.

If you take these six steps now, you'll be far ahead of the great majority of your fellow citizens—including a surprising number of those who have estates large enough to incur significant and unnecessary tax burdens simply because they've failed to plan.

10

ESTATE TAXES AND DEDUCTIONS

In Chapter 9 we outlined the six basic steps that should govern the estate planning process. Now let's consider the specific issues that influence the decisions you make. (We explore other subjects in Chapters 11 and 12 and conclude in Chapter 13.)

THE ABCs OF ESTATE TAX

Federal estate tax is a levy on the transfer of property at death. Your gross estate will include the fair market value of all property to the extent of your interest in it at the time of your death.

Assets Subject to Estate Tax

Here are the types of property included by law in your gross estate:

- Tangible personal property, real estate, and other assets
- Jointly owned property
- Life insurance
- Employee benefits
- Certain gifts
- Gift tax paid within 3 years of death

Tangible Personal Property, Real Estate, and Other Assets. This category includes property you own that is transmitted at death according to provisions of a will or state intestacy laws. Such property is commonly referred to as the *probate estate*. Examples of this category include:

- Real estate
- Stocks, bonds
- Furniture
- Personal effects
- Jewelry
- Works of art
- Interests in a partnership
- Interests in a sole proprietorship
- Bank accounts
- Promissory notes or other evidence of indebtedness

 What's the difference between personal property and real property?

 Real property is land and the buildings on land. Personal property is everything else—cash, stocks and bonds, autos, household items, clothing, jewelry, and so forth. Personal property also includes intellectual property—patents, copyrights, and trademarks.

Jointly Owned Property. Only one-half of the value of property that a husband and wife own as *joint tenants with right of survivorship* (or *tenants by the entirety*) is included in the estate of the first spouse to die. The marital deduction prevents the property transfer from actually causing federal estate tax to be owed. Upon the survivor's death, however, the entire property will be subject to tax (assuming that it's still held at the time of death). See the second half of this chapter for more information on the marital deduction.

If the joint tenants aren't married, the entire value of the property is included in the gross estate of the first to die unless the estate can prove that the other joint owner actually furnished all or part of the payment for acquiring the property. If you and another joint owner acquired property by gift or inheritance, only your fractional share of the property is included. Similarly, if you hold property as a tenant in common with someone else, your estate will include your fractional interest of the property's value.

Life Insurance. Your gross estate will include life insurance proceeds that are receivable (1) by your estate or (2) by other beneficiaries if you possess any *incidents of ownership* in the policies at the time of your death.

Q: What do the incidents of ownership include?

 A: They are:

- The power to change the beneficiary of the policy
- The right to cancel the policy and receive the cash value
- The right to borrow against the policy
- The right to assign the policy

If someone else owns the policy on your life from its inception, the policy's proceeds aren't part of your estate. Also, if you transfer a policy to another party or to a trust and retain no incidents of ownership, the proceeds will generally be removed from your estate once you have survived for 3 years after the gift.

Employee Benefits. The value of payments from qualified pension plans and other retirement plans payable to surviving beneficiaries of an employee (or owner, in the case of a Keogh plan) is generally included in the decedent's gross estate.

Certain Gifts and Gift Tax Paid Within Three Years of Death. Gifts of property made during your lifetime generally aren't included in your gross estate, but they must be figured in the estate tax calculation if they exceed the $10,000 annual gift tax exclusion (see Chapter 11). As noted above, however, life insurance proceeds are includable if you gave away the policies or incidents of ownership within 3 years of your death. Also included is any gift tax you paid within 3 years of your death. Finally, lifetime gifts in which you retain some interest (e.g., life income interest) or control (e.g., voting rights in gifted stock) will be included in your gross debt.

 Allowable Deductions

You can deduct expenses for:

- Funerals
- The estate's administration
- Debts
- Unpaid mortgages
- Other indebtedness on property included in the gross estate

Also allowed are such special deductions as the marital deduction and the charitable deduction. (See the second half of this chapter for details on these deductions.)

Funeral and Administration Expenses

Deductible funeral expenses include:

- Burial costs, such as expenditures for a tombstone, monument, or mausoleum
- Costs for a burial lot
- Costs for future care of a gravesite
- Other related costs

Deductible administration costs include:

- Executor's commissions
- Attorney's fees
- Accounting fees
- Appraisal fees
- Court costs
- Other related costs

Other Deductible Estate Debts

To be deductible, debts must be enforceable personal obligations. Typical examples are your outstanding mortgage or personal bank loan, auto loan, credit card balances, utility bills, and so forth. The deductible amount includes any interest accrued on the debt at the time of your death. Transfers made under a marital property settlement incident to a divorce may be treated as estate expenses. Taxes are also deductible debts if they are accrued and unpaid at the time of your death. Deductible taxes include accrued property taxes, gift taxes unpaid at death, and income taxes. For example, if someone dies in February and his or her income tax return filed for the preceding year reports tax due of $2,000, that amount is a deductible estate expense.

Family-Owned Business Deduction

The estate of a decedent dying after 1997 is allowed a deduction of a portion of the value of a qualifying business interest if the interest comprises a substantial portion of the estate and satisfies family ownership and material participation tests. The maximum excludable amount is the excess of $1.3 million over the allowable unified credit equivalent in the year of the decedent's death (see table on page 181).

Valuation of Estate Property

Property is included in an estate at its fair market value. Property that trades on an established market may be valued easily. For example, publicly traded stocks and bonds are valued based on the average of the high and low selling price on the date of death (or, if elected, the date 6 months after death). However, interests in closely held businesses or partnerships must generally be appraised to take the business's assets, earning capacity, and other factors into account. You're probably familiar with the process of getting a home appraised for purposes of obtaining a mortgage or home equity loan. It's especially important to have a certified appraiser with expertise in appraising the type of property that needs to be appraised. A CPA, attorney, or personal financial planner can assist in identifying an appropriate person to appraise business interests or other difficult-to-value property for estate or gift tax valuation purposes.

Your gross estate is valued as of the *date of your death* or *6 months later*, whichever your personal representative elects. An election to value the estate 6 months after date of death will apply to all assets in the estate. Your executor can make the election only if doing so results in a decrease in estate tax liability. The amount remaining after subtracting any allowable deductions is your taxable estate; it's on this amount that the federal estate tax is computed.

Your executor should determine if using the alternate valuation date produces a tax advantage. He or she must then value all your assets on the date selected. The choice reflects any of several different strategies.

■ Suppose, for instance, that you died at the end of a bull market. Your assets might well be worth less 6 months after the date of your death; your executor thus has the opportunity to use the valuation on the 6-months-after-death date, which reduces the total size of your estate for tax purposes. However, the executor would have to value *all* your assets as of the alternate date. If your house and other tangible assets were appreciating while your stocks were depreciating, the big question would be how everything would balance out. ■

Tax Rates

The federal estate tax is progressive in nature and ranges from the lowest rate of 18% up to a rate of 55% for estates larger than $3 million. There's an additional 5% tax on taxable estates larger than $10 million that is designed to gradually eliminate the benefit of the lower tax brackets. The following table shows illustrative estate tax calculations.

ILLUSTRATIVE ESTATE TAX CALCULATIONS

Taxable Estate	Tax Before Credits	Marginal Estate Tax Rate
$ 150,000	$ 38,800	32%
500,000	155,800	37%
1,000,000	345,800	41%
2,500,000	1,025,800	53%
3,000,000	1,290,800	55%
5,000,000	2,390,800	55%

Note: Each estate is allowed a unified credit as described below.

Credits

In determining the net amount of federal estate tax due, your estate's personal representative can claim certain credits against your tentative tax:

- Unified estate and gift tax credit
- State death tax credit
- Foreign death tax credit
- Credit for tax on prior transfers

Unified Estate and Gift Tax Credit

Each estate is entitled to a unified credit in 1999 equal to the amount of tax generated by a transfer of $650,000. The credit is called a *unified credit* because we have a unified system of gift and estate taxation, and because the credit applies against *both* gift and estate taxes. In other words, no estate or gift taxes will be assessed on the first $650,000 of your combined taxable gifts and transfers at death. You start owing tax once the aggregate amount of your taxable transfers during life and at death exceeds $650,000. At that point, the tax rates start with a 37% bracket and range as high as 55%.

The 1997 Tax Act provides for a gradual increase in the amount of the unified credit equivalent to $1,000,000, as follows:

GRADUAL INCREASE IN THE UNIFIED CREDIT EQUIVALENT	
Year of Death or Gift	Unified Credit Equivalent
2000–2001	675,000
2002–2003	700,000
2004	850,000
2005	950,000
2006–forward	1,000,000

The increase will help restore some of the value of the credit equivalent that has been eroded by inflation since 1986, when it became $600,000.

E X A M P L E

■ Here's a very basic example. Suppose that Frank's estate is $700,000. If he died in 1999, his estate would owe no taxes on the first $650,000. The estate would owe tax at the 37% rate on the remaining $50,000, or $18,500. If he dies in 2000, the additional $25,000 of credit equivalent would reduce the tax to 37% of $25,000, or $9,250. ■

State Death Tax Credit

Your estate receives a credit for estate or inheritance taxes paid to any state or the District of Columbia. The tax must actually be paid on property included in the gross estate. The credit is limited to an amount computed under a graduated rate table based on the amount of the taxable estate reduced by $60,000. Most states only impose a tax on an estate in an amount designed to equal the credit allowable under the federal tax system. This type of state tax is called a "soak-up" (or "pick-up") tax because it *soaks up* the federal credit allowed. Some states do impose higher taxes, however. To the extent that the state death tax does exceed the credit allowed, the estate winds up bearing the extra expense.

Foreign Death Tax Credit

A credit is allowed against the federal estate tax for any death taxes actually paid to a foreign country, Puerto Rico, or the Virgin Islands on property that is also subject to the federal estate tax. The credit is limited to the U.S. tax attributable to the property taxed by the foreign country.

Credit for Tax on Prior Transfers

A credit is allowed against the federal estate tax for part or all of the estate tax paid on property transferred to you before your death or to your estate afterward from someone who died within 10 years before or 2 years after your death. An example might be if you died 2 years after receiving a bequest from a wealthy uncle. The credit prevents two successive taxes from being levied on the same property. Transferred property need not be identified in your estate or even be in existence at the time of your death. It's sufficient that the transfer of property was subjected to federal estate tax in the other person's estate and that you died within the prescribed period.

State Tax Considerations

All states impose some kind of estate and/or inheritance tax. As noted earlier, in many states the estate tax is simply a soak-up tax—the amount of the federal credit for state death taxes. In these states an estate that owes no federal estate tax because of the unified credit will generally owe no state death taxes, either. But remember: Many states impose an inheritance tax on the person that *receives* the property from the decedent. This tax falls heaviest on bequests outside the immediate family. Therefore, in states that have estate or inheritance taxes not tied to the federal credit or other federal rules (such as the unlimited marital deduction), state death tax considerations may influence the form in which you should structure your estate plan.

Illustrative Estate Tax Computations

Your personal representative will be responsible for computing the estate tax for your estate and filing a tax return if the value of the estate is above the unified credit equivalent. The tax will vary not only with the size of your estate but also with the type of beneficiaries you've named, such as a spouse or charity. Your personal representative will compute your gross estate for estate tax purposes by totaling the fair market values of all your assets.

In the tables that follow we show three examples for computing the gross estate, the taxable estate, and the estate tax due for three different-sized estates of married people, each of whom is assumed to have died in 1999 and was the first of the two spouses to die.

COMPUTING THE GROSS ESTATE

	Tom	Harriet	Dick
Assets			
Cash	$ 3,000	$ 15,000	$ 60,000
Marketable securities	7,000	20,000	50,000
Business equity	0	450,000	525,000
Residence	200,000	285,000	185,000
Vacation residence	0	0	90,000
Personal property	95,000	25,000	40,000
Deferred compensation	105,000	25,000	75,000
Ordinary life insurance	10,000	80,000	570,000
Group-term insurance	50,000	50,000	75,000
Gross estate	$470,000	$950,000	$1,670,000

COMPUTING THE TAXABLE ESTATE

	Tom	Harriet	Dick
Gross estate	$470,000	$950,000	$1,670,000
Deductions			
Funeral expenses	3,000	4,000	6,000
Estate administration expenses	2,000	15,000	44,000
Debts	2,000	1,000	2,000
Mortgages	38,000	28,000	48,000
Marital deduction	425,000	250,000	550,000
Charitable deduction	0	2,000	20,000
Total deductions	$470,000	$300,000	$ 670,000
Taxable estate	$ 0	$650,000	$1,000,000

COMPUTING THE ESTATE TAX

	Tom	Harriet	Dick
Gross estate	$470,000	$950,000	$1,670,000
Deductions	470,000	300,000	670,000
Taxable estate	0	650,000	1,000,000
Tentative tax	0	211,300	345,800
Unified credit	0	211,300	211,300
State tax credit	0	0	33,200
Estate tax	$ 0	$ 0	$ 101,300

These three examples show that computing federal estate tax is straightforward. The decedent's representative computes a tentative tax using the tax rate tables. Then the unified credit ($211,300 maximum for 1999) and any allowable credit for state death taxes paid are applied as direct, dollar-for-dollar offsets against the tentative tax specified in the federal estate tax tables for the taxable estate. Remember that the unified credit equivalent is $650,000 in 1999; it increases until it reaches $1,000,000 in 2006.

E X A M P L E

■ At death, Tom had $3,000 in savings and checking accounts, 100 shares of marketable securities worth $70 each, and a residence worth $200,000. Tom's personal property consisted largely of a collection of rare coins valued at $80,000; the balance consisted of his car, clothing, and other personal effects. In addition, Tom had accumulated $105,000 in his employer's deferred bonus and 401(k) plans, and his estate was the beneficiary of one whole life policy and an employer-maintained group term policy.

Besides size, Harriet's and Dick's gross estates differ from Tom's in the following respects: Harriet was the sole proprietor of a consulting business valued at $450,000 at the time of her death, and Dick was a law firm partner whose interest was valued at $525,000 when he died. Dick also owned a beach house, which his father had willed to him outright.

Tom's will provided that his wife should receive his total estate after payment of debts, thereby reducing the taxable value of the estate to zero. Tom could do this because of the unlimited marital deduction (see the discussion of this topic that follows this example).

In Harriet's case, the size of her estate's marital deduction was the product of some planning. Harriet had designed her deduction to dovetail with the unified credit equivalent available in the year of her death, thus eliminating any estate tax liability. In other words, because her death occurred in 1999, she left the first $650,000 of estate value to a trust that would generate tax and "use up" her unified credit; then she left the balance, or residue of her estate, to her husband.

Dick's estate used less than the full amount of the marital deduction needed to eliminate the estate tax; consequently, his estate paid some estate taxes at the lower marginal rates, even with the unified credit. Dick and his wife Elaine had decided that Elaine's anticipated financial needs would not require her outright ownership of all of Dick's estate, so Dick left the balance to his two sons, equally. ■

THE MARITAL DEDUCTION

Our second major topic for this chapter is the *marital deduction*—a feature of both the estate tax and the gift tax. If you're married, you are allowed an unlimited deduction for the value of property transferred to your spouse during life or at the time of your death. To put it bluntly: You can give or bequeath as much as you want to your spouse, and neither you nor your estate will pay gift or estate tax.

The estate tax marital deduction essentially permits you and your spouse to postpone paying estate tax until the second spouse dies. An important feature of the marital deduction is the flexibility to arrange the situation so that your spouse receives a lifetime income interest in the bequeathed property, while you determine who eventually receives that property.

Most married persons should take advantage of both the unified credit and the unlimited marital deduction to reduce the federal estate tax to zero in the estate of the first spouse to die. Harriet's case is an example of how to accomplish this goal. Her marital deduction bequest was calculated to be only $250,000 out of a gross estate of $950,000 (i.e., no more than the amount left after subtracting the 1999 unified credit equivalent of $650,000 and $50,000 of other deductions from the gross estate). As a result of using a "zero-tax" marital deduction, her estate paid no federal estate tax. You can tailor your marital bequest to your specifications. Tom used the full unlimited marital deduction, while Dick used less than the zero-tax amount in order to pay some estate taxes at the lower brackets.

The unlimited marital deduction is unavailable for property transferred by gift or at death to a donee or surviving spouse who isn't a U.S. citizen at the time of the transfer. Instead, the law provides that lifetime gifts to a non-U.S.-citizen spouse will be tax-free to the extent of $101,000 per year as of 1999. (This amount will be increased for inflation.) Also, you can draft your will to place property in a special type of trust for the noncitizen spouse that will postpone the imposition of estate tax until either the property is distributed out of the trust or the surviving spouse dies. Called a

10 Big Mistakes in Estate Planning—#3
Constructing an estate plan that uses the marital deduction to reduce estate taxes when a spouse who isn't a U.S. citizen inherits property
No estate tax marital deduction is available to recipient spouses who are not U.S. citizens unless a Qualified Domestic Trust is used.

Qualified Domestic Trust, it permits property to qualify for the marital deduction if certain requirements are met to prevent ultimate avoidance of the estate tax. Even if the decedent's spouse's will failed to provide for a Qualified Domestic Trust, the surviving spouse can create one and place the inherited assets in it to qualify for the marital deduction.

The Estate Tax Marital Deduction

The estate tax marital deduction permits you to make unlimited transfers to a surviving spouse. The manner in which property passes to a surviving spouse is quite flexible. Property can pass through an outright bequest to the spouse or by operation of law (in the case of joint ownership of property with the right of survivorship). Alternatively, you can arrange for the use of trusts.

The marital deduction provisions ensure that the surviving spouse will actually receive the property to which the deduction relates (or at least the lifetime income from the property). It also ensures that unless subsequently disposed of in either a sale or a transfer subject to gift tax, this property will eventually be taxed in the surviving spouse's estate.

Life Insurance

Any life insurance proceeds included in your estate will qualify for the marital deduction if they are payable in a lump sum to your surviving spouse or to a trust that qualifies for the marital deduction. In addition, insurance proceeds will qualify under certain optional forms of settlement (e.g., an annuity) if either one of the following is true:

- The principal or any remaining unpaid installments are payable to your surviving spouse's estate upon death.
- Your surviving spouse is given a general power of appointment to designate the beneficiary of the principal remaining at death.

As we'll note later, using a life insurance trust will avoid tax on both estates.

Insurance policies offer a variety of options for paying the proceeds to the named beneficiaries. Having the proceeds paid in a lump sum is the most commonly used option. On the other hand, either you or the beneficiary may elect to have the proceeds paid in an annuity over the beneficiary's life.

If your spouse, as beneficiary, is in a financial position where he or she doesn't need the proceeds, some life insurance policies offer an "interest only" option, under which the survivor receives only interest on the principal for life. At death, the principal is paid to beneficiaries named by your spouse. This arrangement will qualify for the marital deduction, but the proceeds will be included in your spouse's estate. Also, insurance proceeds will qualify for the marital deduction, if they are paid to your spouse in a lump sum or in a life annuity with you (or your spouse) having the right to designate the beneficiary of any remaining guaranteed payments. As an additional benefit of using life insurance to provide for your beneficiaries, the proceeds are not subject to the probate process unless they are payable to your estate.

Estate Planning Considerations

Planning is crucial to secure the optimum estate tax marital deduction. Poor planning may result in transferring too much property to the surviving spouse—often referred to as "overfunding" the marital deduction. This would cause an unnecessarily large estate tax at the surviving spouse's death. Typically, you want to plan property transfers to maximize use of the marital deduction and both spouses' unified credits. Here are some alternatives to consider:

- Outright bequest to your spouse
- Jointly owned property
- Insurance arrangements
- Marital deduction trusts
- Marital deduction trusts with charitable remainders

Outright Bequest to Spouse

You can leave property outright to your spouse in your will. As a consequence, your spouse will have absolute ownership of the assets received and may do with them as he or she wishes. Outright bequests qualify for the marital deduction.

An outright transfer gives your spouse the greatest flexibility to react to changing circumstances after your death. On the other hand, outright transfers leave you with the least amount of continuing control over your property. When deciding whether you should leave property outright to your spouse, consider the following issues:

- Your spouse's experience in managing investments
- Your spouse's and other family members' anticipated financial needs
- Concerns you may have over how much of the property transferred to your spouse will eventually pass to your children or other selected heirs
- Whether your marital deduction will be overfunded

Jointly Owned Property

You and your spouse probably hold one or more bank accounts, your home, and perhaps other assets in joint names. In this case, the form of joint ownership will probably result in the property passing to the survivor by operation of law. Joint ownership is popular partly because these assets will avoid probate. However, joint holding of property where the property passes to your survivor removes some of your flexibility in planning for the transfer of those assets. The ownership of excessive amounts of jointly owned property between husband and wife can result in overfunding the marital deduction. This generally increases the amount of taxes that would otherwise be payable at the survivor's death without producing any additional savings in the first estate. You can't pay less than zero tax in the first estate!

Most advisors recommend very limited use of joint property ownership. For estates where combined family assets don't exceed the unified credit exemption amount, unlimited use of jointly owned property generally causes few problems. For larger estates, however, only your residence and a working bank account should usually be in joint names. If the sole joint tenants are husband and wife, only one-half of the property will be included in the estate of the first spouse to die. That one-half will qualify for the marital deduction, and its income tax basis will be stepped up to its fair market value at the date of the first spouse's death. The entire property will be subject to estate tax when the survivor dies (assuming the property is held at death).

Marital Deduction Trusts

For larger estates and estates containing closely held businesses, a marital deduction trust can often serve to provide you more control over assets while still qualifying for the marital deduction. This trust generally includes all property intended to qualify for the marital deduction, other than outright bequests and property interests passing by operation of law. One form of marital trust gives the survivor an income interest for life in the trust property and a general power of appointment exercisable during life or by will. This power enables the survivor to leave the trust property to anyone, including his or her own estate.

 Q: Why should I use a marital deduction trust of this type?

 A: The main reason is that you can appoint a trustee to control and manage property transferred during your surviving spouse's lifetime.

E X A M P L E

■ Let's say that you own a closely held business. Your spouse may not be sufficiently competent or experienced to manage the business effectively after your death. By setting up a general power of appointment marital deduction trust, you can vest voting control in another person (perhaps a family member) who is active in the company; at the same time you ensure that your spouse receives the income from the business during his or her lifetime and retains control over who will ultimately inherit the company. Giving your spouse control over ultimate disposition may be desirable in some cases, as when you want your spouse to distribute the property based on the children's circumstances at his or her death. ■

Additional flexibility is available by using a *qualified terminal interest property (QTIP) trust* as the marital trust. A QTIP trust is an estate tax mechanism that allows you to provide a life income interest for your spouse while determining in *your* will who will take the property after your spouse's death. You can, if you wish, also give your spouse the power to appoint any remaining trust property among a limited class of persons (probably your children) in his or her will. The lifetime income requirement in any marital deduction trust is strict. It can't terminate after a given number of years or upon your spouse's remarriage.

A QTIP transfer qualifies for the marital deduction only to the extent that your executor elects to claim it. This actually provides added flexibility to the estate because it allows the executor to decide if there may be some tax advantage to be gained from paying tax in the first estate. Of course, the surviving spouse's taxable estate will include the portion of the trust property for which the marital deduction was elected.

The QTIP trust can be particularly appropriate when stock of a family business is involved and a family member other than the surviving spouse is active in the company. A QTIP trust is also a convenient way to assure your spouse adequate income during his or her life while ensuring that your assets ultimately go where you want them to go. Thus, if you have children from a previous marriage, or if your spouse remarries after your death, the children named in your will could be assured that they will be the eventual beneficiaries of your estate. This can provide a great sense of comfort: No matter what happens to your family structure following your death, your money will go to your children.

A *bypass trust*—also called a *credit shelter* or *nonmarital trust*—is typically utilized in conjunction with a marital deduction trust. The bypass trust receives just enough assets to absorb the unified credit equivalent remaining at the decedent's death—a maximum of $650,000 for decedents dying in 1999. Although the survivor will generally have an income interest in this trust and can receive trust principal if needed, he or she will have no power over the final disposition of the assets of the trust. It's called a bypass trust because the property, along with any appreciation and income accumulation, will bypass taxation in the surviving spouse's estate.

The estate tax charitable deduction permits you to make an unlimited amount of tax-free transfers to most charitable organizations. The property can pass to charity in the form of an outright bequest or distribution, or through the use of a charitable lead trust or charitable remainder trust created during your lifetime or at your death.

Marital Deduction Trust with Charitable Remainder

In another variation of the marital deduction trust, you can specify a qualified charitable organization to receive the property eventually. The trust would be established following the first spouse's death and would qualify for the marital deduction, since the survivor would be entitled to all the trust's income for life. Following the survivor's death, the property would be included in his or her estate but would not be subject to any federal estate tax, since it would pass to a qualified charity. This may be an ideal way of providing for your spouse and a favorite charity.

 Whom should I choose as my trustee?

 In some families, friction results from disagreements over whether the surviving spouse or someone else—perhaps a grown son or daughter—will administer the trust. You may choose to have your surviving spouse receive benefits from a trust that is intended to allow her or him to live comfortably, yet not necessarily serve as trustee. In a harmonious family, this won't present any problems; the surviving spouse will continue living as before, and the children will readily allow her or him any needed use of the money. In other cases, the situation won't be quite so harmonious, and the spouse or an independent advisor may need to serve alone or as co-trustees. In some cases, a bank or institutional trustee may be advisable if the assets in the trust need professional management. The upshot, then, is to choose carefully as you select both the trustee and the terms of the trust.

Optimum Use of the Marital Deduction

Marital deduction benefits are available during your lifetime or upon your death, and they can be tailored to meet your precise needs. However, planning is essential to obtain maximum benefits. Here's an example. The unlimited marital deduction can reduce your federal estate tax to zero; yet if you die without a will a state intestacy statute may provide that part of your estate will go to your children and not to your spouse. That portion of your estate will not qualify for the marital deduction.

As a result, your estate may pay estate taxes that could have been deferred through proper planning. However, if your spouse is well provided for in his or her own right, a marital bequest may burden his or her estate with significantly more tax than your estate would be saving. This can be especially true if the survivor's estate tax bracket is significantly increased above the bracket that would have applied in the first estate.

A reminder: Using the marital deduction doesn't permanently wipe out estate tax due on the assets owned by the first spouse to die. Instead, it merely *postpones* the payment of the tax until the surviving spouse's death. Be sure that both you and your spouse fully utilize both available unified credit equivalents before using the marital deduction. That is, you should generally leave property worth up to the unified credit equivalent to those beneficiaries you intend to receive the property after your spouse's death. As the amount of the unified credit equivalent increases over the next several years to $1,000,000 as we approach 2006, the amount left to such beneficiaries should also increase in order to maximize estate tax savings. Make sure your will is drafted to take advantage of the unified credit *available under the law in existence at the time of your death*—and is not limited to creating a bypass trust of a specific dollar amount. By using a bypass trust, your spouse can have complete access to the income and principal if it's needed to live on. No estate tax will be due on any assets left in a bypass trust at your death or at your spouse's death, since the property will not be included in his or her estate.

10 Big Mistakes in Estate Planning—#4
Overusing the marital tax deduction
Although the IRS lets you and your spouse leave each other property free from estate tax, you may end up increasing your family's estate tax bill if you leave everything to your spouse. You end up forfeiting all or part of one of the unified credit equivalents available to you.

11

Gift Tax Fundamentals and Generation-Skipping Transfer Tax

The federal government imposes a substantial tax on gifts of money or property above certain levels. The reason? Without such a tax someone with a sizable estate could give away a large portion of their property before death and escape death taxes altogether. If you have a sizable estate, this probably sounds fine to you, but the government thinks otherwise. For this reason, the gift tax acts more or less as a backstop to the estate tax. And yet, few people actually pay a gift tax during their lifetime. A gift program can substantially reduce overall transfer taxes; however, it requires good planning and a commitment to proceed with the gifts before it's too late.

This chapter explores the following topics:

- The advantages of making gifts
- The generation-skipping transfer tax

THE ADVANTAGES OF MAKING GIFTS

You may have many reasons for making gifts. Personal motives for gift giving may reflect your desire to:

- Assist someone in immediate financial need
- Provide financial or psychological security for the recipient
- Give the recipient experience in handling money
- See the recipient enjoy the property

 Q: **Are gifts of jewelry, art, and so on, subject to the same gift tax rules as gifts of money, stock, and so forth?**

 A: Yes. The determining factor for gifts such as jewelry and art, as for other kinds of property, is fair market value.

In addition to satisfying your personal aims, gifts can bring certain tax advantages. The standard arrangements are:

- Annual exclusion gifts
- Marital deduction gifts
- No-gift-tax gift program
- Paying gift tax to reduce overall taxes
- Gifts to minors

Gift Tax Annual Exclusion

Probably the easiest way to reduce the size of your taxable estate is to make regular use of the gift tax annual exclusion. You may give up to $10,000 each year to as many persons as you want without incurring any gift tax. If your spouse joins in making the gift (by consenting on a gift tax return), you may (as a couple) give $20,000 to each person annually without any gift tax liability. Although the $10,000 amount is indexed for inflation beginning in 1998, the first increase—to $11,000—is not likely to occur until around 2002.

10 Big Mistakes in Estate Planning—#5
Failing to maximize usage of the annual $10,000 gift tax exclusion

This annual gift tax exclusion applies only to gifts of present interests. A present interest is the right to use, possess, or enjoy the gift property now or soon. Examples of a gift of a present interest include gifts of money, holiday presents, an income interest in a trust, and so forth. Gifts of future interests do not qualify for the exclusion. Gifts of future interests include reversions, remainder interests, and other interests that won't give the recipient the right to possess or enjoy the property until a future date or time. A gift of a future interest occurs when the beneficiary isn't entitled to immediate enjoyment of the gift property or its income. However, gifts in trust to minors are subject to special rules that may allow an otherwise future interest to qualify for the $10,000 exclusion. (See later sections of this chapter for a discussion of gifts to minors.)

In addition to the $10,000 exclusion, there is an *unlimited gift tax exclusion* available to pay someone's medical or educational expenses. The beneficiary doesn't have to be your dependent or even related to you, although payment of a grandchild's expenses is perhaps the most common use of the exclusion. You must make the payment *directly* to the institution providing the service—the beneficiary himself or herself must not receive the payment. Medical expenses can include health insurance premiums. Educational expenses are restricted to tuition; room and board, books, and other fees do not qualify for the unlimited exclusion, although they do, of course, qualify for the annual $10,000 exclusion. Given the high cost of education today, gifts of this sort can become a significant benefit for your family members or others you choose to be recipients.

Any contribution to a qualified state tuition program will be treated as a gift eligible for the $10,000 gift tax exclusion (see Chapter 19). If a contribution in excess of $10,000 ($20,000 in the case of a married couple) is made in one year, the contributor can elect to have the contribution treated as if made ratably over 5 years, beginning in the year the contribution is made.

Make annual exclusion gifts at the *beginning* of the year—not as a Christmas or Hanukkah present. You'll remove an additional year's income and appreciation on the gifted property, which compounds over time.

Use of the gift tax exclusion in a single year may not affect your estate tax situation significantly, but you can reduce your taxable estate substantially through a planned annual program of $10,000 (or $20,000 if you're married) gifts. All gifts within the exclusion limits are protected from federal estate taxes and most types are protected from generation-skipping transfer taxes (see the discussion below).

In addition to reducing the size of your estate, another major tax advantage of making a gift is the removal of future appreciation in the property's value from your estate. Suppose that you give stocks worth $50,000 to your children now. If you die in 10 years and the stock is worth $130,000, your estate will escape tax on the $80,000 of appreciation.

10 Big Mistakes in Estate Planning—#6
Making gifts to someone who uses the money to pay for medical or educational expenses

Instead, you should pay for that person's medical or educational expenses directly, thus allowing you to exceed the $10,000 annual limit on tax-free gifts.

You can also realize income tax savings when you make gifts of income-producing property to a recipient in a lower-income tax bracket. However, you gain this tax benefit at the expense of forfeiting your future enjoyment and control over the gifted property. And such income-shifting opportunities are sharply curtailed for gifts to children under age 14. That's due to the kiddie tax, which taxes unearned income over $1,400 (adjusted for inflation) of children under 14 at the higher of their parents' or their own tax rate.

There's an unlimited gift tax charitable deduction available for transfers to most charitable organizations. The effect of this deduction is to make such charitable donations nontaxable to the donor; it may also produce an income tax deduction.

Gift Tax Marital Deduction

The gift tax marital deduction allows you to transfer unlimited amounts of property during your lifetime to your spouse without gift tax. Property can be transferred outright or in trust. If structured properly, a gift of a lifetime income interest in property to your spouse can also qualify for the marital deduction.

The gift tax marital deduction can be a useful tool for minimizing taxes of a couple with combined assets over $650,000. Because each spouse can transfer $650,000 tax-free in 1999, a couple should be able to transfer up to $1,300,000 tax-free. But to obtain this benefit if your spouse has an estate of less than $650,000, you may need to make gifts to your spouse so that he or she will have an estate at least equal to the unified credit equivalent amount—$650,000 in 1999 and $675,000 in 2000. Using the gift tax marital deduction will facilitate such transfers.

Three caveats: First, as mentioned earlier, *the unlimited marital deduction isn't allowed for gifts to a spouse who is not a U.S. citizen.* Instead, the $10,000 annual exclusion available for present interest gifts is boosted to $101,000 in 1999 (indexed for inflation) if the recipient is a noncitizen spouse.

Second, *several states also impose a gift tax.* The amount of the gift tax marital deduction for state purposes may differ from the federal amount. It's crucial to get professional advice before making any significant gifts.

Third, the unified credit equivalent amount increases in 2002 to $700,000 and then periodically afterward until it reaches $1,000,000 in 2006. As the equivalent increases you should consider making additional gifts to your spouse of the amount of the increase so that he or she can take full advantage of his or her unified credit.

A No-Gift-Tax Gift Program

E X A M P L E

■ Here's an example illustrating a substantial gift program that incurs no net gift tax. (Note, however, that part of the unified credit is being used.)

During the course of one year, Jordan made outright gifts of $100,000 to his wife, Jackie; $40,000 to each of his three children; and $30,000 to the United Way—for a total of $250,000. The table below illustrates computing the gift tax and shows why Jordan owed no tax on these gifts.

COMPUTING GIFT TAX

	Wife	Three Children	Charity	Total
Gifts by husband	$100,000	$120,000	$30,000	$250,000
Less:				
Annual exclusion, husband	10,000	30,000	10,000	50,000
Annual exclusion, wife	0	30,000	10,000	40,000
Marital deduction	90,000	0	0	90,000
Charitable deduction	0	0	10,000	10,000
Total deductions and exclusions	100,000	60,000	30,000	190,000
Taxable gifts	$ 0	$ 60,000	$ 0	$ 60,000

	Husband	Wife	Total
Tentative gift tax	$ 6,500	$ 6,500	$ 13,000
Unified gift and estate tax credit	6,500	6,500	13,000
Gift tax payable	$ 0	$ 0	$ 0

The Gift to Jackie

Jordan incurred no gift tax on Jackie's gift because of the $10,000 annual exclusion and the unlimited marital deduction.

The Gifts to Jordan's Three Children

Jordan and Jackie were entitled to a total of $60,000 in annual exclusions ($20,000 for each child) because they elected to consider one-half of those gifts as made by Jackie. Nevertheless, a net taxable gift of $60,000 remains. By applying a portion of the unified credit as a dollar-for-dollar offset, Jordan and Jackie can entirely eliminate paying gift tax.

The Gift to the United Way

For gift tax purposes, Jordan and Jackie reduced the $30,000 by their combined $20,000 of exclusions. The remaining $10,000 qualified as a charitable deduction *for gift tax purposes*. In addition, the entire $30,000 charitable gift was deductible by Jordan *for income tax purposes*. ■

Paying Gift Tax to Reduce Overall Taxes

Most of us have a natural aversion to paying taxes, and gift taxes are no exception. However, if you have a sizable estate—one considerably in excess of what you need to live on—you might do well to consider how paying gift taxes *now* can save on estate taxes *later*. The end result is that more of your assets bypass the IRS and actually reach your heirs.

There's a fundamental difference in how estate and gift taxes are calculated that explains why paying gift tax can save you overall transfer taxes. When you make a gift, the tax is computed only on the amount *actually received* by the donee. The gift tax is paid *in addition to* the gift and isn't part of the tax base, which is why the gift tax is called "tax-exclusive."

The estate tax, on the other hand, is computed on the *entire* value of property included in your gross estate—including the amount that will have to go toward paying the estate tax. The estate tax, therefore, is a "tax-inclusive" tax. Your heirs get only what's left after the tax is paid.

E X A M P L E

■ Here's how paying gift tax can put more money in your heirs' hands. We'll compare the situations of two women, Sarah and Marti. Each has survived her spouse. Each now has $2.5 million of liquid assets. Sarah holds on to the full $2.5 million until death, while Marti makes a gift of $1 million to her children (in addition to annual exclusion gifts). Assuming that neither had previously made taxable gifts and that Marti lives for 3 years after the gift, in the table below we show how their taxes would compare if they die in 1999.

COMPARISON OF GIFT TAXES FOR SARAH AND MARTI			
Sarah: No Gift		**Marti: Gift**	
Taxable estate	$2,500,000	Pre-gift estate	$2,500,000
Federal estate tax	814,500	Taxable gift	$1,000,000
Net estate to heirs	$1,685,500	Gift tax paid	153,000
		Estate reduction	1,153,000
		Taxable estate	$1,347,000
		Federal estate tax	586,530
		Net estate to heirs	$ 760,470
		Plus: Gift	1,000,000
Total to heirs	**$1,685,500**	**Total to heirs**	**$1,760,470**

By making the gift and paying gift taxes, the gift tax of $153,000 was removed from Marti's estate. This resulted in $74,970 more of Marti's estate actually getting to Marti's children. And this result doesn't even take into account the benefit of keeping the post-gift appreciation and after-tax income on the $1 million out of Marti's taxable estate. One catch, however: *The gift must be made more than 3 years before death; otherwise, the gift taxes will be brought back into your estate.* In addition, this arrangement assumes that you're comfortable with the nontax consequences of making a large gift—a gift that will deplete your estate to some extent. Finally, there are two other offsetting factors to take into account: First, if the property you give away is highly appreciated, the recipient will ultimately pay capital gains tax when he or she sells the property. This compares to an heir of an estate who gets the property with a cost basis that is equal to the property's value at the time of the decedent's death. This disadvantage will not be as costly with the reduction in long-term capital gains rates under the 1997 Tax Act to 20% (or 10% for gains otherwise within the 15% tax bracket). Second, when you pay gift tax, you lose the time value of money on the tax paid. Overall, however, saving estate tax at rates up to 55% beats paying capital gains tax at a 20% federal rate. ■

Gifts to Minors

As noted earlier, only gifts of present interests qualify for the $10,000 gift tax exclusion. This generally means that the gifted property must be subject to the beneficiary's immediate enjoyment.

In the case of a parent's gift to a minor child, some legal and practical problems arise: The child typically can't manage his or her own affairs.

Moreover, parents usually don't want to give their young children unfettered control over property. In fact, state laws frequently discourage outright gifts to minors. Such laws commonly prohibit or discourage the registration of securities in the name of a minor, for instance, and impose supervisory restrictions upon the sale of a minor's property. Gifts to minors can take different forms and affect the $10,000 annual gift tax exclusion differently.

Here are some ways in which gifts are typically made to minors:

- Outright gifts
- Guardianship
- Custodial arrangements
- Present interest trust
- Crummey trust
- Totten trust

Outright Gifts
Outright gifts to minors are treated as completed gifts. The $10,000 annual gift tax exclusion is available unless the donated property is itself a future interest. Income from the property is taxed to the minor, and the property can be included in the minor's estate. Because of the kiddie tax, however, your child—if under age 14—would generally be taxed at your rates on income over $1,400 (adjusted for inflation) from the property.

10 Big Mistakes in Estate Planning—#7
Saving the unified credit to shelter estate assets at your death
Keep in mind that the unified credit equivalent amount can most effectively be applied to gifts you make during your lifetime, which enables it to be used to remove post-gift appreciation from your estate.

Guardianship
Property held in a guardianship arrangement is under the guardian's legal control subject to formal (and possibly burdensome) accounting to a court. The gift, income, and estate tax consequences are the same as for outright gifts. Thus, such gifts qualify for the $10,000 gift tax exclusion.

Custodial Arrangements

To overcome the legal disability minors have in owning property out-right, all 50 states, the District of Columbia, and the Virgin Islands have adopted the Uniform Gifts (or Transfers) to Minors Act. Under this act, a custodian may hold both cash and securities for the minor until he or she reaches adulthood. Securities may be registered in the name of any bank, trust company, or adult as custodian for the minor. Custodial gifts to minors are completed gifts for gift tax purposes, and the annual gift tax exclusion is available. The income from the gift property during the custodial period is taxable to the minor (subject to kiddie tax provisions). However, income used for your minor child's maintenance and support is taxable to you as the person legally obligated to support the minor *whether or not you are the donor or custodian.*

In general, you should not act as custodian of your own gift to your minor child. The reason: If you die before your child becomes an adult, the current value of your gift will be included in your estate. Instead, your spouse may be the custodian. If you and your spouse are taking advantage of gift-splitting, consider making a third party the custodian.

 Q: Can I designate one person to provide my child's day-to-day care, and another person to look after her financial well-being?

 A: Definitely. The first person is the *guardian*; the second is the *trustee*. The determining factor should be who will best represent your child's interests. Obviously, a good working relationship between the two would be an advantage as well.

Present Interest Trust

Congress has enacted special rules to provide a well-defined method of making gifts to minors that qualify for the annual exclusion. The Internal Revenue Code provides that a gift to a qualifying trust established for an individual under the age of 21 will be considered a gift of a present interest and thus qualify for the $10,000 annual gift tax exclusion. The trust instrument must provide that the gift property and its income:

- May be expended for the benefit of the beneficiary before reaching age 21, and
- To the extent that it's not expended, will pass to the beneficiary upon becoming age 21.

The child must have the right to receive the assets of the trust at age 21. However, the trust assets don't have to be paid automatically to the child upon reaching age 21. It's acceptable if the child is given the *power* to withdraw everything for a period of 30 or 60 days, and is notified of the power. After the withdrawal period expires, the property stays in the trust and is administered according to the terms of the original trust. If the child dies before reaching age 21, the funds must be payable to the child's estate or as the child may appoint under a general power of appointment.

(*Note:* This Internal Revenue Code provision applies to trusts for children under the age of 21 even if a state law has reduced the age of majority to age 18 or 19.)

A present interest trust is useful when accumulating income is desirable for nontax reasons. It may not be suitable for large gifts, however, because of the requirement that the trust funds be payable to (or at least withdrawable by) the minor upon reaching age 21. The child's access to the trust assets at age 21 is something you should carefully consider. Also, the trust income tax brackets will generally tax income retained in a trust more heavily than if it were distributed to a child. The top federal income tax bracket of 39.6% applies to trust taxable income above only $8,450, while a single person can have taxable income of $283,150 in 1999 before reaching that rate.

Crummey Trust

A Crummey trust is a different type of trust, one to which you can transfer property and have the gift qualify for the annual gift tax exclusion. The distinguishing characteristic of a Crummey trust is that it gives the beneficiary the right to demand annual distributions from the trust equal to the lesser of either the amount of the contributions to the trust during the year or a specified amount (e.g., $5,000 or 5% of the trust's value). The beneficiary (or legal guardian) must be notified of the power to withdraw the trust corpus, although the power is permitted to lapse or terminate after a short period of time (such as 30 days). If, following notification that a contribution has been made, the beneficiary fails to make a demand during the window period, the right lapses for that year's contributions. To the extent that the beneficiary (or guardian) has the right to demand distribution of the year's contribution, that contribution is a present interest and therefore qualifies for the annual gift tax exclusion. In practice, the child beneficiary almost never exercises the power, not wishing to bite the hand that feeds him or her, and perhaps causing the gifts to stop. This unspoken threat is the reason that these types of trusts are sometimes called "broken-arm" trusts.

In all other respects, the Crummey trust is very flexible. Once the withdrawal power has lapsed, the trustee can be required to accumulate income until the child reaches a specified age. The trustee can be restricted to using trust assets and income for specific purposes (e.g., college expenses). The trust is also useful as a vehicle for permanently removing assets from the parents' gross estates.

Furthermore, for income tax purposes, the Crummey trust's income is taxed to the beneficiary (or beneficiaries) who allowed their withdrawal right to lapse. Therefore, once the beneficiaries are over 13 years old, the income will be taxed at their rates, which will avoid the punitive tax rates applied to trusts.

Totten Trust

An "in trust for" account or so-called "Totten trust" is created when a donor deposits his own money into a bank account for the benefit of a minor, then names himself as trustee. This is an informal and revocable arrangement under certain states' laws. Upon the donor-trustee's death, the funds avoid probate and pass directly to the minor. However, the trust isn't considered a separate entity for tax purposes because the donor retains complete control over any property in the trust. Accordingly, the donor will be taxed on the income as if the trust were not in existence. Also, assets in the trust account will be includible in the donor's estate.

GENERATION-SKIPPING TRANSFER TAX

An additional tax may apply to gifts or bequests that skip a generation. An example of a generation-skipping transfer is a gift of property directly from a grandparent to a grandchild (which effectively "skips" the intervening generation).

The *generation-skipping transfer tax* is designed to impose the equivalent of the gift or estate tax the intervening generation would have paid. On a direct gift from a grandparent to a grandchild, the generation-skipping tax generally represents the amount of tax that would have been owed if the property had first been transferred to the child, who then died, leaving the property to the grandchild.

However, while the estate tax has a progressive rate structure, the generation-skipping transfer tax is imposed at the maximum estate and gift tax rate of 55%. It's payable *in addition to* any estate or gift tax otherwise payable as a result of the transfer.

The generation-skipping transfer tax is a very significant, if not confiscatory, tax. Fortunately, most people will escape it. First, outright gifts to grandchildren that qualify for the $10,000 annual gift tax exclusion aren't subject to the generation-skipping transfer tax. Similarly, payments of tuition and medical expenses that avoid gift tax also avoid this tax. Second, and perhaps most important, each person is entitled to an aggregate $1 million exemption (which was increased to $1,010,000 for 1999 and will continue to be indexed for inflation) from the tax for lifetime transfers and transfers at death. Since a married couple can "gift-split," they can make just over $2 million in generation-skipping transfers without incurring the tax. And any subsequent appreciation on the transferred property will escape generation-skipping tax.

If you're wealthy, you can maximize your opportunity to avoid the imposition of this tax on transfers to grandchildren and later generations by allocating your available $1 million-plus exemption to trust transfers made during your own lifetime. And if your living descendants are already well provided for, you may be interested in establishing a *dynasty trust*. As its name implies, the trust can provide a huge benefit for future descendants by sheltering assets from estate, gift, and generation-skipping taxes for several generations.

If your wills and revocable trusts were drafted before passage of the 1986 Tax Act, you should review them to determine if they need revision to minimize the impact of the generation-skipping transfer tax. A personal financial counselor can help with this review.

12

SOPHISTICATED ASSET PLANNING TECHNIQUES

Two other techniques that you should consider as part of your estate planning are:

- Trusts
- Sophisticated asset transfer

Both of these techniques can provide flexibility for your estate and reduce the taxes that your family would have to pay following your death.

TRUSTS: THE MOST USEFUL PLANNING TOOL

Aside from a written plan itself, trusts are possibly the most useful personal financial planning tool. A trust is an arrangement under which one person or institution holds legal title to real or personal property for the benefit of another person or persons, usually under the terms of a written document setting forth all parties' rights and responsibilities. A trust can hold property set aside under the management of a competent trustee for the benefit of other persons, present and future, and often avoid some taxes that otherwise would have to be paid.

Our discussions of estate planning so far have already referred to various kinds of trusts. You can probably understand this subject best in terms of particular *kinds* of trusts designed to achieve certain limited goals. Two of the most basic types of trusts are *irrevocable trusts* and *revocable trusts*.

Irrevocable Trusts

As is evident in its name, an irrevocable trust may not be changed or revoked after you create it. This type of trust is usually created to remove property and its future income and appreciation from your estate. The present interest and Crummey trusts are irrevocable trusts. You might also use an irrevocable trust if you want to make a gift to someone but want to prevent that person from spending the assets too quickly. Another purpose for an irrevocable trust is to prevent a beneficiary's creditors—or even a child's spouse in a divorce action—from reaching the property.

Property placed in an irrevocable trust will not be removed from your estate if you retain certain interests or powers in the trust, such as a life income interest or the power to determine which beneficiaries will receive distributions. Furthermore, any transfer to an irrevocable trust will be subject to gift tax if you relinquish all control over the property. If someone else will receive the income from the trust currently, or if it's a present interest trust, the $10,000 annual gift tax exclusion can shield at least part of the transfer from gift tax.

Besides saving you estate tax, irrevocable trusts created for your children may provide a limited income tax benefit. The amount of this benefit depends on how much other income your children already receive and whether the kiddie tax applies to them. In addition, very strict rules minimize the type of control you or your spouse may keep over the trust without causing the income to be taxed to you. Finally, the income will be taxed to you if it's used to pay for an item that you're legally obligated to provide as support for the beneficiary.

Revocable Trusts

A revocable trust (also known as a *living trust*) is created during your lifetime, and you may amend or revoke it at any time. The trust instrument directs how the assets held by it are to be managed during your lifetime. It can also act very much like a will by instructing how its assets should be distributed after your death.

What distinguishes a revocable trust from other kinds of trust arrangements is that *you keep the power to reclaim the trust assets*. You can amend the terms of the trust or even terminate it altogether whenever you wish. This means that by setting up a revocable trust, you really haven't committed yourself to anything—at least until you die and the trust becomes irrevocable. For all practical purposes, you continue to own the trust property beneficially; the trust merely gets bare legal title.

Since you keep complete control over the trust and its assets, the property held in it will be included in your gross estate for estate tax purposes. Also, all income and deductions attributable to the property in the trust flow back to you. On the other hand, your retained control means that your contributing assets to the trust won't trigger gift tax. This is the case even though the trust names the beneficiaries who will take the property following your death. However, a gift *will* occur if you give up your power to revoke or amend the trust, or if income or principal is actually paid to someone else.

The Advantages of Revocable Trusts. There are essentially no tax advantages gained by establishing a revocable trust; however, there can be some real financial and administrative advantages, including:

- Avoiding probate and ancillary administration
- Avoiding legal guardianship
- Relief from financial responsibility

Avoiding Probate and Ancillary Administration

Revocable trust assets pass to the beneficiaries you name in the trust document and are not controlled by your will. This cuts out the costs and delays that arise in some states as part of the probate process. Unlike probate, with a revocable trust the identity of beneficiaries and instructions for distributing estate property aren't part of the public record. This allows you to maintain your privacy.

For those owning real property located outside their state of domicile at the time of death, ancillary probate proceedings will generally be required by each state in which such realty is located. By placing this property into a revocable trust, your estate can escape these multiple probate proceedings.

Avoiding Legal Guardianship

If you become incapacitated, the assets kept in your living trust would be managed automatically by a trustee you named in the trust document. Otherwise, the determination of whether and to what extent you're disabled or incompetent and who is going to handle your affairs could be left to public and potentially costly guardianship proceedings. (*Note: A durable power of attorney* can also be an effective tool for prearranging the management of your affairs in the event you become incapacitated. See Chapter 13 in this regard.)

Relief from Financial Responsibility

If you desire, you can use an independent trustee immediately to relieve you of the details of managing your property and investments, record-keeping chores, and preparation and filing of income tax returns. An *agency account* managed by a bank trust department can perform these functions, too, but it doesn't provide the other benefits of using a revocable trust.

The Disadvantages of Revocable Trusts. Predictably, revocable trusts have some drawbacks, too, and aren't suited to everyone. Among them are:

- Legal fees and expenses
- Uncertain savings
- Taxation of gifts made directly by a trustee
- Title issues

Legal Fees and Expenses

Expect to pay legal fees and other expenses, such as real estate recording fees, to set up the trust and transfer property to it. You will also owe recurring trustee and administrative charges if you use a corporate trustee in lieu of managing the trust yourself.

Uncertain Savings

Probate cost savings may not be dramatic when you use a revocable trust. Many states have adopted streamlined probate procedures; this means that probate for a variety of estates can be completed more easily and less expensively than in the past, often with minimal court supervision. Moreover, using a living trust won't necessarily save on other legal, accounting, and executor's fees paid to handle your estate. Whether your assets are held in a living trust or pass through probate, the same sort of work will generally be needed to value your assets, prepare federal and state tax returns, settle creditors' claims, and resolve disputes among beneficiaries.

Taxation of Gifts Made Directly by a Trustee

Prior to the enactment of the 1997 Tax Act, gifts made directly from a revocable trust within three years of death could be caught by a trap for the unwary and brought back into your estate. Fortunately, this problem has now been solved and gifts made by the trustee of a revocable trust pursuant to a power in the trust document will be respected for estate tax purposes.

10 Big Mistakes in Estate Planning—#8
Setting up a living trust instead of a will to reduce your estate tax bill

In fact, living trusts have no impact on your estate tax liability. Also, no one transfers *all* of their assets to a revocable trust. There will always be some assets held outside the trust that will pass by state intestate laws without a will.

Title Issues

Finally, be sure that any property you want to have covered by the benefits of a revocable trust is legally titled in the trustee's name. This is a straightforward point but one that often ends up overlooked. It also means that after you create the trust, you must remember to conduct your personal business affairs through this vehicle. Doing so isn't difficult, but sometimes it becomes a burden. Except for life insurance proceeds and property held jointly with right of survivorship, which pass by operation of law, property held outside the trust at your death will still be subject to probate.

Life Insurance Trusts

Next to your home, life insurance policies may well be your most valuable assets. You may not realize, however, that life insurance proceeds payable to your estate will be included in your gross estate for estate tax purposes. You may also not realize that merely retaining even one of the incidents of ownership (mentioned earlier) will cause the proceeds to be included in the estate—*regardless of who the policy's beneficiary may be.*

What's the solution to this problem? One possibility is that to minimize estate taxes, you shouldn't own any life insurance policies. This doesn't mean that you shouldn't *have* life insurance; rather, it means that by transferring the policy and all incidents of ownership to your children or to a trust for your family's benefit, you can reap significant tax advantages. However, to be effective in keeping the proceeds out of your estate, you must make the gift more than 3 years before you die. You can avoid the 3-year waiting period for a newly purchased policy if you take proper steps to have someone else (e.g., a trustee of an irrevocable trust) apply for the policy. An ideal way to structure these types of irrevocable life insurance trusts enables you to apply your annual gift tax exclusion to cover contributions of money you make each year to the trust for paying premiums. The trust can therefore be used as a powerful way to leverage the annual exclusion to get insurance proceeds to your heirs without income, gift, or estate tax.

How a Trust Can Save Taxes

Life insurance proceeds are free from *income* taxes when they're paid to your survivors. However, the death benefits on policies you own are included in your estate and can be taxed at a rate as high as 55% at the federal level. An irrevocable life insurance trust avoids estate taxes because it's a separate legal entity in which you retain no interest. Once you transfer assets to this type of trust, you forfeit all control and ownership rights and therefore relieve yourself of the resulting tax liabilities. The idea of the life insurance trust is therefore to remove the policy proceeds from your own and your spouse's taxable estates. Proper drafting can accomplish this goal while allowing your spouse to receive income for life and principal as needed. You can achieve similar estate tax benefits by assigning ownership of the policy to your children. However, this alternative obviously lacks the planning flexibility offered by a life insurance trust.

How They Work

A trustee manages the life insurance trust, maintaining the policy during your life by paying the premiums. At your death, the trustee receives the policy proceeds and acts in accordance with your instructions in the trust document. You could direct that the death benefits be distributed immediately to named beneficiaries. In addition to being free from estate taxes, the death benefits are paid to your survivors without the costs and delays of probate (i.e., estate settlement). Alternatively, you can have the trustee manage the life insurance proceeds after your death, disbursing the money to your survivors over a specified period of time.

10 Big Mistakes in Estate Planning—#9
Making no plans to shelter taxable life insurance proceeds
Since life insurance benefits may push your estate past the unified credit equivalent amount, even after it is phased up to $1,000,000 (or push your and your surviving spouse's combined estate past the $2 million mark by 2007), you should transfer ownership of the policy to your children or other heirs. Alternatively, you can fund a life insurance trust.

Transferring a Policy

You can create a life insurance trust by transferring an existing policy to an irrevocable trust. The transfer is considered a taxable gift, but the tax is calculated on the surrender value of the policy, which, for cash value-type policies, is most often substantially less than the death benefit. Term insurance policies can also be transferred with the gift amount being only the amount of the current year's premium paid in as of the transfer. The tax cost of transferring a policy during your lifetime could therefore be substantially less than the estate taxes due upon your death. (*Note:* If you die within 3 years of the transfer, the policy proceeds would be included in your taxable estate.)

Setting Up a Trust with a New Policy

You can also set up a trust and have the trustee apply for a new policy on your life. You can transfer cash to the trust each year to enable the trustee to make the premium payments. These cash transfers are taxable gifts unless beneficiaries are given withdrawal powers (i.e., Crummey powers) that annually total more than the premium payments. Because the trustee applied for a new policy in which you never had any owner-ship rights, the policy proceeds would not be included in your estate, even if you were to die within 3 years.

10 Big Mistakes in Estate Planning—#10
Not keeping your beneficiary designations up to date
You must name beneficiaries on many assets, including life insurance policies, retirement plans, and bank and brokerage accounts.

Once you create an irrevocable life insurance trust, it's carved in stone. You can't cancel or amend the trust or withdraw the assets. You also lose control over the life insurance policy, including the ability to borrow from or surrender the cash value or change the beneficiary. If you feel an irrevocable life insurance trust may serve your purposes, be sure to enlist the support of qualified professionals to draft and administer your trust. These arrangements require sophisticated tax and estate planning expertise. Ask about the costs to set up and administer the trust, but remember that these fees can be more than offset by the tax savings.

SOPHISTICATED ASSET TRANSFER TECHNIQUES

As you have gathered from the previous chapters, making lifetime gifts of property to children or other chosen beneficiaries saves estate taxes by removing future income and appreciation from your estate. Outright gifts accomplish this, but may put more control in the hands of the donee than you would like, and may be cumbersome for partial interest gifts of certain assets, like real estate. There are a few more complex techniques that can solve these non-tax concerns, as well as provide the opportunity to move greater amounts of property in a more tax efficient manner.

Fractional Interest Discounts

Recall that property is valued for transfer tax purposes at its "fair market value" (see Chapter 10). Determining a property's fair market value is relatively straightforward for marketable property (e.g., publicly traded securities). Making this determination is more difficult, however, for property that is not freely tradable or if less than an entire interest in property is transferred. In such cases, the value of the transfer may be less than a pro rata share of the underlying property.

For example, if the sole owner of a closely held business were to transfer a 20% interest in the business to his or her child, the child would receive a "minority interest." Since a minority interest (generally no more than 50% ownership) lacks voting control, its holder cannot force the business to distribute profits or compel a liquidation. Thus, for transfer tax purposes, the value of the interest transferred could be discounted, since a hypothetical buyer would offer something less than 20% of the underlying assets to purchase the noncontrolling business interest.

In addition, the holder of an interest in a closely held business typically cannot freely sell his or her interest to outside parties due to the presence of shareholder or partnership agreements. The lack of an "established market" for such interests enables the transferor to claim a valuation discount for lack of marketability. The combination of minority and marketability valuation discounts creates an attractive opportunity for shifting wealth to younger generations at a reduced transfer tax cost. Following are several asset transfer techniques that take advantage of these valuation discounts.

Grantor Retained Annuity Trust (GRAT)

A GRAT can enable a business owner to transfer a large amount of stock—or an interest in a partnership—to his or her children at a reduced gift tax cost. While the GRAT works best for closely held business owners, it can also be very effective for publicly traded stock or real estate that is expected to appreciate significantly.

To establish a GRAT, you would transfer property to a trust for a fixed term of years. During the trust term, you receive a fixed stream of annuity payments. When the term of the GRAT expires, any property remaining in the GRAT after payment of your annuity would pass to your children. The present value of this retained annuity is subtracted from the value of the transferred property in order to determine the taxable gift to the children. By setting the annuity payout high enough, the value of the annuity will approximately equal the value of the property transferred to the trust. This reduces the value of the taxable gift to the children to a very small fraction of the value of the transferred property. Transfer tax benefits are realized from the GRAT if the assets transferred produce a total return in excess of the IRS assumed rate of return used in valuing the annuity. For example, if the applicable federal interest rate is 7.6% when a GRAT is created and the assets transferred produce a 12% average rate of return over the GRAT term, the 4.4% compounded excess return will pass to your children. Thus, when interest rates are low, the GRAT can be especially attractive because it provides a leveraged way to move a significant amount of the appreciation on the transferred assets to children at an insignificant gift tax cost.

A GRAT should be set up as a grantor trust for income tax purposes, regardless of the type of property transferred to the trust. For S corporation stock this is important, because a grantor trust is qualified to hold S corporation stock. In addition, grantor trust status prevents capital gains from being triggered if some of the trust property is used to satisfy the annuity payments. As the deemed "owner" of the trust, you will still report all the income and capital gains associated with the trust property on your income tax return.

There is one other important element involved in making the GRAT successful. *The trust property will be includible in your estate if you die during the trust term.* Therefore, the trust term should be one that you expect to survive. Nevertheless, even if death were to occur during the trust term—pulling the property back into your estate—you'd end up in about the same position as if you had not created a GRAT.

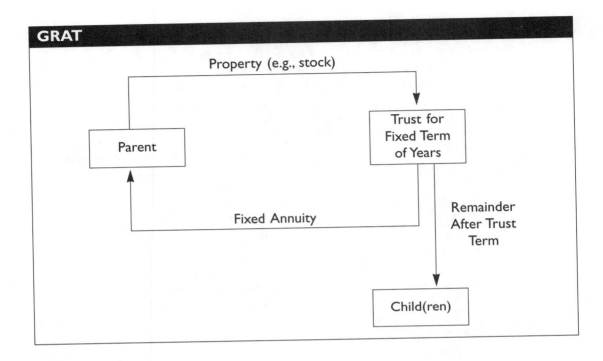

GRAT

Property (e.g., stock)

Parent

Trust for
Fixed Term
of Years

Fixed Annuity

Remainder
After Trust
Term

Child(ren)

Personal Residence Grantor Retained Interest Trust

The Personal Residence Grantor Retained Interest Trust (Residence GRIT) offers an opportunity to achieve significant gift and estate tax savings with virtually no risk. A Residence GRIT is an arrangement in which you transfer either a principal residence or vacation home to a trust, retaining (1) the right to income for a period of years (i.e., the right to live in the house during the trust term), and (2) the right to have the trust property returned to your estate if you die during the trust term. At the end of the trust term, the home goes to your children outright or remains in the trust for their benefit. The trust is irrevocable and the transfer is considered a gift of the present value of the property that will pass to your children in the future.

The GRIT offers transfer tax "leverage" because the amount of the gift for gift tax purposes will be considerably less than the current value of the home transferred to the trust.

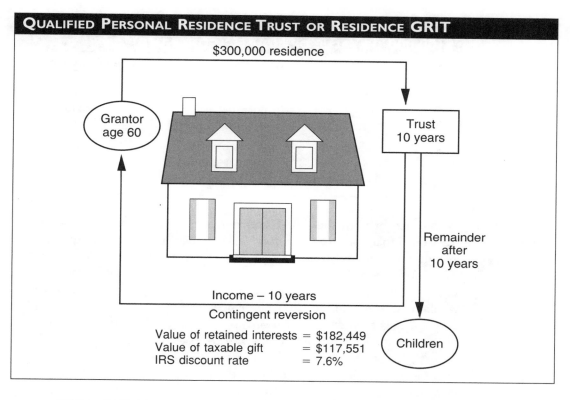

QUALIFIED PERSONAL RESIDENCE TRUST OR RESIDENCE GRIT

$300,000 residence

Grantor
age 60

Trust
10 years

Remainder
after
10 years

Income – 10 years

Contingent reversion

Value of retained interests = $182,449
Value of taxable gift = $117,551
IRS discount rate = 7.6%

Children

E X A M P L E

■ Let's say you're 60 years old. You transfer your home to a 10-year GRIT. The reportable gift is just over 39% of your home's value (assuming an IRS discount rate of 7.6%), as shown in the illustration above. For a $300,000 home, the gift would be $117,551—only a fraction of the unified credit equivalent. If your home appreciates 3% per year during the 10-year trust term, there will be $403,175 of value passing to your children at the end of the 10 years—more than three times the amount of the taxable gift. ■

RESIDENCE GRITs— TAXABLE GIFT PER $100,000 OF VALUE OF HOUSE*		
Age	**Trust Term**	**Value of Taxable Gift**
40	25	$13,014
45	20	19,036
50	15	28,078

(continued)

Age	Trust Term	Value of Taxable Gift
55	12	34,704
60	10	39,184
65	8	44,515
70	5	57,702
75	5	52,708
80	3	63,383
83	3	58,767

RESIDENCE GRITS— TAXABLE GIFT PER $100,000 OF VALUE OF HOUSE* (CONTINUED)

*Assume IRS discount rate of 7.6%.

In the case of both the GRAT and the GRIT, it's important to select a trust term that you expect to survive. That's because the property will be included in your estate at its date-of-death value if you die during the trust term. Nevertheless, there's really no downside tax risk to the GRIT, since if death *did* occur during the term, you'd merely end up where you would have been had the GRIT never been created. If you've already used up your unified credit and owe gift tax when you create the trust, death during the trust term would cause you to lose the time value of money on the gift tax paid. By surviving at least three years, this would be more than offset by your savings resulting from removing the gift tax from your taxable estate. (See Chapter 11.) Your financial advisor can provide more information on reducing transfer taxes with GRITs and GRATs.

Family Limited Partnership (FLP)

The FLP allows you to transfer ownership of significant assets to family members—typically, children and grandchildren—during your lifetime without having to relinquish control. An FLP is also an ideal vehicle for dividing assets into portions to facilitate using your $10,000 annual gift tax exclusion and making other large gifts. However, to be respected for tax purposes, the FLP must have a bona fide business purpose (e.g., your desire for centralized management of family assets).

Once transferred through a gift of a partnership interest, a portion of valuable assets are removed from your estate, thus freezing your gift and estate tax burden. But the benefits of an FLP go beyond that. By carefully structuring the partnership, state laws will restrict a limited partner's ability to liquidate his or her interest. By lowering the value that a "willing buyer" would pay for the partnership interest, the gift and estate tax values of assets transferred to an FLP can be reduced. An FLP also provides a degree of protection from potential creditors, who generally cannot reach the partnership's underlying assets or cause a dissolution of the partnership.

An FLP is established and operates like any limited partnership. At least two individuals (e.g., you along with your spouse and/or child) would contribute property to the FLP in exchange for a partnership interest. The general partner, who manages the FLP, can be you—or perhaps a corporate entity, such as a limited liability company (see below). Each partner would hold a portion (generally at least 1%) of the ownership. You would contribute most of the assets and would receive most of the limited partnership interest. You would then make gifts of limited partnership interests to your children and/or grandchildren.

Just as in a regular limited partnership, the general partner(s) in an FLP is/are fully liable for all debts, while the limited partners are liable only up to the amount of their investments. In addition, limited partners have no voice or control in the management of the partnership or its assets. Thus, as general partner, you or your spouse could maintain management control over partnership assets while enjoying significant transfer tax benefits.

Limited Liability Company (LLC)

LLCs have become an increasingly popular form of business entity, combining the liability protection of a corporation with the "pass-through" income tax treatment associated with limited partnerships. It is this combination of features that gives LLCs their appeal. An LLC may be appropriate if you own a family business and seek personal protection against business liabilities, or if you want to keep management control over your business while transferring ownership to the next generation. The gift and estate tax valuation discounts available for transfers of interests in an FLP or closely held corporation are also available to LLC interests.

As a member of an LLC, you are not personally liable for the entity's debts or obligations. You are only subject to the claims of the business's creditors to the extent of your capital contribution to the LLC or to the extent to which you are obligated to contribute in the future (i.e., under the LLC agreement). Contrast this with limited partnerships, where general partners have unlimited liability and limited partners lose their "limited liability status" if they participate in the management of the partnership. In addition to their many non-tax advantages, LLCs are not subject to a separate income tax (unless the LLC's members *elect* to be taxed as a corporation). Instead, similar to a partnership, the LLC's income, deductions, gains, losses and credits are reported directly on the members' personal income tax returns. Thus, LLCs avoid the "double taxation" of income associated with C corporations. Furthermore, LLCs allow more flexibility than S corporations in various respects. For instance, LLCs may have an unlimited number of investors (S corporations are limited to 75), and tax benefits may be allocated to members in a disproportionate manner (S corporations must make pro rata allocations to their shareholders). Since converting an existing corporation to an LLC can result in a significant tax cost, and due to the variation of state laws affecting LLCs, you should consult with your tax and financial advisors if you believe an LLC would be right for you.

Gifts of Transferable Stock Options

A compensatory stock option gives an employee/holder the right to purchase shares of employer stock at a predetermined price at some time in the future. While many U.S. companies today issue nonqualified stock options (NQSOs) to key executives, officers, and directors, a growing number are expanding their option-granting base to include rank-and-file employees. Due to the extended "bull maket," many option holders have seen significant increases in the value of their options. Because of the potential estate tax consequences of this growth in value, more companies are currently permitting their employees to transfer unexercised NQSOs to family members and trusts for their benefit.

Giving away an option is most advantageous if the gift occurs before the option has a large "spread" (i.e., the excess of the stock's value over the option's exercise price). That's when the gift tax value of the option is lowest.

It's important to be aware that even though your *donee* exercises the option you gifted, *you* would still be required to include the option spread at the time of exercise in your taxable income. Nevertheless, from an estate and gift tax standpoint, you still benefit from this technique. Your payment of income tax further reduces the size of your estate while increasing the property owned by your children—with no additional gift tax. However, this rule generally makes gifts of compensatory stock options to charity an unfavorable tax strategy since you would remain liable for the income tax at the time the charity exercises the option.

Secure an Accurate Appraisal

Each of the above wealth transfer techniques may involve difficult-to-value assets. An expert appraisal that takes advantage of all available discounts and yet will be likely to withstand an IRS challenge is a critical element of a successful valuation "freeze" for transfer tax purposes.

13

ESTATE LIQUIDITY, POWERS OF ATTORNEY, AND LIVING WILLS

Now for some Last Things—in this case, three topics to conclude our discussion of estate planning, plus a reminder.

- Estate liquidity
- Durable powers of attorney
- Living wills and health care powers of attorney
- The importance of periodic review

ESTATE LIQUIDITY: RAISING CASH TO PAY DEATH TAXES

If you own a closely held business, your estate may not have sufficient cash to pay all the estate's obligations, including estate taxes, following your death. Indeed, the principal estate asset may be the business itself. Without sufficient liquidity, the estate may be forced to sell a portion of the business to raise enough cash to satisfy these obligations. The techniques described below can help alleviate liquidity problems. These techniques are *buy–sell agreements, stock redemptions to pay death taxes,* and *installment payment of estate tax.*

Buy–Sell Agreements

One way of attempting to fix the estate tax value of a business interest is to use a buy–sell agreement. Buy–sell agreements can actually fulfill three objectives:

First, the *buy–sell agreement can ensure that inside parties will retain control of a closely held business.* For example, a buy–sell agreement may prohibit the acquisition of closely held business stock by relatives, employees, or outsiders who are inactive or incapable of running the business. Thus management control can be retained by those most capable of managing the business.

Second, *a buy–sell agreement can ensure that your heirs can dispose of your interest in a closely held business at a fair price when you die.* In this way, the agreement provides a source of liquidity for the shareholders' estate.

Third, *a valid and binding buy–sell agreement can be used to try to fix the estate tax value of stock in a closely held business* when unrelated parties are involved. This used to be accomplished by fixing the future price of the stock at a reasonable fixed amount or by basing the sales price on a formula. However, buy–sell agreements among family members that are entered into after October 8, 1990, will not control the estate tax valuation of a business interest unless evidence (such as actual agreements in other businesses) can be produced that unrelated parties would enter into a similar agreement. Once a buy–sell agreement is executed, the involved parties should ensure that funds will be available to implement the agreement at the time of a "triggering event" (e.g., a co-owner's death). This is often accomplished through the use of life insurance that covers the lives of the involved parties. The policies could be owned by the business entity, by the parties themselves, or by a third party (e.g., an irrevocable life insurance trust). At the death of an insured, insurance proceeds would be available to purchase the decedent's business interest, thereby providing cash to his or her surviving family members. Although not all buy–sell agreements are funded with life insurance (i.e., the business entity or surviving business owners may have other adequate sources of cash), an agreement that lacks an identifiable source of funding may not fulfill its intended purpose.

Stock Redemptions to Pay Death Taxes

A special tax law provision—Section 303 of the Internal Revenue Code—allows a tax-favored redemption of stock where the decedent owned a substantial interest in a closely held business. Absent the special rule, the redemption might be treated as a dividend, meaning that the entire payment for the stock would be income to the estate. Assuming that the technical requirements of this provision are met, the redemption will be given capital gain treatment. This is a real benefit in this situation because the estate will have a new basis in the decedent's stock equal to its fair market value at the date of the death. The result is that only post-death appreciation will be taxed upon the redemption, and only up to the maximum capital gains tax rate of 20%.

To qualify for a Section 303 redemption, the value of all the corporation's stock included in the decedent's gross estate must exceed 35% of the decedent's adjusted gross estate. The adjusted gross estate is the gross estate less the allowable deductions for funeral and administration expenses, debts, and certain losses (but before any charitable deduction or marital deduction).

A qualifying redemption under Section 303 is limited in amount to the sum of the following items:

- Federal and state death taxes
- Funeral expenses
- Estate administration expenses

An estate doesn't actually have to be illiquid for Section 303 to apply. In other words, an estate may take advantage of the provisions of Section 303 and redeem stock up to the maximum amount referred to above, even if the estate otherwise has sufficient liquid assets to take care of its expenses and taxes. It's often desirable to redeem stock under Section 303 because it may be difficult for your heirs to withdraw funds from the corporation without paying tax at ordinary income rates.

Installment Payment of Estate Tax

To further relieve the tax burden on an estate holding a closely held business, your heirs can pay estate taxes attributable to your interest in such a business over a 14-year period if certain conditions are met. This 14-year payout offers a very favorable interest rate plus a 5-year deferral of the first installment of estate taxes. The tax is then paid in 10 installments. This deferral provision only applies to an "interest in a closely held business." To qualify for the 14-year payout, the value of the closely held business must exceed 35% of the adjusted gross estate.

The amount of estate tax that qualifies for a deferred payout is limited to the portion of the total tax that is attributable to the business interest. For example, if the decedent's qualifying stock constitutes 62% of the adjusted gross estate, 62% of the total estate tax liability may be deferred.

The executor of an estate owning a qualified business interest who makes the election to defer payment will pay none of the tax attributable to the business interest for 5 years. However, interest on the tax for the first 4 years must be paid annually. After the fifth year of deferral, the estate tax liability must begin to be paid with interest in up to 10 yearly installments.

A favorable rate of 2% is charged on the deferred estate tax attributable to the first $1 million in value of the closely held business interest for decedents dying after 1997. An interest rate equal to 45 percent of the rate applicable to underpayments of tax applies to the deferred estate tax in excess of that amount.

DURABLE POWERS OF ATTORNEY

Suppose that you've prepared a valid will to provide for the proper management and disposition of your estate after you die. It's safely tucked away. Now you can relax, right? Maybe so. If you were to suffer an illness or injury, however, you might end up incapable of managing your financial affairs. Under such circumstances, the will you've so thoughtfully prepared won't help a bit.

Confronting your disability, your family might have to have a court appoint a guardian or conservator for you so that your finances continue to be properly managed. That could mean delays, legal expenses, and perhaps public disclosure of your infirmity. Meanwhile, your bills and taxes might remain unpaid. Couldn't your spouse just step in and take over for you? Often, that's not possible. He or she wouldn't have the legal authority to perform certain acts on your behalf. As a result, your family might end up in a state of financial limbo until the courts granted a guardianship or conservatorship.

The Simple Alternative

■ **TIP:** The good news is that there's a simple alternative to guardianship. A *durable power of attorney* is one of the safest, simplest, and cheapest ways of continuing the management of your affairs in the event of your incapacity.

It's a short legal document that your lawyer prepares, stating simply that you (the *principal*) grant authority to one or more individuals [*your attorney(s)-in-fact*] to manage your financial affairs (and personal affairs such as health care, if you wish) on your behalf.

You retain the right to modify or revoke the power at any time. The document terminates automatically on your death. One caveat: If you do revoke the power without informing third parties (e.g., a bank), they can continue to rely on the directions of your attorney-in-fact without penalty. Also, if a guardian is appointed for you, that guardian can revoke the power just as you yourself could have.

The power is *durable* because the underlying document creating it specifically states that it remains in force even if you become disabled or incapacitated. This feature is what gives the power its value in ensuring continuity of your financial management. ■

General and Special Powers

Your durable power of attorney can be as broad or as narrow as you wish. A *general durable power* grants your attorney-in-fact the authority to handle virtually all financial matters that you would ordinarily manage yourself. If you prefer, you can grant a *special durable power*, under which the attorney-in-fact's authority is restricted to one or more specific functions designated by you. The general power is better designed to avoid the problem of guardianship.

If you own a business, you might execute two durable powers with separate attorneys-in-fact: a spouse or other close relative to handle your personal affairs, and a business associate or trusted advisor to handle your business. The underlying document could provide that the latter receives a fee for services.

Springing Powers

Typically, a durable power takes effect when it is created, so that the designated attorney-in-fact can assume responsibility as soon as it becomes necessary. To be sure that control is not assumed prematurely, you may want to give the underlying document to your lawyer or accountant for safekeeping, since your attorney-in-fact cannot legally act for you without possession of the document.

Another way you might deal with the problem of premature exercise is through a *springing durable power*, which is worded so that it becomes effective only in the event of your disability. One drawback to the springing power, however, is this: While all 50 states and the District of Columbia recognize durable powers, the validity of a springing power is unclear in some states and specifically denied in a few others.

Another problem is that since its operation is triggered (or sprung) by disability, it could be difficult in some cases to convince the attorney-in-fact that disability has actually occurred and that it's safe to begin acting for the principal. Thus the document must contain a clear definition of disability: for example, certification by two designated physicians.

Combining Durable Powers and Revocable Trusts

As we discussed in Chapter 12, revocable trusts can provide for the management of your assets during life and after death. Revocable trusts can also provide the same benefit in the event of disability.

Under these circumstances, you don't even have to fund the trust fully. You can create it with a nominal amount (say, $10) and make it available as a *standby trust*. The durable power of attorney can be drafted to direct the powerholder to fund the trust with selected assets, or with your entire estate, if you become incapacitated.

Options

As principal, you can authorize your attorney-in-fact to do any number of things in your stead, limited only by the laws of your state. For example, you can give your attorney-in-fact the power to continue implementing your plan to reduce the size of your estate with annual tax-free gifts to your heirs (see Chapter 11 regarding gift tax). You can also provide for charitable donations, payment of medical bills, and tuition disbursements. Note that absent *explicit* authorization in the document, the powerholder will not have the legal authority to make gifts on your behalf under most state laws.

Here are other tasks your attorney-in-fact can perform for you:

- Manage your investment portfolio
- Forgive or collect debts owed to you
- File tax returns and pay taxes
- Represent you in legal matters
- Manage your business
- Provide for your medical care

Two Caveats. Some financial institutions (e.g., banks and brokerage houses) will honor *only* powers executed on forms that their own staffs have prepared; you may need to create more than one document to cover all needs. Also, one thing your attorney-in-fact cannot do is change your will.

Choosing Your Attorney-in-Fact

It goes without saying that the person you choose as your attorney-in-fact must be someone you trust completely. This person should also have some knowledge of financial matters—especially if you contemplate a general power. Ideally, your attorney-in-fact should also have some understanding of your financial objectives so as to be better equipped to carry out your plans. Accordingly, spouses often name each other as their attorneys. Whomever you pick for this important task, you should designate an alternate as well, since your first choice may be unavailable when the time comes. Finally, your attorney-in-fact must be of legal age when the power is exercised.

 Can one of my relatives challenge the legality of my appointing another relative to be my attorney-in-fact?

 Someone can certainly *challenge* the legality of the appointment, but doing so successfully is another matter. Provided that your durable power of attorney is properly written and executed, your wishes would stand up in court.

Spread the Word

A durable power of attorney is especially important for aged parents and older close relatives. You should encourage these relatives to consider a durable power in your favor to relieve you of a significant burden if and when they are unable to shoulder their own responsibilities. Here's an example: Your widowed parent suddenly becomes incapacitated and is unable to write checks. Without a durable power in place, you might have to pay the bills out of your own pocket, at least temporarily, and you would be powerless to make other important decisions on your parent's behalf.

A durable power of attorney won't solve all your financial management problems, but it can certainly reduce the physical, psychological, and financial burdens that will fall on your family if you became disabled. And the durable powers for which you are attorney-in-fact will do the same for older members of your family. *Note:* Although some form of this financial planning tool exists throughout the United States, the state laws aren't identical. Consult your legal advisor before proceeding.

LIVING WILLS AND HEALTH CARE POWERS OF ATTORNEY

You may recall that during the final weeks of his life, former President Richard Nixon refused "heroic measures" and received only palliative (discomfort-easing) care at his home in New Jersey. Similarly, former First Lady Jacqueline Kennedy Onassis refused life-prolonging medical intervention before her death from non-Hodgkins lymphoma. Former President Nixon and Mrs. Onassis both retained control over their final medical care through use of a *living will* and a *health care power of attorney*.

Perhaps you've reflected on your own wishes if you were to face a similar situation. Although no one likes to imagine the possibility of being in such a helpless state, the statistical possibility of such an event remains fairly high. This is why it's wise to ensure that your wishes will be respected if you become incapacitated.

Documents That Declare Your Wishes

Living wills and durable health care powers of attorney (sometimes called *health care proxies* or *medical powers of attorney*) are legal instruments similar to durable powers of attorney. Their purpose is to make sure that your wishes regarding health care issues will be carried out.

A *living will* is a statement that allows you to specify clearly your wishes concerning life-sustaining medical treatment. In this way, a court has evidence of your wishes regarding the refusal of medical treatment. The living will describes what sort of physical condition you wish to trigger the document's provisions, and it lists the types of treatments you wish to avoid.

A *durable health care power of attorney* picks up where the living will leaves off. It's an instrument through which you can appoint a person to make medical and health care decisions on your behalf in the event of your temporary or permanent incapacity. It's called a *durable* power because it remains valid and operative despite any subsequent incapacity you may suffer. You direct the designated powerholder to make decisions based on your previously expressed wishes—or, in the absence of a clear expression, to act in your best interests based on what this person knows about you.

Most states have enacted legislation recognizing both living wills and some form of durable health care powers of attorney. Because each state's legal requirements may differ for proper execution of these documents, you should consult a lawyer familiar with the rules in your state. If you live in a state that lacks legislation on these instruments, it's still crucial for you to state your wishes in writing as completely and explicitly as possible. Explicitness may also be necessary if you later take up residence in a state other than the one in which you drafted the document. If you split your time between two states during the year, you may need to draft *two* living wills and durable health care powers of attorney; this will provide documents that comply with each state's requirements.

Q: Do medical personnel really follow the wishes you state in health care powers of attorney and living wills? Aren't they too afraid of lawsuits to comply?

A: Many states now regard a living will as a legal document. Medical practitioners are more likely than before to follow your wishes as stated in your living will. However, not all physicians or institutions are equally responsive either to the general concept of the living will or to specific provisions. You should discuss in detail all your views on the situation with your attorney and with your doctor.

Why You Should Have Both

Because a living will can't cover every circumstance, the extra step of executing a durable health care power of attorney will help assure that the powerholder will carry out your intentions to the extent that the living will doesn't specifically define them. The powerholder you select should be someone you have complete confidence in, of course, since this person will have broad powers to deal with unanticipated circumstances. The ideal person is someone who knows you well enough to have a clear idea of your preferences in such a situation.

You should update your living will and durable health care power of attorney periodically to reflect any change in your intentions. Updating is also generally advisable every couple of years so that a judge or a hospital will regard them as accurately expressing your current thinking. You reduce the threat of someone challenging the validity of a living will or durable health care power of attorney when you keep the document current.

Implementation

Here are some steps to follow if you're concerned enough to take action:

Step 1. Reflect on your wishes regarding medical treatment and discuss them with your doctor and family.

Step 2. Properly execute a living will. With your attorney's help, be as clear as possible about your intentions in a variety of circumstances.

Step 3. Execute *two* originals of a durable power of attorney authorizing someone to make medical decisions for you in the event of your incapacity. Give one of the originals to the appointee.

Step 4. Give appropriate doctors a copy of each document and emphasize your specific wishes to them.

Step 5. Inform your family members of these documents, tell them the contents, and make sure the documents are accessible to them in a time of urgent need. In other words, don't keep your documents locked away.

Step 6. From time to time, you should update your living will and durable power of attorney.

Besides providing you with the ability to control more aspects of your medical care (not to mention the possibility of sparing your family the pain of a prolonged ordeal) these documents can indirectly help to preserve your estate for your heirs. If you have clarified that you don't want artificial support systems to prolong your life, there's less danger that escalating medical care expenses will drain your estate.

■ **TIP:** For more information about living wills, contact the National Council for the Right to Die, 200 Varick Street, 10th floor, New York, NY 10014. Phone: (212) 366-5540. ■

PERIODIC REVIEW AND FOLLOW-UP

In light of the frequent changes in all phases of taxation in recent years, a periodic review of your personal financial plan makes common sense. Filing an annual income tax return forces most taxpayers to look over their situations at least once a year; however, many people—perhaps most—allow years to go by without adequately considering possible changes in property holdings or key provisions in wills and trust instruments. Inflation and increased life insurance coverage push a large number of unaware families into high estate tax brackets.

The Six Basic Considerations

To be safe, you should reappraise the following six basic tax and financial considerations from time to time.

One: Tax Laws and Rulings. Have there been any changes in the tax laws (e.g., the 1997 Tax Act) or rulings that might affect your present estate plan?

Two: Liquidity. Does your estate have sufficient liquidity to take care of debts, taxes, funeral expenses, and estate administration expenses?

Three: Family Circumstances. Have there been any changes in your family's circumstances (such as births, adoptions, deaths, marriages, illness or disability, special schooling needs, etc.) that might call for revisions in the estate plan?

Four: Gifts. Should a gift program be initiated or continued? If prior gifts exhausted your unified credit equivalent of $600,000, you may want to consider additional gifts as the credit increases. Which assets are most appropriate for such a gift program?

Five: Ownership of Family Property. Is the present form of ownership of family property suitable for flexibility and savings in taxes and expenses?

Six: Forms of Payment and Designation. Has the proper form of payment and beneficiary designation been selected for distributions from qualified employee benefit plans?

What many people overlook in their personal financial planning is the opportunity to make lifetime gifts that take advantage of available exclusions. Too often, people also ignore the desirability of separating most jointly owned property because of tax and administrative considerations. The result of inaction is often one of paying taxes that could have been minimized.

Checklist for a Follow-Up

To jog your thinking, take a look at the following checklist for follow-up.

CHECKLIST FOR FOLLOW-UP

If any adult member of your family doesn't have a will, or if any wills haven't been reviewed within the last 3 years, contact your CPA or your attorney. This is especially important in light of the frequency of tax legislation. ☐

Compile a record location schedule of all important financial and legal papers and inform all appropriate persons of its location. ☐

Compile information on the cost and approximate purchase date of all your assets, including your residence. ☐

If you haven't already done so, be sure that your spouse or whomever you designate as your personal representative knows your attorney, CPA, trust officer, broker, insurance advisor, and other appropriate persons. ☐

To reduce federal estate taxes, consider assigning ownership rights of your group-term life insurance to your spouse, a trust, or other appropriate recipient. ☐

Review the beneficiary designations for your employee retirement or Keogh plan and other employee benefits. ☐

Review the disposition of your property not subject to probate (jointly owned property, life insurance) to determine if you have overfunded the marital deduction. ☐

CHECKLIST FOR FOLLOW-UP *(continued)*

Make sure that you've provided for the legal guardianship and personal custody of your minor children. ☐

Review your wills or trust instruments with your attorney to ascertain whether the provisions, if any, concerning simultaneous death produce the desired marital deduction result. ☐

If you and your spouse don't have durable powers of attorney, consider having them drawn up soon. ☐

Special Problems Alert

If your answer to any of the following questions is yes, you may need assistance to determine whether there are tax problems on the horizon. Remember: *A yes is a warning flag* but not necessarily a signal that there is a problem.

Are you:

Making significant cash gifts to members of your family that are likely to continue indefinitely?

Planning to make gifts to grandchildren within the next few years? In your will?

Anticipating a significant inheritance? Is your spouse?

Do you:

Hold assets jointly with your spouse, other than your residence and a working banking account?

Have a simple will that leaves all property you own at the date of your death outright to your spouse?

Own any real property in a state other than the state of your residence?

Have a child or other relative with a serious medical problem that may require special consideration in your will or trust instrument?

Need relief from the management of your investments?

Have substantially more or less property than your spouse?

Have you:

Moved your residence to a different state since you last executed your will?

Named your estate as the beneficiary of your life insurance or your retirement plan benefits?

Lived a part of your married life in a community property state?

PART II

THE LIFE EVENT APPROACH TO FINANCIAL PLANNING

14

GETTING MARRIED

Most people who marry do so for love—and rightly so. However, marriage generally results in the couple entering into a financial partnership as well. No matter how rich in love, a couple that ignores its money matters will undergo stresses that another couple may well avoid by keeping their financial house in order.

As a result, getting married can be one of the major life events from a financial standpoint just as it is in so many other ways. Income may increase, but so do responsibilities. The ability to plan ahead may develop, but so will the variety of goals that require planning. Simply tracking income and expenses can grow so much more complex that even the accounting tasks involved may lead to disagreements and quarreling. In short, the financial and emotional dimensions of marriage aren't always neatly compartmentalized. Ignoring financial planning issues can cause marital conflicts; conversely, collaboration on financial planning tasks can aid in maintaining marital harmony.

To help in understanding the financial issues during marriage, we explore the following topics in this chapter:

- Timing your marriage from a tax standpoint
- Integrating insurance and other benefits
- Discussing finances
- Investment planning for couples
- Estate planning for couples
- Prenuptial agreements
- Sharing costs and assets without marriage

Timing Your Marriage From a Tax Standpoint

Although it seems decidedly unromantic to consider marriage from a tax standpoint, the fact remains: Getting married affects the amount of income tax you pay. No doubt this is a particularly obvious situation in which "you shouldn't let the tax tail wag the dog." However, it's worthwhile to note the tax consequences of how you time your marriage. This may be especially important for couples who, whether living together before marriage or not, see getting married chiefly as a means of formalizing an already long-term relationship.

There are two especially relevant questions here: *Will you and your spouse have one income or two?* and *What's your situation regarding tax losses?*

One Income or Two?

Whether the amount of tax that you and your spouse will pay as a married couple will be higher or lower than when you were single depends partly on whether you will be generating one income or two. If you're marrying someone who generates a lot of income, getting married can hurt you from a tax standpoint. Here's why.

Two-Income Couples

As a married couple, you have only two options for how you file your income tax returns: You either file *married-filing-jointly* or *married-filing-separately*. Married-filing-separately generally causes you to pay more tax than does married-filing-jointly. However, *the total amount of tax is typically higher for a couple filing married-filing-jointly than for two unmarried persons filing single returns.* The upshot is that you may end up paying more tax together as a married couple than you did before you "tied the knot." So if both you and your spouse work, and if this tax issue swings a lot of weight for you, you'll benefit financially by postponing marriage for as long as possible.

One-Income Couples

If your spouse-to-be doesn't generate any income, your tax situation will actually *improve* once you marry. You'll benefit in two ways:

- Your spouse won't add any income to your tax return, yet you can now take advantage of a second personal exemption deduction.
- You'll be using different tax tables to compute your tax—and the married-filing-jointly tax tables are actually more beneficial than the single tax tables.

Combined, these changes may reduce your tax burden considerably.

What About Tax Losses?

The other issue concerns tax losses that your spouse may bring to your shared financial situation. If you're marrying someone who has a tax loss every year, or a tax loss that carries forward from prior years, you may or may not be better off from a tax standpoint once you're married.

E X A M P L E

Capital Losses

■ Let's say that your spouse-to-be is an investor who recently lost a lot of money in the stock market. Losses of this sort carry over from year to year indefinitely. However, there's a limit on how much anyone can deduct per year: an amount equal to that year's capital gains plus $3,000. As a single taxpayer, your spouse-to-be can deduct $3,000 of his or her capital loss each year plus offset all capital gains until the loss is used up. If your own investments produce capital gains, marriage would be beneficial. However, if they generate capital losses as well, getting married may result in delaying the benefits of your capital losses. If you get married, you can use your spouse's losses to offset both of your capital gains as well as $3,000 of your combined income. But if you both would have been able to deduct $3,000 against each of your incomes, getting married will mean that you can deduct only $3,000 of your combined losses rather than $6,000. ■

Other Losses

Among the other losses that you might use to your advantage are:

• Business losses
• Net operating losses
• Passive activity losses

If your spouse-to-be has any of these losses, the losses may reduce your tax burden. Tax considerations in such situations may influence your decision to marry sooner rather than later. On the other hand, if you or your spouse-to-be have losses from rental property, combining your incomes on one tax return may cause you to be unable to deduct losses that used to be deductible, because of the tax rules that phase out the deductibility of these losses based on income levels.

The tax consequences of these rules will obviously vary from one marriage to another. Some couples find that their financial circumstances improve; many others find that getting married leaves them owing more, not less, to Uncle Sam. Especially at high income levels, it's almost as if the government exacts a toll for people getting married. (CPAs and other counselors refer to this as the "marriage penalty.") As to why the tax laws should essentially penalize some couples for getting married, that's something of a mystery. Perhaps this is ultimately a question not so much for your financial counselor as for your representatives in Congress.

Other Tax Consequences

The Taxpayer Relief Act of 1997 creates a number of new income limitations for various tax benefits—including the child tax credit, deductible IRAs, Roth IRAs, deductibility of student loan interest, educational credits, and others. These benefits are phased out depending on your adjusted gross income. In most cases, the AGI limits for married couples filing jointly are less than twice the limit for single filers. You should consider these limits for the year that you're considering for your marriage.

INTEGRATING INSURANCE AND OTHER BENEFITS

Once you marry, you and your spouse may find that your situation has changed regarding insurance and other benefits that you obtain from your workplace. You may, for instance, be able to reduce your costs for health care coverage by taking advantage of spousal benefits from one of your employers. In addition, by combining your households, your insurance costs may go down, thus enabling you to take advantage of retirement savings opportunities at one or both employers.

For this reason, you and your spouse should coordinate your company plans to obtain maximum benefits at the minimum cost. The most common issues here are:

- Health insurance coverage
- Other insurance plans
- Flexible spending accounts
- 401(k) plans

Health Insurance Coverage

If both you and your spouse are working, and if you both have health insurance coverage at the time of your marriage, you should look at your two insurance plans and determine which offers you greater benefits. Plans vary enormously in cost and range of benefits. (For a more detailed overview of what benefits you need, review Chapter 8.) Once you complete the necessary paperwork to cover you both under the plan you choose, you should drop the other plan.

Health care coverage for a married couple is generally cheaper than separate coverage for two individuals. However, here are some important caveats.

Conditions for Reinstatement. Let's say that you and your spouse-to-be both have coverage through your respective employers. You then get married. At that point you decide to cancel your own coverage in favor of being covered through your spouse's program, which offers better benefits. Suppose, however, that soon thereafter your spouse gets fired, and you wish to resume coverage under your own employer. No problem? Maybe, maybe not. In fact, you may have to pass a physical exam to regain the health care coverage you had earlier. Check ahead to make sure that your options are flexible.

Exclusions for Preexisting Conditions. A variation on this scenario is that you may end up regaining your coverage but face possible exclusions for preexisting conditions. You should examine the terms of your present coverage to find out what restrictions may apply. Is it possible that your coverage will be more limited than if you hadn't dropped it, then gotten reinstated?

You should be aware that, under the Health Insurance Portability and Accountability Act of 1996, coverage exclusions under group health plans for preexisting conditions are limited.

A group health plan may exclude coverage for preexisting conditions only for 12 months. This period is reduced, however, by counting certain prior coverage under other health plans toward the exclusion period. Employees with 12 months of coverage with one employer may, therefore, move to a new employer with new coverage without becoming subject to the preexisting condition exclusion of the new employer.

Other Insurance Plans

Insurance coverage of other sorts may start to seem far more important than before you got married. Many single people have little or no life insurance at all, for instance, since they have no dependents. This situation changes overnight when you get married. For this reason, you should carefully assess your needs for life insurance (to provide for your spouse's economic well-being in the event of your death) and disability insurance (to provide income in case you become seriously ill or injured).

Note, however, that many employers specify a window of opportunity during which you can sign up for these kinds of coverage. Your change of marital status may allow you a period of time to consider obtaining insurance; however, the length of time varies from one employer to the next. Check with your employer's personnel or employee benefits department for specifics. (In Chapters 7 and 8 we explain the various kinds of insurance coverage in greater detail.)

Flexible Spending Accounts

Some companies allow certain employees a benefit that may provide you with a tax benefit for your health care costs. This is called a *flexible spending account*. Flexible spending accounts can be a significant perk if you either pay for your own medical expenses or for substantial child-care costs. (We discuss this issue again in Chapter 15 with special reference to child care.)

Let's say that you pay for 100% of your health care insurance premiums and out-of-pocket medical costs. Generally speaking, you'll receive no tax deduction for these expenditures. In a situation like this, a flexible spending account can give you a tax break. Here's how it works.

E X A M P L E

■ Suppose that you can predict your medical expenses at $1,200 during the coming year. You then have $100 withheld on a monthly basis from your paycheck and put into a flexible spending account. Here's where the benefit occurs: The income placed into a flexible spending account isn't taxable. As a result, you essentially receive a $1,200 tax deduction for the money you put in the account. The flexible spending account then pays you back the money you spend on medical care when you incur the expenses, up to $1,200.

Note, however, that if you fail to use the funds in your flexible spending account by the end of a given year, you forfeit the money, which then goes back to your employer. But the risk of this happening probably diminishes after marriage, when both your and your spouse's health care costs can be covered. When November rolls around, you can assess both your own and your spouse's relatively optional medical costs (e.g., eyeglasses, contact lenses, dental and medical appointments, etc.) and decide which ones to accelerate into the current year. ■

401(k) Plans

401(k) plans are one of the most flexible and powerful forms of retirement plan available today. 401(k)s differ enormously, however, with a wide variety of terms available. In Chapters 2 and 24, we discuss retirement planning in detail. For the moment, though, let's consider just a few aspects of what 401(k) planning entails for married couples who have the opportunity to utilize the 401(k) plans of both spouses' employers.

After you marry, it's important to understand all aspects of both of your employers' 401(k) plans thoroughly to take advantage of their benefits.

The key is to take advantage of the better one first. Which is better? Here's a brief rundown of some deciding factors:

- Employer match
- Investment options
- Loan provisions

Employer Match. One or both of your employers may match your 401(k) contribution. In general, you should concentrate on the plan that includes the best matching arrangement, and you should try to take full advantage of the match. The ideal situation is when both of your employers match your contribution to your respective plans. However, the degree and the extent to which the employer matches will differ. For example, your employer may match on a dollar-for-dollar basis up to 2% of compensation, while your spouse's employer may match $0.50 on the dollar up to 6% of his or her compensation. In this case, you'd probably want to contribute 2% of your contribution to your employer's 401(k) plan first, then contribute to your spouse's plan. After you've reached both plans' match limits, you may want to contribute to your plan in an effort to keep your assets more or less even.

Investment Options. The investment options in your own plan compared to your spouse's 401(k) plan are important as well. Although history doesn't necessarily repeat itself, and it can be difficult to compare one mutual fund with another (e.g., the stock fund in your plan may be quite different from the stock fund in your spouse's plan), it may nonetheless be useful to compare the past performance of the funds available in your 401(k) plan with the performance of funds in your spouse's plan. This can be done by analyzing the rates of return over 3-, 5-, and 10-year periods, as well as the risk and other performance information provided by the 401(k) plan sponsors.

The interest rate paid on guaranteed investment contracts (GICs) is often determined in advance. If your investment strategy dictates utilizing the GIC investment choice, you may be able to compare what the GIC rate will be in the two plans over the next year. If your plan's GIC rate will be 7% at the same time that your spouse's plan's GIC rate is 7.2%, you have a fairly straightforward means for determining which plan will provide a higher rate of return—at least for the next year.

Some 401(k) plans offer more leeway than others in how many investment options you can choose among. Your own plan may have just a few options; by comparison, your spouse's plan may offer an entire laundry list of mutual funds for possible investment. When you decide which plan warrants higher contributions, you should consider your latitude in making investment choices. You may feel that one plan offers too few choices for your individual purposes; or you may feel that the other plan offers too many.

Another aspect of this situation is ease in making the investment selection. Some employers offer a lot of guidance to employees in making investments within their 401(k) plans; other employers provide very little advice in this regard. If guidance in selecting which funds to use is important to you, this issue might be a consideration influencing your decision as to which plan to fund more heavily. When selecting which 401(k) plan to contribute to based on investment options, it's important to keep in mind that the funds will be committed for a long time. If the investment choice needs to change for any reason in the future, it's important that the 401(k) plan have an acceptable alternative.

Loan Provisions. Some 401(k)s have loan provisions; others don't. Whether the presence or absence of loan provisions matters to you significantly will depend on whether you're planning to use these funds for goals (such as funding your children's education costs) prior to retirement. If you use your 401(k) plan to fund shorter-term goals (e.g., if you're saving to purchase a house or a car), the loan provisions of your 401(k) plans will be more important. On the other hand, if you're saving for retirement, the existence of a loan provision would be nice but is probably the least important factor in deciding which 401(k) plan to use. See Chapter 19 for more on 401(k) plans' loan provisions.

DISCUSSING FINANCES

Many sociologists and family counselors attest that financial issues can be the source of intense marital conflicts. Of course, for some couples, disagreements over money may be the effect, not the cause, of these conflicts. But because finances may cause trouble *either as cause or as effect*, spouses can do each other a big favor by understanding how finances can influence their marriage.

Shortfalls are only one source of friction. Who spends what, and for what purposes, are common irritants as well. Other difficulties arise from differences of opinion over recordkeeping, cash flow, and goals for saving money. Unfortunately, many couples intensify their money problems simply by refusing to deal with them. For this reason, discussing these matters can potentially ease tensions between you and your spouse; it can also help you work together to take control of your finances.

Here are four fundamental issues that many couples find contentious:

- Determining short- and long-term objectives
- Paying the bills
- Keeping a budget
- Setting up a savings plan

Determining Short- and Long-Term Objectives

In Chapter 1 we discussed the importance of determining your financial objectives. That discussion focused on your individual perceptions of this issue. Even if you filled out the checklists in that chapter and reached some insights about your own goals, however, there's another dimension to this issue once you're married. *What are your financial objectives in relation to your spouse's objectives?* Do the two of you agree about what you want to achieve, financially speaking? Or do you disagree about some or all of your objectives? The issue of agreement is crucial—something that can severely strain even otherwise happy marriages.

What can happen is that spouses have different expectations about how they should earn, save, and spend money together, with tensions resulting over the differences. This can be problematic if they end up quarreling over these different objectives. (On the other hand, it can be even more problematic if they *don't* quarrel, perhaps because they simply suppress or ignore the subject altogether.) Sometimes one spouse wants to attain a higher standard of living while the other spouse feels a desire to increase the couple's level of saving. Or one spouse wants to invest very conservatively while the other prefers higher potential return despite an increased level of risk. The disparities between objectives are almost as varied as individual personalities and financial circumstances. The central issue here is simply that differences of opinion often exist regarding financial matters. If you and your spouse find yourselves at odds over these issues, you should try to reconcile your opinions as a way of helping you deal with your finances creatively.

How can you deal with this situation? First, go over your objectives together. Revisiting Chapter 1 and filling out the financial objectives checklists may be a good place to start. Each of you should now fill out a separate copy, then compare your responses. This exercise allows you a simple way to see where you stand. Here are some questions that you can ask yourselves about the results:

- Are your objectives the same?
- If not, how different are they?
- Is there some overlap between your images of what you want to attain?
- Where is there room for compromise?

This discussion can be especially difficult if one spouse wants to spend more money and the other prefers to save. Each of you may have good reasons for particular opinions. Even if you disagree, however, you should approach these issues as partners, not as adversaries. It's important to discuss these issues in a way that allows each spouse to express his or her opinions without immediate feedback (especially negative feedback) from the other. Try to avoid having one of you overwhelm the other with his or her financial vision or world view.

Another step to this process is running some numbers. Again, you may have done so already. But have you done so *together*? Have you used a spreadsheet or financial planning software program to see the actual consequences of your respective scenarios? Seeing the numbers can be illuminating, and it can assist you in reconciling your opposing conclusions.

E X A M P L E

■ Let's say that one spouse wants to cut back on work hours and spend more time at home. What does the decrease in income do to your net cash flow? What are its consequences on plans to move into a new home or to save for your retirement? Or perhaps one spouse anticipates saving $800 per month—an amount that the other finds excessive. What are the consequences of saving only $500 per month instead? Is it possible that properly invested, $500 per month will generate more long-term income than you thought? ■

In these and other instances, the purpose of the exercise is to create some objective reference points that help you reconcile your differences. Projecting your financial situation according to several alternative scenarios will cause you to see the anticipated long-term implications of your decision. The long-term impact of the strategies needed to achieve your objectives may project a result that you never anticipated.

Paying the Bills

Figuring out an appropriate way to pay your bills is one of the most important financial tasks during married life. Well-thought-out methods that both spouses find agreeable will prevent misunderstandings and cash flow problems; ill-considered methods that seem unfair to either or both spouses will almost certainly lead to resentment. The main considerations here are *accuracy and fairness*. Accuracy is a matter of keeping good records and paying bills in a timely fashion. Fairness is a matter of finding an agreed-upon division of labor and responsibility that suits your purposes. There are myriad possible methods for paying bills, of which we'll focus on these:

- Automatic debit plans
- Computerized check writing

- Standard checking accounts
- Effective use of credit cards

Using Automatic Debit Plans

One option that may simplify your bill paying is using automatic debit plans. By making arrangements with your bank and creditors, you can have some monthly payments debited directly from your checking account. Typical automatic debits are payments for your mortgage, car loan, charitable contributions, and insurance premiums. It's often possible to have a series of automatic debits pay all monthly fixed costs, leaving you to manage only your variable expenses. In addition, some companies allow you to pay your bills by using a touch-tone phone.

Advantages. The advantages of automatic debit plans are most significant from a standpoint of time: The arrangements spare you the hassle of writing checks, filling out payment slips, and addressing envelopes. This approach also helps prevent late payments, which is beneficial in avoiding additional charges and—more important—in maintaining a good credit record. In addition, you save $0.33 in postage for each bill you would have had to mail. This may seem a minor advantage, but it adds up fast. There's a special advantage, too, if you use this method as part of a savings plan: The automatic debit transfers a predetermined sum directly to savings, thus sparing you (at least temporarily) from the temptation to spend it.

Disadvantages. The main disadvantage here is that you may lose track of certain payments if you don't log them carefully in your checkbook. Errors would foster the illusion that you have a greater balance than you really do. In addition, you might forget to take certain expenses into account for tax purposes, such as a contribution to charity. However, good recordkeeping can eliminate these risks.

Computerized Check Writing

Many people have found that using a computerized check-writing system is beneficial for several reasons. These allow you to designate which expenses should be paid through your checking account. At a convenient time, you enter the information for your checks: payee, amount, payment date, and so on. On the appropriate date, the program can direct your bank to transfer the money electronically from your checking account to the payer to the extent possible or, alternatively, to print the checks for you.

Advantages. As is true for many high-tech variations on standard tasks, computerized check writing reduces the amount of drudgery you face. The initial time you spend setting up the system pays off quickly once you're paying your monthly bills. In this sense, computerized check writing bears some resemblance to automatic debits—it's another fancy way of doing something you'll have to do in any case. The difference is that this kind of check writing doesn't work just for fixed expenses, as is true for automatic debits; it's as good or better for variable expenses. You'll save lots of time. However, the biggest benefit concerns recordkeeping. Computerized check writing will maintain complete records for whatever you've spent as long as you use it consistently and completely.

Disadvantages. Typical of other computerized functions, however, this one has a few drawbacks. One risk you run by paying bills this way is that your computer knows you've paid them but *you* don't. Or you may have paid bills manually and failed to inform the computer. As a result, you may lose track of your bank balance and the total of your expenses. It's also possible to make inputting errors, such as typing $2000 instead of $20.00 or paying last month's bill twice.

Paying Bills Manually

This payment method is the old standby. It seems rather ordinary nowadays, but it's flexible, simple, and familiar. Many people swear by this method, and it can potentially serve you well. Your dilemma following marriage will be deciding whether to use the *one-account method* or the *multiple-account method*.

The One-Account Method. The one-account method means simply that both you and your spouse write checks drawn from the same account, typically a *joint checking account.*

Advantages. The main advantage of this method is that you only need to maintain one account. If you can keep track of what you deposit into and withdraw from this account, you may end up with simpler accounting tasks. This payment method tends to be more straightforward and less paper intensive. Obviously, it works best if both spouses keep good records.

Disadvantages. The chief disadvantage of the one-account method is that it easily leads to errors. Most couples with one checking account use two checkbooks, which means that each spouse can make payments without telling the other. This situation may lead to both spouses writing checks without informing each other, thus losing track of the bank balance and overdrawing the account. Many couples spend considerable time retracing their steps to determine who spent, deposited, or withdrew which amounts—or else they throw up their hands in frustration and simply give up trying to balance their account at all.

Some people leave larger-than-necessary balances in their account simply because they have no idea how much is available. They want to avoid the risk of overdrawing. Rather than figure out where things stand, they just pad in an extra (and often non-interest-earning) cushion just in case.

Another response—also counterproductive—is for one spouse to abandon the account to the other spouse, thereby abdicating a degree of control and responsibility over the family finances. This response can lead to mutual resentment and, in some marriages, one spouse's ignorance pertaining to his or her personal financial position.

The Multiple-Account Method. Alternatively, you and your spouse could maintain two separate accounts, one for each of you, with each account having a single checkbook. You pay "your" bills separately. In addition to each spouse's separate account, some couples also have another checking account for paying "their" bills.

The multiple-account method requires the spouses to divide up the bills. For example, spouse A is responsible for paying the mortgage payment and car payment; spouse B is responsible for paying all other bills. Based on how much income the spouses have coming into each account, the particular division of payments can involve a complex breakdown. But overall, this method has more advantages than disadvantages.

Advantages. There are three reasons that the multiple-account method is advantageous.

First, it tends to result in the fewest errors. With two separate accounts, you're more likely to know what the account balances are. This method also works well if each spouse feels a need to have his or her own personal account (as opposed to one half of a joint account).

Second, both spouses have control over the financial situation. They're more likely to understand what's involved in decisions, and they're more likely to share day-to-day responsibility over money matters.

Third, the two-account system allows for a degree of financial privacy. This can be important even for couples who are committed to sharing the work of financial planning. For instance, keeping two accounts means that when each spouse purchases gifts for the other, the costs involved can remain secret.

Disadvantages. There are two main drawbacks to the multiple-account system. One is financial; the other isn't so much a financial issue as it is marital.

The financial issue has to do with a couple's overview of their finances. Having separate accounts means that you may not have the "big picture" of your financial situation. You may not know the sum of the money you have in all your checking accounts. You may therefore be uncertain about what you're spending and what you're saving. In a sense, you've decentralized your finances. This can leave each of you wondering what the other has received in income or paid in expenses. It's not difficult to go from this situation to one where you're actually losing control over your finances.

The other drawback is that if you use separate accounts to pay your bills, you or your spouse may end up feeling a lack of control over how much money is in his or her account. That is, one of you may feel that your share of the family funds is more easily depleted by unpredictable circumstances. Unless you're careful to ensure that an equivalent share of the variable expenses winds up the responsibility of each spouse, one spouse's share of overall expenses may end up disproportionate. Alternatively, many spouses simply divide their bills based on whether they are fixed or variable, giving the responsibility of paying variable expenses to the spouse with the better cash management skills.

E X A M P L E

■ For example, let's assume that spouse A brings in $4,000 per month, while spouse B earns only $2,000. Assume as well that A's cash management skills are considerably better than B's. In this case, spouse A should take over $4,000 of variable expenses, including payments to savings. Spouse B should pay the fixed expenses—mortgage, car payment, savings, and so on—equal to $2,000 per month. ■

Some couples have a joint checking account in addition to their separate accounts. This is typically used to pay large fixed expenses, such as the mortgage payment. The advantage of having a joint checking account as well is that you can arrange each spouse's contribution requirement to the account in an equitable way, and you can have the account pay all or some nondiscretionary expenses. Then each spouse's other expenses can be paid from that person's separate account, thus eliminating some of the disadvantages of the two-account method. Of course, this three-account method is even more complicated and requires greater recordkeeping.

Effective Use of Credit Cards

In Chapter 1 we outlined the risks that credit cards can pose to your financial health. There's no question that indiscriminate use of credit cards can limit your ability to avoid debt and save money wisely. Used effectively, however, credit cards are actually an excellent way to pay your bills. However, such use assumes that you pay off your accumulated charges each month, thus avoiding interest charges.

Advantages. Among the advantages that credit cards allow are:

- Time value of money
- Simplicity of use
- Organized, detailed records
- Somewhat lower costs (e.g., postage and the charge for checks)
- Consolidation of payments
- Potential secondary benefits (such as frequent-flier miles)

Disadvantages. Credit cards have significant disadvantages, most of which we noted in Chapter 1. Their ease of use is all too tempting; you can rack up big bills effortlessly. You're charged interest on any expense left unpaid past 30 days, and any new expense added to an existing balance generally causes more interest charges from day 1 onward. You must also typically pay an annual membership fee.

If you believe that your own situation is such that the drawbacks of using credit cards don't outweigh the advantages, it's still important that both spouses have sufficient recordkeeping skills to use the cards effectively. Using credit cards to pay as many of your bills as possible obviously requires a strong sense of purpose by *both* spouses. Without this commitment, you may end up damaging both your financial position and your marital harmony.

How can you ease the tensions that paying bills often creates? The answer: Use a family budget.

Keeping a Budget

In Chapter 1 we discussed budgets and how they can simplify both short- and long-term financial planning. The recommendations made there hold true for married couples just as for singles.

There's another dimension to the situation, however: implementing a long-term budget as a couple. Even the best budget won't serve you well if it's only a historical document—a snapshot of your income and expenses at a particular time. Rather, you need to use your budget as a way of shaping (and generally that means *limiting*) present and future expenditures. This means making the budget conspicuous in some way that influences your decisions day to day.

How is this achieved? You can choose among any of several options. One way is to have the budget printed out and "posted" somewhere that you and your spouse can see easily. For instance, you might tack it on a kitchen bulletin board. The document lists the various categories of monthly expenses and your target goals for each category. In addition, the document has a blank column for you to note current expenditures. Whenever one of you charges something or spends money on a particular category, you write down the amount in the proper place.

E X A M P L E ■ Let's suppose that you've budgeted $200 per month for entertainment. You and your spouse go out on the first day of the month and charge $63. You come home and write $63 in the entertainment category. Then you both know that you have $137 remaining for additional entertainment costs that month. The numbers for this and the other categories provide a continuous reminder of where you stand for that month's expenditures. ■

The advantages of this arrangement should be obvious. You and your spouse don't necessarily have to notify each other following each purchase; the information is right there in black and white. This ongoing process is beneficial in the long run, assuming enough discipline to note the expenditures consistently. Most couples find that simply noting expenditures as they occur somehow exerts a subtle pressure to keep spending under control.

If you find this arrangement too complex, you can try a more casual approach. This would simply involve each spouse reporting to the other that they've made certain expenditures; then you both keep track of how much is left in the checkbook to cover your expenses. The advantage here is a less intricate, rigorous system; the disadvantage is that it's far easier to forget what you've spent, thus letting expenditures exceed what you've designated in your budget.

No matter what method you choose, your goal should be to create a system you can live with. Set it up, then stick with it. Even the best budget serves no purpose unless you actually use it.

Something else to keep in mind: Some money matters aren't just financial. No matter how carefully you keep your budget, crunch numbers, and save, you're in for a rough ride unless you keep an eye on the big picture. Some of the issues here aren't financial, but personal. For instance, consider the issue of buying cars and homes. Having a new car is nice, but the cost of replacing a car every few years can be exorbitant. If you feel that your lifestyle dictates a new car every other year, so be it. But if you don't really *need* a new car, consider postponing the purchase or purchasing a used car instead. The same holds true for buying a home. It costs a lot to move, redecorate, and furnish a home. Try to anticipate your future needs and wants when you buy your home so that you can own just three homes during your lifetime—a starter home, a family home, and a retirement home.

The general questions you should ask yourself include:

- How much do I really need these things?
- Do I truly *need* or simply *want* them?
- Can I have both my short-term wants and my long-term needs?

Setting Up a Savings Plan

In Chapter 3, we discussed the various kinds of savings plans you can design to serve your purposes. If you need to review your options in that regard, it's worthwhile to review that chapter. From the standpoint of marriage, however, we should stress three other aspects that affect savings plans.

- Savings as a shared commitment
- Savings on a per-month basis
- Savings as a long-term project

Savings as a Shared Commitment. The most important issue is that you and your spouse should "sign on" to a savings plan as a shared commitment. Avoid situations in which one spouse imposes a savings plan on the other. This will invariably backfire. If you disagree on a particular savings plan, rework the plan until you've designed something that you both find comfortable. Also, you should try to avoid taking your savings plan to an extreme. Some couples become so obsessed with their savings plan that they concentrate on it to the exclusion of all else. You don't want saving money to be your main priority. Enjoy life, but think ahead and don't waste money.

Savings on a Per-Month Basis. Consider a savings plan from the standpoint of what you think you can save per month. Let's say that your financial planner recommends that you start saving $300 per month. The most you feel you can save, however, is $130 per month. It's easy to find the discrepancy so discouraging that you drop the notion of a savings plan altogether. However, the most crucial step is simply to get started. Even if you're saving $130 instead of $300, you've at least begun the process.

There's another important but hidden issue here. If you're like most middle-class Americans, your standard of living gradually improves without your taking advantage of the improvement. Every time you get a pay raise, you spend a little more. (This is a corollary of Parkinson's law: "Expenditures rise to meet income.") You may or may not be enjoying the incremental increase in your prosperity; the odds are, though, that you're spending most or all of the extra money coming your way. Regardless of your good intentions, you're probably not as disciplined in your spending habits as you'd like to be. Instead of scrutinizing prices and considering what material goods you truly need, you just reach for your checkbook and credit cards. The money is there, right? Maybe so. But even if you're getting a good deal for what you buy, do you really need it? Is this new possession so important after all—or would you be better off saving the money and eventually discovering that you can retire a year or two earlier than you'd expected?

This is why a savings plan is so important. It's all too easy to let your standard of living rise so high that you'll eventually find retirement difficult. You simply won't have saved enough to maintain the affluence that you've come to enjoy. (And don't forget about the consequences of inflation.) A good savings plan will help counteract this pattern. Instead of allowing yourself to spend more and more, a savings plan will put the brakes on habitual or inadvertent spending. When your compensation rises, keep control of the surplus.

Savings as a Long-Term Project. Like many people, you may assume that your current capacity to save will stay the same throughout the future. The truth may turn out to be different from what you imagine. In fact, you probably have a greater capacity for saving than you think. The reason is that in your later years, your savings potential may far exceed what you can realistically save earlier. During the early years of your career, you may well end up spending almost everything you earn. Once you reach your desired standard of living, however, you'll have a greater capacity to save as your compensation continues to increase. You may be capable of saving only $130 per month now, but the amount may rise to $400 or $500 per month in 5 or 6 years. Grab the chance to increase your savings when it presents itself so that you can make sure to fund your retirement years adequately.

Consequently, you should view your savings plan as something that will happen over the long term. This means first and foremost that you try to project your needs as far into the future as possible. What are your financial goals? How much money do you anticipate needing to attain them? Here again, the cash flow analyses and goal-setting exercises in Chapter 1 can be useful in deciding where you stand. Typical issues are:

- What sources of income you need in general
- What level of affluence you wish to attain
- When you plan to retire
- How much money will be available for saving each year
- How you will fund any anticipated periods of negative cash flow

If you haven't yet done those analyses and exercises *as a couple*, consider doing so now. You may be able to use them to determine how much money you and your spouse can save to attain your goals. This is a crucial reference point.

Creating a Contingency Fund

Part of your savings plan should be a contingency fund (or "financial cushion") to help out during emergencies and lean times. A contingency account is absolutely crucial for the self-employed. Given economic uncertainties and the leaner corporate workplace, an account of this sort is also important even if you have what you consider a bomb-proof job.

As noted in Chapters 1 and 2, most financial advisors suggest that your contingency fund should equal at least 3 to 6 months of expenses. That amount should be enough to tide you over through emergencies or brief periods of unemployment. However, the contingency fund may need to be larger if you're self-employed or if you have reason to believe that finding a new job would involve a protracted search.

Let's look next at three other issues to consider as you make decisions about a contingency account.

Cushion vs. Investment

You may be so eager to get started on implementing your investment strategy that you postpone building your contingency fund. Perhaps you feel that by the time you have enough saved to cover 6 months' worth of expenses, many years of investment opportunities will have passed. This is a legitimate concern. However, you should consider the overall situation from the perspectives of risk and peace of mind. Longer-term investments earmarked to fund contingencies may result in unnecessary principal loss (not to mention sleepless nights) if they occur at the wrong time.

Line of Credit

One way to supplement your contingency fund's ability to provide you with ready access to cash during an emergency is to establish a line of credit and other readily available borrowing opportunities (i.e., credit cards). Quick and easy access to money through a borrowing mechanism may enable you to maintain a smaller contingency fund. Keep in mind, however, that the cost of utilizing borrowed funds when an unanticipated need arises would probably be much more expensive than withdrawing money held in a contingency account.

Kinds of Accounts

Appropriate accounts for a contingency fund are those that are completely liquid and have no risk to your principal. Typical of these accounts are passbook savings accounts, money market mutual funds, and short-term certificates of deposit. Whatever account you select, your main goal is to make sure that your funds are safe. You should also be able to access the money on short notice. Consequently, attributes such as check-writing privileges and the absence of a penalty for early withdrawal are advantageous. In addition, the account should be convenient. The reason for the stress on convenience is that there's often only minimal difference between the yields on an inconvenient account and on a convenient one. If you already have an account established with a stockbroker, for example, it may be much easier to use the money market mutual fund available through that brokerage house rather than to invest directly in a money market mutual fund that your stockbroker can't sell.

If you determine that the most appropriate account for your purposes is a money market mutual fund, you have two different types to consider: *taxable* or *tax-exempt*. Which you should use depends on your tax bracket. See Chapters 2 and 3 to determine whether you'd be better off with a tax-exempt account.

INVESTMENT PLANNING FOR COUPLES

The process of investment planning for couples is much like the process for single persons. In Chapters 3 through 6 we have described the investment planning process in detail, so we won't duplicate that discussion in this chapter. What's worth noting here, however, is that given the financial constraints affecting many married couples—especially during the early years of a marriage—you would do well to plan your investments with great care and foresight.

Cash Flow Analysis

Your first step is careful cash flow analysis. Looking 10 years ahead is ideal; 3 to 5 years seems the workable minimum. What you need to establish are sources of income and expenses to be funded. (See Chapter 1 for a discussion of cash flow analysis, including worksheets.) As part of projecting income, you should determine how much money you'll be able to save annually. As part of projecting expenses, you should try to predict what objectives to fund within the next 3, 5, or 10 years.

Typical financial objectives include:

- Furnishing/decorating/improving your home
- Moving to a new state
- Buying a home
- Having children
- Planning for retirement
- Taking an expensive vacation
- Buying a new car, another car, a boat, and so on

Funding Your Objectives

Once you have a clear enough sense of your cash flow, you can start to fund your objectives. To do so effectively, however, you have to separate them into three categories:

- Short-term
- Medium-term
- Long-term

Short-Term Objectives
If the goal you want to fund will arise within the short term—"short" meaning one year or less—you want to put your money in a cash-type account, such as your contingency account. Suitable for this purpose would be a passbook savings account, money market mutual fund, or similar liquid investment. The factors determining which type of cash management account are safety of principal (first and foremost) as well as ready access, convenience, and after-tax rate of return.

Medium-Term Objectives
If you're funding an objective you expect to be 1 to 7 years distant, you may want to invest in a dedicated bond—that is, a bond or similar investment that matures at the same time that you need the money. For example, you can purchase a 2-year bond or certificate of deposit (CD) if you expect the expenditure to be 2 years away. Bonds and longer-term CDs typically pay higher interest than money market mutual funds and other liquid investments. However, they are less liquid. If you predict the

timing of your expenditure wrong and end up needing the money prior to the bond's or CD's maturity date, you run the risk of losing some principal (or, in the case of the CD, paying an early-withdrawal penalty).

A way to avoid this potential problem—and perhaps even to receive a modest tax benefit—is to use U.S. Series EE bonds. These bonds can be redeemed without risking loss of principal at any time after you've held them for 6 months.

Long-Term Objectives

The third category of financial objectives includes everything past the 7-year time horizon. Typical objectives in this category are retirement and college expenses for younger children. For objectives falling into this category, virtually all assets are appropriate. You should consider your choices, however, in light of your personal risk tolerance and asset allocation. (See Chapters 4 and 5 on these subjects.) Generally, most people invest their money in common stocks or stock mutual funds to fund these goals, but you never want to take on more risk in your overall portfolio than you find comfortable. In addition, you should make sure to change your investment type to a dedicated-type bond or cash investment as the time of the expenditure draws nearer.

ESTATE PLANNING FOR COUPLES

Getting married is a major life event from many standpoints, and the estate planning standpoint is no exception. At the very least, you'll now have decisions to make about the nature of your estate and how much of it you and your spouse want each other to receive in the event of death. In addition, you may need to plan carefully if one of you is financially dependent on the other. Many couples, feeling uneasy with this entire subject, balk even at discussing it; however, the start of a marriage is actually one of the best times to start this process. You gain nothing by procrastination, and you run the risk of financial calamity. To review the estate planning fundamentals, see Chapters 9 to 13.

Here are five subjects you should consider:

- Wills
- Trusts
- Overuse of joint tenancy ownership

- Durable powers of attorney and living wills
- Beneficiary designations

Wills

Writing a will is one of the most important estate planning steps. Dying *intestate* (without a will) may cost your spouse a considerable portion of your estate—not to mention untold heartache. By contrast, having a properly written and executed will can allow you great peace of mind. Arranging to write a will is generally a straightforward matter and (barring a highly complex estate) much less expensive than many people imagine.

Among the questions that you should address at the time of writing your will are:

- How big is your estate, and how big is it likely to get?
- Who should be your executor?
- Who do you want to receive your property, and when?
- How should your properties be held?
- Should you set up trusts for tax-saving or asset-protection purposes?

Trusts

As discussed in Chapter 12, trusts are legal arrangements in which you transfer assets to be held by a fiduciary (the trustee) for the benefit of some person—either yourself or someone else. Marriage may occasion planning for the use of trusts, since you may be able to provide funds to your spouse in a more effective way than would be possible without the trust. Among the suitable arrangements are:

- *Support trusts*: provide enough money for the beneficiary to live on comfortably while preserving trust principal.
- *QTIP trusts*: allow you to make the most of your unlimited marital deduction and still control who inherits your assets after your spouse dies.
- *Irrevocable life insurance trusts*: ensure that the death benefit from your life insurance policy is not included in your estate, thereby pushing the estate past the unified credit threshold and triggering estate taxes.

For details on these and other trusts, refer to Chapter 12.

Overuse of Joint Tenancy Ownership

Many couples tend to acquire all of their assets as joint tenants with right of survivorship. However, as the size of the combined estate grows, overuse of .

this form of ownership can be costly. The problem arises because all of the joint property passes directly to the surviving spouse. This can cause the marital deduction to be "overfunded," as explained in Chapter 10.

Durable Powers of Attorney and Living Wills

As we discussed in Part I of this book, a *durable power of attorney* is a legal document that allows someone to act on your behalf if you become incapacitated. More and more Americans are executing these documents to avoid paralysis of their personal, legal, and financial decisions. For details on durable powers of attorney, see Chapter 13.

Perhaps you find it unpleasant to think about planning for incapacity when embarking on a new marriage. After all, isn't a new marriage a time of joy? True. However, accidents and debilitating illnesses can strike at any time; even newlyweds aren't exempt from misfortune. The fact remains that financial and legal hassles might well worsen the tragedy of an illness or accident if you haven't taken the necessary steps to look after one another's affairs. Failing to execute a durable power of attorney for your spouse could require him or her to petition the court and be named your guardian; alternatively, he or she might have to sell some assets simply to pay your bills. It's hard to exaggerate the importance of taking proper steps *in advance* of an emergency.

Beneficiary Designations

Finally, you should make sure that all beneficiary designations are current at the time of your marriage, or you should change them to reflect your wishes. Relevant documents include wills, pension plans, IRAs, and insurance policies.

PRENUPTIAL AGREEMENTS

Prenuptial agreements are legal documents specifying the nature of assets that individuals bring to a marriage, indicating which of these assets will remain individual or joint property, and designating to what degree future assets will be shared or kept separate. Typical issues discussed in prenuptial agreements are:

- The intent of your relationship
- Who will pay which expenses
- Who will get which assets if you separate

Having a prenuptial agreement can serve you well as a couple if one or both of you bring substantial assets to the marriage. The more assets you have, the more important a prenuptial agreement would be. The advantage is simply that it clarifies who owns what before the marriage begins. There's less room for misunderstanding the nature of ownership, and a legal document indicates where things stand if there is a misunderstanding later.

In addition, prenuptial agreements can discuss assets acquired after marriage. If you currently have assets likely to generate a lot of income, or if you're generating more wealth after marriage as a result of a great job, a prenuptial agreement may ease any concerns about your assets in the event of divorce. A related issue: If you have children from a prior marriage, a prenuptial agreement may simplify your task of ensuring that your children eventually inherit your assets.

That being said, however, it's important to emphasize that state law will prevail as to who owns what in case of divorce or death. And the law varies substantially from one state to another. The 9 community property states differ greatly from the other 41 in settlements following divorce or one spouse's death.

On the negative side, using prenuptial agreements can be counterproductive because of the arguments they can cause. The big problem is that some people feel a legal agreement of this sort is a sign of distrust. "If you really want to marry me," your future spouse may say, "you wouldn't need to have every last *i* dotted and *t* crossed." As a result, what starts out as an effort merely to specify who will own which assets gradually turns into a legalistic struggle that can sour the marital relationship even before it starts. You may end up feeling that you're getting divorced long before you're married.

SHARING COSTS AND ASSETS WITHOUT MARRIAGE

If you have a domestic partner, many of the financial issues that you must deal with will resemble those that face married couples. Sort through the topics we've discussed to see which apply to your situation. Take careful note, however: *Many laws pertaining to married couples won't necessarily cover unmarried partners.*

Domestic Partner Agreements

Just as some couples create a prenuptial agreement as the foundation for the financial aspects of their relationship, you may want to create something similar with your domestic partner. This is an issue that requires close consultation with your attorney, since each state has its own rules about how such agreements are enforced. A domestic partner agreement would serve the same kinds of purposes as a prenuptial agreement: it would specify which partner pays which costs; what obligations each partner has to the other; and what the assumptions are about long-term plans, including the aftermath of separation, retirement, or death. In addition, a domestic partner agreement might address the issues of any children affected by the relationship. Among these issues are:

- Rights and responsibilities of the domestic partner who isn't the child's parent
- Guardianship/custody
- Payment of expenses

Whether or not you create a domestic partner agreement, your record-keeping must be just as accurate as (or even more accurate than) that which a married couple must maintain. You need to be able to keep track of what you've brought to the relationship, financially speaking, in the event of separation or your partner's death.

Other Issues Facing Domestic Partners

One of the main reasons that agreements of this sort are so important is that domestic partnerships exist in a near-limbo, legally speaking, with potentially problematic consequences for either or both partners. Let's turn now to the most common issues and how they may affect you. We'll consider:

- Financial arrangements planning
- Retirement planning
- Estate planning

Financial Arrangements Planning. Regarding certain financial arrangements of domestic partners, there are essentially no laws for domestic partners equivalent to those that protect spouses. Many of the laws affecting spouses have to do with the transfer of property between one spouse and another. For instance, one spouse can transfer an unlimited amount of cash or real property tax-free to his or her spouse. (See Chapter 10 regarding the marital deductions.) No such provision is allowed to domestic partners. Transfers of property between you and your domestic partner may actually be considered gifts—and thus subject to gift taxation. (An important exception: If you pay your domestic partner's medical bills or educational tuition costs *directly*, your contributions for these purposes are exempt from taxation.)

Retirement Planning. By federal law, a spouse generally has a 50% interest in his or her spouse's pension plan. That is, if someone receiving a pension benefit dies, his or her spouse can receive a benefit equal to 50% of what the deceased spouse was receiving. Similarly, if someone covered by a pension plan dies before benefits start, his or her spouse can receive 50% of whatever the accrued benefit was at that time. However, neither rule applies to domestic partners. Most companies don't provide many (if any) survivor pension plan benefits for domestic partners upon the death of the employee. Partners must often fund their partner's retirement benefits by other means, including the purchase of significant life insurance.

Given this situation, you should carefully consider what you're counting on from each other's pension plans. Will you fund your retirement jointly? Alternatively, will you each be responsible for funding your own retirement? Because so few companies provide benefits to domestic partners, you need to do your retirement planning even more cautiously than you would otherwise.

Estate Planning. In addition, estate planning may present a number of concerns for domestic partners. Many of these concerns focus on how property is held and will be transferred after death. Moreover, since there is no marital deduction for property passing from someone to a nonspouse, the tax ramifications of transfers at death may be a concern. (See Chapter 10 regarding the marital deduction.)

From an estate tax perspective, holding joint assets as a married couple means that half of those assets are considered your property; if you're not married, however, any account you hold jointly will be considered to be owned by the first to die, except to the extent that the survivor can establish his or her contributions. If your contribution to a joint account was one-third, then one-third is considered yours. It's crucial for you to keep records that will document what you truly contributed.

Married couples most often hold property jointly with survivorship rights. Following one spouse's death, the survivor receives the entire property. This may or may not be what domestic partners want, however; you should be careful about deciding whether you and your partner want to own property jointly with rights of survivorship or as tenants in common.

E X A M P L E

■ Two domestic partners decide to purchase a house together. One of them has a child from a prior relationship. If they own the property jointly with rights of survivorship and one partner dies, the survivor becomes the sole owner. The child doesn't receive anything. If they own it as tenants in common, however, the surviving partner and the estate each own half of the property following the death of one partner. Depending on how the will or state inheritance laws work, the child may get half of the property. ■

E
X
A
M
P
L
E

■ One more tax consideration. If you sell a home that you owned and used as your principal residence for at least 2 of the 5 years before the sale, you may be able to exclude up to $500,000, as a married taxpayer filing jointly, of the gain on the sale provided certain tests are met. (Single taxpayers can only exclude $250,000.) However, if one of you is not eligible to use the exclusion because of the 2-out-of-5-years rule, the other may still use the exclusion, but the exclusion cannot exceed $250,000. For example, assume on May 15, 1999, Betty, who is single, sells the home she has been living in as a principal residence for the past 4 years, and has a gain of $50,000 on the sale. The entire $50,000 qualifies for the capital gain sale exclusion. On November 1, 1999, Betty marries Mike. On January 1, 2000, Mike sells the home he has owned and been living in as a principal residence for over 2 years and has a capital gain of $350,000 on the sale. Mike can only exclude $250,000 of the gain even if he and Betty file a joint tax return. The $500,000 exclusion does not apply since Betty did not use Mike's home as her principal residence for at least 2 of the 5 years before the sale.

See Chapter 18 for more details on these rules. ■

Since the law is rather vague on issues relating to domestic partners, how should you respond to the situation? Once again it's hard to make general recommendations. The safest course is to consider carefully how you want to hold and distribute property, then seek advice to determine what's best *given the specifics of your situation*.

Marriage

Domestic partners who contemplate getting married often wonder what the overall financial consequences for them will be. Our brief discussion should suggest that there are some significant advantages to marriage. However, it's worth noting the so-called "marriage penalty" as well: Two wage earners who aren't married filing income tax returns separately usually pay lower taxes than those paid by a married couple. As we noted earlier, whether the advantages counterbalance the disadvantages is something only you and your advisor can decide. One way or another, it's crucial that you seek knowledgeable counsel to determine the course of action that best suits your particular needs.

E
X
A
M
P
L
E

■ By way of illustration, let's consider two people who are domestic partners. One partner has a salaried job; the other is unemployed. The non-income-earning partner receives benefits that include housing, joint ownership of a car, and spending money for food, clothes, fuel, and medical expenses. From a tax law standpoint, are these benefits considered compensation for services? Alternatively, are they a gratuitous transfer from the other partner and therefore a gift? ■

To date, the IRS hasn't tended to take action on these sorts of domestic partner issues. The reasons aren't altogether clear. However, it is important to note that Congress may consider taxing some of these transfers in the future. See your tax advisor before transferring substantial amounts of cash or property to your domestic partner.

15

RAISING A FAMILY

A father of two children recently reminisced about the stages of life that he has experienced so far: "When I went off to college, everyone told me my life was about to change forever. But it didn't really change. Then I went into the service, and people told me my life would change. It did—at least for a while—but once I got out, my life returned to normal. Then I got married, and people told me how much my life would change. And I'll admit it changed, though not as much as I'd expected. Then I had kids. Everybody told me yet again how much my life would change. And this time they were right. My life really, really changed. Man, did it change!"

For many people, parenthood is the single greatest transformation of adulthood. It's not just the breadth of their new responsibilities that changes their lives, but also the responsibilities' duration. Once a parent, always a parent. As a result, there's probably no single life event that prompts so many people to become thoughtful, careful, and forward-looking.

In this chapter we examine the various ways in which parenthood changes your finances and offer suggestions on how to keep financial control of your life throughout the ups and downs of raising a family. The topics we discuss are:

- The decision as to whether to earn one or two incomes
- New costs, new budgets
- Investment planning for parents
- Insurance planning for parents
- Estate planning for parents
- Income tax planning for parents

- Teaching your children about money
- Your children's wedding costs

In the next chapter we discuss the special financial issues affecting single parents.

THE DECISION AS TO WHETHER TO EARN ONE OR TWO INCOMES

The decision as to whether to earn one income or two is often especially difficult for couples with children. One income means less money to spend and invest, but it generally has the advantage of allowing one parent to stay home with the children. Two incomes mean more money but more complexity in child-care arrangements, thus potentially more strain on family dynamics. Couples have many reasons for choosing one arrangement over the other, although sheer economic necessity is first and foremost for many people. One issue you should consider, though: Will a dual income really produce the financial payoff you anticipate?

When you think through whether you and your spouse should have one income or two, focus on what you're really earning after you subtract all the costs that are likely to diminish your gross income. It's your net income, not the gross, that should enter into the financial side of your decision. Is that income what you thought it would be? Or does it fall short? Either way, does this income counterbalance what you'll trade off in nonmaterial terms: time with your children, relative simplicity of day-to-day arrangements, and so forth?

Let's consider this issue from three perspectives:

- The unexpected tax bite
- Other costs
- Non-bottom-line factors

The Unexpected Tax Bite

You've probably assumed that you'll have income tax subtracted from your compensation. But have you thought through what you'll pay for FICA or self-employment tax? The situation is probably more complex than you think. If the second spouse isn't going to earn a lot relative to the first spouse's income, the FICA tax can be a substantial burden because *it may not provide any real benefit in the future.*

E
X
A
M
P
L
E

■ Fern Martin has decided to do freelance word processing for college students and faculty in her community. She works part-time and thus earns considerably less than her husband. In addition to paying nearly 40% federal and state income tax, Fern pays approximately 12% self-employment tax (net of the federal and state tax benefit). *More than half of her income goes to the government.* What shocked Fern even more than that fact was learning that she may not realize any benefit from the money she pays to Social Security through self-employment tax. The rule is that when you retire, you generally get the greater of what you qualify for, based on your earnings, or half of your spouse's Social Security benefit. Fern's self-employment tax payments may be all for nought. ■

 My wife's business generates a loss that allows us to take a deduction against my income. From a tax standpoint, doesn't it make sense for her to keep working?

 No. The best you'll manage is to share the loss with the government, but you'll never come out ahead. The higher your income, the greater the government's share of the loss. But based on current tax rates, it can't be more than about a 50-50 split.

Other Costs (Hidden and Otherwise)

Taxes are only the beginning of what you'll pay when the second spouse starts working. Here are some other expenses that you may find increase dramatically to enable both spouses to work outside the home:

- Child care
- Transportation to and from work
- Work-related attire
- Work-related charitable contributions (e.g., United Way)
- Domestic costs (e.g., housekeeping services)
- Children's entertainment
- Eating out (e.g., lunch at work, dinners at restaurants because of less time to cook)

These costs are usually more difficult to determine than taxes are; there are no neat formulas for calculating what you're likely to pay. The main point is simply this: *Don't underestimate the costs associated with being employed.* To the degree possible, try to estimate these costs accurately and weigh their consequences carefully. At first blush, your spouse's reentry into the workforce with a $20,000 annual salary may seem like the answer to your financial worries. If you find that you get to keep only $4,000 after deducting all the costs, however, you may still need to keep a close eye on your family budget.

Caveat: Don't let your standard of living increase more than the extra spendable income you've gained when the second spouse goes back to work. This may seem self-evident, but it's a tactic that many couples fail to implement. It's all too easy to let your standard of living rise to meet the increased income.

The Non-Bottom-Line Factors

Whether to earn one income or two is a decision that many couples have to make solely for economic reasons. In many cases, there's simply no choice; even a marginally better net income settles the matter. Other couples have more leeway: Either the pay is good and the bottom line is very favorable, or there are nonfinancial issues that carry a lot of weight. Perhaps your job is intellectually, emotionally, or spiritually satisfying. Perhaps you enjoy a sense of community among your peers. Perhaps you take the long view on career advancement. Perhaps your work is simply fun. If any of these reasons is persuasive, the nonfinancial reasons may well override the financial dimensions.

New Costs, New Budgets

Whether both spouses work will affect the net income portion of your budget. Your budget will also probably be affected on the expense side when you begin your family. When you're raising a family, expenses have a tendency to crop up even faster than you expected.

No matter how glibly people may reassure you about the minimal costs of raising children—"Oh, they hardly eat a thing!"—the fact remains: Having a family is expensive. For this reason, one of your primary financial tasks during the parenting years is to take all these new costs into account and plan for them accordingly. In short, you have to revise your budget.

In general, the budget you create as you raise your family will be similar to what you might use as a married couple without children. You simply broaden your earlier budget to encompass your new family members and new parental responsibilities. Many of the expense categories will remain the same; so will your fundamental task in using the budget. Certain specific aspects of the situation, however, may differ somewhat. Your budget has to be more flexible, since parenthood is nothing if not unpredictable.

The expenses that many parents have to fund include:

- Hiring a babysitter or paying for day care
- Moving to a bigger home
- Adding onto an existing home
- Buying a bigger or more reliable car
- Moving to a neighborhood with better schools
- Paying for children's extracurricular activities
- Sending children to school
- Traveling to visit grandparents
- Taking family vacations
- Paying for orthodontia
- Expanding insurance coverage
- Paying increased medical bills

The Expanded Role for Savings

Your budget should also try to assign an expanded role for savings, since you now have greater expenses to anticipate for the future, including those for weddings (see the final section of this chapter) and those for the college years (see Chapter 19). Although your own personal circumstances will influence the particular categories you create (as well as how you fund them), here are some situations that may or may not seem likely now but that will need to be accommodated if they crop up in the future:

- *New arrivals.* Even a birth planned well in advance will stress most couples' finances. And there's nothing like a "surprise" baby to wreak havoc on even the best-planned budget.
- *Educational needs.* One or more of your children may need private schooling, tutoring, or other forms of education that differ from those you've anticipated.
- *Multigenerational demands.* You may end up involved in caring simultaneously for your aging parents and your children.
- *Emergencies.* A child's illness or accident may create financial demands far exceeding those covered by your health insurance and ordinary savings.

More About Flexible Spending Accounts

It's worth noting that you can deal with employment-related child-care costs by means of flexible spending accounts. We discussed flexible spending accounts relating to medical expenses in Chapter 14. Here's how they work for child-care costs:

- You estimate your employment-related child-care expenses for the year.

- You contribute the lesser of that amount or $5,000 to the flexible spending account from your paycheck on a pretax basis during the year.
- You pay your costs and receive reimbursement out of the account.
- You never pay income or FICA tax on the amount you contribute to the account.
- You may not claim an income tax credit for child-care costs reimbursed by the account.
- You forfeit any amount contributed to the account that isn't spent on employment-related child-care costs during the year.

Since most parents can accurately predict how much they'll spend on child care each year, this kind of flexible spending account can be straightforward and convenient. However, because you cannot claim the child-care credit if you've been reimbursed for the full $5,000, before you sign up for this type of plan, you should determine which will give you the greater savings: the child-care credit or excluding the earnings under your employer's plan.

As a parent, you may also find a flexible spending account convenient for medical expenses, given the health care costs associated with raising your family. A caveat, however: Be careful to anticipate accurately what you're going to spend on these costs, since estimating incorrectly can cause you to forefeit money at the end of the year.

E X A M P L E

■ Let's suppose you estimate that you'll be spending $1,200 in medical expenses this year. This means that $100 a month goes into your flexible spending account. However, if you didn't incur medical expenses equal to or more than $1,200 during the year, you'll lose any additional amount over the medical expenses incurred. In short, you have to predict correctly. If by November you know you won't be able to use your entire flexible spending account, you might want to proceed with an optional medical procedure, such as having your eyes examined this year rather than next year. You need to incur expenses up to the amount of money deposited into your flexible spending account by December 31; otherwise, you'll just lose the money regardless. If you incur the expenses before December 31, the law allows you to get reimbursed in the following year. ■

Here are some situations in which using a flexible spending account isn't worthwhile for covering your medical and child-care expenses:

- Your medical expenses are very low anyway.
- You're already getting a tax deduction for your medical expenses.
- Your child-care costs aren't employment-related.
- The child-care credit provides a greater tax savings, due to your relatively low income.

Finally, it's important to note that flexible spending accounts aren't an option for the self-employed.

INVESTMENT PLANNING FOR PARENTS

The investment planning process for parents is no different from that described in Chapters 3 through 6. It can be more challenging, however, if you're in the early stages of parenthood because you probably have more goals to fund. For this reason, the key is to do a good job of setting your financial goals and forecasting your cash flow situation through the point at which your children become self-sufficient. Once you've set goals and forecasted your cash flow, you can select appropriate investments to fund the negative cash flow years, based on whether they'll occur in the short term, midterm, or long term.

Let's consider three aspects of this situation:

- Funding high cash flow needs
- The (even greater) necessity of a contingency fund
- Financial discipline

Funding High Cash Flow Needs

Certain phases of parenthood will cause an unusually heavy drain on your cash flow. Typically, the first of these will be the preschool phase, when you may be paying day-care costs. (These costs will obviously continue—and may even increase—for parents whose children attend private elementary and secondary schools.) The second phase will be the teen years, when children start to travel more, incur greater costs for extracurricular activities, and start to drive. The third phase will be the late teens and early 20s, when sons and daughters start college and, in some cases, get married. Anticipating any high cash flow needs will help you to fund them with as little financial disruption as possible. The longer in advance you can project your expenses, the better off you'll be.

How you fund these expenses is basically the same as we described in Chapter 14. Pay careful attention to whether you're funding short-, mid-, or long-term goals.

The (Even Greater) Necessity of a Contingency Fund

If you didn't have a sufficient contingency fund before, you definitely need one now. There's nothing like having kids to bring home the need for a financial cushion. And the need for a contingency fund grows with the number of children in your family.

Here again, the nature of the contingency fund itself is pretty much as we've discussed elsewhere in the book. The rule of thumb is that you should have at least 3 to 6 months of fixed and variable expenses in an account that is liquid and has no risk of loss of principal. However, is that amount enough if you should lose your job tomorrow or experience some other financial setback? Compared to the situation when you're single or married without children, you tend to have less flexibility regarding your cash flow during a financial crisis when you have a family.

Given your potentially increased need for funds during the parenting years, you may want to consider a second "tier" to your contingency fund. This would mean creating a readily accessible source of credit. You can set up this source of credit in several ways:

- Lines of credit
- Credit cards
- 401(k) plan loans
- Life insurance loans

Lines of Credit. Most financial institutions make lines of credit available to their customers based on the customer's ability to pay back the loan. The financial institution may require the line of credit to be secured by the customer's home or other assets. *Home equity lines of credit* are secured by a mortgage on your home. Home equity lines of credit have a built-in tax advantage: The interest that the bank charges you for your debt is generally tax deductible. This makes this kind of line of credit preferable to the others.

An unsecured line of credit is simply backed by your promise to pay; it may or may not be available based on your compensation and financial situation. From a tax standpoint, whether the line of credit is secured by something other than a residence has no bearing on the deductibility of interest payments. What matters is what you do with the loan proceeds. If you spend the money on a personal-use asset (for example, a new bedroom set), the interest won't be deductible even if the loan is secured by your stocks or bonds. On the other hand, if you use the funds to acquire investment property, the interest is generally deductible.

To set up a line of credit, you should explore the various options (e.g., check with area banks and other financial institutions) and weigh their pros and cons. It is important to shop around for the best terms and interest rates. Many banks charge an annual fee for these credit arrangements, but you may not incur charges if you haven't actually used the account. The most important point regarding what you choose *is to make arrangements in advance of your need for credit.* The reality of the situation is that you can probably obtain credit when you don't need it more easily than when you need it.

Credit Cards. Credit cards provide an acceptable form of credit that tends to be easily available. However, you need to stay clearheaded about the risks involved. Credit cards incur much higher interest rates for your debt than would a line of credit, and the interest you pay for your credit card debt is generally *not* tax-deductible. As discussed earlier, credit cards also tend to offer a greater temptation for inappropriate use than does a line of credit.

401(k) Plan Loans. Your 401(k) plan may be an additional source of funds. Not all 401(k) plans have loan options, but those that do allow you to pay the interest to *yourself* rather than to another party. However, in general, you cannot receive an income tax deduction for the interest payments. You may not necessarily be able to borrow your entire 401(k) plan balance. The amount of the loan is generally limited to 50% of your 401(k) plan account balance. In addition, the loan must generally be repaid over a 5-year period or less. An exception to this rule is in the case of a home purchase, for which the 401(k) loan's term can be longer.

Make sure that your 401(k) plan includes the loan option before you assume that you'll have access to funds. Absent an available loan, your ability to access the funds in your 401(k) plan will be precluded unless you are:

- At least age 59½
- Disabled
- Retired or otherwise separated from service
- Able to meet the hardship withdrawal requirements

Hardship Withdrawal

You can withdraw funds from your 401(k) plan if the reason for the withdrawal meets the definition of a *hardship withdrawal*. To qualify for a hardship withdrawal, you must have an immediate and heavy financial need that cannot be accommodated by other resources. Examples of expenses that meet this financial need test are:

- Purchase of a home
- College costs
- Medical expenses

Hardship withdrawals are typically less advantageous than 401(k) plan loans in that they require you to pay income tax, and possibly a penalty tax, on the amount withdrawn.

Life Insurance Loans. Loans against cash value insurance policies are another possibility. You can borrow funds up to the full amount of your accumulated cash value. Interest rates are generally about two or three percentage points above prime rate—a much lower rate than you'd pay on a credit card. If either 401(k) loans or cash value insurance loans are feasible, they may provide a relatively beneficial alternative to other sources of credit. Similar to lines of credit, the interest payments on life insurance loans are deductible only to the extent the loan proceeds are used to purchase taxable investments or invest in a business.

Financial Discipline

Precisely because parenthood involves so many demands on your time, energy, and money, financial planning is unusually difficult while you're raising a family. It's no great secret that children are expensive to feed, clothe, entertain, and educate. Most parents muddle through, and their efforts along the way are laudable. But the rigors of the situation complicate the task of staying your financial course. It's hard to save money when you have so many demands (often conflicting demands) on your resources.

There are two things you can do to minimize this problem. One is maintaining your financial discipline; the other is teaching your children about finances. Maintaining your financial discipline is chiefly a matter of what we've discussed throughout the book: Determining your financial objectives, making a strategy, and pursuing your goals steadfastly. The difference is simply that you have to proceed with even greater clarity of mind than you would otherwise. This isn't easy in a consumer culture that frequently confuses wants with needs. It's especially difficult when your children, barraged as they are by endless advertisements, are convinced they'll die of embarrassment without the latest fashions, toys, electronic gadgets, foods, activities, and so on. Still, succumbing to their peers' pressure (or to your own, for that matter) can ruin even the best-laid financial plans.

Teaching your children about finances is not only part of the solution but also an important phase of their education in other ways. Because this is such an important topic, though, we explore it separately later in this chapter.

INSURANCE PLANNING FOR PARENTS

Becoming a parent dramatically changes your insurance equation. Just as parenthood brings so many other intense and complex responsibilities into your life, it also intensifies and complicates your responsibilities for selecting insurance products that will protect your family. You must now make sure that to the degree possible you have shielded yourself, your spouse, and your children from the risks affecting you.

The planning implications become much more complicated. Your insurance needs increase, of course: You now have more dependents. But your response isn't just a question of adding more life insurance coverage. If you've both held a job until now, you or your spouse may decide not to work outside the home. Quitting the job cuts off a source of income and benefits, including health care coverage. Yet your long-term needs for income not only remain, they increase. You still need all the various sorts of insurance you've needed before—and you need them *precisely at a time when your income may have diminished.*

How should you respond to these changes? The specific recommendations vary according to your individual circumstances, of course, but here are some general suggestions pertaining to:

• Life insurance
• Health insurance
• Disability and property/casualty insurance

We'll consider these kinds of insurance in relation to two separate stages of parenthood: the early years (essentially the first decade) and the later years (essentially the second decade).

Note, however, that in all instances, you need to start with the sorts of capital needs analysis we discussed in Chapter 7. You need to run the numbers to determine what your income is now and what your income would be if you or your spouse were to die or become disabled. You also need to take into account the specific circumstances you face, such as anticipating disruptions to your income or having a child with special needs.

Limited discretionary income will probably constrain your insurance choices during the early years of parenthood. You probably don't have a lot of extra cash available as you start your family. At the same time, this is one of the most crucial times for you to cover your needs. Here are characteristic choices that many couples make under these circumstances.

Life Insurance

During the early years of parenthood, most young couples cover their life insurance needs with term products. If your discretionary income permits, you should consider investing in at least some cash value insurance. You may find, however, that you simply can't spare the money. The truth is that you're better off adequately insured through term products than underinsured through cash value policies. You have to make sure that your spouse and children will have sufficient income in the aftermath of your death; for a couple in the early years of parenthood, term insurance is generally the best route to this goal.

The later years of parenthood present circumstances similar to those in the earlier years but some new opportunities start to appear. On the one hand, your expenses probably remain high. You have more than just the standard children's expenses—food, clothes, toys, sports equipment, travel, and so forth. You also have new expenses, including saving for college costs. On the other hand, your income may well have risen over the years. You probably have somewhat more discretionary income than you had during the first 10 years of parenthood. This widens the range of insurance choices you can make. Your life insurance policies are probably predominantly term products; if so, fine. However, cash value policies are now even more worthwhile than before. The reason? They offer various savings and tax advantages, and they may ease your worries in a decade or two as you approach retirement. As before, though, one of the main determining factors is simply whether you have sufficient discretionary income to purchase cash value insurance without ending up underinsured.

Disabled Child. There's another issue that can affect your life insurance needs as a parent. This is the presence of a child with special needs. Depending on the nature of your child's disability, he or she may be qualified for government benefits from your state or from the federal Social Security Administration. Note, however, that *these benefits may terminate if your life insurance policy's death benefit creates an income stream to your child exceeding certain threshholds.* If that seems likely, you should consider making the insurance benefit payable to your spouse or to a trust that you set up to take care of your child without disqualifying him or her from government benefits. In short, you must consider insurance planning *and* estate planning to cover the situation.

E X A M P L E

■ Suppose for a moment that you have two sons. One is healthy and thriving. The other, recently diagnosed with a serious neuromuscular disorder, will require long-term medical care and educational attention. When you do your capital needs analysis, you soon realize the difference between your financial obligations to the two boys. The first will require support only until he's out of college. You'll pay for his schooling, and you'll make sure there's enough food in the fridge and clothes in his closet until he reaches his majority. But your other son has special needs; he isn't going to function well on his own. You'll be supporting him well past his turning 21.

How should you respond? For starters, you should investigate all means of support. You can also increase your life insurance coverage by a figure corresponding to an amount of money sufficient to support this child's need in the aftermath of your death. If you do purchase life insurance to provide for your disabled child, consider making the proceeds payable to a trust for his benefit. ■

Health Insurance

Obtaining sufficient health insurance coverage for your family is as important as having enough life insurance. Your choices in this situation, however, are generally far more limited than they are for selecting life insurance policies. You'll probably receive your health care coverage through your employer. From within the confines of that plan, you'll select the options that best suit your situation. Beyond that, you don't have much maneuvering room. Individual health care policies are very expensive. Group policies through professional or trade associations are a possibility if you're self-employed—but here, too, you'll have just a limited set of choices.

During the early years of parenthood, you may end up having to alter your health care coverage if one spouse quits a job to spend time with your children. That is, you may have to reconfigure your coverage if you lose one source of health insurance. This may simplify your situation—you now have fewer choices to consider—but it's not a reassuring kind of simplicity. You end up simply taking whatever coverage you can.

Later years of parenthood may offer you slightly more options. As your children grow older, both you and your spouse may end up working outside the home. Two incomes won't necessarily increase your choices for health care coverage, but two jobs may give you two plans from which to choose. For more details about how to evaluate the alternatives, see Chapter 20.

An aside about special-needs children. One of the quandaries you'll face with a special-needs child is that your child will age, yet your option for covering his or her health care needs will end when he or she reaches 21. At that point, dependent children are no longer eligible for coverage under your plan. Your response at this point—or, more responsibly, at a point long before this actual transition—you'll have to arrange with the state to obtain special health insurance benefits. Most states have programs for this purpose. Your child may also be eligible for Social Security benefits. If you're unable to make these arrangements, however, you'll have no choice but to pay your child's health care costs out of pocket.

Disability and Property/Casualty Insurance

Having children will change your needs for disability as well as property/casualty insurance. Property/casualty insurance includes homeowners and automobile coverage as well as liability insurance coverage. For the most part, the issues remain what they were before you had children. You need to:

- Guarantee both spouses' ability to cover the family's fixed and variable expenses in the event of disability.
- Safeguard your investment in your home.
- Protect your family against the possibility of litigation.
- Insure against injury and property damage from an accident.

However, you may need to increase the level of coverage, and you may end up altering the kinds of coverage as well. Here are some specific suggestions that parents may find helpful in dealing with insurance issues:

Try to obtain the coverage you want from the company you want as soon as possible. The reason? Once your children reach their teens and begin to drive, you may have difficulty increasing your coverage or changing insurance carriers.

Personal Injury Protection—sometimes called medical payments—can be a useful addition to your property/casualty coverage. Consider adding this endorsement to your homeowner's and auto insurance policies. This is important during the parenting years because it provides flexibility in protecting yourself if one of your children's playmates ends up getting injured on your property or in your car. Carrying the maximum personal injury protection lets you pick up more of the other family's medical bills without hardship to yourself.

For a rundown on insurance issues in general, refer to Chapters 7 and 8.

Estate Planning for Parents

Yet another way in which parenthood transforms your life is how it affects estate planning. Now that you have children, it's all the more important for you to get your house in order. Review Chapters 9 through 13 for an overview of estate planning issues. Meanwhile, here are three especially crucial issues for you to consider:

- The importance of a will
- The importance of trusts
- The usefulness of a testamentary letter

The Importance of a Will

Even if you have minimal assets, make sure that you have a valid will. Your will designates your child's *guardian* and the *trustee* of any trusts established to manage your assets and make distributions in keeping with your wishes. In both cases you want to determine who is best suited to look after your child's well-being. If you and your spouse are raising the family together, you can't assume that both of you won't die simultaneously. (Technically, this is called a *common disaster*.) If you're a single parent, you have even more reason to clarify your wishes about guardianship and set them forth in a legal document. Failing to take these steps may result in your child being raised by someone you would never have chosen for this role.

> ***Guardian:*** *the person responsible for your child's day-to-day well-being following your death. More specifically, the* guardian of the person *is responsible for your child's day-to-day care; the* guardian of the estate *is responsible for your child's financial well-being.*
>
> ***Trustee:*** *the person or institution (e.g., a bank) you've appointed to manage the assets in a specific trust. In certain cases, it may be appropriate to name an individual and an institution as co-trustees.*

Designating your child's guardian in your will allows you a degree of control over who raises your child and in what manner. In many instances the issue isn't just who the guardian should be and what assets the child receives, but how more complex arrangements will be worked out.

E X A M P L E

■ Lucy and Jed have written their will to stipulate that if they die simultaneously, Lucy's sister Meg will raise their two children. However, Meg lives in a one-bedroom apartment. Lucy and Jed have therefore included a provision in their will allowing Meg a share of the estate that will fund her purchase of a bigger home. This will let the couple's children move in with their aunt without creating hardships for Meg. ■

■ Harry and Beth have a somewhat more complex situation to face. They've worked out an arrangement in which Harry's brother and sister-in-law will take in Harry and Beth's daughter following a common disaster. Frank and Sandi (Harry's brother and sister-in-law) are comfortable with the situation; they have plenty of space at home. However, Harry and Beth have always sent their daughter, Adele, to private schools. They'd want Adele to continue attending private school if at all possible. But they worry that Frank and Sandi's twin boys might feel left out if they attended public schools while their cousin received a private education. For this reason, Harry and Beth have included a provision in their wills allowing their estate to fund their nephews' education if necessary. ■

Your will allows you to designate who will take care of your children after you're gone as well as who receives many of your assets in the event of your death. Your will, combined with your beneficiary designations, serves to help you ensure your children's material safety for the future.

When your children are born, you should make sure to review your primary and contingent beneficiary designations. Typical assets you hold that require beneficiary designations are:

- Insurance policies
- 401(k) plans
- Other employee benefits
- IRAs and Keoghs

The Importance of Trusts

Another crucial decision you must face as parents is who will handle the money from your estate and when your children will receive their inheritance. Most state laws restrict how much money a minor may receive by this means; guardianship is a response to these restrictions. However, you still have to decide what will happen when your children reach adulthood. If your bequest is substantial enough that considerable funds will remain even after your children attain their majority, you have another issue to face: Should you simply allow them access to the money at age 21? Or should you create a trust so that they don't get the money all at once?

Various sorts of trusts can allow you flexibility in dealing with these situations. For instance, you might designate that your children receive one-third of their inheritance at age 25, with later distributions at ages 30 and 35. Other sequences are 21, 25, and 30; 30, 35, and 40; and so forth. You can specify any other ages you prefer. The point is simply that these sequenced distributions allow your children an opportunity to learn how to manage money without risking their entire nest egg all at once.

If your estate is large enough, you might also make arrangements to have the trust remain in existence for an indefinite period. That is, you might have your children receive all of the income from the trust's investments and that amount of trust principal that the trustee deems necessary to carry out your wishes as stated in the trust. An arrangement of this sort safeguards your children's long-term financial safety by making the principal itself inaccessible to their creditors.

Are you worried that your children may end up financially irresponsible even as adults? One way to safeguard their inheritance from foolish decisions is to have a *spendthrift clause* written into the trust documents and allow the trust to remain in existence for their lifetimes. These clauses protect your estate from creditors that might dun your heirs as a consequence of bad financial choices they've made.

The Testamentary Letter

In addition to a will, you should consider writing a *testamentary letter*—a handwritten document that sets forth your wishes about the distribution of personal belongings. This is a way of indicating "who gets what" among special family items. Although your will may settle the issue of the more valuable assets in your estate that are legally titled, the testamentary letter is important for specifying how to divide up other possessions: china, furniture, photographs, family mementos, and so forth. If handwritten and referenced in your will, the testamentary letter is a holographic codicil to your will and thus legally binding. Whether legally binding or not, use of a testamentary letter can simplify your executor's task and also avoid conflicts among your children over material possessions. Be sure to read Chapters 9 through 13 for more about estate planning.

INCOME TAX PLANNING FOR PARENTS

The Child Tax Credit

A tax credit is now available for each qualifying child under the age of 17. The per-child credit is $500. A qualifying child is someone you claim as dependent on your tax return. (A grandparent may claim a child credit if the grandchild is claimed as a dependent on the grandparent's tax return.) The credit is phased out based on your adjusted gross income (AGI) and the number of qualifying children. The maximum child credit is reduced by

$50 for each $1,000 by which your AGI exceeds a certain threshold. See the chart below for the details. You will notice that the income level at which the child credit is phased out is higher with each additional child.

CHILD TAX CREDIT					
Maximum Amount of Credit Available				**When AGI reaches:**	
Number of Qualifying Children			**Single Head of Household**	**Married Filing Jointly**	**Married Filing Separately**
1	3	5			
$500	$1500	$2500	$75,000	$110,000	$55,000
0	$1000	$2000	$85,000	$120,000	$65,000
0	$500	$1500	$95,000	$130,000	$75,000
0	0	$1000	$110,000	$140,000	$85,000
0	0	$500	$120,000	$150,000	$95,000
0	0	0	$130,000 and above	$160,000 and above	$105,000 and above

Generally, the credit will not be refundable beyond your income tax liability. However, exceptions do exist for families with three or more qualifying children and for some families with low income levels.

Caveat: You should note that using the child tax credit as well as other credits in the new law (e.g., the Hope Scholarship tax credit discussed in Chapter 19) could subject you to the alternative minimum tax (AMT) depending on the extent to which you have reduced your income tax through tax preference items such as high real estate taxes or state and local income taxes. The AMT was designed to apply when taxpayers significantly reduce their taxes through the use of certain deductions and tax credits. Because the child and education tax credits are generous, middle-income and upper-middle-income families might reduce their regular tax liability by 20% to 50%, and possibly subject themselves to AMT. Be sure to complete the AMT calculation when preparing your income tax return if you have taken advantage of many of these credits and other income tax deductions. The Tax and Trade Relief Extension Act of 1998 provided a break for 1998. In 1998 you were, in effect, able to reduce your AMT by the amount of these credits. As of the date of this publication, no one is sure what the rules will be after 1998.

TEACHING YOUR CHILDREN ABOUT MONEY

Some parents feel that it's a mistake to talk with their children about finances. Money matters will only make children anxious, they say; children have no business knowing what their parents make; they shouldn't even worry about how much things costs. Sentiments such as these are unquestionably well intended. However, even these good intentions can backfire. Growing up in an affluent and money-minded culture, children learn about money whether or not their parents decide to teach them. By sidestepping the issues, parents may end up abdicating their role as guides in a situation where children badly need their guidance.

Budgets

Consider the issue of your family budget. It's not as if your children need to know what you earn or the details of what the family spends. But letting them in on certain aspects of the overall picture at carefully chosen stages of their development can be salutary. Do your kids know why you sometimes refuse their requests for this or that purchase? Do they imagine that your refusals are totally arbitrary? Or, by starting to understand the realities of family finances, do they grasp that you have reasons for letting them buy a special toy now and then but not every new gizmo and gadget they want? Sharing information about the budget can help them not only understand the importance of specific budget items, but also the importance of budgeting as a process.

One implication of this issue is that you set the right example. If you stress the importance of the family budget but ignore it yourself, your "party line" won't be persuasive. You need parameters for the entire family. Suppose that your monthly allotment for entertainment is $200. You're

SAMPLE CHILD'S BUDGET

	WEEK OF _____		WEEK OF _____		WEEK OF _____		WEEK OF _____	
	PLANNED	ACTUAL	PLANNED	ACTUAL	PLANNED	ACTUAL	PLANNED	ACTUAL
Inflows:								
Allowance								
Extra jobs								
Gifts								
Total	$	$	$	$	$	$	$	$
Outflows:								
Savings								
Snacks								
Entertainment								
Charity								
Gifts								
_____								
_____								
Total	$	$	$	$	$	$	$	$

already up to the $200 line this month, but now your children want $5 apiece to go see a movie. Even though it's only $5 per kid you'll be spending, it's much more beneficial for everyone if you say, "Sorry, we're almost over budget" and hold the line instead of making an exception. Otherwise, your message is that budgets don't really matter.

Allowances

Giving your children an appropriate allowance is one of the best ways to help them understand the value of money. This is an opportunity for children to learn at least three important lessons:

- The benefits of working
- The importance of keeping a budget
- The consequences of their financial choices

They learn the benefits of working by gaining a material reward for their efforts. They learn the importance of keeping a budget by having to keep track of what they've earned and spent. And they learn the consequences of their financial choices by experiencing the pleasures both of saving and of making thoughtful purchases, as well as the discomfort of ill-considered spending.

The amount of the allowance is less important than how your children gain it and how they're allowed to use it. Ideally, the allowance might come from two sources: (1) the "base case," money that the children receive for doing a standard set of chores; and (2) additional money for additional work. Any number of variations on this basic theme are possible. Typical chores for the base case might be the children's cleaning up their rooms and making their beds. Additional jobs might include setting and clearing the table, washing the car, mowing the lawn, and so forth. By this means, the children learn that they actually receive financial rewards for expending additional effort—effort that creates incentive and accustoms them to working at an early age.

Savings

One of the long-term goals for teaching children about finances is, of course, to instill the value of saving money. Keeping a budget and earning an allowance can both serve as means to this end. A clear emphasis on the discipline of saving is important, however; otherwise, children may not grasp how these separate pieces of the picture fit together.

For this reason, it's important not only to pay an allowance but also to help your children do something constructive with the money. Otherwise, they may think of money simply as a toy—something to play with or handle. It should be more goal oriented than that. The goal can involve either purchasing an item or saving the money in an account.

EXAMPLE

■ Your 6-year-old daughter receives an allowance of $1 per week. She often saves her weekly allowance for a particular item she wants. This item costs $15. She needs to know that saving her allowance will mean waiting 15 weeks to reach her goal. This situation makes the value of a dollar much more concrete to a child than any amount of parental lecturing. It also may help her to understand the situation if she realizes that she can either wait 15 weeks to save enough allowance money, or she can do extra chores around the house and reach her goal in 10 or even fewer weeks. ■

Another issue is *how* children save money. Rather than simply accumulating coins and bills in a jar, your children can learn to deal with a savings vehicle and financial institutions. A passbook savings account is probably the most common way that kids start this process. However, there may be some practical obstacles in this regard, since some banks require a minimum of $100 to open an account or won't accept small additions to an existing account. You have to consider the situation from a standpoint of what's practical. Check with your local bank to see what is available.

BUILDER

One savings vehicle that some parents and children seem to like is a U.S. Series EE bond. There are several significant advantages to this arrangement:

• The minimum investment is only $25, which allows your child to save enough money for an investment fairly fast.
• The bond your child receives looks impressive, with its face value double the amount of the child's initial investment.
• The disparity between the investment and the face amount can spur discussions of interest rates, compounding, and so on.

The most important aspect of this issue is simply to start teaching your children to save for the future. If they get it in their minds that this is simply part of what one must do, they'll be much better off for the rest of their lives.

Charity

One last money matter that you may want your children to learn about: the importance of charity. Here again, this is something children find easiest to understand in concrete terms. There's no better way to teach them charity than simply by encouraging them to do the giving. Among the ways in which your child can participate in charitable giving are:

- Giving of themselves—such as contributing to a neighborhood cleanup project or baking cookies for a local food bank
- Raising money—through walkathons, school fund-raisers, or other fund drives
- Donating some of the child's own money—through a place of worship or a program at the child's school
- Donating some of the child's used toys or clothing
- Contributing some of your own money or property—to school or other institutions and programs

Some children enjoy assisting their parents in making a family contribution; however, they may benefit even more from this experience if they're donating money that's actually theirs—part of their allowance, perhaps, or money they've earned through some sort of fund-raiser.

Moneyopolis

To help parents teach their children about financial planning, Ernst & Young, in cooperation with the U.S. Department of Education, has established a free web site called Moneyopolis (www.moneyopolis.org). The site has games and other features that teach and reinforce financial concepts in a fun way. Visit it with your children.

YOUR CHILDREN'S WEDDING COSTS

If you're like most parents, you've probably given little thought to wedding costs during the long years of parenthood. The notion of your little darlings going off and getting married themselves somehow doesn't quite compute. Like so many other aspects of parenthood, however, this one will come rushing at you with bewildering speed. It's worth thinking over well before the fact.

There are two main issues to consider in this regard. One issue has more to do with personal expectations than with finances. The other is more strictly financial.

How Personal Expectations Affect Wedding Costs

There's a tendency for many parents to give their son or daughter *carte blanche* in planning a wedding. To some degree this is understandable,

Setting a Limit on Your Contribution

Setting a limit on your contribution to the wedding costs can be a positive message you send about financial responsibility, especially if you combine this statement about limits with allowing your child to make some real budgetary decisions. Let's say that at most you'll pay $5,000. Your daughter and her fiancé can then decide if they want to spend that entire sum on the wedding or, alternatively, spend $4,000 on the wedding and use the remaining $1,000 toward a down payment on a house. Giving them a dollar amount *and* a degree of fiscal responsibility can be highly beneficial.

Prefunding Your Child's Wedding

Just as you can prefund your child's college costs (see Chapter 19), you can prefund wedding expenses. Here, too, you can make a gift of the funds to your child in advance and have the income earned on the investments taxed at your child's income tax rate. Alternatively, you can simply designate a particular fund as what you believe you'll use for this purpose. This would not shift the income tax burden to your child. Whichever method you select, the advantage is that by starting early, you can let the compounding of your initial investment take some of the long-term weight off your shoulders. Typical investment vehicles for this purpose are similar to what you'd use for other midterm objectives, such as funding a college education. See Chapter 19 for a full discussion of investment strategies and vehicles.

Determining When to Make the Gift

The question of *when* to provide your son or daughter with this money is largely a matter of personal preference. However, it's worth considering some of the side effects of making your contribution at particular times. If you make your gift early, you may have a larger fund as a consequence of income tax savings. The investment income earned on the funds transferred may be taxed at a lower tax bracket than your own, creating a larger available fund. On the other hand, knowing that he or she has this money in advance may prompt your child eventually to feel that the fund has been his or hers all along, in which case you may feel some pressure to provide even more funds for the wedding than those you've already given.

given most people's desire to acknowledge how special the occasion will be for everyone. However, it's important to keep the situation in perspective— not only for you and your spouse as the parents but for your child and his or her spouse-to-be. Deciding *not* to write a blank check may be one of the ways you give them a good start as they make their new life together.

Two ways of dealing with the situation are shown on page 285.

Wedding Costs: The End of Your Parental Expenses?

In paying your children's wedding costs, you see the final stage of your financial responsibilities as a parent. Right?

Wrong! Your children may now have children of their own, at which point you'll start facing financial responsibilities as a *grandparent*—responsibilities you'll probably face with delight and creativity.

16

COPING WITH DIVORCE

Although statistically common, divorce is almost invariably a traumatic experience. The process of dismantling a marriage is often emotionally wrenching for both spouses, their children, their respective families, and their friends. To make matters worse, the process is usually expensive and legally complex. Most people emerge from the experience feeling traumatized and exhausted.

Specialists from many fields—psychology, sociology, jurisprudence, and others—have written books to help people cope with divorce. Many of these books are helpful resources. Unfortunately, few of them touch on an important aspect of the subject: the potentially traumatic *financial* aspects of divorce. In fact, many people who are in the process of divorce (or who are dealing with its aftermath) receive only minimal advice on adjusting to how divorce will affect them financially. Divorce attorneys address certain financial issues, of course. Property settlements, alimony, child support, and other matters are all within their professional purview, and their advice is often useful. Unless an attorney has specific training in financial planning, however, that advice may not go far enough.

The truth is that if you're going through a divorce, your financial situation will almost certainly be transformed. For most people the transformation is not a change for the better. Each spouse may end up experiencing a decline in his or her standard of living. Not just current but also future cash flow may lead to reduced financial expectations. However, this situation isn't cause for despair. As with other aspects of divorce, proper planning can allow a measure of flexibility, good grounds for compromise, and a method for starting to build a new life. Some of that planning should be financial planning.

Divorce is, in fact, a classic opportunity for financial planning. And not just an opportunity—it's a necessity. For the changes that result from a divorce will require careful, imaginative responses if you are to limit their effects on you and allow you to keep your options open.

To address these issues, here are the topics we'll address in this chapter:

- Working with advisors
- Calculating total assets and liabilities
- Determining new living expenses
- Determining the financial planning consequences of alimony
- Determining the financial planning consequences of child support
- Determining the financial planning consequences of property divisions
- Dealing with the investment aspects of divorce
- Dealing with the retirement planning aspects of divorce
- Dealing with the insurance aspects of divorce
- Dealing with the estate planning aspects of divorce

WORKING WITH ADVISORS

Divorce attorneys may or may not have an extensive knowledge of financial planning, including the tax aspects of the subject. Yet the issues involved are crucial. If you miss certain opportunities from a tax standpoint, you may end up paying for the consequences—literally—for years to come. (A brief example: If all your payments are structured as child support, they won't be tax-deductible for you.) Even for the divorce process itself, you need to work with someone who has a full understanding of financial and tax planning.

The same holds true for post-divorce issues. Your entire financial picture will have changed by the time your divorce has been finalized. To take hold of your situation, you'll almost certainly need advice from an advisor who can help you plan for the long run. Is that advisor your attorney? Rather than assume that it is, you should ask your attorney what sort of background he or she has in financial matters—and whether this background includes financial planning *for the long term*. If you feel that you need to supplement your attorney's advice with information and recommendations from other advisors, then you should consider obtaining help from a financial planner, and perhaps from certain other professionals as well.

Financial Planners

If you decide to hire a financial planner, he or she should consult with you and your attorney to become familiar with the nature of the divorce proceedings and relevant issues concerning support and property. After initial consultations, the planner should analyze and calculate your financial needs and resources. Among the considerations will be the total amount of your family's financial assets. This is especially important because maintaining your accustomed standard of living will be more difficult for two households than it was for one household before the divorce.

To help you plan effectively, your financial planner will need all the data you have available regarding:

- Employment
  - Recent wage and salary data, including raise notifications, W-2's, pay stubs, etc.
  - Contracts, if any
  - Benefit statements
  - Partnership or S-corporation K-1's
  - Business tax returns
- Home ownership/rental
  - Purchase documents
  - Leases
  - Insurance data
  - Appraisals
- Income tax returns
- Life, health, and disability insurance policies
- Will and trust documents
- Investment portfolio information
- Data concerning income, expenses, and debts
- Other important information regarding assets, liabilities, income, and expenses

Using information of these kinds, your financial planner can perform a variety of tasks, including:

- Accumulating and analyzing data
- Expressing opinions to the courts on the value of marital property
- Projecting cash flow
- Preparing reports or serving as an expert witness during the divorce proceedings
- Projecting tax consequences
- Providing data and professional opinions on financial issues
- Helping you make financial decisions

Regarding this final point—help on financial decisions—the planner can help you make financial choices about a variety of issues. Some will be specific to divorce, such as estimating the amount of temporary support, alimony, and child support. Other choices will concern more generic financial planning tasks, such as determining how to fund children's educations, dealing with debt, and doing various kinds of investment, insurance, and estate planning.

Once the divorce process is complete, you may find your financial planner helpful in assisting with longer-term personal financial planning matters. Help of this sort will generally resemble financial planning services in a nondivorce context.

Other Advisors

Your financial planner will probably provide the most comprehensive financial advice of the various advisors working with you on your divorce. However, other professionals may be involved as well, such as bankers, insurance specialists, money managers, appraisers, and others.

Consult with your financial planner if you feel that you need these advisors' services. The planner may be able to recommend specific persons to help you and may also coordinate interactions between them on your behalf.

CALCULATING TOTAL ASSETS AND LIABILITIES

One of the first financial tasks that your attorney and your financial planner will perform is determining the total assets and liabilities that you and your spouse have. This is usually required by the courts and, among other things, would be done pursuant to a property settlement in which it would be decided who would take permanent possession of what assets, and when. What follows is a worksheet for making these calculations.

ASSETS AND LIABILITIES AS OF_____

ASSETS

Cash Equivalents

Checking accounts	$_____	U.S. Treasury bills	_____
Savings accounts	_____	Cash value of life insurance	_____
Money market accounts	_____	Total	$_____
Money market fund accounts	_____	**Investments**	
Certificates of deposit	_____	Stocks	_____

ASSETS AND LIABILITIES AS OF _____ *(continued)*

Bonds	_____	Total	$_____
Mutual fund investments	_____	**Total Assets**	$_____
Partnership interests	_____		
Other investments	_____	**LIABILITIES**	
Total	$_____	Charge account balances	_____
Retirement funds		Personal loans	_____
		Student loans	_____
Pension (present lump-sum value)	_____	Auto loans	_____
IRAs and Keogh accounts	_____	401(k) loans	_____
Employee savings plans (e.g., 401(k), SEP, ESOP)	_____	Investment loans (margin, real estate, etc.)	_____
Total	$_____	Home mortgages	_____
Personal assets		Home equity loans	_____
Principal residence	_____	Life insurance policy loans	_____
Second residence	_____	Projected income tax liability	_____
Collectibles/art/antiques	_____	Other liabilities	_____
Automobiles	_____	**Total Liabilities**	$(_____)
Home furnishings	_____		
Furs and jewelry	_____	**Net Worth**	$_____
Other assets	_____		

The difference between determining assets and liabilities in connection with a divorce compared to financial planning calculations you may perform later is that you'll need to specify individual as well as joint ownership. This may mean three sets of worksheets: "His," "Hers," and "Ours." To complicate matters, the various state laws will influence how these assets and liabilities must be divided. The states that have community property laws, for instance, divide property differently than the other states do. This is just one of many issues for which a financial planner's advice may be useful.

Once you've set forth your total assets and liabilities, you'll also have to identify your items of income and expenditure. This analysis is an important component in negotiating such items as temporary support, alimony, and child support. It also forms the basis for cash flow financial planning for the future. The following worksheet will be helpful in making these calculations:

PREPARING FOR DIVORCE: MONTHLY CASH FLOW ANALYSIS

INCOME WORKSHEET

GROSS MONTHLY INCOME FROM	HUSBAND	WIFE	TOTAL
a. Salary and wages (including commissions, allowance, and overtime)	$	$	$
b. Bonuses (annual, semiannual, or quarterly)			
c. Income from royalties, trusts, or estates			
d. Gains derived from dealing in property			
e. Business income from sources such as self-employment, partnerships, etc.			
f. Pensions and retirement			
g. Social security			
h. Disability and unemployment compensation			
i. Child support from any previous marriage			
j. Interest and dividends			
k. Rental income (net of expenses)			
l. All other sources (specify)			
_____			
_____			
_____			
Total Monthly Income	$	$	$

EXPENSE WORKSHEET

1. HOUSEHOLD EXPENSES

	HUSBAND	WIFE	TOTAL
a. Monthly rent/mortgage payment		$	
b. Property taxes (monthly basis)			
c. Repairs and maintenance			
d. Groceries and household items			
e. Meals outside the home			
f. Services:			
Gardener/landscaping	$		
Housekeeper			
Pool service			

PREPARING FOR DIVORCE: MONTHLY CASH FLOW ANALYSIS (continued)

	HUSBAND	WIFE	TOTAL
Trash collection			
Security service			
Other _____			
Total Services		$ _____	
g. Utilities:			
Water and sewage	$ _____		
Telephone			
Gas/oil/electricity			
Cable television			
Other			
Total Utilities		$ _____	
Total Household Expenses			$ _____

2. AUTOMOBILE/TRANSPORTATION EXPENSES: (SPLIT HUSBAND/WIFE)

	HUSBAND	WIFE	TOTAL
a. Monthly payment/lease	$ _____	$ _____	
b. Gasoline and oil			
c. Repairs and maintenance			
d. Auto tags and license			
e. Public transportation			
Total Automobile/ Transportation Expenses			$ _____

3. PERSONAL EXPENSES

	HUSBAND	WIFE	TOTAL
a. Toiletries/cosmetics	$ _____	$ _____	
b. Nonprescription drugs			
c. Dry cleaning/laundry			
d. Clothing purchases			
e. Grooming/hygiene			
f. Gifts			
g. Entertainment			
h. Vacations/travel			
i. Publications/records			

PREPARING FOR DIVORCE: MONTHLY CASH FLOW ANALYSIS (continued)

	HUSBAND	WIFE	TOTAL
j. Dues/club memberships	_____	_____	
k. Charitable contributions	_____	_____	
l. Other personal expenses	_____	_____	
_____	_____	_____	
_____	_____	_____	
_____	_____	_____	
Subtotals	$ _____	$ _____	
Total Personal Expenses			$ _____

4. HEALTH CARE EXPENSES

	HUSBAND	WIFE	TOTAL
a. Medical	$ _____	$ _____	
b. Dental	_____	_____	
c. Prescription drugs	_____	_____	
d. Vision	_____	_____	
e. Nonprescription drugs	_____	_____	
Subtotals	$ _____	$ _____	
Total Health Care Expenses			$ _____

5. CHILD(REN)'S EXPENSES

	HUSBAND	WIFE	TOTAL
a. Day care		$ _____	
b. School tuition/supplies		_____	
c. Lunch money		_____	
d. Allowance		_____	
e. Clothing		_____	
f. Grooming/hygiene		_____	
g. Gifts		_____	
h. Entertainment/activities/lessons		_____	
i. Medical		_____	
j. Dental		_____	
k. Prescription drugs		_____	
l. Vision		_____	
Total Child(ren)'s Expenses			$ _____

PREPARING FOR DIVORCE: MONTHLY CASH FLOW ANALYSIS *(continued)*

	HUSBAND	WIFE	TOTAL

6. INSURANCE PREMIUMS

a. Homeowner $_____

b. Automobile   _____

c. Life   _____

d. Medical/hospital   _____

e. Disability   _____

f. Personal property   _____

g. Other _____   _____

Total Insurance Expenses (monthly) $_____ (TOTAL)

7. OTHER MONTHLY EXPENSES

a. Alimony to any previous spouse $_____ (HUSBAND) $_____ (WIFE)

b. Child support to any previous spouse   _____   _____

_____   _____   _____

_____   _____   _____

_____   _____   _____

Subtotals $_____ (HUSBAND) $_____ (WIFE)

Total Other Monthly Expenses $_____ (TOTAL)

8. PAYMENTS TO CREDITORS

Creditor   Balance Owed   Monthly Payment

_____ $_____ $_____

_____ $_____ $_____

_____ $_____ $_____

_____ $_____ $_____

_____ $_____ $_____

Total Monthly Payments to Creditors $_____ (WIFE column)

Total Monthly Expenses $_____ (TOTAL)

Net Worth $_____ (TOTAL)

DETERMINING NEW LIVING EXPENSES

You will also need a second set of calculations to help you clarify your sources of income and living expenses. Many divorcing spouses don't realize how dramatically their financial picture is about to change; it's crucial that you look ahead and start to determine both what expenses you'll have and how you'll pay for them.

The issues involved in this regard are numerous and complex, and a single chapter in a book can only begin to address them. However, the issues that your attorney and financial planner should broach with you include:

- What will one spouse *need* to receive in terms of alimony and child support?
- What will the other spouse *have* to pay in terms of alimony and child support?
- What are the family's total current living expenses, and what are the living expenses that each spouse pays, and how will these change following the divorce?
- What modifications will be necessary in spending patterns given the probable reduction in income to both spouses?

To answer these questions, you'll have to take the living expenses you've identified and scrutinize them more closely to determine which are core expenses, which are discretionary, and which may be altogether unnecessary. You'll also have to look ahead to how expenses will change following the divorce. The spouse who retains the couple's residence, for instance, will face expenses such as the mortgage, property taxes, and homeowners' insurance. The spouse who relinquishes the residence will have to find a new place to live. The spouse who pays child support and/or alimony will have those costs to pay. Both spouses may have to face increased expenses for transportation. Since two people living together generally live more inexpensively than two people living apart, costs may increase overall, thus requiring both spouses to cut back on spending.

The process of sizing up these expenses may well strike you as daunting, even depressing. However, it's important to keep in mind that the situation isn't permanent. Many divorced spouses find that the initial increase in costs doesn't last indefinitely. Formerly dependent spouses start their own careers and earn an income of their own. Alimony-paying spouses find that since alimony isn't usually adjusted for inflation, the burden of payments becomes easier over time. Initial cutbacks may last several years but not forever. In short, *the numbers you use for financial planning in the early years following a divorce aren't static.* But you can't plan properly for the future unless you take some initial steps to size up your situation as accurately and thoughtfully as possible. Your attorney and financial planner can help you assess your specific situation and decide on the best response to it.

DETERMINING THE FINANCIAL PLANNING CONSEQUENCES OF ALIMONY

Alimony is an amount of money paid to a spouse under a divorce or separation agreement. You are allowed a tax deduction for alimony payments you make. The rules regarding alimony vary. In some states, determining payments includes factors such as the duration of the marriage and marital fault, but all states consider the spouses' needs and their abilities to pay.

Some alimony situations are "classic" cases: One spouse has greater needs; the other has a greater ability to pay. As a result of the changes in spousal earnings during recent decades, however, many situations are less clear-cut than they used to be. For instance, there may be no alimony paid if the spouses' projected post-divorce income levels are roughly equal.

We'll look at the following subjects that pertain to alimony:

- Cash flow and budgeting after divorce
- Tax treatment of alimony
- Requirements for alimony and separate maintenance payments
- Alimony recapture rules
- Alimony paid to nonresident aliens
- Prepaid alimony

Cash Flow and Budgeting After Divorce

Although both parties are often at odds at the time of the divorce, both must plan ahead with the same objectives of taking steps necessary to ensure adequate cash flow after divorce. Among the factors that your financial planner will consider in determining either your ability to pay or your need for support will be how long you or your spouse will receive the income. Issues in this regard include the likely date of retirement and the start of Social Security benefits for the spouse receiving the alimony.

Divorcing spouses don't necessarily either over- or underestimate their expenses. However, the spouse who receives support may tend to overestimate expenses, since guessing high may lead to more child support or alimony; similarly, the spouse who pays support may also overestimate expenses, since that may indicate greater difficulty in meeting the support obligation. Yet the opposite situation may be true as well. In amicable divorces, for instance, one spouse or the other may express confidence in his or her ability to "get by" without help. Unfortunately, unrealistic assessments of expenses—whether high or low—can backfire, resulting in a payee spouse having insufficient support, or a payor spouse being excessively burdened by too high a level of alimony compared to his or her ability to pay.

You should also take a close look at what your income sources will be. Although you may be optimistic when you consider future pay raises, it makes sense to plan as if you won't be receiving raises of this sort. Be conservative about the funds that you'll have coming in. If you or your spouse haven't worked outside the home for a while, you should be especially cautious about assuming how easy re-entering the workplace will be.

For each of these reasons, it's extremely important for you to go through all your records in detail. Be as accurate as possible about your expenses. Look at your credit card records, automated teller receipts, and checkbook entries to construct an accurate sense of what your family spends and of what you're likely to spend as a single person or single parent. Use the cash flow analysis sheets we've included to clarify those expenses.

Your financial planner can help you assess each spouse's financial needs. Complete, accurate data will clarify the income and expenses likely for each spouse. To assess expenses accurately, your financial planner should factor in the effects of inflation and the tendency of certain expenses (such as health insurance and life insurance) to increase more quickly than the normal rate of inflation.

Tax Treatment of Alimony

If you receive cash payments of alimony or separate maintenance, you must include them in figuring your gross income. Conversely, if you pay alimony or separate maintenance to a former spouse, you may deduct such payments from your gross income. Payments received from a property settlement or for child support are not considered alimony and therefore are not considered income to the recipient (or deductible to the payer).

The tax consequences of alimony as opposed to other payments need to be carefully considered in working out divorce or separation agreements. For example, if you receive property with a tax basis that is substantially less than its current value, you will be subject to tax when you sell the property on the difference between the tax basis of the property and what you receive. You should consult your tax advisor on such matters.

What Qualifies as Alimony? To qualify for a deduction as alimony, payments stipulated in the divorce or separation agreement should not be designated as something other than alimony. In addition, the parties to the divorce or legal separation must not be members of the same household at the time of payment, and there must be no liability for payments to continue after the death of the spouse receiving the money. Payments made under a divorce or separation decree executed after 1984 must be in cash or its equivalent. For example, transferring securities to satisfy payments due under a divorce or separation agreement does not qualify as alimony. Cash payments made to a third party, however—such as medical expenses paid to doctors or hospitals, on behalf of the spouse or former spouse at his or her request—will qualify as alimony, assuming all other requirements are met.

If you pay medical expenses for your spouse or former spouse, you should deduct the payment as alimony, not as medical expenses. Alimony is fully deductible from your adjusted gross income (whether or not you itemize your deductions), whereas only the portion of your medical expenses that exceeds 7.5% of your adjusted gross income will be deductible.

Deductible alimony payments made under divorce or separation agreements executed after 1984 are subject to recapture rules when payments are "front loaded." In other words, if the payments decrease by more than a designated amount during the first three post-separation years, you may be required to recapture and include in your gross income some portion of alimony that you deducted in a prior tax year. On the other hand, if you received the payment, you deduct any recaptured amount from your income in the computation year.

Exceptions to the recapture rules apply when alimony payments end because either party dies, the spouse receiving the payments remarries before the end of the third post-separation year, or the payments are subject to fluctuation because they are tied to the payer's compensation or income from a business or property.

The recipient spouse can treat alimony as earned income for purposes of contributing to an IRA.

DETERMINING THE FINANCIAL PLANNING CONSEQUENCES OF CHILD SUPPORT

The financial planning issues for divorcing spouses with children are complex and often contentious. Just as the presence of children complicates a divorce in many other ways, it also raises the stakes, evokes strong emotions, and intensifies the situation financially. This is true even aside from the loaded issue of child custody. Even if the spouses agree as to which of them should have custody of the children, there may be severe arguments over who pays for child support, how much should be paid, and for how long.

Among the issues involved are:

- How much support is adequate?
- What are the provisions for specifying child support?
- What are the means for determining child support?
- Income tax treatment of child support
- Insurance issues
- Planning for educational expenses

How Much Support Is Adequate?

Your financial planner can prepare a budget of living expenses as a way of determining the proper level of child support. Overall fixed and variable costs are the fundamental basis for determining this level. However, other factors influencing the amount of support are:

- *The number of children.* Each state's law determines amounts or percentages per child.
- *Education.* Children may require private schooling or tutoring.
- *Recreational and social activities.* These may include vacations, sports, camps, and so on.
- *The child's own assets.* If your child has received gifts or an inheritance, his or her own assets may influence the amount of support.

What Are the Provisions for Specifying Child Support?

You should try to make provisions of the child support agreement as specific and clear as possible, as this will help to prevent disagreements in the future. Try to make provisions for:

- Intervals during which the financially dependent parent doesn't have custody of the children. Support may need to be reduced or suspended during such intervals.
- Circumstances in which the children no longer need support. Typical arrangements stipulate that payments stop when the child attains majority, is adopted by a stepparent, or dies.
- Timing of payment dates so that both parents can plan their cash flow adequately.
- Medical and dental coverage.

What Are the Means for Determining Child Support?

Each state has guidelines for determining the minimum level of child support by means of several different formulas. Your divorce attorney will be familiar with the formulas applicable to your state of residence and with their application to your individual case. You may find that higher levels of child support are more appropriate, or that alternate means of payment may serve your purposes. For example, since alimony payments are tax-deductible and child support payments are not, structuring payments more heavily toward alimony may work to your advantage and still serve the purpose of supporting the child. There is some flexibility within the constraints of the law, depending on the state in question.

Tax Treatment of Child Support

Child support payments are neither deductible by the payor nor included as income by the spouse who receives them. If any portion of payments that were agreed to be alimony could be reduced because of circumstances relating to a child (e.g., the child's leaving school or the family household, becoming employed, getting married, or dying), that portion may be reclassified as nondeductible and nontaxable child support. This can occur even when the divorce or separation agreement specifically provides for separate child support payments.

Payments are presumed to be child support if a reduction is scheduled to occur within 6 months before or after a child reaches age 18, 21, or the local age of majority, or when two or more reductions are scheduled within one year of a child reaching an age between 18 and 24 that is designated in the agreement. Payments that represent property settlements or child support are not treated as alimony.

Deciding whether payments should be classified as alimony, a nontaxable property settlement, or child support is relevant if the spouse who will be making the payments will be in a higher tax bracket than the spouse receiving them. The spouse making the payment typically wants it to be tax-deductible alimony to minimize his or her out-of-pocket costs. At the same time, the spouse receiving the payment doesn't want to see it eaten up by taxes.

A way to solve the problem is to share the overall tax saving realized by treating the payment as alimony. For example, if the spouse making the payment offered to "gross up" the payment to cover the taxes the recipient would owe, both on the amount of the payment originally expected and the "extra" alimony offered, the payer could wind up paying less out-of-pocket (after deductions) than if the initially-agreed-to level of the payment was treated as a nondeductible property settlement.

Insurance Issues

Ideally, both parents should obtain and maintain sufficient life and disability insurance to protect the child's financial well-being. One way of ensuring that the payments are paid is for each parent to own the policy on the other. See Chapter 7 regarding life insurance and Chapter 8 regarding disability insurance.

Planning for Educational Expenses

Because the education expenses are so high, you should plan to fund these costs well in advance. (See Chapter 19 on the subject of funding your children's education.) Other issues that fall within the purview of education funding include:

- Special schooling
- Psychological counseling
- Repaying student loans
- Funding graduate or other professional programs

DETERMINING THE FINANCIAL PLANNING CONSEQUENCES OF PROPERTY DIVISIONS

One of the most important tasks in divorce proceedings is classifying and dividing each spouse's property. Among the issues determining who owns which assets are the couple's state of residence, where the assets are located, and where, when, and how the assets were acquired.

The 50 states' laws vary in defining marital property. For the most part, however, *marital property* includes all property that either spouse has acquired during the marriage, except for property acquired by inheritance or gift. *Separate property* is property that each spouse has acquired before the marriage, through inheritance or gift during the marriage, and after separation. Most states assume that assets acquired during the marriage are marital. A spouse may need to trace the origins of funds used to acquire property in order to prove that the property is separate.

The fundamental concept in property divisions is *equitable distribution*. By means of this concept, each spouse has a legal right during marriage to the other spouse's earnings and to the assets acquired by means of those earnings. The court must therefore (1) classify all assets either as marital or separate, (2) value the assets, and (3) distribute the assets equitably.

The courts consider several factors relevant to spouses' contributions and needs when they determine equitable distribution. These factors include the duration of the marriage; marital fault; monetary and nonmonetary contributions to the marriage; the spouses' earning ability, separate property, age, and health; custody of children, and many other factors.

In addition, nine states use the concept of *community property*. According to community property rules, the marriage creates a partnership. Community property rules therefore apply to property acquired during marriage, while the couple is living together. Each spouse acquires a 50 percent undivided interest in property acquired with community earnings or community assets during marriage. However, despite this interest, giving each party half of each asset is generally impossible or impractical. Examples of impractical divisions are the principal residence, closely held business interests, investment portfolios, and so on. To distribute these assets, one or the other spouse must obtain some or all of one asset or group of assets. Otherwise the assets must be sold to obtain the liquidity sufficient to provide each spouse with an equitable share.

The nine community property states are:

- Arizona
- California
- Idaho
- Louisiana
- Nevada
- New Mexico
- Texas
- Washington
- Wisconsin

By contrast, gifts and inheritances that each spouse receives during marriage remain separate property. Assets acquired before marriage are likewise separate property.

Determining whether property is marital or separate may be difficult. If you've received or acquired separate property before your marriage, the divorce proceedings may involve determining what has happened to the property. Here are some of the possibilities:

- Separate property may have been used to acquire other property.
- Separate property may have been commingled with marital property.
- The separate property's value may have increased.

Your financial planner and attorney can help you to classify your property as marital or separate and to determine its value.

Tax Aspects of Property Settlements

Generally, a transfer of property from one spouse to the other "incident to the divorce" is tax-free—that is, no gain or loss is recognized by the transferor spouse. Such transfers can include sales or exchanges of property between ex-spouses within one year after the marriage ends and transfers pursuant to a divorce or separation agreement generally occurring within six years after the marriage ends.

These transfers are treated as gifts for tax purposes even if there were actually a bona fide sale; that is, the transferee spouse will be required to recognize gain or loss when the property is ultimately sold or otherwise disposed of.

When dividing up appreciated property in a divorce settlement, remember that the value of a particular property may be overstated if it does not take into account potential taxes that would be due on the built-in gain if the property is subsequently sold. The spouse receiving the property should consider having the divorce or separation agreement provide for reimbursement when the property is actually sold or otherwise disposed of.

Principal Residence Issues. In most cases, a couple's home is their most significant asset. Usually, when couples divorce or separate, one spouse stays in the home with the children while the other finds separate living accommodations. In many cases, the departing spouse pays the entire mortgage on the jointly owned home until it can be sold and the proceeds are split. In other circumstances, the departing spouse will transfer ownership of the home entirely to the remaining spouse. Each of these and other alternative arrangements have their own peculiar tax and financial implications.

An especially important issue is the tax treatment of mortgage payments by the divorced spouses. Specifically, can the absentee spouse deduct the mortgage payments he or she makes after leaving a jointly owned home? If both spouses are liable for the mortgage, half of each payment of principal and interest may qualify as deductible alimony for the departed spouse (and income to the occupying spouse). Each spouse is then considered to have paid half of the mortgage interest.

If the departing spouse is solely responsible for the mortgage, then he or she will be deemed to have paid all of the mortgage interest. Regardless of whether the non-occupying spouse is seen to have paid all or half of the mortgage interest, the question becomes—can he or she deduct this interest?

How the Home Is Classified. A taxpayer can only deduct mortgage interest paid on a principal or secondary residence. Once the departing spouse moves out of the jointly owned home, he or she can no longer claim that house as a primary residence. On the other hand, the non-occupying spouse may still be able to claim the home as a secondary residence, even though he or she no longer lives there.

A secondary residence is defined by certain special tax rules which your financial planner or tax advisor will be familiar with. Divorced taxpayers who do not have children living with the occupying ex-spouse may not be able to deduct the interest they pay as mortgage interest. The reason for this is that their former homes may not qualify as either their principal or secondary residences. If they do not, the mortgage interest paid by these divorced taxpayers in these circumstances would likely be considered personal interest, which is not deductible. However, a second home may be treated as a "qualified residence" regardless of personal use, as long as it is not rented at any time during the year. The rules are somewhat ambiguous, but there is support for permitting a post-divorce departing spouse to deduct mortgage interest that he or she pays on the house occupied by the former spouse, if the former spouse lives in the house rent-free. This is especially tricky and you should contact your financial planner and/or tax advisor for proper guidance with this issue.

An Alternative Strategy. One way to avoid potential problems or ambiguity regarding an interest deduction in this situation is to provide for sufficient alimony (in addition to any other alimony otherwise anticipated) to cover the mortgage payment. That way, the payer spouse can deduct the payment as alimony. The payee spouse will generally be able to offset most of the income from the extra alimony received to cover mortgage payments by claiming a mortgage interest deduction for the interest paid (repayments of principal are not deductible). But proceed with caution. The separation agreement or divorce decree should not explicitly provide that a portion of the alimony paid by the non-occupying spouse is to cover mortgage payments.

Of course, every situation should be planned for independently and your financial planner or tax advisor can help you here. Regardless of how the parties work out the payment and tax aspects of the mortgage, the non-resident partner may not roll over any capital gain from the sale of a former residence.

DEALING WITH THE INVESTMENT ASPECTS OF DIVORCE

Because divorce changes so many aspects of your life—including, in large measure, your financial situation—you may need to change your investment objectives. Here are some questions that you should ask yourself as you reconsider investment objectives and strategies:

- What are your cash flow requirements now?
- How has your tax picture changed? (That is, are you in a different bracket? Do you need to liquidate investments and incur capital gains?)
- Has your risk tolerance changed because of your new financial standpoint? (That is, are you prepared to accept more risk because of your need to invest in vehicles presenting an expectation of higher returns?)
- What are your requirements for liquidity?
- Do you need to change your means of managing investments (e.g., from managing themselves to investing through mutual funds)?

Many divorcing spouses feel pressured to sell assets so that they can divide the proceeds between them. Be careful about this approach; consider the alternatives before proceeding hastily. There are two reasons why:

- Forced liquidations may create lower sales proceeds. (Example: Sale of real property.)
- The tax effect of selling assets may reduce the net return on the investment, thus also on capital available to divide or borrow against.

Many spouses find that they must change their investment philosophies following divorce. Since funds may be designated for specific purposes (e.g., funding a child's education), you may end up with a lower tolerance for risk. Conversely, the need for greater income may give rise to a willingness to accept greater risk. You may need to coordinate investments with your former spouse to avoid misunderstandings and tensions.

Because good investment planning is now so crucial, consider revisiting Chapters 3 through 6 regarding the investment planning process.

DEALING WITH THE RETIREMENT PLANNING ASPECTS OF DIVORCE

Divorce may have dramatic consequences for your retirement plans. Perhaps you anticipated relying on your spouse's pension or retirement plan benefits and Social Security benefits. Perhaps your plans had prompted you to underfund your own IRA or Keogh. No matter what your situation, you should review your retirement plans and alter them to the degree necessary in light of your changed situation. See Chapters 24 and 25 for an overview of retirement planning issues.

In the meantime, three specific issues pertaining to divorce are how it affects use of qualified and nonqualified plans as well as Social Security. (For more information about both qualified and nonqualified plans, see Chapter 2.)

Qualified Plans

Most states regard the present value of pension plan benefits as marital property subject to distribution. You must obtain a valuation of these benefits coinciding as nearly as possible to either the date of divorce or the date of separation. Marital property retains its character as marital property in most states up to the date of divorce. For this reason, the valuation may be critical. Provide your financial planner with relevant documents to determine your plans' valuation and consult with your attorney about the requirements in your state regarding qualified plan accumulations and their distribution at the time of divorce. Also remember that plan assets will be subject to tax when paid out to the recipient spouse.

Nonqualified Plans

Nonqualified plans generally present fewer complexities, for they aren't eligible for tax deferred treatment. You must treat them like other assets that you and your spouse owned at the time of divorce. These assets are also taxable when paid but generally to the transferor spouse.

Social Security

You *can* receive Social Security benefits based on your former spouse's work contributions *if* you meet these conditions:

- Your marriage must have lasted at least 10 years.
- You must be at least 62 years old and unmarried.
- Your former spouse must also be at least 62 years old.

Your receiving Social Security benefits as a divorcee won't reduce your former spouse's benefits to a current spouse. For more information about Social Security benefits, see Chapter 24.

DEALING WITH THE INSURANCE ASPECTS OF DIVORCE

All of your insurance coverage may be affected by your divorce. For this reason, insurance planning is crucial at the time of divorce. The main issues are:

- Life and disability insurance
- Medical insurance
- Property insurance
- Automobile insurance

Life and Disability Insurance

You should assess your own life insurance and disability insurance needs—as well as your spouse's and dependents' needs—in the aftermath of divorce. Among the questions that you may need to answer are:

- Do you need more or less coverage than before?
- Do you need different kinds of coverage than what you had before?
- To whom should you change your beneficiary designations?

One of the common issues that people face is whether the financially dependent spouse needs additional coverage in case the earning spouse becomes disabled or dies. Similarly, more extensive disability coverage may be in order, given the possibility of the principal earner becoming disabled, thus affecting payments of alimony and child support.

You may want to change the beneficiary designations of life insurance policies currently in force. However, you should determine first whether separation agreements or court orders prohibit you from changing beneficiaries.

Medical Insurance

One of the most important issues will be medical insurance. Precisely because your financial picture has changed so radically, determining your needs for health care coverage will be paramount. Even a relatively minor illness may now have severe financial consequences. Here are some issues that you should broach with your financial planner:

COBRA. A nonworking spouse is eligible for up to 36 months in the group plan sponsored by the working spouse's employer. This is advantageous for many reasons. Not least is that the insurance premiums for such group coverage are typically lower than those for a privately purchased health insurance policy.

Note: Coverage under COBRA is not automatic. You must contact your former spouse's employer within 60 days of notification that you are eligible for COBRA coverage; if you don't respond within the 60-day period, you lose your right to coverage under COBRA. See Chapter 8 for more information about COBRA.

Individual Policies. Since individual coverage varies greatly in cost from one insurer to another, you should compare which policy suits you best and is priced most competitively.

Group Policies. The option of obtaining group health insurance may have an impact on the financially dependent spouse's decisions to return to the workplace or not.

See Chapter 8 for further information about health care insurance, including use of COBRA to extend coverage.

Here are some suggestions about health care coverage:

- To the degree possible, shop around. Health care premiums vary enormously.
- If you decide to purchase an individual policy, you can lower your costs by purchasing policies with higher deductibles or copayments.
- Consider HMOs as a way of controlling your premiums while making sure that your coverage is sufficient.

Property Insurance

You must insure your own real and personal property. Make sure that when you and your spouse change ownership of real property, you modify or rewrite your insurance policies to reflect the actual owner as the insured party.

Automobile Insurance

After you and your spouse divorce, make sure to obtain separate automobile insurance policies. You should also change vehicle ownership documents to make sure that you've insured the vehicles you actually own.

See Chapter 8 for information about property/casualty and automobile insurance.

DEALING WITH THE ESTATE PLANNING ASPECTS OF DIVORCE

In the aftermath of divorce, your estate planning goals will probably focus on preserving your assets, disposing of them according to your wishes, and simultaneously reducing the potential estate tax liability while providing adequate liquidity. These are typical goals for most people's estate planning anyway. Yet divorce presents special issues that you should broach with your financial planner so as to avoid problems later.

Here are four issues to consider carefully:

- Changing designations
- Child custody succession
- Gift tax
- Absence of the unlimited deduction

Personal Representatives

Make the necessary changes to ensure that your spouse isn't designated the personal representative, successor trustee, holder of powers, or beneficiary on relevant estate planning documents.

Child Custody Succession

Make sure that the divorce decree addresses the issue of child custody succession following the death or disability of the custodial parent.

Gift Tax

Your property settlements may require you to transfer assets to third parties. An example: funding children's educational expenses. Note that such transfers will generally not be subject to gift tax.

Absence of the Unlimited Deduction

If you have a large estate, you may have to face the consequences of estate planning without an unlimited marital deduction. You may have depleted your liquid assets to fund the property settlement; your estate may now be illiquid. One possible response to this situation is using life insurance to provide liquidity.

Precisely because divorce is such a traumatic experience for both spouses, it's easy to lose track of the complex practical issues at hand. This is understandable; emotions often overwhelm attempts at issues-oriented thinking. Long-term financial planning may seem especially difficult at such a time. However, so much is at stake that it's important to redouble your efforts and plan ahead as thoughtfully as possible. Your financial well-being for decades to come may depend on actions you take now.

Remember: You don't have to "go it alone." Just as you wouldn't handle the legal aspects of divorce by yourself, you needn't handle the financial aspects, either. Your financial planner can help you determine what assets you bring to the divorce proceedings, what you will contribute or take away in their aftermath, and what you can do to safeguard your financial well-being for the future.

17

BEING A
SINGLE PARENT

The financial issues affecting single parents resemble those affecting two-parent families; they differ mostly in degree. If you're a single parent, you know how fully your family's well-being rests on your shoulders. You probably have costs similar to those faced by two-income families, but you're the sole breadwinner. For this reason, it's especially important for you to closely attend to the issues discussed in Chapter 15, "Raising a Family."

You must have:

- A good cash flow plan
- A realistic budget
- A sufficient contingency fund
- Adequate health care coverage
- Adequate insurance (life, disability, property/casualty, and auto)
- A properly executed will, including guardianship provisions, and probably a trust

None of these aspects of financial planning are fundamentally different for single parents than for two-parent families. However, the stakes are higher. You are your own safety net.

BECOMING A SINGLE PARENT

Single parenthood is reached in one of three ways:

1. Death of a spouse or partner.
2. Divorce or breakup of a relationship.
3. A conscious decision to become a single parent by conceiving a child with a plan to raise it alone or by adopting a child.

Single parenthood used to be thought of as a "woman's" issue. However, there have always been widowers. Today more men are retaining custody after divorce and adopting children on their own.

The conscious decision gives you time for planning, and the change from a childless condition to one of having children is analogous to the situation for two-parent families. So this chapter will focus more on the special issues that previous partners in two-parent families will find when they suddenly become single parents. The last few pages of Chapter 14, "Getting Married," discuss financial planning issues for domestic partners.

Becoming a single parent is the ultimate in downsizing. Being downsized is a difficult aspect of life and one many of us would prefer to deny. Whether the reason be death or divorce, you must get beyond denial and face the hidden costs and potentially reduced opportunities for you and your family.

THE EXPENSE SIDE—MANY HIDDEN COSTS

When you sit down to do your budget and cash flow statement as a newly single parent, things you previously took for granted may become significant.

Between you and your partner, you barely had time to get the housework and yardwork done. With only one of you, you may not have any time at all. You may need a cleaning service, or a yard service, even if on an infrequent basis. You need to include this added expense in your budget and not wait for the cost to occur, then hope you can find the cash somewhere to pay for it.

With the two of you splitting drop-off and pick-up at day care, school, or after-school care, you still got caught short once in a while and had to call on a friend or family member. Now, you need to think about extending your child(ren)'s hours in day care, after-school, or extended-day programs. You need to think about having an after-school in-home babysitter. Again, you need to budget for this.

Picking up that overtime hour each day, or extra evening a week, or the Saturday shift was always good for some extra cash. But now the extra demands on your time as a single parent may not allow you to take on this extra work. And if you do, it may cost as much for child care as you will earn after tax, even at the overtime rate.

By the time the three kids were done going through the chicken pox last year, you and your spouse or partner had both taken all your sick days and half your vacation days. What will happen this year if it's a bad flu season, or if one of the children has recurrent strep throat? Will you have enough days? How can you go an entire year with no vacation?

Perhaps your spouse or partner was a teacher, and stayed at home with the kids during the summer. This year, and in the future, they will need to go to camp—all of them! Fortunately, many of us still have friends and other family members willing to pitch in to help, at least in the short term.

Asking the grandparents to babysit one evening a week or one weekend a month so you can work overtime might be okay, but you can't ask them to do it all the time so that you can try to replace your spouse's income with overtime.

It's important to maintain adequate insurance. This may cost more now, as you add individual policies to any benefits you receive through your work. You may want to raise deductibles on property and casualty insurance to offset the increased cost of added life and disability insurance. You need to make sure beneficiaries are properly designated. In a divorce situation, you and your ex-spouse may want to own policies on each other's lives to make sure there are adequate funds for raising children in the event one of you should die.

In that regard, it's important to make sure your will is up-to-date and conforms to the terms of any divorce settlement with respect to the guardianship for any minor children and who will take care of their financial affairs. Clarity in terms of guardianship is also important for widows or widowers and for those living with a domestic partner who has no automatic right of custody for any of your children.

THINKING OF NUMBER ONE

Being solely responsible for your children puts a number of burdens on a custodial parent. While you are thinking of how you can maintain at least your child(ren)'s lifestyle as closely as possible to current circumstances, you cannot sacrifice your own goals and needs completely.

Reducing or stopping payments to your retirement fund adds cash now, but at what cost? If you're stressed out about your inability to save for retirement, that will affect your children, possibly more than reducing their current lifestyle will.

The same is true for your personal entertainment and vacations. Even though the money might be useful elsewhere, you need to pay for some child care once in a while so you can go out and relax, whether it's with friends, family, or associates from work.

Often, divorced parents feel terrible guilt about the situation they have put their children in. One way some people try to mollify their own guilt is to "buy back" their child(ren), by overspending in general and buying whatever the child impulsively wants. This is a trap you need to keep yourself from falling into right from the start.

Sources of Income

On the income side of your income statement, there are a number of potential sources of income, depending on how well you and your former partner did your financial planning while you were together.

First, of course, there is your own income. Because your tax-filing status will probably change, from married filing jointly to head of household, you may be able to increase your take-home income by adjusting your withholding. This will clearly be the case in a death-of-spouse situation; in a divorce situation it will be more complicated and depend on the provisions of your divorce agreement regarding who claims the children as a dependent, and so on. We'll discuss this in more detail in the section on "Financial Planning as Part of the Divorce Agreement."

You may also work overtime, take a second job, or start your own business or freelance/consulting practice to generate extra income. When thinking this through, be sure to look at whether the extra income will offset the cash costs of child care and other expenses, as well as the impact this extra working will have on your already stressed schedule—working, keeping up a home, and raising a child or children on your own.

If you become a single parent through a death, you may be the recipient of life insurance proceeds, leaving you with the decision of how to best use these funds. (See Chapter 23 on widowhood.) The first and most fundamental decision is whether you should invest the proceeds or pay off existing debt. While you may be tempted to pay off the mortgage on your primary residence, it's important to consider the following: (1) any debt that may be more appropriate to pay off; (2) the income stream and related income taxes resulting from investing the funds; and (3) the cash stream requirement and related tax deduction available from retaining the mortgage. For example, suppose that you received $100,000 in insurance proceeds, and are in the 28% tax bracket. You have a mortgage balance of $100,000 that charges you an interest rate of 8%. This means that you pay $8,000 per year in interest and receive a tax benefit of $2,240. By paying off the mortgage, you will save $5,760 after taxes. Alternatively, suppose that you invested the $100,000 in a taxable bond fund earning 9%. This investment would generate a cash flow of $9,000 and a tax liability of $2,520. After taxes, your return on your investment would be $6,480. The benefit of earning $6,480 annual investment return clearly exceeds the benefit of eliminating the annual mortgage cost of $5,760. Therefore, investing the money and continuing to pay the mortgage with the investment earnings would be the best strategy.

Widows or widowers may also be able to claim some Social Security survivor benefits, if not for themselves at least for their children. Benefits for surviving widow(er)s with dependent children end when the youngest child turns age 16, and for each child it ends when he or she turns age 18. Benefits are also phased out as the widow(er)s income increases.

In a divorce situation, your income may include alimony or child support payments, or a combination of both. Alimony is taxable to the individual receiving it, and deductible for the individual paying it. Child support is not taxable and not deductible. Therefore, if you are taking custody of the children, you want as much support from your former spouse as possible to be paid in the form of child support.

You can also add a little income by taking as cash any dividends you receive from stocks or mutual funds rather than reinvesting them. You pay tax on the income from stock or mutual fund dividends, even if you reinvest them. The cash might be very helpful. But remember, if you take cash you are reducing the growth of your investment portfolio. If this portfolio was your major college-savings tool, taking cash now is robbing Peter to pay Paul. You may want to change to a cash payout to add income during your transition period; then once you get a handle on your expenses move back to reinvesting the dividends.

If you find yourself in a home that is too big after a death, divorce, or breakup but you don't want to move, you may want to rent out a room. If feasible, you may even be able to create a rental apartment in part of your home. Of course, you need to consider the zoning issues and capital costs of doing this and the tax implications of renting. For more information on this subject see *The Ernst & Young Tax Guide.*

Reducing your contribution to your retirement plan is also a way to increase income to cover short-term cash needs. If you fund your own IRA, SIMPLE, Keogh, or SEP-type plan, you can defer the decision on how much you will contribute at least until April 15 of the next year. Even if you contribute to a 401(k) or 403(b) plan, some plans allow you to reduce your weekly or monthly contribution and make a lump-sum contribution before the next year's tax filing deadline if your finances should improve.

The last resort for increasing income should be borrowing. This should only be done for short-term cash needs. Look to the possibility of borrowing from your life insurance or retirement account, and check out the equity you have in your home, since home equity loans are generally tax deductible. This is discussed in greater detail in Chapters 7 and 19 on "Life Insurance" and on "Funding a College Education," respectively. There are also discussions in *The Ernst & Young Tax Guide.*

SAVING FOR COLLEGE

You thought saving for college was tough when there were two parents. Try doing it yourself. The task can look insurmountable. The key to keep in mind is that you have to do something. Even if you can only save a few hundred dollars a year, that amount can be invested so that your child(ren) will have something for tuition. See the chart on page 354 in Chapter 19.

Now that you are single, if your income is reduced you may now be below the income threshold so that you would benefit by saving for college through Series EE U.S. Savings bonds. When these bonds are held to maturity and cashed to pay for higher education, their interest is tax free for single- or two-parent families below particular income levels. The level is adjusted up for inflation.

Some states also sell tax-free zero-coupon bonds with varying lengths of maturity, which pay off right at tuition time. For children who won't be going to school for 12 or 15 years, you may be able to get these bonds for only one-third or so of the face amount. They are often offered in $1,000 face amounts. Whether zero-coupon bonds are viewed as a good investment depends a great deal on other options available to you and the level of risk you are willing to take with your investments.

Other benefits under the tax law can help you finance a child's education. These include:

- Education IRA
- Qualifed state tuition programs
- Hope Scholarship Credit
- Lifetime Learning Credit
- Deduction for student loan interest
- Penalty-free IRA distributions
- Exclusion for employer-provided educational assistance

These benefits are discussed in more detail in Chapter 19.

An additional, often overlooked consideration is financial aid. In broadest terms, financial aid is largely dependent on the income and assets of not only the child, but the parents as well. A child's assets must be applied toward college costs. Parents are expected to contribute a percentage, lower than the child's, of their assets as well. Retirement plans such as pensions, IRAs, and Keoghs are not counted toward the family's contribution. Since a single parent will generally have a lower income and asset base than a two-parent family, you may be close to qualifying for aid. If so, consider shifting income or assets into retirement plans that will not be counted against you. However, you must consider the cash flow effect of shifting current disposable income to your retirement plans.

FINANCIAL PLANNING AS PART OF THE DIVORCE AGREEMENT

While many divorce proceedings are hardly the time grown-ups act their most rational, if a couple is truly thinking about what's best for their children, they have some financial planning opportunities they must consider when creating a divorce agreement.

First, and simplest, is the issue of alimony or child support, discussed earlier. (Alimony and child support issues are also covered in more detail in Chapter 16—Coping With Divorce.)

After that there are a host of other issues:

- Who gets the home, or in the case of more than one, who gets which property? Who pays for mortgage, taxes, and upkeep?
- Who takes the children as exemptions on their income tax return?
- Who claims the dependent care credit?
- Who covers the children on health insurance, and how?
- Who creates college funds, and what do the parents agree on as to where the children may go and how much tuition support they will provide?

PROPERTY

Let's say you and your soon-to-be ex-spouse own two homes, your primary residence and a second home you used to live in and now rent out. The fair market value, existing mortgage, net equity, and original cost basis are as follows:

Assumptions		Primary Residence	Secondary Residence
A.	Fair Market Value	$ 210,000	$125,000
B.	Existing Mortgage	(170,000)	(55,000)
C.	Net Equity	$ 40,000	$ 70,000
D.	Cost Basis	$ 185,000	$ 40,000
Calculation of After-Tax Proceeds			
E.	Potential Gain (A-D)	$ 25,000	$ 85,000
F.	Potential Capital Gain Tax @ 20%	—0—	(17,000)
G.	Net Sale Proceeds (C-F)	$ 40,000	$ 53,000

As the parent who will retain custody of two children, which house do you want? (Remember that you can exclude up to $250,000 of gain on the sale of a principal residence.) The maximum tax rate on gain from the sale of real estate held more than 12 months is 20%; however, the portion of the gain attributable to depreciation may be taxed as high as 25%.

On its face, you may think that the home with the highest fair market value, the primary residence, would be the best choice. However, you would also need to consider any outstanding mortgage balance due. For example, let's say you need to tap into your home equity to increase cash flow, or you are moving away from the area and want the most cash from a sale. The secondary residence clearly has greater net equity available ($30,000 greater) than the primary residence. Even after taking into account a capital gain tax upon its sale, the secondary residence would yield greater after-tax proceeds ($13,000 greater) than the primary residence. Other considerations include the cost of maintenance (i.e., real estate taxes, upkeep, and relative mortgage terms and interest rates). Finally, you need to consider the potential for appreciation, as well as the strength of the national, regional, and local real estate markets.

You also need to consider the issues of the emotional stability of your children; moving can make the divorce doubly traumatic. As well, if you take the current rental property, but it is in a community where you feel you may have to send the children to private school, you may be defeating the financial purpose of keeping the house.

Declaring Children as Dependents

Essentially, unless the custodial parent signs IRS Form 8332 and waives the right to claim the child(ren) as his or her dependent(s), the custodial parent receives the exemption.

SUPPORT TEST FOR CHILDREN OF DIVORCED OR SEPARATED PARENTS

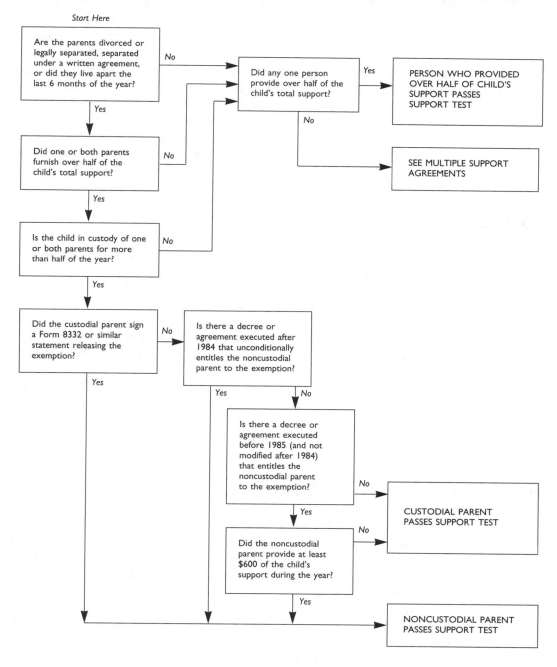

The same test applies for purposes of determining who gets the child tax credit.

When might it be advantageous for the noncustodial parent to waive this right? If the noncustodial parent is in a much higher tax bracket than the custodial parent, the custodial parent may want to exchange the right to claim the exemption for an increase in support greater than the amount he or she would realize in tax saving from the exemption.

If the noncustodial parent's medical insurance would allow the children to continue being covered provided they were claimed as dependents on the noncustodial parent's tax return, then the saving to the custodial parent of only having to obtain health insurance for him- or herself could easily outweigh the tax benefit of the claiming the exemption.

Remember, even if you give up the dependent exemption, you may be able to claim a dependent care credit for child care expenses.

College Funds

Too often, noncustodial parents think custodial parents are putting aside some of child support for college, only to find when high school graduation nears that the custodial parent expects the noncustodial parent to pay for the majority of the child's college expenses.

In terms of a divorce situation, the time to start doing financial planning for your children's college education is when you are writing your divorce agreement. Both parents should take some responsibility, and what responsibilities each takes should be clearly stated.

At its simplest, such an agreement could require the custodial parent to put aside a percentage of child support payments for higher education and the noncustodial parent to create a fund that would provide tuition support equal to the amount of support paid until the child graduated high school.

Involving Children in Financial Planning

One way to help children—especially those who are in the later primary school years and older—understand the family's financial circumstances is to include them in financial planning. Teaching children about budgeting, allowance, saving, and making charitable contributions are valuable lessons and are covered in Chapter 15.

You need to do this without burdening the children with the particulars of your financial situation. You may want to start by thinking through the part of your budget that has been "discretionary" and asking the kids for some help ranking those items—"Given the fact that we can't afford everything, if you had a choice of going to soccer camp for a week or buying some new tennis equipment and a baseball glove, which would you prefer to do?" And, don't forget to visit www.moneyopolis.org.

IT'S YOUR CALL

Remember, as the parent who is raising your child(ren) after a death or divorce or a breakup, you have to set the goals and make the rules regarding finances. You need to be firm with a noncustodial ex-spouse, ex-partner, or the family of a deceased spouse about stating your authority in these matters, even if it means hurting their feelings. It's important for kids to maintain a relationship with a noncustodial parent, or with a deceased parent's parents and other family, but that relationship shouldn't involve "buying the child."

Gifts for birthdays or other occasions should not be larger than life. Children should not be encouraged to call dad or mom or the grandparents to get things they can't get from you because it simply isn't in the family's budget.

It's important to remember through all of this that, while financial planning as a single parent may involve a little less flexibility than planning within a two-parent household, the goals and objectives are the same—to maintain a reasonable current lifestyle while saving adequately for the large life-cycle events that wait down the road.

18

BUYING AND SELLING A HOME

If asked to explain their idea of the good life, a majority of Americans would probably mention home ownership in their descriptions. The specific images would range widely. From suburban split-levels to urban brownstones to resort condos to high-rise apartments, all sorts of properties suit people's purposes and tastes. What these many kinds of real estate have in common, however, isn't just a way of satisfying the primal human need for shelter. It's also a way of gratifying people's desire for a piece of turf to call their own. This is one of the reasons why people take the quest for home ownership so seriously.

Another reason for taking home ownership seriously, of course, is the magnitude of the investment. Buying a home is probably the single biggest financial investment you'll ever make. The task of finding and financing a house, condo, or coop is complex and often stressful. Like other life events, however, buying a home is a task that you can control to some degree with forethought and careful planning. This is especially true for the financial dimension of home ownership.

In this chapter we discuss the following aspects of home ownership:

- Buying versus renting
- Financing your home
- Selecting your home
- Refinancing your mortgage
- Selling your home

Buying versus Renting

There's no question that deciding whether to buy or rent often hinges substantially on financial factors. You may prefer to rent a home simply because you don't have the funds available to buy one; on the other hand, you may prefer to own a home rather than rent because you prefer the significant tax breaks that ownership provides. Other financial factors may enter into the decision. However, it's important to stress that *nonfinancial* factors can play an important role as well. Your career may require you to move frequently, which makes renting easier and far less stressful than the complex process of buying. You may also feel uneasy if the real estate market is sluggish in your area, thus prompting caution in how you invest your money. Whatever your reasoning, it's important that you make the decision about whether to buy or rent as carefully as possible. Let's look at some of the issues.

Advantages and Disadvantages of Renting

Renting is notable for its flexibility and potentially lower expense; on the other hand, renting is in many ways a less secure arrangement than buying, and even its apparent cost-effectiveness isn't always what it seems.

Advantages. Although home ownership is a state that most Americans consider worth achieving, renting a house or apartment has its own benefits. The most significant are:

More space for the money. You can generally afford the monthly costs of a larger property when you rent rather than buy. In addition, the initial deposits for a rental property are much smaller than the startup costs associated with purchasing a house or apartment.

Economic flexibility. You can upgrade or downgrade the quality of your rental property in keeping with your own financial ups and downs or other changes in your personal circumstances.

Freedom to invest elsewhere. You may have more discretionary income to invest when you rent, since your money isn't tied up in the rental property.

Freedom to move. You have no long-term obligation to the rental property beyond the period of time designated on the lease you've signed.

Less commitment to upkeep. You aren't ultimately responsible for maintaining and improving a rental property; you can demand that the landlord correct problems or hire contractors to do so.

Decreased concern over your investment. You have less vested interest in the long-term value of a rental property, and you will be less affected by a downturn in property values.

Disadvantages. At the same time, there are downsides to renting. The most common are:

Risk of involuntary relocation. You may have to move if your landlord sells the property.

Lack of freedom to change the property. You won't have much leeway to decorate, renovate, and so forth.

Absence of tax deductions. Rental payments aren't tax-deductible.

Absence of leverage. You can't borrow against the value of rental property.

Advantages and Disadvantages of Buying

Home ownership exerts a strong pull for many people, and its positive aspects often outweigh the negative ones. Here are what's typical of each:

Advantages. Among the potential positive factors are:

Value as a tax shelter. With home ownership you receive one of the last big tax advantages: deducting mortgage interest and property tax payments. This is a tax break that no other investment can match. Up to $1 million of mortgage debt for a home you buy or build is fully deductible.

Capital gain exclusion on sale of principal home. Once every two years, you can exclude up to $250,000 ($500,000 for joint taxpayers) of capital gains from the sale of a primary residence if certain conditions are met. This means that you may keep up to $250,000 ($500,000) profit completely tax-free.

Leverage. You can purchase a home with a down payment (a small amount of your own money) while someone else (the bank or mortgage company) provides the rest. This means that you may end up profiting from price increases on an asset that you have not yet fully paid for.

Inflation hedge. You have an investment that has historically appreciated faster than the cost of living in general.

Disadvantages. There are some notable drawbacks to home ownership, however, of which these are probably the most common:

Burden of maintenance. You have to maintain the property yourself. Under the best of circumstances, you have a series of household chores and projects to do yourself or to hire someone else to do. Under the worst-case scenario, you end up with a "money pit" that drains your resources, energy, time, and patience.

Higher monthly costs. You must pay a combination of mortgage payments, taxes, and insurance premiums that may far exceed the costs of an equivalent rental property.

Risk of losses. You may lose money if your property depreciates in a declining market.

Lack of flexibility. You can't move as spontaneously as you can when you rent.

FINANCING YOUR HOME

Buying a home may well be the biggest single financial decision of your life. Before you start shopping around, ask yourself what you can really afford. Determine the answer to this question as soon as possible. Otherwise, you may end up wasting a lot of time and disappointing yourself by considering purchases that aren't financially wise—or even feasible.

What You'll Pay

The costs of buying a home can generally be split into two categories:

- Up-front costs for the down payment and closing
- Monthly payments for principal, interest, taxes, insurance, repairs, and utilities

Down Payment and Closing Costs. Most lenders will require you to put down between 10% and 20% of a property's price. Here's a worksheet for figuring out how much of a down payment you can afford:

DETERMINING AN AFFORDABLE DOWN PAYMENT

AVAILABLE FUNDS

Equity in present home (less sales commission)	$ _____	
Savings	_____	
Investments	_____	
Insurance (cash value)	_____	
Family assistance (if available)	_____	
Less: Cash reserve	(_____)	
Total Funds Available		$ _____

ANTICIPATED EXPENSES

Settlement costs[a] (5% of home price)	$ _____	
Needed fix-up costs	_____	
Furniture, decorating expenses	_____	
Moving costs	_____	
Other	_____	
Total Expenses Anticipated		$(_____)
AMOUNT AVAILABLE FOR DOWN PAYMENT		$ _____

[a]As indicated in the worksheet, settlement costs usually equal about 5% of the selling price. Such costs may include attorney's fees, points, transfer taxes, a property survey, title insurance, recording fees, and termite inspection. There will also be adjustments for expenses paid by the seller. For example, the seller might have prepaid 6 months of property taxes, in which case you'll have to reimburse the seller for your share. Keep in mind, however, that the actual amount of closing costs can change dramatically depending on location.

While you may be tempted to put down as little as possible to maintain your cash reserves, don't overestimate your savings needs. Compare the added income you expect to earn on the reserves to the interest cost you could have saved with a smaller mortgage. Generally, your cost of borrowing will be higher than your current return on investments. In an emergency, you can tap your home's equity.

The law allows you to withdraw up to $10,000 from an IRA without being subject to the 10% premature distribution penalty if you use the money to buy a home and you're a first-time home buyer. Unless this is a last resort for your down payment, this wouldn't make sense since you may have to pay income tax and you're reducing your retirement assets.

Closing Costs. In addition to the down payment, you'll also pay *closing costs*—expenses you'll pay when you actually sign the documents transferring ownership from the seller to you. Generally, you'll have a clear idea of how much money the closing costs will be, although last-minute changes are possible. The total amount of these closing costs is generally about 2% to 5% of your home's total cost. For a detailed list of closing costs, see the section entitled "Closing the Sale" at the end of this chapter.

Points. Points are additional interest charges collected up front on your loan. One point equals 1% of the mortgage. You may have to pay one or more points when you obtain your mortgage, then the remaining point(s) when you close the sale. While you're out shopping for mortgages, you'll probably notice that institutions offer various combinations of interest rates and points. On a 30-year mortgage, each ⅛-percentage point reduction on the mortgage rate will generally cost you one point. If you don't plan to stay in your new home longer than the average homeowner—7 years—you may be better off paying a higher interest rate and fewer points. That's because the number of points charged to cut your interest rate is figured on the assumption that you'll keep your mortgage as long as will the average homeowner.

Your points will be fully tax-deductible if they meet these tests:
You've incurred them in connection with buying or improving your principal residence. Points paid to refinance a mortgage are generally not currently deductible. Instead, the deduction is stretched out evenly over the life of the new loan. You can also elect to stretch out the deduction for points paid in connection with buying or improving your principal residence, if it's advantageous to do so.
For points paid on loans to acquire your primary residence, the total of your down payment plus other cash paid by the time you close must be at

least as much as the number of points charged. This rule holds whether or not the points are actually paid separately or are added to the total amount borrowed. Points paid on home improvement loans will be immediately deductible if paid with separate funds—that is, funds that did not come from the loan proceeds.

The payment of points is an established business practice in the area where your loan is made.

The number of points doesn't exceed the number of points generally charged in your area. Beware: Some lenders try to pass off other costs as points when these costs aren't actually interest charges. These additional charges may not be tax-deductible.

The Monthly Payments

One rule of thumb in estimating an affordable monthly payment is to limit mortgage principal and interest, taxes, and homeowner's insurance (generally abbreviated as *PITI*) to 28% of your gross income. For example, if your total household income is $70,000, this guideline would suggest that your total monthly payment should not exceed $1,633 ($70,000 divided by 12, times 28%).

Another guideline is to limit your payments on all debt, not just home debt, to about 35% of gross income. If credit card and car loan payments account for 12% of your income, for example, you can only afford to spend another 23% on housing.

You should expect the bank personnel reviewing your mortgage application to consider both guidelines. Making a realistic estimate up front will help you to buy the most house you can afford without incurring too great a risk of having your mortgage denied.

Financing Your New Home

Once you've found the house that feels "just right," the next step is to secure adequate financing. Your first decision is whether to apply for a fixed-rate or an adjustable-rate mortgage (ARM).

Fixed-Rate Loans. The traditional fixed-rate loan offers a predetermined rate of interest throughout the life of the loan. These loans offer you the security of being locked into a rate regardless of market conditions; as a result, they have a higher initial interest rate than ARMs. Their advantage is that you don't have to worry about the roller-coaster movements of the interest rate market. If this alternative appeals to you, you should opt for the predictable monthly payment that a fixed-rate loan offers. A fixed-rate loan can be especially appealing if you expect to own your home for the long term. If you do choose a fixed-rate loan, make sure that there are no prepayment penalties, however; the absence of these penalties means that you'll pay less to refinance in the future.

Some fixed-rate loans offer you the option of refinancing at reduced rates. You should check on the availability and cost of this option (called a *conversion provision*) if interest rates are relatively high when you apply for your mortgage.

Choosing Between a 15- or a 30-Year Mortgage. Mortgage loans are typically offered for 15- or 30-year terms. Which one is right for you?

30-Year Mortgages

If you're looking to buy the most house you can and if the monthly payment you can afford is fixed, you'll probably want a 30-year loan. The same monthly payment will get you a larger loan if it's to be paid over 30 years instead of 15. Also, if interest rates are low, you may benefit from locking in your mortgage at the low rate for as long as possible.

15-Year Mortgages

On the other hand, many home buyers find 15-year mortgages attractive. Compared to 30-year loans, 15-year mortgages promise much more rapid buildup in equity and full home ownership in half the time. At first glance, the opportunity to avoid paying an extra 15 years of interest translates to an astounding amount of interest saved. However, a little probing shows that the benefits of a 15-year mortgage may not be as dramatic as they seem.

Comparing 15- to 30-Year Mortgages. Let's see how a 15-year loan really stacks up against a 30-year mortgage.

EXAMPLE

■ We'll compare a $150,000 loan for 30 years at 8½% to the same amount borrowed for a 15-year term at 8¼%. (Rates offered on 15-year loans typically are slightly lower than comparable 30-year loans.) Monthly payments on the 15-year note would be $1,455. Compared to the $1,153 monthly payment on the 30-year loan, you'd pay $302 more each month on the 15-year loan. By shortening the mortgage term to 15 years, it appears that you can slash the overall interest costs from about $265,000 to $112,000—a whopping $153,000 total savings!

Very impressive—but it's only part of the story. The extra $302 per month required for the 15-year mortgage could have been invested elsewhere. Also, the apparent interest savings ignores the fact that the extra interest paid on the 30-year loan is tax-deductible. ■

When you're deciding whether to choose a 15- or a 30-year mortgage, you should focus on whether the after-tax interest cost on your mortgage is higher or lower than the return you could achieve elsewhere. The scenario above can work for you if you're disciplined enough to invest each monthly payment difference as well as the extra tax savings generated from paying more interest on the 30-year loan. Your investment also needs to achieve a high-enough yield. Many homeowners may find this approach impractical, preferring instead the "forced savings" inherent in a 15-year loan. Perhaps just as important is the emotionally gratifying prospect of owning a home free and clear in just half the time.

■ **TIP:** You can obtain information about mortgage rates from these sources:

- HSH Associates, 1200 Route 23, Butler, NJ 07405. Phone: (201) 838-3330 or (800) 873-2837. Information about more than 2,000 lenders in more than 30 states and many metropolitan areas.
- Gary Myers and Associates, 181 Waukegan Rd., North Field, IL 60093. Phone: (312) 642-9000 or (800) 472-6463. Reports mortgage rates weekly for Boston, Chicago, Cincinnati, Dallas, Detroit, Houston, Los Angeles, Madison (Wisconsin), New York City, Norwich (Connecticut), and Washington, DC. It also provides rate information to some 150 newspapers in 46 states.
- National Mortgage Weekly, P.O. Box 360991, Cleveland, OH 44136. Phone: (216) 273-6605 or (800) 669-0133. Covers the metropolitan Cleveland, Columbus, and Detroit areas.
- Peeke LoanFax Inc., 101 Chestnut Street, Suite 200, Gaithersburg, MD 20877. Phone: (301) 840-5752. Provides mortgage reports for the Washington, DC, area, including northern Virginia and suburban Maryland. Individual rate quotes free by dialing (301) 258-1000. ■

ARMs. Adjustable-rate mortgages (ARMs) allow you to play your mortgage as you'd play the bond market. In each case, you benefit if interest rates either decline or remain constant. ARMs are much more complicated than fixed-rate loans; you must be aware of the risks and rewards that ARMs offer before you can decide if one is right for you.

ARMs were an invention born of necessity—a response to the very high interest rates of the early 1980s. Lenders wanted protection from rising interest rates and were willing to offer slightly lower initial rates to home buyers willing to accept a floating rate. So far, so good. However, in choosing an ARM, you must sort through the many provisions protecting the lender and the borrower.

How ARMs Work. The interest rate on an ARM is generally tied to one of two independent indices: U.S. Treasury securities or the cost that banks and S&Ls pay to borrow funds. A margin of 2% to 3% is then added to the index rate, resulting in your mortgage rate for an "adjustment period." The adjustment period is the amount of time between rate adjustments. A "3-year ARM," for example, has a 3-year adjustment period.

When interest rates and the index increase, the amount of your monthly mortgage payment will also increase. For this reason, you should be sure to review the historic and anticipated volatility of the index before selecting an ARM. Large swings in the index rate can cause substantial changes in your payments. In response, ceilings (or caps) are typically placed on any increase or decrease that may occur after any one adjustment period. Look for an ARM that has such annual caps—preferably no more than 2% per adjustment period—and also make sure there is a cap on the total adjustment that can be made during the life of the loan.

When the dollar amount of your payment is capped but the interest rate isn't (or isn't capped as much), negative amortization can occur. Negative amortization means that your monthly payment is being outpaced by increases in interest charges. In other words, the principal amount on your loan is increasing rather than decreasing. Lenders are usually required to let you pay the additional amount to avoid the possibility of your owing more after 10 years of payments than when the mortgage was acquired.

The Pros and Cons of "Teasers"

If you're shopping for an ARM, beware of "teasers." Teasers are ARMs that offer an attractively low initial interest rate. Make sure that you can afford the mortgage *without* the "teaser rate" or you could be in over your head when the rate is adjusted.

ARMs with an attractive teaser rate can be a good way of financing a house that you don't expect to own for more than a few years. The payments in the early years are often lower than those of their counterpart—the fixed-rate mortgage. And if you're going to move in a couple of years, your *average* annual interest rate may be lower with the ARM, even if the rate increases the maximum amount each year. One last word, however: in case your plans change, consider whether you anticipate being able to handle the maximum possible changes in your payment cap.

The APR: A Useful Guide

Lenders must provide an annual percentage rate (APR) for all loans. Comparing an APR for a fixed-rate mortgage with one for an ARM is like comparing apples and oranges, because the rate used to calculate the APR for the ARM is likely to change. However, the APR is a useful starting point because it allows you to compare mortgages offered by different lenders.

■ **TIP:** To help you choose the type of mortgage that suits you best, you may want to send for *How to Shop for a Mortgage* from the Mortgage Bankers Association of America, 20th Street and C, NW, Washington, DC 20551. Be sure to include a self-addressed, stamped envelope. You can also obtain a copy of the *Consumer Handbook on Adjustable Rate Mortgages* by calling the Federal Reserve Board at (202) 452-3000. ■

Variations on the Theme. In addition to the relatively basic forms of ARMs, many lenders offer one or more variations on the basic theme. Here's a sampling of what you might consider:

- *Convertible ARM.* This is an adjustable rate mortgage that allows you the option of converting to a fixed-rate loan. The potential advantage is locking into a lower rate after a few years. Convertible ARMs are generally preferable to nonconvertible ARMs, although conversion fees and slightly higher rates may apply.
- *Two-step mortgage.* Sometimes called 5/25 and 7/23 mortgages, these are amortized over 30 years, but with a fixed rate for the first phase of 5 or 7 years, then an adjusted rate when the first phase ends. Two-steps offer the advantage of a lower rate than regular fixed-rate loans; they're especially useful if you know you'll be selling your house before the adjustment at the 5- or 7-year point.
- *Growing equity mortgage (GEM).* A GEM increases your payments each year for a specific period of years; then the payments level off. The loan term is shorter than usual because your payments include more principal than is typical of normal amortization.
- *Graduated payment mortgage* (GPM). By contrast, GPMs start out with lower initial payments than normal. The payments rise gradually (a 5- to 10-year period is typical) and then level off. This arrangement is advantageous to home buyers who want low payments at the outset but assume that their income will rise to meet higher future payments over the long haul.

Amortization: the systematic liquidation or reduction of a financial obligation.

Where to Obtain Financing

Let's say that you've decided to buy a home and you've determined that you can afford a mortgage. What are your options for obtaining a loan? These are the standard sources for a home mortgage:

Savings and Loans (S&Ls). Traditionally the largest lenders of home mortgage loans, S&Ls have considerable expertise in this area.

Savings Banks. Savings banks are generally an east coast variant of S&Ls.

Credit Unions. If your workplace has a credit union, you may be able to obtain unusually favorable terms on a home mortgage.

Mortgage Banks. Mortgage banks are organizations that borrow money from investors or institutions, make mortgage loans, then resell the loans to other investors.

Mortgage Brokers. Most mortgage brokers don't lend their own money; instead, they locate the best loans for buyers who seek their services. There is a fee for this service.

Sellers. Some sellers will offer to arrange financing with you directly. This arrangement is to the seller's advantage because it may cut red tape and speed up the process; it's to your advantage because it may reduce your overall purchase costs.

Your Family. Many people obtain funds—either as a gift or as a loan—from one or more family members. This kind of arrangement has its risks, but there are genuine advantages as well. For instance, a family member's loan or gift may be what puts you "over the top" in having enough money for a down payment. Be aware, however, that there may be income tax and/or gift tax implications in this type of arrangement.

Whatever source of mortgages you choose, you should make sure to compare prices as thoroughly as possible. Mortgage lending is an extremely competitive business; careful research may uncover price breaks that could save you thousands of dollars in the long run. Be sure to compare *all* the costs involved. The interest rate charged on your mortgage is only one aspect of what you'll pay.

SELECTING YOUR HOME

In addition to sizing up your finances and determining what kind of mortgage to use, the other task you face—whether simultaneously with the first or sequentially—is finding the home that suits your tastes and needs. This is a far less precise task than crunching numbers, yet it's potentially strenuous in its own way.

For most people, these are the most important initial questions about a prospective home:

- *What's the best location for your property?*
  - Should it be in an urban, suburban, or rural setting?
  - How close is it to your work?
  - How convenient are local roads, highways, and mass transit?
  - How convenient are local shops, restaurants, recreation areas, and schools?
  - How safe is the neighborhood?
  - Are there nearby natural or artificial hazards (e.g., flooding, pollution, etc.)?

- *How big a home do you want?*
  - Does it meet your present needs?
  - Will it be sufficient for future needs (e.g., if you have children)?
  - Will it be excessive in the future (e.g., given impending retirement)?
  - Are additions/renovations feasible given the property's structure?
  - Are additions/renovations even allowable (i.e., if it's a condo/coop)?

- *How well maintained is the property?*
  - Is it structurally sound?
  - Is there insect/water or other forms of damage?
  - Are the plumbing/heating/electrical systems sound?
  - What are your probable maintenance costs (for a house)?
  - What are the probable maintenance fees (for a condo/coop)?

- *Do I want a house or a condo/coop?*
  - Are you willing to trade a degree of privacy for freedom from household maintenance?
  - Do you prefer total control over your own property or relinquishing some control to a board empowered to make decisions?
  - How important to you are the amenities (e.g., swimming pool, game room, tennis court, lawn care) that may accompany ownership in a condo/coop?

- To what degree do you prefer paying for your own household upkeep versus paying a share of community upkeep?

House, Coop, or Condo?

Answering these questions will guide you toward one of the fundamental decisions that should precede home ownership: Do you prefer owning a house, a coop, or a condo? Here are the fundamental differences of ownership:

House. This is the most traditional property, of course. You own the house and are completely responsible for its upkeep.

Advantages. The main positive factors in owning a house are:

- Relative privacy
- Self-determination as to decorating and renovating
- More space (generally speaking)

Disadvantages. The chief drawbacks are:

- Responsibility for routine maintenance
- Full financial burden for renovation, upgrades, and so forth

Coop. Cooperatives (coops) are an arrangement in which you don't hold title to your individual unit; instead, you own stock in a corporation that owns the development. You are essentially a tenant of a corporation entitled to occupancy because you own stock. In addition, you pay a monthly maintenance fee to the cooperative corporation, which is then responsible for maintaining the building, grounds, and real estate taxes. You are able to deduct your share of the corporation's mortgage interest and taxes.

Advantages. The main advantages to owning a coop are:

- Lower price than for a detached house in a similar neighborhood
- Amenities (e.g., swimming pool, sports facilities, activity centers, etc.)
- Maintenance-free lifestyle (e.g., no lawn care, household repairs, etc.)
- Potential for increased security (e.g., walled premises, security guards, etc.)

Disadvantages. The significant drawbacks to coop ownership are:

- Relative lack of privacy
- Unpredictable future increases of maintenance fees
- Relative lack of freedom to decorate or renovate your unit
- Risk of insufficient reserves in corporation's maintenance fund
- Potential for conflict with the corporation board
- Potential for mismanagement of property by corporation board

■ **TIP:** For information about buying into a cooperative, contact the National Association of Housing Co-operatives, 1614 King Street, Alexandria, VA 22314-2719. Phone: (703) 549-5201. ■

Condo. By contrast, condominiums are an arrangement in which you actually hold title to the unit you live in; you also own an interest in the development's land and common areas. The condominium properties can take many forms, including apartments, townhouses, beach communities, offices, and warehouse space. Governing the development takes place through an owners' association. Most condos have a hired on-site manager.

Advantages and Disadvantages. Owning a condo generally presents pros and cons similar to those of owning a coop. See above.

Finding the Home You Want

Next comes the search itself. Your work, educational commitments, or family needs may determine the particular community in which you'll search for the right property; otherwise, you'll need to narrow your search from wider regions to more specific towns or cities. Then you can narrow the search through one or more of the standard means. Ways to find a home include:

- Tips from friends, relatives, or neighbors
- Classified ads you read in newspapers
- Responses to classified ads you place in newspapers
- Properties you spot yourself
- Properties you learn about through real estate agents

Using an Agent

Many people find that using an agent simplifies the task of house hunting. Real estate agents have access to listings and detailed information about more homes than you're likely to find on your own; in addition, agents know the general area you're exploring, and many will respond to your specific real estate needs with tips and suggestions. However, you should keep in mind that generally speaking, *the agent represents the seller*. Even a congenial, energetic, helpful agent isn't committed primarily to your interests as the buyer. For this reason, you should avoid divulging your overall strategy for purchasing a home, including your top price.

An alternative possibility: Hire your own agent to represent you and serve your own specific interests. If you take this course of action, make sure that you have a contract specifying all duties and fees. Specific clauses should indicate:

- How the agent will be paid (fees and/or commissions)
- What services the agent will perform
- How conflicts of interest between your agent and the seller's agent will be resolved
- How you and the agent will resolve disputes

Checking Out Properties

Most people find house hunting alternately (or simultaneously) exciting and exhausting. On the one hand, it's often fun to see different homes, to imagine the experience of living in them, and to develop your skills in sizing up their various advantages and disadvantages. On the other hand, it's usually hard work. You can see only so many houses before the pros and cons jumble together and your recollections of the properties intermingle into one big blur. Despite the fatigue that usually sets in, however, it's important to persist in keeping the details straight. You're about to make a major investment. Clearsightedness about the homes you've visited is crucial.

Checking out properties ultimately involves a sequence of specific steps in evaluating the home you consider your best bet. These steps are:

- Inspecting the property
- Appraising the property
- Negotiating the price

Inspecting the Property. Regardless of how much you like the home you're considering, you should have it assessed by a professional building inspector to identify problems inherent in the property. Most realtors can recommend one or more inspectors in the area. If you have any doubts about their impartiality, you can obtain references for inspectors from any of several professional associations.

■ **TIP:** Here are two associations of building inspectors:

- The American Society of Home Inspectors, 85 West Algonquin Road, Suite 360, Arlington Heights, IL 60005-4423. Phone: (708) 290-1919.
- The National Association of Property Inspectors, 303 West Cypress, San Antonio, TX 78212-0528. Phone: (800) 486-3676. ■

The inspector you hire should check for specific problems in the following general systems:

- Structural integrity
  - Foundation
  - Floors
  - Supporting columns
  - Other weight-bearing structures
  - Walls
  - Ceilings
  - Roof

- Exterior
  - Walls
  - Doors and windows
  - Porches, steps, walkways, driveways
  - Balconies, decks, and patios
  - Eaves and soffits
  - Gutters and downspouts
  - Chimneys and flashing

- Interior
  - Walls
  - Floors
  - Ceilings
  - Doors and windows
  - Staircases

- Heating system
  - Furnace or boiler
  - Water heater
  - Heat pump
  - Radiators or ducts and vents
  - Thermostats and safety controls

- Air-conditioning system
  - Central units
  - Pumps and fans
  - Ducts and filters
  - Central controls and safety features

- Electrical system
  - Fuse boxes and circuit breakers
  - Wiring
  - Grounding equipment
  - Voltage and amperage ratings

- Fixtures
- Wall receptacles
- Plumbing system
  - Pipes
  - Drains
  - Kitchen, bathroom, and laundry room fixtures

Appraising the Property. Assuming that the home receives the inspector's passing grade, your next step is to have the property appraised. Many mortgage lenders will select an appraiser for you and bill you for the appraisal. You can arrange your own appraisal for an additional fee. Although this is more out-of-pocket expense, you may find it worthwhile: The appraisal can influence the course of subsequent bargaining over the property. (The appraisal may also make a difference as to how big a loan the mortgage lender will provide, since institutions will lend only a specific percentage of a property's appraised value.)

■ **TIP:** Here are two sources of information to help you locate an appraiser:

- The National Association of Master Appraisers, P.O. Box 12617, 303 West Cypress Street, San Antonio, TX 78212-0617. Phone: (210) 271-0781 or (800) 229-NAMA.
- The Appraisal Institute, 875 North Michigan Avenue, Suite 2400, Chicago, IL 60611-1980. Phone: (312) 335-4100. ■

Negotiating the Property's Price. Now comes the nitty-gritty. Armed with the inspection report and the appraisal, you can negotiate with the seller over a mutually acceptable price for the property. How well you do obviously depends on your (or your agent's) bargaining skills, but you'll also have to face the side effects of general economic conditions, the local real estate market, the seller's relative eagerness or reluctance to sell, and the presence or absence of other potential buyers.

Whether you negotiate with the seller face to face or through an agent is your own choice. Either way, however, you can try to use any of the property's identifiable flaws as a means of lowering the price. Probable repair costs may provide a means for deducting specified amounts from the property's overall cost. In addition, you can negotiate on what furnishings, appliances, or fixtures remain in the home when the seller moves out.

Closing the Sale

Your final step in purchasing a home is to close the sale. This is a process in which you sign the documents that transfer the property from seller to buyer; in addition, you write a series of checks to complete the financial part of the transaction. Generally in attendance at the closing will be the buyer, the seller, both parties' real estate agents, their respective attorneys, someone representing the bank, and someone representing the title insurance company. (Sometimes one or both of the attorneys will represent the bank and/or the title insurance company.)

A federal law called the Real Estate Settlement Procedures Act (RESPA) covers the process of closing a sale. You should have a clear sense of the costs you'll have to pay at this time, although there may be some variations in response to last-minute negotiations. Here's a list of typical closing costs:

- Down payment (less the earnest money you paid earlier)
- First mortgage payment
- Mortgage insurance premiums
- First year's property tax payments
- Mortgage application fees
- Loan origination fees (the bank's loan processing fees)
- Loan assumption fee (if you're assuming the seller's mortgage)
- Credit report fees
- Appraisal fees
- Survey fees
- Inspection fees
- Fees for recording the deed
- First year's homeowner's insurance premiums
- Escrow account reserves (sometimes required by the lender to cover insurance payments or property taxes)
- Your attorney's fees
- The bank's attorney's fees
- Settlement company's fees
- Fees for title search and title insurance premiums
- Mortgage recording fees
- Points

As noted earlier, closing costs are generally about 2% to 5% of the total cost of your home.

REFINANCING YOUR MORTGAGE

What if you've already purchased a house but have now decided it's time to refinance? If interest rates have dropped sufficiently in the time since you obtained your mortgage, refinancing may be worth your while. However, refinancing involves signficant costs and abundant paperwork; think carefully whether it's in your best interest to refinance.

When Should You Refinance?

Generally speaking, your new mortgage should be at least two percentage points lower than your existing mortgage for refinancing to pay off. The reason for this rule of thumb is that obtaining a new mortgage requires you to pay costs similar to those you paid when applying for a mortgage the first time around. Such costs include:

- Points
- Application fees
- Credit report fees
- Appraisal fees
- Inspection fees
- Title insurance fees
- Mortgage recording fees
- Legal fees

For your new mortgage to be cost-effective, the new rate needs to be low enough that your new payments compensate for these refinancing charges in a relatively short period of time. Otherwise, you might well be better off to keep the old mortgage instead. Also, don't forget to take into account that the interest payments are tax deductible.

To determine whether refinancing makes sense in your case, fill out the worksheet below.

REFINANCING WORKSHEET

	Example	Your Mortgage
1. Present monthly mortgage payment (after tax)	$1,000	
2. Mortgage payment after refinancing (after tax)	$ 900	
3. Monthly savings (subtract item 2 from item 1)	$ 100	
4. Total fees, closing costs, and prepayment penalties	$3,000	
5. Time needed to break even (divide item 4 by item 3)	30 months	

If you decide to refinance, here are your main options:

- *Replace your fixed-rate loan with a lower-interest fixed-rate loan of the same term (i.e., 30-year to 30-year or 15-year to 15-year).* This will lower your monthly payment; the payment itself will remain constant.

- *Replace a 30-year fixed-rate loan with a 15-year fixed-rate loan*. You may find that your monthly payment stays approximately the same, although you'll be paying off the loan much more quickly.
- *Replace your fixed-rate loan with an ARM*. Here, too, your monthly payment will drop. However, you now face the possibility of higher payments in the future.
- *Replace an ARM with a fixed-rate loan*. This will almost certainly result in increased monthly payments. The advantage is that they will be stable, which may provide peace of mind.

Whichever of these arrangements you prefer, you should scrutinize interest rates, points, and other aspects of loans as carefully as you did for your old mortgage. Consider applying first to your current lender, who may offer favorable terms to keep your business. It pays to shop around, however, to find the best deal possible.

Selling Your Home

If you're selling your home, your first decision (and perhaps the most important one) will be whether to sell the property yourself or use a real estate agent. Some people prefer to work on their own, figuring that pocketing what they'd spend on an agent's fee justifies the work involved. The majority, however, find an agent's expertise well worth the cost. Here are the pros and cons.

Selling Your Home Yourself

Avoiding the services of a real estate agent may appeal to you from a cost standpoint: You don't have to pay the usual 5% to 7% commission. Even on a home with an average price, this amounts to a significant saving. There are nonfinancial aspects of the decision as well, however, including the possibility that you simply prefer to handle the whole process yourself. That being said, you should still be careful not to underestimate the task of selling your own home. These tasks include:

- *Getting the home appraised*. You must be realistic about its current fair market value. Especially for owners who purchased homes in the overheated late-1980s real estate market, your property values may be far lower than you've expected.
- *Fixing up your property*. You'll have to follow your own hunches about your home's strengths and weaknesses and about what features need improvement before you're likely to sell.

- *Dealing with potential buyers.* Since you're representing yourself, you'll have to face all the browsers, uninvited prospective buyers, and others who stop by to see the property. Perhaps you enjoy these sorts of interactions. If not, think twice about the potential for disruption from unpredictable visits.
- *Negotiating the sale.* You'll be on your own when you actually have properly qualified buyers to bargain with. There will be no "buffer" between you and the person or people who are intent on purchasing your home for the lowest possible price.

Selling Your Home Through a Real Estate Agent

Alternatively, working with a real estate agent means relinquishing a percentage of your proceeds but also sparing yourself a certain amount of work and anxiety. This may appeal to you, especially if you dislike the notion of going head to head with prospective buyers or if you lack the time or knowledge to get involved in the first place.

Before discussing the possibilities further, it's worth a brief digression to note the terminology within the real estate industry. *Agents* are salespeople licensed to work for a real estate broker. *Brokers* are licensed to negotiate real estate transactions for a fee. Both agents and brokers may call themselves agents, since they serve clients in this capacity. In addition, some brokers and agents may call themselves *Realtors*. Realtors and *Realtor Associates* are members of the National Association of Realtors, a trade and lobbying organization within the real estate industry.

Finding an Agent. You can find an agent to represent you by any of several different means.

- Ask friends and business associates for recommendations.
- Check the local newspapers.
- Determine which real estate brokerage firms seem most prominent in the area.

Once you've narrowed your search, interview several successful agents in each of two or three firms. Your primary concerns are breadth of professional experience, overall sales record, a professional manner, and a personality that you find congenial. Since selling your house can be a stressful and sometimes protracted experience, you want to work with someone who seems compatible with your own attitudes. More to the point, you're the one who's paying, so it's ultimately your choice.

What an Agent Costs. Most agents charge commissions of 5% to 7% of the home's selling price. This fee is negotiable; however, the "wiggle room" is minimal unless your property has features that would prompt the agent to lower his or her fee. It's worth noting, too, that a good agent may bring you a sale worth considerably more than what you might have negotiated yourself, so the commission may be more cost-effective than it seems.

Listing Your Property. After deciding on which agent you wish to represent you, your next decision is how to list your property. The usual arrangements are:

- *Exclusive right to sell.* You'll owe a commission to the listing broker no matter who sells the property.
- *Exclusive agency.* Although similar to exclusive right to sell, exclusive agency means that you don't owe the broker a commission *if you sell your property yourself.*
- *Open listing.* This agreement allows you to list your property with several brokers simultaneously. You owe a commission to the first agent to produce an acceptable buyer.

The *listing agreement*—the legally binding contract you sign with your agent—stipulates various terms, including:

- The type of listing
- A description of your property
- The price
- The terms of sale
- The fee or commission

Most contracts run approximately 30 to 90 days. Generally speaking, you shouldn't lock yourself into an initial contract that seems longer than you want since you can always extend past the initial term.

Here's what your agent should do for you in trying to sell your house:

- *Write a full description of the property.* This should include data about the home's features, tax costs, and utility rates and information about the property's neighborhood, including local schools, parks, and public transportation options.
- *Indicate what you should do to improve the home's appearance.* Suggestions might include painting and decoration, removing some items of furniture (to make the home appear less cluttered), making home improvements or repairs, and cleaning up the exterior and yard.

- *Assist in setting the price.* Although you have the ultimate say in determining your asking price, the agent will provide information about sales of comparable homes in your neighborhood to serve as a guideline for pricing your home.
- *Prepare information sheets or other data for prospective buyers.* Until recently, these forms of information always involved printed write-ups that detailed a property's features and terms of sale. During recent years, however, information has begun to take a more high-tech form, including computerized databases that allow prospective buyers in the agent's office to "tour" available properties through interactive media.
- *Show the property.* The agent or an associate should be available to show prospective buyers your home during regular business hours and some evenings and weekends.
- *Screen prospects.* Which prospective buyers are serious about purchasing your home and are financially able to afford it? Your agent should screen genuine offers from frivolous offers and provide advice on potential problems.
- *Help you transact the sale.* Your agent should serve as your representative in negotiations for the property and, once you have a deal, represent you at the closing.

TAX CONSEQUENCES OF A HOME SALE

When it comes to your primary residence, tax planning and financial planning go hand-in-hand.

The gain on the sale of a home is considered a gain on the sale of a capital asset. Any taxable profit you make is subject to a maximum long-term capital gain rate of 20% (10% for gains in the 15% federal income tax bracket) if you owned the house for more than 12 months. Gain on the sale of a home may only be taxable to the extent it exceeds $250,000 ($500,000 for joint filers) if certain conditions discussed below are met.

To determine your profit, you subtract your *basis* from the sale price minus all costs and commissions. For instance, if you sell a house for $235,000, and must pay your broker 6% of the sale price—or $14,100—your sale price for determining capital gain tax is $220,900 ($235,000 minus $14,100).

Say you bought that house 30 years ago, for $25,000. You have since redone the kitchen, put in new thermal windows, added a family room, turned the garage into an office, put on vinyl siding and a new roof. Your *basis* in the house is $25,000 plus the cost of all of the capital improvements you have made, providing you have paperwork to verify the costs. We'll assume you keep good records, and the total cost of those improvements over the 30 years you owned the home is $50,000, many of them having been done in the 1970s. In such a case, your *basis* would be $75,000. Your capital gain would be $220,900 minus $75,000, or $145,900. If you are in the 28% federal tax bracket or higher, your capital gain tax on your home sale would be $29,180 unless you use the principal residence exclusion.

A $250,000 exclusion for single filers ($500,000 for joint filers) is now available to all taxpayers. You can claim the exclusion once every 2 years. To be eligible, you must have owned the residence and occupied it as a principal residence for at least 2 of the 5 years before the sale or exchange (occupancy by a divorced spouse is treated as yours). If you fail to meet these requirements (the 2-out-of-5-years ownership rule or the once-every-2-years use of exclusion rule) by reason of a change of place of employment, health, or other unforeseen circumstances you can exclude the fraction of the $250,000 ($500,000 if married filing a joint return) equal to the fraction of 2 years that these requirements are met.

E X A M P L E

■ Martin and Fern purchase a home in 1999. In 2000, Martin's employer transfers him to another city. They owned the home as their principal residence for 12 months. They can exclude up to $250,000 of gain ($500,000 times ratio of 12 months/24 months). ■

Limiting the exclusion to only one sale every 2 years does not prevent a husband and wife filing a joint return from each excluding up to $250,000 of gain from the sale or exchange of each spouse's principal residence, provided that each spouse could exclude up to $250,000 of gain if they filed separate returns.

If you acquired your current residence in an old law rollover transaction, periods of ownership and use of the prior residence would be taken into account in determining ownership and use of the current residence.

The exclusion will not be an advantage for taxpayers who have traded up over a long period under the old rollover rules and now must sell a high-priced home and realize a significant profit.

■ The Garners are married filing jointly. They bought a home in 1965 for $20,000, sold it later for $50,000, and purchased a replacement home for $60,000. They repeatedly sell and buy homes over the years, each time purchasing a more expensive replacement home. The Garners have owned a home for the past 5 years that now is worth $800,000, with accumulated profits of $600,000. If they were to sell that home for $800,000, the capital gains tax (20%) would be imposed on $100,000 (the $600,000 of accumulated profit minus the $500,000 exclusion). ■

For more details on tax planning and your home, see *The Ernst & Young Tax Guide* and *The Ernst & Young Tax Saver's Guide.*

19

FUNDING A COLLEGE EDUCATION

Most parents—including many who are financially secure—worry a lot about how to fund their children's college education. It would be wonderful if financial planners could reassure them that there's no cause for concern. Unfortunately, funding higher education is a daunting task for most families—a task made even more difficult because many people are saving simultaneously for other goals, such as retirement. Unlike retirement savings, college savings don't generally receive much support from governmental or corporate sources. As a result, funding a college education may end up being the single greatest financial burden you face as a parent.

Is this situation really as bleak as it seems? Not at all. In fact, careful plans can make college funding manageable—a challenging but feasible part of your overall financial strategy. In this chapter we discuss what you need to know to fund your children's higher education and offer specific suggestions to make the whole task easier.

Here are the topics we cover:

- Starting early
- Choosing an affordable college
- Determining how much you'll need
- Developing a savings program

- Selecting investments
- Saving money through your child's tax bracket
- Borrowing to pay for college
- Purchasing a rental property during your child's college years
- Obtaining financial aid and scholarships

Starting Early

To reach your goals for college funding, your best bet is to start your child's college fund as early as possible. That's easier said than done, of course: You probably find it difficult to put away money for a distant goal when so many more immediate expenses drain your resources and leave little or no surplus to invest. Still, starting early provides you with your best opportunities. Like many parents, you may find that when your children enter public elementary school, you have some extra money. Some parents end up financially better off because of reduced child-care costs; for others, the net gain results because a spouse previously at home with the kids can now return to the workforce. Either way, setting aside the extra money for your children's higher education makes good sense.

The Importance of Projecting Income and Expenses

Starting early is more than just a matter of beginning to save. As with other financial planning tasks, it's important for you to take stock of where you are and where you're trying to go. This means quantifying how much you'll need to take from savings to pay these anticipated college expenses in the future. In addition, it means determining if you can fund that savings pool currently or if, like most people, you'll need to establish a plan to fund this need over time.

The best way to take stock is to do some cash flow projections. Depending on your children's ages, you may need to project 20 or more years ahead to determine what sources of income and what kinds of expenditures you anticipate. You won't be able to pin down everything. The greater your accuracy, however, the better you'll be able to assess the variables that influence your financial future. Here are some of those variables:

Income. Consider these points:

- How consistent are your raises and cost-of-living adjustments?
- How consistent are your bonuses or other forms of nonsalary compensation?

- How secure is your job overall?
- Do you anticipate working the same number of days/hours as you work now?
- If you're married, will both you and your spouse work outside the home?
- If you're divorced, how reliable are your alimony and child support payments?
- To what degree can you expect college funding assistance from financial aid, scholarships, or relatives?

Expenses. When (if ever) do you anticipate:

- Needing to move to a new home?
- Making major home repairs or improvements?
- Buying a new car?
- Paying for child care or private school tuition?
- Funding more than one child's college expenses?
- Saving for retirement?

Answering these questions will help you determine what funds you'll have available for funding college expenses over the time span that you're projecting. Your actual income and expenses will probably differ from what you project; even so, you're still better off knowing more rather than less about what to expect. And even a somewhat discouraging answer regarding your finances puts you in a position of increased strength. For example, let's say that you learn you'll need $25,000 for your daughter's first year of college. Your financial projections indicate that your savings will amount to only $15,000 for that year. The $10,000 shortfall is understandably discouraging; however, having an actual figure at least lets you know where you stand. With that relatively concrete number (as opposed to a vague sense that your funding is inadequate), you can take specific steps to close the gap. After all, funding a $10,000 shortfall over many years is a lot easier than tackling it in her first year of college.

If it turns out that you don't have enough money set aside to pay your child's college costs when the time comes, you may have a variety of options to choose from to help you meet your goal. Among these possible options are:

- Using current income
- Taking out loans
- Using your child's own part-time employment income
- Obtaining student loans
- Obtaining scholarships

We discuss most of these options later in the chapter.

Choosing an Affordable College

Another important step that you can take is clarifying your child's collegiate aspirations. How many years of undergraduate coursework will you pay for? Will you also pay for graduate school, law school, medical school, and so on? Is she intent on a private college, or is a state school within her range of choices? It's no secret that college costs vary enormously. For example, the cost of a baccalaureate degree from an Ivy League school is much more expensive than an associate degree from a community college. Knowing what sorts of costs you face is clearly half the task of knowing how much you have to save. For an overview of what many schools cost, you can consult any of several reference books designed for precisely this purpose.

■ **TIP:** Two sources of information about college costs are *The College Cost and Financial Aid Handbook 1999* and *Paying for College: A Guide for Parents,* both available from the College Board, 45 Columbus Avenue, New York, NY 10023, (212) 713-8000, www.collegeboard.org. ■

Your son's or daughter's definition of a "good" school can be based more on image than on fact. Many Americans assume that a private college is inherently better than a state school. (The Ivy League colleges tend to be regarded as the be-all-and-end-all of higher education.) Although private schools can offer an excellent education, what matters most is the specific match between what your child needs and what particular schools have to offer. Choosing a school according to popular images or snob appeal may not serve your son or daughter well. In addition, you may spend a staggering amount of money over and above what you could have spent elsewhere for a superior education, *given your child's individual academic and career goals.*

Determining How Much You'll Need

To anticipate what the college costs will be when your son or daughter starts school, you should first determine what these costs are today, based on the school or type of school you expect your child to attend. Most schools will provide you with that information upon request, and they may even indicate what they think college costs will be when your children reach college age. With this information, you can begin the process of determining how much money you'll need in the future, as well as how to fund what you need.

To determine how much money you'll need to send your children to college, it's important to obtain as accurate information as possible on the schools your child may attend. As noted earlier, you can obtain this kind of information by calling college or university admissions offices, or by checking individual college catalogs. However, the amounts they specify may not encompass all the college costs you need to fund.

In addition to tuition, room and board, and additional college costs, there will be other expenses that you should estimate yourself. The most expensive is probably travel. How far away will your child's school be— clear across the country, or two towns over? The difference in travel expenses projected over 4 years may be more than the cost of a year's tuition. Another frequently overlooked expense is that of long-distance phone calls. To the degree possible, size up these costs and factor them into your college budget.

The important thing is to ensure that you have a plan to set aside as much money as you can as early as possible to fund your children's college educations. When estimating how much you'll need in the future for these costs, you will need to forecast inflation—and the inflation rate for college costs may be higher than the average inflation rate. Therefore, be sure to estimate high. If inflation is 5%, for example, you might assume that college expenses will increase by 7% per year. A good rule of thumb is to assume that tuition costs will increase by at least two percentage points more than inflation each year. However, the rate could be even higher.

As a result, it's best to try to get information directly from the specific college or colleges in which your child is interested. Request information regarding tuition, room and board, and other college costs for the forthcoming year, as well as what their past and current increases have been compared to inflation. You should also ask them for their expectations for future increases, as this will help you develop a reasonable savings plan for this purpose. The key is to obtain as much accurate information as possible. When in doubt, estimate high. The only downside of guessing high is that your fund may end up larger than you need, in which case you'll have some money left over to help fund other future goals, such as your children's weddings or your retirement.

Once you've determined how much your college costs will be, you should project your net cash flow position on an annual basis through your children's college years to determine how much of these costs need to be funded. This process will enable you to take into consideration any ability to pay college costs out of cash inflows during the college years if your cash inflows exceed outflows other than college costs.

After you've projected your annual net cash flow position, you can then identify how much your shortfall will be for any negative cash flow years and determine how much money you must set aside to fund those negative amounts. The amount you need to set aside will be less than the sum of the negative amounts because those amounts already include inflation, and the money set aside today should grow based on the investments selected.

The table below provides you with a point of reference regarding the projected costs for 4 years of college and the funds necessary to pay for these costs, assuming that:

- Current college costs are $10,000 per year.
- College costs will rise at a rate of 7% per year.
- You'll earn 6% after-tax return on investments used to fund this goal.

The table shows how much you would need to save, given these assumptions, if the money is set aside in a lump sum annually, or on a monthly basis, depending on how old your child is now.

PROJECTED COST AND REQUIRED FUNDING FOR FOUR YEARS OF COLLEGE ASSUMING 7% INFLATION RATE, 6% AFTER-TAX RATE OF RETURN

Child's Current Age	Projected 4-Year College Cost	Required Funding		
		Single Payment	Annual	Monthly
1	$140,250	$52,084	$4,690	$395
2	131,074	51,597	4,817	406
3	122,499	51,115	4,965	419
4	114,485	50,637	5,139	434
5	106,996	50,164	5,346	452
6	99,996	49,695	5,592	473
7	93,454	49,231	5,889	499
8	87,340	48,770	6,251	530
9	81,627	48,315	6,701	569
10	76,286	47,863	7,271	618
11	71,296	47,416	8,013	682
12	66,632	46,973	9,012	767
13	62,272	46,534	10,422	888
14	58,199	46,099	12,551	1,070
15	54,391	45,668	16,118	1,376
16	50,833	45,241	23,279	1,989
17	47,507	44,818	44,818	3,832

What are the implications? The table offers you a general sense of how high college costs will be in the future and how much money you'll have to invest to meet those costs. It's truly staggering to see that college costs of

$10,000 per year today will cost you over $140,000 (assuming 7% annual inflation) for the 4-year term of a child who is currently 1 year old. With numbers this large, you can see why it's advisable to get a more specific estimate of what you'll need.

DEVELOPING A SAVINGS PROGRAM

The simplest way to save for college costs is to set aside an appropriate sum that will grow until it's adequate to pay all your children's college costs. However, most middle-class Americans simply don't have enough money sitting around to invest a lump sum toward college funding. Even though there may be advantages associated with investing a larger amount of principal early on, you may have to proceed by other means. The most common programs for accumulating college funds involve investing in a longer-term, more systematic way.

E
X
A
M
P
L
E

■ Let's suppose that you decide you'll need $25,000 per year for 4 years beginning when your daughter (now 7 years old) turns 18 and needs funds to pay for college. If you have the money, you could simply invest a total of $50,000 in four zero-coupon bonds now. Assuming a yield of about 6%, each bond could be set to mature at $25,000 the summer preceding each of your daughter's collegiate years. Since the bonds provide $25,000 during each of the 4 years your daughter will be in college, you presumably have sufficient funds to pay her college costs at that time.

Alternatively, assuming that you can earn a rate of return of 6% per year, you could set aside $560 per month for the next 10 years to accomplish the same thing. It may be impractical to purchase zero-coupon bonds with your smaller investment amount, however. For this reason, you may need to use a different investment, such as U.S. Series EE bonds or mutual funds, or you may need to accumulate your $560 monthly deposits in a cash investment until you have enough money to buy your zero-coupon bonds. ■

Your savings program for college funding generally involves using the kind of investment planning process that we've explored elsewhere in this book (see Chapters 3 through 5). During this process you need to:

- *Quantify your financial goal.* How much money do you need for your child's college education?
- *Identify the amount of money you currently have available to fund that goal.* How does this limit the universe of investment vehicles from which you can choose?

- *Determine your investment horizon (short-term, medium-term, or long-term).* When do you need the money?
- *Select appropriate investment vehicles.* What are your risk and return constraints?
- *Select the specific investment.* Does it meet your risk and return criteria, as well as your liquidity needs?

This process isn't static. The passage of time and other factors may cause you to change the investment selection periodically. Therefore, you should repeat this process on an annual basis.

SELECTING INVESTMENTS

Generally speaking, if the college costs will begin more than 7 years in the future, you can invest your money using any investment vehicle that meets your risk and return criteria. Bonds, stocks, and mutual funds will all serve your purposes. As the payment dates approach, however, the need for liquidity becomes more important. Therefore, it becomes prudent to change from stocks or bond mutual funds to bonds with specific maturities or cash investments.

Using Stocks to Fund Your Child's College Expenses

Stocks are expected to produce a higher rate of return over time than bonds or cash investments. However, they are much riskier investments in the short term. When you invest in stocks, you accept a great deal of uncertainty regarding what the value of the investment will be on a particular date in the future. Since this uncertainty becomes more stressful as that date approaches, stocks become less and less desirable as a college funding investment as the college start date approaches. As your investment horizon shortens, you become less able to cope with the stock market's risk.

It is important to identify in advance when you'll change the investment choice from stocks to a more liquid asset if you fund college costs initially with stocks. More important, you need to make the change when it's appropriate. Although rate of return is always important, it's crucial to make sure that you have the money available to pay your costs when they become due.

How Bonds Can Simplify Saving for Higher Education

A simpler strategy for funding a college education is to purchase one or more dedicated bonds. This means that you purchase a bond (or bonds) intended specifically to pay a particular cost at a particular time. The bond's maturity date coincides with the point in time at which you need the money. Generally speaking, this means that you purchase a bond maturing in July or August before your child's academic year begins.

Bonds that reinvest their interest income automatically are particularly popular for this purpose. This is because you don't need any income from the investment until the future date when you'll pay the college costs. Consequently, zero-coupon bonds and Series EE bonds are frequently selected so that the investor doesn't have to reinvest interest income on a semi-annual basis. These bonds are discussed in detail in Chapter 3. Here we'll discuss a special advantage that Series EE can provide in a college funding context if certain criteria are met.

Specifically, the interest you earn on U.S. Series EE Bonds purchased after 1989 may be exempt from federal and state income tax to the extent that you redeem the bonds to pay tuition and fees at a qualified college or graduate school. (Certain nursing or vocational schools also qualify.) To be eligible for the tax exemption, the person to whom the bond is issued must be at least 24 years old, and you must use the bond proceeds to pay either your own or your spouse's or dependents' qualified higher education expenses. (As a result, bonds purchased by grandparents or parents in the name of a child who is younger than 24 won't qualify.)

There are other conditions as well. The exclusion from federal taxable income only applies to parents with income below certain limits, and those limits change every year with inflation. For 1999, the tax break phases out for married taxpayers filing jointly who have adjusted gross income of between $79,650 and $109,650. For single taxpayers and head-of-household filers, the phaseout range is between $53,100 and $68,100. No exclusion is allowed for married taxpayers filing separately. *Note:* The phaseout is figured on gross income in the year the bond is *redeemed*, not the year the bond was purchased. Consequently, you may not be able to have the exclusion if your income rises significantly before your child goes off to college. The phaseout ranges are adjusted each year for inflation.

The amount of qualified higher education expenses must be reduced by the expenses used to calculate the Hope Scholarship and Lifetime Learning Credits (see below).

■ **TIP:** For more information on Series EE bonds, contact the Office of Public Affairs, U.S. Savings Bonds Division, Washington, DC 20226, (202) 447-1775, www.ustreas.gov. ■

Qualified State Tuition Programs

Is there a good alternative to purchasing an investment and hoping it will grow to become large enough to fund your children's college educations? One option is to utilize a qualified state tuition program.

Many states have set up these programs. Some work by guaranteeing you coverage of your child's tuition costs at a state college if you make a predetermined cash payment up front. The size of the payment depends on current tuition and how close your child is to entering college. The money is then invested in a fund that the state has set up; the state then accumulates your payments until your child is ready to enroll; your child's tuition is then prepaid. Other programs allow you to set aside funds to be used for tuition at a school in that state or any state; the amount accumulated pays a certain amount of tuition—you pay the balance.

Advantages. The main positive side to these programs is that they offer a means to a specific end. You pay your money; your child's college tuition, room and board, and so forth are substantially or fully covered by the time that he or she registers for first-year classes. To this end, these programs offer considerable peace of mind.

- You pay your money and your child's college expenses are substantially or fully covered.
- There are no income limitations restricting who may contribute to a prepaid tuition program.
- The income earned is tax deferred.
- The income is taxed at your child's bracket, presumably lower, when withdrawn.

Disadvantages. Although tuition prepayments have notable advantages, they aren't without potential drawbacks. Consider these closely before enrolling in any program:

- You may be able to achieve better returns on alternative investments.
- You usually can't touch your investment without penalty until your child reaches college age.
- Your child's choice of colleges may be limited.
- If your child doesn't attend college, you may not get all your money back (in most cases you receive less due to administrative charges).

For gift tax purposes, any contribution to a qualified tuition program will be treated as a gift eligible for the $10,000 gift tax exclusion.

If a contribution in excess of $10,000 ($20,000 in the case of a married couple) is made in 1 year, the contributor can elect to have the contribution treated as if made ratably over 5 years beginning in the year the contribution is made.

E
X
A
M
P
L
E

■ A single contributor making a $30,000 contribution to a qualified state tuition program could elect to treat the contribution as five annual contributions of $6,000 and, therefore, could make up to $4,000 in other transfers to the beneficiary in each of those 5 years without triggering the gift tax. ■

College Savings Plans

These funding alternatives are sponsored by individual states. They allow tax-deferred savings to be used toward the education costs of a child or other family member. The child is not limited to a specific university, and the withdrawals may be exempt from state taxation. Each state has specific rules, but most allow for federally tax-deferred savings, professional money management, school choice, and annual contributions.

Education IRAs

Many taxpayers can make a nondeductible contribution of up to $500 per year per beneficiary until the beneficiary reaches age 18. The advantage to Education IRAs is that withdrawals to pay for qualified higher education expenses are free from federal tax. Education IRA benefits are not available for everyone because income limits of the allowable contribution is phased out once income reaches $150,000 for married taxpayers filing jointly. Married taxpayers filing separately cannot contribute to Education IRAs. And you can't contribute to an Education IRA for a child who has had a contribution made on his or her behalf to a Qualified State Tuition Program in the same year.

SAVING MONEY THROUGH YOUR CHILD'S TAX BRACKET

Before 1986 tax reform, many parents' favorite college-funding strategy was to shift taxable income to children so that the income would be taxed at the children's lower tax brackets. The idea was to create a bigger fund after taxes. While tax reform reduced the benefits of income shifting, it still remains a worthwhile technique for saving for college, especially as tax rates have been climbing.

Your children's unearned income (interest, dividends, and capital gains) is taxed at their rate only if they are age 14 or older. For children under 14, unearned income in excess of $1,400 is taxed at their parents' tax rate in 1999. Therefore, if you transfer assets into the name of a child—regardless of age—that generate $1,400 of annual investment income, the child would owe a federal income tax of only $105 per year. By comparison, the same income could incur a federal income tax as high as $555 if taxed to you. That may seem a relatively minor matter, but saving $466 of income taxes per child each year can really add up when you compound it over a period of years. For this reason, it makes tax sense to consider shifting assets to your children.

How Much Income Can You Shift to Your Children?

The tax laws allow you to take much greater advantage of income-shifting for children age 14 or older. In 1999, children under age 14 are exempt from paying tax on the first $700 of income and are taxed at a 15% federal income tax rate only on the next $700 of income. Income over $1,400 is then taxed at their parents' marginal tax rate. However, children age 14 or older pay zero tax on the first $700 of income, 15% tax on the next $25,750 of income, and 28% tax on the next $36,700 of income in 1999.

E X A M P L E

■ Suppose you have $10,000 of investment income that could be shifted to your child. By retaining it subject to your tax rate of, say, 28%, you would have only $7,200 left to invest after taxes ($6,900, if your tax rate were 31%). The same income in the hands of a child 14 or older might leave $8,605 after federal tax in the college fund. ■

In addition to greater income tax shifting benefits for making transfers of assets to children age 14 or older, this may also be a better time to give assets to children because college costs are more imminent and you can better predict whether your child may use the money for a purpose other than the intended college education. Moreover, the fund may be becoming larger, and you may be investing in bonds rather than stocks at this point, due to the investment time horizon. As the amount of investment income that is subject to ordinary income taxation currently becomes larger, you may become more inclined to transfer the assets to your child so that you can pay income tax at your child's rate rather than at your own.

One caveat, however. Although transferring assets to your child for college funding is advantageous for two reasons—(1) using the child's lower tax bracket, and (2) encouraging their financial discipline to save—it can have some serious drawbacks as well. It's very important to keep in mind that shifting assets to your child is irrevocable; once you transfer the assets, your child owns them.

Income-shifting strategies may make sense as a way of maximizing your college-fund investments. However, shifting income to your children may backfire if you hit a snag in your career or other financial catastrophe. What would happen, for example, if you shifted significant assets to your son or daughter, then suffered a major setback, such as losing your job or becoming disabled? You might end up with a greatly heightened need for the assets or income you've transferred to your child.

In short, you should consider more than just the tax advantages of income-shifting strategies. Take the long view. Plan your college funding in ways that allow flexibility over as long a time horizon as possible, given the uncertainties of life.

Another consideration is that having funds in your child's name can be an impediment to securing college financial aid. The reason? The funding formula generally requires children's funds to be completely spent *before* the family can secure financial aid. Moreover, gifted assets belong to your children, not to you. Some parents decide that income tax savings are not sufficient to outweigh their concerns over losing control of the assets.

Using Trusts to Shift Income

To take advantage of the income tax savings associated with income-shifting, you must actually transfer assets to your children. Even if you remain as custodian of the property (e.g., under the Uniform Transfers to Minors Act), your child will have unrestricted access to the funds at some point (the age of majority in the state where the child resides) without any obligation to use these funds for education. If you're concerned that 2 years of hanging out at a beach resort may fascinate your child more than 4 years in college, income-shifting may not be right for you.

You can retain some control over your child's assets by putting them in trust. If you put assets into a trust, the income earned for the year on those assets will generally be subject to tax at the trust level (not on your or your child's tax return) as long as the money isn't withdrawn during the year. The typical kinds of trust selected for this purpose are the *minor's trust* and the *Crummey trust*.

Minor's Trust

Congress has enacted special rules to provide a method for making gifts to minors that qualify for the gift tax annual exclusion, even though the child doesn't necessarily have access to the gift property or its income until he or she turns 21. The trust instrument must satisfy certain requirements concerning the gift property and its income—the key requirement being that any property remaining in the trust when the child turns 21 will pass to (or become available to) him or her at that time. Also, if the child dies before reaching age 21, the funds must be payable to the child's estate or as the child designates under a general power of appointment.

The chief concern when using a minor's trust is that the beneficiary can withdraw all the assets when turning 21; however, the trust can be structured to continue beyond that time if the beneficiary doesn't withdraw the funds within a designated period (e.g., within 90 days of his or her 21st birthday).

A minor's trust is taxed at trust rates. You can save a considerable amount of taxes over time using this sort of trust.

Once a trust's taxable income reaches $8,450 in 1999, it is in the 39.6% bracket. So once the trust's income becomes more substantial, the tax advantage disappears. When that happens you might want to distribute the trust's income so that it's taxed at the child's lower bracket.

However, setting up a trust for college costs can have its own drawbacks as well. One such drawback is the cost of setting up the trust. Another drawback is the complexity of doing an annual income tax return for the trust. Whether or not setting up a trust for your child's college funding is worthwhile depends partly on how much tax you expect to save over time, but mostly on how important it is to be able to have some degree of control over the assets.

> **Gift Tax Annual Exclusion:** the tax rule that allows you to give up to $10,000 each year to as many individuals as you want without incurring any gift tax. (If your spouse joins in making the gift by consenting on a gift tax return, you may give $20,000 to each person annually without any gift tax liability.)

Crummey Trust

Another trust often used for educational savings is the Crummey trust. The distinguishing characteristic of a Crummey trust is that it gives the beneficiary the annual right to demand a distribution of all or part of new contributions to the trust. Generally, this right to withdraw money from the trust is equal to the lesser of the amount of the contributions to the trust during the year or some specified amount (e.g., $5,000 or 5% of the trust's value). A Crummey trust taxes income to the beneficiaries, which will mean tax at the parent's rate or the children's rate depending on their ages.

With a Crummey trust, you can transfer property and have the gift qualify for the gift tax annual exclusion to the extent that the beneficiary has the right to withdraw from the trust. The beneficiary (or legal guardian) must be notified of the power to withdraw the money from the trust, although the power is permitted to lapse or terminate after a short period of time, such as 30 days. Even if the beneficiary fails to make a demand during the specified window period (after being notified that a contribution was made) and thus can't access the money unless the trust otherwise provides for distribution, the gift will qualify for the gift tax annual exclusion.

The Crummey trust can be very flexible. It can be set up to preclude access to any trust income or principal until the child reaches a specified age even beyond age 21. The trustee also can be restricted to using trust assets and income for specific purposes, such as the payment of college costs.

Tax-Advantaged Investments

Another way to have Uncle Sam help fund your child's college education is to use tax-advantaged investments such as the following:

- U.S. Series EE bonds
- Tax-exempt bonds
- Growth stocks
- Certificates of deposit

The income tax savings opportunities of these investments can be beneficial for you whether you decide to hold the asset in your own name or, alternatively, to transfer it to your child.

U.S. Series EE Bonds

Series EE bonds allow income to accrue without being taxed until redeemed. If you own the Series EE bond, this tax deferral may be beneficial, and as we discussed earlier, you may never have to pay tax on the interest income. If, on the other hand, the bonds are titled in your child's name, the built-up income on bonds will be taxed at your child's tax rate as long as he or she waits until after his or her 13th birthday before redeeming them. The interest earned on these bonds is always exempt from state income taxes.

Tax-Exempt Bonds

These bonds pay interest that is generally exempt from federal tax and in some cases may also be exempt from state income tax. These bonds are typically used in cases where the parents decide to own the bonds or for children under the age of 14 who already generate $1,400 of investment income annually. Tax-exempt zero-coupon bonds are popular investments for these situations because they eliminate the problem of having to invest the interest payments received. However, shop around and compare interest on an after-tax basis with similar bonds (i.e., U.S. Series EE bonds and interest-paying tax-exempt bonds) to ensure that the return is beneficial.

Growth Stocks and Growth-Oriented Mutual Funds

These pay little or no dividends and are expected to produce a rate of return that's primarily capital gain income. Since capital gain income doesn't generally have to be taxed until the stocks are sold, and since they may be subject to a lower tax rate at that time—especially after your child turns 14—these may be beneficial investments for the same people as would benefit from tax-exempt bonds. However, most growth stocks are significantly riskier investments than are high-quality dedicated tax-exempt bonds.

Certificates of Deposit

Certificates of deposit are often used to defer income to the following year for yourself or, for that matter, for your children as they near age 14. Typically, this is accomplished by purchasing a one-year CD in January. The result is that the interest income earned on the CD will not be subject to tax until it matures the following year. By investing some of your child's money in a one-year CD in the year *before* he or she turns 14, tax will be imposed on the CD's interest income in the following year based on his or her tax rate. Your tax savings comes from the income being taxed at your child's income tax rate—a rate that's probably lower than the kiddie tax that would be imposed on income earned at age 13. In addition, since the taxable income will be reported on your child's next year's income tax return, you may receive a time-value-of-money benefit.

Education IRAs

An Education IRA is a trust or custodial account that is created exclusively to pay qualified higher eduction expenses.

Anybody who is eligible can make a nondeductible contribution of up to $500 per year per beneficiary into an Education IRA. Eligible contributions must be in cash and made until the time the beneficiary reaches age 18.

(*Note:* An Education IRA is not considered an IRA for purposes of the aggregate $2,000 annual limit on contributions to all other IRAs.)

The contributor does not have to be related to the beneficiary, and there is no limit on the number of individual beneficiaries for whom one contributor can set up an Education IRA (as long as the person making the contribution has modified AGI within the established limits, and each contribution for each individual does not exceed $500 annually). Multiple Education IRAs may be created for one beneficiary, but the contribution limit of all contributions for a single beneficiary is $500 in any one tax year.

No contribution may be made by any person to an Education IRA during any year in which any contributions are made by anyone to a qualified state tuition program on behalf of the same beneficiary.

EXAMPLE

■ If grandparents contribute to a qualified state tuition program on behalf of a child, and the parents establish an Education IRA for the same child, the parents cannot make the $500 annual contribution to the Education IRA in any tax year in which the grandparents have made a contribution to the state tuition program on that child's behalf. ■

Income Limits. The $500 annual contribution limit for Education IRAs is phased out ratably for single contributors with modified AGI between $95,000 and $110,000 ($150,000 and $160,000 for couples filing jointly). Individuals with modified AGI above the phase-out range cannot make contributions to an education IRA established on behalf of any other individual.

Distributions. Distributions from an Education IRA are excludable from gross income to the extent that the distribution does not exceed qualified higher education expenses (i.e., post-secondary tuition, fees, books, supplies, equipment, and certain room and board expenses) incurred by the beneficiary during the year the distribution is made. The beneficiary can be enrolled at an eligible educational institution on a full-time, half-time, or less than half-time basis. However, certain room and board expenses are qualified higher education expenses only if the student incurring such expenses is enrolled at an eligible educational institution on at least a half-time basis. (*Note:* Any account where distributions are taxable also are subject to a 10% penalty, unless the distribution is made on account of death or disability or made to cover educational expenses that exceed expenses paid by scholarships or through an employer's education reimbursement plan.)

Special Rules. Any balance remaining in an Education IRA at the time a beneficiary becomes 30 years old must be distributed, and the earnings portion of such a distribution will be includible in gross income of the beneficiary and subject to an additional 10% income tax because the distribution was not for educational purposes. The new law allows tax-free (and penalty-free) transfers and rollovers of account balances from one Education IRA benefiting one beneficiary to another Education IRA benefiting a different beneficiary (as well as redesignations of the named beneficiary), provided that the new beneficiary is a member of the family of the prior beneficiary and that the transfer or rollover is made before the prior beneficiary reaches age 30.

If a beneficiary's interest in an Education IRA is rolled over to another beneficiary, there are no transfer tax consequences as long as the two beneficiaries are in the same generation. If a beneficiary's interest is rolled over to a beneficiary in a lower generation (e.g., parent to child or uncle to niece), the 5-year averaging rule described earlier in connection with qualified state tuition programs may be applied to exempt up to $50,000 of the transfer from gift tax.

Penalty-Free Withdrawals from All IRAs to Cover Education Expenses

The 10% early withdrawal penalty does not apply to distributions from retirement IRAs if you use the amounts to pay qualified higher education expenses (including those related to graduate-level courses) for yourself, your spouse, your child, or your grandchild.

Any distribution from a retirement IRA for education expenses that is exempt from the 10% early withdrawal penalty also reduces the amount of education costs that are eligible for a Hope or Lifetime Learning tax credit. Before making any IRA withdrawal to cover these costs, parents and grandparents should analyze whether the waiver of penalty exceeds the loss of a portion of the tax credit.

The credits are phased out ratably for single taxpayers with modified AGI of $40,000 to $50,000 and for couples filing jointly with modified AGI

The New Hope Scholarship Tax Credit and Lifetime Learning Credit

You can elect either a nonrefundable Hope Scholarship tax credit or a Lifetime Learning credit for eligible higher education expenses.

These two credits, as well as the tax-free withdrawals from education IRAs (see above), are mutually exclusive. For each eligible student in each tax year, you must elect either one of the tax credits or the exclusion from gross income for withdrawals from education IRAs.

between $80,000 and $100,000. The credits are not available to married taxpayers filing separately.

The Hope Scholarship Credit

The Hope Scholarship tax credit is equal to 100% of the first $1,000 of eligible expenses, and 50% of the next $1,000 of expenses, for the first 2 years of college. Such expenses include qualified tuition and related expenses, but not room, board, or books. The qualified tuition and related expenses must be incurred by you, your spouse, or your dependent.

Limitations on the Hope credit:

1. The student must be at least a half-time student for at least one academic period that begins during the year.
2. The Hope credit is permitted only for the first 2 academic years of post-secondary education.
3. The credit is disallowed if the student is convicted of a felony drug offense.

The Lifetime Learning Credit

The Lifetime Learning credit is equal to 20% of qualified tuition and fees incurred during the tax year on behalf of you, your spouse, or your dependent. For expenses paid before January 1, 2003, up to $5,000 of qualified tuition and fees per taxpayer return will be eligible for the 20% Lifetime Learning credit (i.e., the maximum credit per taxpayer return will be $1,000). For expenses paid after December 31, 2002, up to $10,000 of qualified tuition and fees per taxpayer return will be eligible for the 20% Lifetime Learning credit (i.e., the maximum credit per taxpayer return will be $2,000).

Unlike the Hope credit, a taxpayer may claim the Lifetime Learning credit for an unlimited number of tax years, but the maximum amount of the Lifetime Learning credit that can be claimed on a taxpayer's return per year is capped as just described.

Qualified tuition and fees for the Lifetime Learning credit include amounts incurred for undergraduate or graduate-level (and professional degree) courses. The credit is available for the tuition and fees of a student who attends classes on at least a half-time basis as part of a degree or certificate program. It also is available for any course of instruction at an eligible educational institution (whether the student is enrolled on a full-time, half-time, or less than half-time basis) to acquire or improve the student's job skills.

The interaction between the Hope Scholarship and Lifetime Learning tax credits can present interesting tax planning issues depending on the situation. You should remember to layer on to your tax planning the interaction between these tax credits and the income exclusion for Education IRAs. If you have an Education IRA, the tax benefits of the income exclusion versus the value of a tax credit for a particular student must be analyzed. For example, the family may want to make withdrawals from an Education IRA only in those years when the family has greatly exceeded the maximum amount of expenses eligible for tax credits.

In addition, these tax credits add another factor in determining dependency status of working students. For example, depending on the particular facts, it may be more advantageous for a working student to file his or her own tax return if the parents have income above the threshold for claiming these tax credits.

Deduction for Student Loan Interest

An above-the-line deduction (meaning it is taken when determining adjusted gross income and therefore is available for non-itemizers) is allowed for interest expense on qualified education loans. A qualified loan is a loan you took out to pay for qualified higher education expenses for the benefit of you, your spouse, or any dependent at the time the indebtedness is incurred.

The deduction is allowed only for interest paid on a qualified education loan during the first 60 months in which interest payments are required on each loan outstanding (the original loan or loans and subsequent refinancing of those loans are treated as one loan for purposes of counting the first 60 months). An individual claimed as a dependent on another taxpayer's return for the tax year cannot claim a deduction for the interest paid on a qualified education loan during such year.

The maximum deduction is phased in with a $1,500 maximum deduction in 1999, $2,000 in 2000, and $2,500 in 2001. The maximum deduction amount is not indexed for inflation.

The deduction is phased out ratably for single taxpayers with modified AGI of $40,000 to $55,000 and for couples filing jointly with modified AGI of $60,000 to $75,000.

BORROWING TO PAY FOR COLLEGE

Even the most rigorous savings and investment program may leave you short on college funds. Your child's choice of a particular school may result in higher expenses than you anticipated, or other financial obligations may diminish the funds you've set aside. As a result, you may have to consider borrowing money to close the funding gap. Under these circumstances, you have a variety of options to choose from, including:

• Qualified plan (401(k)) loans
• Home equity loans
• Life insurance loans
• Special loan programs

Qualified Plan (401(k)) Loans

Many 401(k) plans allow employees to borrow a portion of the money in them for purposes such as paying college tuition. Loan provisions vary, but many work to your benefit. A particular advantage of this option is that the interest incurred on your loan is actually paid back into your fund. This doesn't put you ahead, but you don't lose any money, either. The disadvantage of these loans is that there's no tax deduction on the interest you're paying. (For more information about 401(k) plans, see Chapter 15.)

Home Equity Loans

You can also borrow money through a home equity line of credit to pay for college costs. You would obtain this sort of loan from a bank or S&L, just as you would if borrowing money for some other purpose. The disadvantage here is that you'll be paying interest to the institution, not to yourself. The advantage, however, is that the interest you pay is tax-deductible as long as your total home equity indebtedness does not exceed $100,000.

Life Insurance Loans

In the context of college funding, life insurance can provide another financing opportunity. You can borrow from the cash surrender value of most life insurance policies without incurring any tax on the amount received. Alternatively, you can cancel the policy just when the funds are needed to pay for college; however, in this case, you may recognize taxable income. The taxable amount equals the difference between what you received and the total amount of premiums you paid into the policy.

Special Loan Programs

If you don't qualify for financial aid, consider some of the special loan programs available, including:

- Stafford loans
- Student Loan Marketing Association (Sallie Mae) loans
- ExtraCredit loans
- Educational Resources Institute loans

■ **TIP:** Review *The College Costs and Financial Aid Handbook 1999* by the College Board or *The Student Guide: Financial Aid from the U.S. Department of Education 1999–2000* for a more comprehensive list of loan programs available; call (800) 433-3243 to order the *Student Guide.* ■

Stafford Loans

Formally called guaranteed student loans, Stafford loans allow college freshmen to borrow up to $2,625. Sophomores are eligible for up to $3,500, while juniors and seniors can borrow up to $5,500 annually. Graduate students are also eligible for up to $8,500 each year. Stafford loans are available in "subsidized" and "unsubsidized" versions. Eligibility for subsidized loans depends on demonstrated financial need. Unsubsidized loans are available without proving financial need. Although the loan limits and terms are identical for subsidized and unsubsidized Stafford loans, the federal government pays the interest due on subsidized loans while the student is still in school. Also, repayment of subsidized loans is deferred until 6 months after graduation. Unsubsidized borrowers must make interest payments while in school. Alternatively, unsubsidized borrowers may defer interest payments until after graduation, when the cumulative interest becomes added to the principal of the loan.

Student Loan Marketing Association (Sallie Mae) Loans

Sallie Mae offers PLUS loans to parents regardless of financial need. The interest rate charged is variable (based on the 52-week U.S. Treasury bill rate plus 3.10%) and is capped at 10%. The yearly limit on loans is figured on the student's "cost of education" less other financial aid to be received for the school year. Deferred repayment is unavailable.

■ **TIP:** To find out more about Sallie Mae loans, call the Student Loan Marketing Association at (800) 831-LOAN. ■

ExtraCredit Loans

Sponsored through the College Board, ExtraCredit loans offer parents a line of credit for up to 100% of college costs, including tuition, fees, books, supplies, and room and board. Repayment starts when you borrow the funds. The loan's variable interest rate is adjusted quarterly to 4.5% above the prevailing rate on 13-week Treasury bills. If you choose, the loan may be available as a home equity loan. The benefit: The entire amount of interest paid on up to $100,000 of home equity loans is fully deductible.

■ **TIP:** To find out more about ExtraCredit loans, call (800) 874-9390. ■

The Educational Resources Institute (TERI) Loans
TERI loans are available through local designated banks. Loan amounts begin at $2,000 per year and can be as high as the total cost of education determined by the school. The interest rate is variable, but it is limited to the prime rate plus 1.5% to 2%. (It varies among lenders.) At the borrower's option, you can defer repayment of principal, but you must make interest payments currently and repay everything within 25 years.

■ **TIP:** To find out more about TERI loans, call (800) 255-8374. ■

PURCHASING A RENTAL PROPERTY DURING YOUR CHILD'S COLLEGE YEARS

Some parents find that if their finances permit, purchasing a rental property in their child's college neighborhood can diminish expenses and generate funds during the college years. A real estate investment of this sort offers several significant advantages.

- Your child has reliable housing.
- Your housing expenses will essentially be paid to yourself, not to someone else.
- Some of the costs (e.g., real estate taxes and mortgage interest) will be tax-deductible.
- The property may appreciate in value.
- Some properties (e.g., a duplex or triplex) may provide rental income.
- Travel costs to visit your child may be tax-deductible if you need to work on your rental property.

Many parents of college-aged children find this sort of arrangement cost-effective. Obviously, proceeding along these lines assumes sufficient income to make the investment; moreover, you must be willing to attend to the additional responsibilities of purchasing and maintaining the property. You should carefully compare the costs of maintaining the property versus simply paying rent on a property that you don't own. If the property's value doesn't actually appreciate, paying rent may end up less expensive, less risky, and less time-consuming.

OBTAINING FINANCIAL AID AND SCHOLARSHIPS

Exploring financial aid and scholarship opportunities can prove worthwhile in uncovering all possible sources of funds to help you pay for college. Even if you have a high income, don't give up entirely on applying for financial aid. You may be eligible depending on your other assets and liabilities; another factor is how many children you have attending college simultaneously. To determine whether you qualify for federal aid, you should complete the Free Application for Federal Student Aid (FAFSA) and submit it to the College Scholarship Service (CSS) for consideration. Some applicants for non-federal aid must also complete the CSS & Financial Aid Profile. Filling out the form is time consuming, but it may be well worth your time in the long run.

Without question, scholarships can be a great source of funds if your child satisfies the criteria. Some scholarships are given to students with special talents or interests; others are available to students from a specific geographical area; still others are based on grades or activities. Need isn't always a factor. Although most scholarships are highly competitive, others go unclaimed. The research you do may pay big dividends.

■ **TIP:** Helpful Telephone Numbers
College Board (212) 713-8000
College Scholarship Service (CSS) (609) 771-7725
FAFSA Questions and Information (1995–96) (319) 337-1000
FAFSA Questions and Information (1996–97) (319) 337-5615
Federal Student Aid Hotline (U.S. Dept. of Education) (800) 433-3243 ■

20

TAKING ADVANTAGE OF EMPLOYMENT BENEFITS

Second only to your private life, your job probably consumes the most time and energy of all your commitments. Your job may even demand more of your attention than other aspects of your life. As a result, it's crucial that you deal with your job in ways that maximize the financial gains you derive from your employment. Doing so effectively, however, means that you should view these financial gains as more than what salary alone provides; you must take advantage of other benefits that directly affect your overall financial health. Most of these benefits fall into one of three general categories:

- Insurance options
- Savings opportunities
- Income tax reduction vehicles

In this chapter we will focus on these three categories of benefits. For a more general overview of retirement planning issues, see Chapters 24 and 25.

INSURANCE OPTIONS

In evaluating company insurance options, it's important to make sure that you understand what benefits are available, then evaluate which of them best serve your purposes. Most companies offer their employees a fairly specific set of options to choose from. For most people, these insurance benefits fall into three categories:

- Health care
- Life insurance
- Disability insurance

Health Care Insurance Options

One of your most substantial benefits—and certainly one of the most crucial—is your health care coverage. From the standpoint of both your actual physical health *and* your financial health, your employer's health care plan can make an enormous difference to your quality of life. Consequently, you should size up the options before you and determine which suits you best.

Most employers' health care coverage is some form of:

- Fee-for-service (indemnity) program
- Health maintenance organization
- Preferred provider organization

Fee-for-Service Programs. With fee-for-service programs, you have the most flexibility in your choice of physicians and other health care providers. You receive medical treatment and submit your medical bills to the insurance company, which then pays a portion of your expenses. Some expenses you must pay 100% of the amount (deductibles and exclusions). After your deductible is met you make a copayment, which is often 20% of the amount. The degree of coverage depends on the specific plan you have joined; limitations (in the form of deductibles, copayments, stop-loss provisions, and exclusions) apply to almost all programs.

E
X
A
M
P
L
E

■ Courtney has $3,500 of medical expenses. Suppose her plan has a $500 annual deductible, after which the plan pays 80%. Courtney must make a 20% copayment. The plan's stop-loss provision provides that Courtney's maximum out-of-pocket payment is $1,000 per year. The plan pays only for reasonable and customary charges and excludes well-baby care and routine physical exams (exclusions).

Expenses	$3,500
Deductible	$ 500
20% copayment	
(20% × $3,000	
limited to the $1,000 stop loss)	500
Courtney's out-of-pocket (plus premiums)	$1,000 ■

In evaluating different fee-for-service plans, you need to project total costs under each plan: premiums or price tags for the insurance *plus* out-of-pocket costs for deductibles, copayments, and uncovered charges. Check the numbers carefully: Often the plan with the lowest deductible is the most expensive.

Health Maintenance Organizations (HMOs). HMOs provide comprehensive service by a single provider. You have fewer choices as to which physicians you can use and whether you can use specialists without prior approval. But costs are often lower than for fee-for-service plans. Although HMOs are increasingly common, they are most abundant in urban areas, so that ease of access should be just one factor in deciding whether to join one.

Preferred Provider Organizations (PPOs). Offering a compromise between fee-for-service programs and HMOs, PPOs offer you more latitude in choosing your physicians plus discounted fees for using health care providers with whom the PPO has made special arrangements.

It's worth noting that the issue of finding the best health care option often leads to a quandary. On the one hand, most employers will offer you several options to choose from. On the other hand, the list of options may be fairly limited. You may be able to select from programs A, B, and C—with a few variations for each program—yet you probably won't have any leeway beyond those choices. It's true that you could obtain individual health care policies, but these are prohibitively expensive for most people. The reality of the situation is that the health care plan that you choose at work is almost certain to provide the extent of your health care coverage. Choose carefully. For help in sorting through the options, contact your company's personnel department or employee benefits department. (Chapter 8 includes an overview of health care plans.)

Life Insurance Options

The life insurance coverage you obtain on the job is probably a supplement to policies you already own. (For more information on life insurance, see Chapter 7.) Options will be either group term insurance or group universal life insurance.

Group Term Life Insurance. The most common life insurance option that employers offer is group term coverage. Term insurance of this sort has two main advantages. One is that it's generally inexpensive and convenient. The second advantage is that the first $50,000 of coverage of employer-provided group term is tax-free to the employee. As a result of these two advantages, you may be able to obtain substantial life insurance coverage for a relatively small expense.

That being said, it's important for you to consider two other aspects of the situation.

First, *competitive pricing*. Obviously, group term insurance isn't free; the cost will be deducted from your monthly paycheck. Could you obtain more competitive coverage on your own? Perhaps. The answer to that question depends on what your employer charges for the coverage and what you might find from another carrier. It is a good idea to shop around and compare the cost of an individually purchased policy with the cost of the group insurance.

Second, *portability*. In addition to the issue of price, you should consider what happens if you leave your job. Generally, you'll have the right to convert the group *term* coverage to an individual *whole life* policy, but perhaps not on as attractive a basis as you'd do on your own. Consider your needs and preferences for the long term; you may be better off to purchase an individual policy that will stay in force regardless of where you're employed.

Group Universal Life Insurance. Many employers now offer group universal life policies. (For a discussion of universal life insurance, see Chapter 7.) Policies of this sort have several distinct advantages.

First, *flexibility*. One of the most appealing features of universal life is its flexibility. Group universal life policies typically offer all of the flexibility that individual universal life coverage provides, including flexibility in determining premium payments and the policy's face amount. Universal life policies, unlike term insurance, offer the opportunity to save money within the policy: cash value. The cash value builds up within the policy at a tax-free rate and you can borrow these cash values from the policy.

Second, *competitive rates*. Group universal life policies are often very competitive with quality individual universal life coverage. Other than the premiums themselves, you're likely to pay only administrative charges and a premium tax. There are usually no commissions or surrender charges, so you'll have more cash value in the early years than with many individual products. As a result, group programs of this sort can compete with individual universal life policies. Another reason group universal is attractive is that your own employer will be monitoring the insurer, thus keeping rates on a fairly even keel.

Third, *portability*. Unlike most group term policies, group universal policies are portable. When you leave your current job, you can take the coverage with you as a universal life policy, though the rates for the insurance will often eventually increase as a result of your leaving your employer's group.

Disability Insurance Options

Many firms offer group disability insurance. If your employer does, you should consider this kind of coverage very carefully, since it is a crucial kind of insurance that most people neglect to carry. Group disability insurance is also often cheaper than individual coverage. (See Chapter 8 for more about disability insurance.) However, it's important to realize that your options will be limited and the group coverage itself is generally inferior to individual coverage. For example, the policy might not provide you coverage until age 65 if you're partially disabled. Or it might not give you a cost-of-living increase to benefits. Benefit payments will be fully taxable unless you pay the premium with after-tax dollars. You may have few choices in what sorts of coverage you can obtain.

If you're lucky, you'll have the option of either short- or long-term policies. Short-term coverage generally functions as a kind of sick leave from your job. By contrast, long-term disability coverage serves to protect a portion of your salary—generally, 60% of your compensation up to a certain amount per month—between the time at which you become disabled and age 65. Most advisors would recommend that you seriously consider buying the maximum amount of disability insurance that your employer offers, and if you're offered the choice, it's often wise to pay the premium yourself with after-tax dollars.

Other limitations on group disability coverage are that it may not be convertible to an attractive individual policy if you leave, and it also may lack certain options you want, such as residual benefits or cost of living riders.

Other Insurance Options

A few employers are now offering long-term care insurance—policies that pay your expenses if you require nursing home or convalescent home care following an accident or illness. If you have an opportunity to obtain coverage of this sort, you should think seriously about taking it. You'll need to consider whether long-term care insurance is your *priority* or whether some other goal—such as retirement or education funding—is a higher priority for you at this time.

Are Company Benefits Enough?

Regardless of the benefits that your employer offers, you should do some needs analysis to determine if you're properly covered. The two big concerns here are retirement planning and overall insurance coverage. As noted earlier, in Chapters 24 and 25 we explore retirement planning in detail. As for insurance coverage, your two biggest concerns are life insurance and disability insurance. (Health care coverage is obviously of paramount importance; however, as noted earlier, you're unlikely to be able to afford the high costs of an individual health care policy, so in many respects the issue is a moot point.)

Life Insurance. Is your life insurance coverage adequate? Don't assume that you've covered your family well enough through group policies alone: Most provide only a foundation with additional coverage needed. If you don't have individual term or cash value insurance, you should investigate the possibility of obtaining sufficient coverage in the form of individual insurance.

Disability Insurance. As we noted in Chapter 8, many Americans ignore the need for disability insurance. You may or may not have the option of disability coverage through your work; if not, however, consider obtaining an individual policy, ideally to meet the 60% to 70% of income threshold that most insurance companies will allow.

Savings Opportunities

The savings opportunities that your job may provide can be extremely beneficial. The specific options available will vary from employer to employer. Whatever your particular options, however, you should make sure to take full advantage of them, as the money you save by these means may provide the foundation not only for your retirement fund but also for attaining other financial planning objectives. Some options may also provide income tax benefits—a situation we'll discuss shortly. With or without income tax benefits, however, the savings opportunities are typically beneficial because they provide disciplined savings. It's hard to spend money you don't receive because it has been contributed to a company-sponsored savings vehicle already.

Here are the savings opportunities we'll consider:

- Contributory company retirement plans
- Company stock purchase plans
- U.S. Series EE bonds
- Credit unions

Contributory Company Retirement Plans

Contributory company retirement plans are plans that companies set up to enable you to contribute some portion of your salary to fund your retirement. 401(k) and 403(b) plans are the most prevalent types (see Chapter 2 for more information). Think of these plans as long-term retirement plans—not savings plans (despite their names) for a second home, a dream vacation or even a child's college. These plans may limit the amount you may contribute, but they may also provide income tax benefits. In some plans, the employer may match the employee's contribution with its own contribution. Thus 401(k)s and 403(b)s provide strong incentives to save for retirement. In addition, 401(k)s and 403(b)s often offer specific additional features, including:

- Flexible investment options—you can make investment choices about portions of your own portfolio
- Loan provisions
- Special withdrawal arrangements

After-Tax Contributions. In addition to contributions to plans such as 401(k)s and 403(b)s, which provide a tax benefit at the time of making the contribution, your employer may allow you to contribute additional funds to these or other qualified retirement plans. Making after-tax contributions is an attractive way to invest more money for your retirement.

Company Stock Purchase Plans

Some companies offer programs to encourage their employees to purchase company stock. These programs can benefit the employer and employee alike because employees frequently perform better when they have an ownership interest in the company. The program may be one in which employees can simply purchase the stock directly from the company without incurring any commission, or it may be a formalized plan in which employees also receive an income tax benefit. The two plans we discuss in which there is an opportunity to buy more stock less expensively are *ESOPs* and *ESPPs*.

Employee Stock Ownership Plans (ESOPs). ESOPs and other stock bonus plans are qualified plans designed to invest primarily in employer stock. Similar to 401(k) plans, these plans can allow employees to contribute to the plan up to an annual maximum limitation. The benefit of purchasing employer stock through such contributions is that, up to an annual maximum amount, the amount of money spent to buy the stock won't be subject to income tax until the stock is distributed from the plan. The result: You can buy more stock.

E X A M P L E

■ If you can afford to save $100 per month and you want to invest that sum in your company's stock, you'd be able to buy more shares of stock through an ESOP than you would if buying the stock outright. Assume that your income tax bracket is 28%. The stock price is $20 per share. If you buy the stock outright with $100 of your monthly paycheck, you'd purchase five shares each month. However, you'd have the same amount of spendable cash each month and be able to buy seven shares per month if you buy the stock through contributions to an ESOP. The extra two shares are essentially *loaned* to you by the government, interest-free, and you won't have to pay back this "loan" until you receive a distribution from the ESOP. ■

ESOP distributions are taxed similarly to other qualified plan distributions with a potential benefit: Tax on the capital gain can be further deferred until the stock is actually sold and, if it is held more than one year, it will be taxed at the potentially lower capital gains rate.

Employee Stock Purchase Plans (ESPPs). Employee stock purchase plans are stock option plans that provide employees with favorable tax consequences. Since these plans are relatively cumbersome for employers and may present securities problems for smaller companies, they aren't commonly available. However, if your employer makes the plan available, it may be a very beneficial way for you to acquire your employer's stock.

These plans often allow employees the opportunity to buy their employer's stock at a reduced price up to certain limitations. The ESPP gives the employee the right to buy the company stock on a future date for an amount that's no higher than the current price of the stock. If the stock price increases between the time this right is granted and the time the employee purchases the stock, the employee can buy the stock at the lower value. Moreover, even though the employee receives a benefit at the time of purchase, he or she will not be subject to tax on the benefits received from this plan until the stock is sold. If the stock is held long enough, some or all of the benefit will receive beneficial capital gains treatment when taxed.

E
X
A
M
P
L
E

■ Assume that your company's ESPP provides you with the opportunity to buy your employer's stock on December 31 each year for the price the stock sold for on the prior January 1. Furthermore, assume that the stock price is $8 on January 1 and $10 on December 31, and that you choose to contribute $100 per month to the ESPP. Your $1,200 will buy you 150 shares of stock under this plan on December 31. If you had not participated in the ESPP, your $1,200 would have bought you only 120 shares on December 31. The extra 30 shares you receive from the ESPP aren't subject to tax until you sell the stock. ■

Some employers' ESPPs also allow their employees to purchase the stock for less than what the stock sold at on the day this right was granted, up to 15% lower. The result: You'd get over 56 extra shares in this example if the ESPP enabled you to buy the stock at a price equal to 85% of the January 1 stock price. Again, this benefit isn't taxed until the stock is sold.

U.S. Series EE Bonds

As noted in Chapters 3 and 17, U.S. Series EE bonds are cash investments that can provide relatively high interest rates and distinct tax advantages. Interest grows tax-deferred and its eventual payment is exempt from state and local taxes. Sales may be exempt from federal tax in certain situations when used to pay for tuition. For more information on Series EE bonds, see *The Ernst & Young Tax Guide,* published annually by John Wiley & Sons, Inc.

Many employers support programs where employees can elect to have the company purchase Series EE savings bonds for time through automatic payroll deductions. Their chief advantage is disciplined savings, though you can arrange to have automatic payments made from your bank account into a wide selection of mutual funds and other investments. The reason is that instead of receiving your entire paycheck, you receive some portion (as little as $25) of your paycheck in the form of a bond that can't be redeemed for 6 months. In addition, this employee savings arrangement enables employees to buy an investment easily that is affordable, safe, and flexible. Call 1-800-US BONDS for more information.

Credit Unions

Similarly, some companies provide their employees with the ability to make deposits to a savings account at their credit union or another financial institution (e.g., mutual funds) through automatic payroll deductions. Although savings accounts at credit unions don't provide tax benefits, they provide employees with safety of principal, an immediate and high degree of liquidity, and frequently, relatively high rates of return. Credit unions are banking cooperatives that operate for the benefit of their members. The members are the stockholders of a nonprofit corporation; for this reason, any surplus generated is paid to account holders as dividends or rebates of loan interest each fiscal year.

Income Tax Reduction Vehicles

In addition to providing access to beneficial insurance and savings opportunities, many employers provide their employees with the ability to reduce their income tax burdens. These income tax reduction vehicles typically allow you to spend a whole dollar to pay for a dollar's worth of the item covered, as opposed to having first to pay income tax on that dollar. For example, if an expense costs $100 and you pay income tax at the 28% marginal tax bracket (your marginal tax bracket is the tax rate on your next dollar of income), you would have to earn about $139 to have $100 to pay for that item. If, instead, your employer offers a program that enables you to buy that item for $100 pretax, you would be better off by $39.

As you can see, the ability to make investments and/or to use pretax dollars through your employer to pay for some of your expenses can be very beneficial. Unfortunately, only a few of your expenses and investments can be paid for in this way.

We have already discussed the income tax benefits associated with making contributions to 401(k) plans, 403(b) plans, employer stock ownership plans (ESOPs), and employee stock purchase plans (ESPPs). To the extent that these plans are available through your employer, you should consider participating in them to take advantage of their income savings benefits. Here are typical tax-advantaged comployee benefits:

- Disability insurance
- Health insurance plans
- Group term insurance (up to $50,000)
- Dependent care and health care "spending" or flexible reimbursement plans

To summarize: Your job may provide you with the ability to acquire the insurance coverage you need more cheaply, as well as the ability to more easily meet your tax and financial planning objectives.

SEPARATING FROM A JOB

Separating from a job, either voluntarily through early retirement or a company buy-out, or involuntarily due to a layoff, is an increasing concern to many Americans.

Whether you are considering a voluntary separation or have been notified of an involuntary layoff, you need to spend some time creating a rational financial plan. Such planning can help to ease your transition into early retirement, starting your own business or freelance/consulting practice, or job hunting.

When separating from a job, there are four key questions you need to ask yourself:

1. What changes do I need to make in my expenses, assets, and debts to compensate for the period of time when I will have little or no earned income?
2. What are the tax and financial considerations of the separation offer and the distribution from my retirement plans?
3. What kind of investment program should I have for my plan distributions?
4. Do I need to replace or supplement my health, disability, or life insurance?

Assets

During the transition period, you need added liquidity in order to provide "transition pay." To accomplish this, you need to have a cash reserve to cover planned expenses, and extra cash to meet extraordinary expenses. You should probably adopt a less risky investment profile, possibly taking such steps as shifting money from small-capitalization, growth-oriented mutual funds to equity and income or high income funds. You may want to take gains from equities when you can and shift the money into money market funds or staggered certificates of deposit.

If you find you need cash you may also want to consider selling any "luxury" assets, such as a boat, recreational vehicle, or a vacation home, but with adequate planning you may not have to do this.

Liabilities

Restructuring debt is the name of the game on the liabilities side of your balance sheet. You may want to refinance an old mortgage, both to reduce the interest rate if that is possible and to free up cash. Or you could take out a home equity loan but keep in mind that you will have to come up with cash to make the home equity loan payments. In either case, the first proceeds from this new loan should go to pay off any consumer debt, such as credit cards, car loans, or personal loans.

This is because both mortgage debt and home equity debt are usually tax deductible, while consumer debt is never deductible.

Tax and Financial Considerations of Retirement Plan Distributions

The key question you have to ask yourself here is whether to leave your retirement funds in the company's plan or take a rollover into your own IRA.

Assuming you choose to take a rollover, it is not taxable if it is paid from the trustee of your company's plan directly to the trustee of an IRA you establish for the purpose of accepting the rollover. The IRA would be tax deferred, and distributions made at retirement would be fully taxable. You could begin taking distribution any time after age 59½, and you must begin taking distribution by age 70½.

Any amount not rolled over is subject to tax, at your federal tax bracket, and subject to a 10% early distribution tax if you are under age 55 when you separated from service. For instance, if you have $40,000 in your company's 401(k), and elect to roll over $30,000 and take $10,000 in cash distribution, you would pay a $1,000 early withdrawal penalty plus your applicable federal income tax on the cash distribution.

If you need to begin drawing from your retirement plan savings, you can avoid the 10% withdrawal penalty by taking a distribution in *substantial equal payments* over your life expectancy. This is complex and you should probably consult a professional to help you work through it; there is a discussion in *The Ernst & Young Tax Guide* and *Ernst & Young's Retirement Planning Guide*.

Insurance

On employment separation, you need to consider your insurance needs carefully.

If your compensation benefit package included health insurance, the federal law known as COBRA allows you to purchase the insurance previously paid for by your company for up to 18 months. Many insurance carriers also allow you to convert from a company-paid plan to an individual plan. If you have a standard fee-for-service plan, you may want to increase your deductible to reduce premiums, or you may want to switch to a less expensive HMO-type plan.

You can take distributions from your IRA to pay health insurance premiums while you're unemployed without being subject to 10% premature distribution penalty tax.

Your group term life insurance policy may allow you to convert to an individual term policy or even an individual whole life or universal life policy.

If your group policy was universal, you may want to reduce the amount you contribute each year, or eliminate it altogether during the transition and allow your built-up cash value to pay the premiums. You also may be able to borrow against your cash value for short-term cash needs.

Maintain your individual policy. Do not let policies lapse. If you have whole life policies you can use the annual dividends to reduce or even offset the premium. If you have excess dividends, you might want to use them to purchase additional term life. If you need to, borrow against the cash value. You can reduce to a minimum the payments necessary to keep any individual universal policies in force; or let the cash value pay the premiums.

See if you can convert a company-paid disability policy into one you own individually if you are moving into self-employment as a consultant or freelancer.

21

Starting Your Own Business

One can easily make a case that the United States has always been a nation of entrepreneurs. In addition to seeking political and religious freedom, many immigrants to this country have sought opportunities to work for themselves rather than for others; the traditions of self-reliant merchants and innovators have been strong within our culture. These traditions vary and change over the years, and large organizations are certainly a major cultural force as well. Even so, the entrepreneurial option remains attractive to many Americans.

If you've considered starting your own business—or perhaps going into business for yourself in some other way—you have many options to choose from. You can take your own idea, obtain funding, organize a company, and seek success on your own. You can buy someone else's existing business and run it yourself. You can purchase a franchise with a recognizable product, existing supply network, and uniform business procedures. You can become an independent consultant. No matter which route you take, however, you need to proceed carefully and consider all aspects of the situation before you commit yourself.

To this end, in this chapter we explore the following aspects of going into business for yourself:

- Determining how to start
- Creating a business plan
- Deciding which business structure makes sense
- Deciding whether (and how) to use advisors
- Determining capital needs and capital sources
- Using your home as your office
- Hiring employees—and dealing with their costs

DETERMINING HOW TO START

Even if you have a strong inclination toward going into business for yourself, you may be unsure how to start. You may be unclear about your options. You may be uncertain about the sequence of events to follow as you get yourself organized. You may even be unsure if you should be an entrepreneur at all. In fact, it's that final issue that you should address first, so let's examine it before proceeding to other topics.

Are You an Entrepreneur?

Although entrepreneurship has been a powerful tradition in America for hundreds of years, it's not a way of life that suits everyone. More problematically, it's a way of life that lends itself to certain false assumptions. The powerful image of the entrepreneur in American culture makes it difficult for many people to distinguish myth from reality. Thus the earlier you determine if the day-to-day substance of entrepreneurial life truly suits you, the better off you'll be.

Here are some myths about entrepreneurship, along with the realities of the situation:

Myth 1: When you run your own business, you don't have to answer to a boss. You have complete autonomy.

Reality: You may not answer to a boss, but you must still answer to your clients or customers—many of whom may be at least as demanding as a boss.

Myth 2: Running your own business is easier than working for a corporation.

Reality: Most entrepreneurs work even harder than they did when employed by someone else. One reason is that they themselves are in charge now; another is that they're often personally obsessed with the tasks at hand, hence more driven than they were when responding to someone else's priorities.

Myth 3: Becoming an entrepreneur is a cut-and-dried decision.

Reality: Most entrepreneurs are initially uncertain about whether to start their own business. They perceive good reasons to proceed and good reasons to choose some other expression of their talents.

How can you find out whether you have what it takes to start your own business? Perhaps the most systematic way is to seek guidance from one of the firms that offer assistance to people making a transition from the corporate world to self-employment. Firms of this kind provide testing, counseling, and planning that can help you decide that entrepreneurship either does or doesn't meet your needs. If you prefer to take a more self-guided route, however, consider the exercises below.

EXERCISE 1: EVALUATING WHY ENTREPRENEURSHIP INTERESTS YOU

What follows are some of the statements that may explain why entrepreneurship interests you. All of these are statements that people commonly make regarding why they want to go into business for themselves. There are no "right" or "wrong" statements; the goal is simply to clarify your reasons for becoming an entrepreneur.

Check all that apply:

____ You prefer to be your own boss.
____ You feel dissatisfied in a corporate environment.
____ You've determined that your opportunities for advancement are limited in your current position.
____ You have a business idea that you want to explore.
____ You want to change your goals.
____ You're tired of hunting for jobs in the marketplace.
____ You want to take advantage of an opportunity that has arisen.
____ You want to avoid relocating in another geographical area to pursue your current occupation.
____ You need to express your creativity.
____ You believe that you can make more money by running your own company.
____ You need employment that's more personally satisfying.
____ You want to make good use of a financial windfall.
____ You want to see if you can succeed on your own.

Now review the checklist that you've just filled out. Select the three statements you've checked that most fully express your interest in entrepreneurship. Prioritize them from the most personally important to the least.

EXERCISE 2: EVALUATING HOW YOUR LIFE WILL CHANGE

How will your life change if you run your own business? Consider the factors listed below. Each factor involves a dimension of your life that will change during and after the transition to self-employment. On a sheet of paper, note what changes you anticipate in each factor.

- Time
- Sense of personal identity
- Lifestyle
- Family relationships
- Other personal relationships
- Business relationships
- Accountability
- Stress level
- Reward/risk balance
- Support system
- Other

If possible, discuss these issues with your family, business associates, and friends. Given what you've noted here, what do you perceive to be the greatest change to your life if you become an entrepreneur?

EXERCISE 3: EVALUATING FINANCIAL RESOURCES

Becoming an entrepreneur invariably involves a significant financial investment—almost certainly your own, and probably someone else's as well. In a later section of this chapter we provide an overview of funding sources. As you decide for or against running your own business, however, there's another issue you must face: financial resources for the transition to self-employment. You should assess this issue by answering the following questions:

- How much money do you currently have?
- What are the sources of this money (your own income, your spouse's income, severance pay, unemployment benefits, etc.)?
- What are your current assets?
- Which of these are liquid and which are illiquid?
- What is the available credit on your credit cards?
- What other sources do you have for funding the transition between your current occupation and running your own business?
- What are your outstanding debts?
- How much money do you need to meet fixed and variable expenses during your transitional phase?
- How many of these expenses are discretionary?
- What insurance (life, health, disability, property–casualty) do you have in force? Are the policies portable?
- How will you maintain insurance coverage during your transitional phase?

Answering these questions will provide an overview to your immediate financial situation. If you decide more conclusively to pursue self-employment, however, you should take the task a step further and perform a complete cash flow analysis. Chapter 1 contains a worksheet for this purpose.

Considering Your Options

As an entrepreneur, you have four basic options:

- Starting your own business
- Purchasing an existing business
- Becoming an independent consultant
- Purchasing a franchise

Each of these options has advantages and disadvantages, so we'll review them in general terms.

Starting Your Own Business. The most common form that starting your own business will take is probably that of producing and selling products or services. This can mean anything from manufacturing computer supplies to selling ice cream at the local mall. To succeed in this kind of venture, you must be as enthusiastic about people as about the product or service you're selling.

Advantages. The typical positive factors in starting your own business are:

- Being your own boss
- Taking your idea from inception to successful completion
- Having extensive or even total input into the process
- Reaping the fruits of your labor—possible wealth and fame
- Expressing your prior knowledge of the field or endeavor

Disadvantages. The drawbacks of this form of entrepreneurship are:

- Working in relative isolation
- Carrying the full burden of responsibility
- Lacking a built-in support system
- Learning mostly or entirely on the job
- Weathering cash flow fluctuations
- Accepting total responsibility for the business—which usually translates into reduced personal time

Purchasing an Existing Business. If you like the idea of running your own business but don't wish to endure the rigors of starting it yourself, you can consider buying an existing enterprise. This allows you not only to circumvent the startup stage; you may also benefit from ongoing advantages.

A history of profits, a network of relationships with suppliers and distributors, a customer base, an already known location—all of these are aspects of buying an existing business that may make this option attractive.

Advantages. The additional advantages of this arrangement are:

- Having an ongoing relationship with lenders and investors
- Earning a salary through ongoing cash flow
- Limiting the need for intial investment
- Having the possibility of seller financing
- Gaining the seller's assistance in a transitional phase, including training
- Having a chance to size up the history of the business, which can reveal "real" books and records, not just projected numbers

Disadvantages. The drawbacks of purchasing an existing business are:

- Committing time to finding the right company to buy
- Avoiding the risk of overpayment at the time of purchase
- Dealing with the potential for a slower growth rate
- Lacking the fun of creating your own business
- Lacking the opportunity to "phase yourself in"

Becoming an Independent Consultant. Independent consultants serve a wide variety of roles within the corporate world, as well as in the legal, medical, academic, and political spheres. Consultants provide information or advice that can influence a person, group, or organization, but they lack a mandate to change the client directly. Despite the ambiguities inherent in this role, the number of consultants in the United States has grown dramatically since the 1980s. Given the trend of corporate downsizing and hiring of nonstaff contractors, it seems likely that an increasing number of people will position themselves as consultants.

Advantages. The main advantages of being a consultant are:

- Taking advantage of the general trend toward corporate downsizing and reliance on external staff on a temporary basis
- Eliminating the likelihood of becoming enmeshed in company politics and procedural red tape
- Limiting your capital investment and overhead expenses
- Allowing flexibility for controlling your time
- Lacking a mandatory retirement age
- Having the potential for high annual income

Disadvantages. The drawbacks to being a consultant are:

- Competing with the large number of other consultants
- Lacking a built-in support system
- Lacking an organizational authority to mediate or impose solutions
- Lacking a schedule or set routine
- Lacking a clear dividing line between work and leisure time
- Dealing with irregular cash flow

Purchasing a Franchise. Finally, you have the alternative of purchasing a franchise. This course of action involves a legal arrangement in which you gain access to products, services, trademarks, and business concepts. Ideally, this arrangement allows you access to a customer base that responds to the products or services as a known quantity. On the other hand, purchasing a franchise allows you considerably less latitude in the products or services you sell and how you present them to your customers. Franchising has consistently grown at a rate that outstrips the American economy's general growth rate, and this growth seems likely to continue.

Advantages. The positive factors in purchasing a franchise are:

- Using a recognized name, trademark, and business appearance
- Gaining the benefits of the franchisor's previous track record
- Having the advantages of standardized products or services
- Benefiting from proven concepts, training, approaches, or methods
- Lacking the need to come up with your own business idea
- Gaining access to packaged financing

Disadvantages. The downsides to owning a franchise are:

- Limiting your flexibility as to products, suppliers, operating budget, and advertising budget
- Risking the consequences if the franchisor has exaggerated the success or benefits of the firm's approaches
- Dealing with the consequences of litigation against the franchisor
- Dealing with the need to protect the franchise locations

Selecting the Right Option

Many people who go into business for themselves start with a clear sense of what they want to accomplish and how they want to proceed. It's possible that you are among the entrepreneurs whose image of the task is so clear-cut. If the situation isn't so obvious, however, you're probably in the majority. This doesn't mean that self-employment isn't in your future; rather, it means that you need to sort through your options more systematically. One way to do so involves reviewing the advantages and disadvantages listed for each of the four options above. Here's one way to proceed:

- Note which pros and cons seem most compelling, given your own personal situation.
- Try "weighting" the pros and cons you note on a scale of 1 to 5 (with 1 = least compelling and 5 = most compelling).
- Total the weighted pros and cons to see which options seem most and least persuasive.

CREATING A BUSINESS PLAN

If you're like many entrepreneurs, you'd probably rather be on the battlefield—the cutting edge of business—than behind the lines planning your assault. In addition, you may have difficulty articulating the business concepts that may have already become second nature to you. One of the most difficult chores you face may therefore be that of preparing and writing a business plan. No matter how difficult this task may be, however, a plan is an absolute necessity for your business.

Why You Need a Business Plan

A business plan serves three functions.

- *First, it helps you develop ideas about how you should conduct your business*. It's a chance to refine strategies and "make mistakes on paper" rather than in the real world by examining the company from all perspectives, such as marketing, finance, and operations.
- *Second, it's a retrospective tool you can use to assess your company's actual performance over time*. For example, you can use the financial part of a business plan as the basis for an operating budget and as a way of seeing how closely the business sticks to that budget.
- *Third, it's a tool to help you raise money*. Most lenders or investors won't put money into a business without seeing a business plan. A large part of the process of raising money involves your preparing a plan and then letting potential lenders examine it closely.

If you were to present an idea to a commercial lender or a potential investor without a business plan, that lender or investor would ask you to come back only after you've drafted a plan to present. Worse yet, the potential source of money might not even take you seriously or ask you back at all. Given the importance of a convincing plan, you may wish to seek professional assistance in the effort of writing it. A consultant or accountant may be a suitable source of help. Whatever your means of producing the plan, however, *you must prepare a suitable document if you expect your venture and your funding to be taken seriously. The Ernst & Young Business Plan Guide* provides a comprehensive overview of a business plan, as well as an annotated model business plan.

The Nature of a Business Plan

A business plan is a document designed to map out a company's course over a specific period of time. Many companies write annual business plans, which focus intently on the coming 12 months and give more general attention about the following 1 to 4 years. Few business plans project beyond 5 years.

Because the business plan is a hybrid document—part pragmatic projection and part sales tool—it must walk a fine line in content and tone of presentation. The information must be accurate, yet it must convey a sense of optimism and excitement. Although risks must be acknowledged, you shouldn't dwell on them. The tone should be businesslike. The people who read business plans are practical people. They'll respond to a positive, interesting presentation; they'll be turned off by one that's vague, long-winded, or not carefully considered and organized. An imaginative (but not flamboyant) presentation style may work to your advantage. Even minor errors in spelling and grammar may work against you—and therefore against your enterprise as well. Have someone skilled in this area review the plan to eliminate these minor annoyances, since they may have a disproportionate impact on the reader.

Three specific purposes that your business plan will serve:

- A planning document
- A retrospective yardstick
- A financing tool

Purpose 1: Your Business Plan as a Planning Document. For a startup company, the business plan is often your first crack at strategic planning. For an ongoing business, the business plan serves to develop consensus and consistency throughout the company. Writing the plan can involve nearly everyone managing a small business; it's a chance for them to create their vision for the company.

The business plan is also an implementation tool. You can use it to test theories of how you should run your company and to calculate possible outcomes. You can then use the plan to check those ideas as they're implemented to see if the projections were accurate. This step provides an early warning system and allows you time to correct problems. The truth is that many of the questions you need to ask when preparing a business plan must be answered successfully—or at least put in the "can't be answered at this time but must be monitored" file. Otherwise, your company will have far less chance for success. Neglecting to ask these questions in the business plan stage may be fatal.

E X A M P L E

■ The entrepreneurs starting a small specialty chemical company forgot to ask about the impact of federal environmental regulations before starting up their business. The company went into production in 1983, anticipating the first sales in 1984. Management hired personnel, opened an office, and began marketing. With the meter running—the company was incurring significant overhead—the company finally discovered that it would need the federal Environmental Protection Agency (EPA) to review its products before it could start marketing them. The company nearly bled itself dry maintaining its facilities and personnel while its product was tied up in review. This particular company made it, but others aren't so lucky. ■

Purpose 2: Your Business Plan as a Retrospective Yardstick. The second major purpose of your business plan is to be a benchmark against which you measure the company's actual performance. Last year's business plan can tell you whether your strategy and implementation were effective or ineffective. Examining the actual performance of your business against the plan can identify strengths and organizational weaknesses that separate strategy from effective implementation.

You can use your business plan's financial section as an objective, concrete means of monitoring the business's performance. Your initial financial projections became the basis for the budget under which the company tried to operate; now deviations from that budget will point out areas where you misjudged either the necessary resources or the controls during the period the business plan covered.

Other people besides yourself will use the business plan as a monitoring tool. Financial sources—both lenders and investors—will note deviations between the plan and your company's actual performance; they'll also ask why those deviations occurred. This is one of the reasons why you shouldn't hype your business in the plan you've written. Try to make realistic projections. If you aspire to being superhuman and then fail to meet your projections, you'll end up painting yourself into a corner. A little more modesty will produce projections that are much more easily attained—or even exceeded—thereby keeping lenders happy and still providing investors with a healthy rate of return.

Purpose 3: Your Business Plan as a Financing Tool. The third major purpose for writing a business plan is the one that most people think of first: helping to raise cash. Without an effective business plan, you're unlikely to obtain the funding you need to start your business.

There's another side to this situation, however. Viewing your business plan exclusively or primarily as a sales tool to raise cash can get you into trouble. This emphasis can lead you to write a hyped-up plan that lacks the objectivity needed for the plan to fulfill its other two roles. In fact, it's better to write an objective business plan and fail to obtain financing because your business is a bad risk than to hypnotize yourself into underestimating the risk. Hyped projections in your plan present a sham—deliberately or not—to funding sources; as a result, your house of cards may come tumbling down later. Bankruptcy court is a genuine possibility following this course of action. Avoid it if at all possible. For this reason, it's in this task of raising cash that your business plan walks a fine line between providing an objective analysis of the company's future and providing a sales document.

Your plan's ultimate test is how much interest it can generate from reviewers in as little time as possible. In reality, the business plan is really only the start of the money-raising process. It's the first in a series of documents the reviewer will receive. If it conveys the company's basic goals and methods in a clear, readable, and acceptable form, the reviewers will pay attention. If they want more information, reviewers won't be shy about asking for more detail.

Here are two aspects of this situation to keep in mind:

The plan is a negotiating tool. When preparing a plan, you should be specific about what you want from the lender or investor but be vague about what you're willing to give up. This puts the ball in the investor's or lender's court. By holding back a card or two (without being misleading), you'll allow the reviewer to establish the first negotiating point.

The plan is a confidential document. You should distribute it only to those who need to see it, such as members of the management team, professional advisors, and potential sources of money. Those who receive copies of the plan should sign confidentiality forms (see below). There's no reason to produce a large quantity of copies. Neither is there reason to produce glossy bound volumes. A glitzy document will make updating the plan difficult and expensive to update, and it will imply that many people were seeing the plan. (Sources of financing often get a queasy feeling if they think a plan is being "shopped around.") You should initially send your plan to at least 3 but fewer than 10 possible sources of financing. Plans should never be sent to professional sources sequentially. You'll end up waiting for a reply from each before moving to the next—an approach that could postpone success for years.

The plan should go only to carefully selected sources. Do thorough research about who may be interested in your field. Some banks lend only in certain geographic areas; some investors invest only in certain types of businesses. Within a given organization, there may be several people or departments that deal with business plans. They may also be divided geographically, by business group, or in another way, so make sure you get your plan to the right group—and ideally to the right person.

Your Business Plan's Structure

Business plans follow a standardized formal structure that reviewers will expect in any document you submit. Within this structure there's room for creativity, but you should adhere to the standard form to avoid confusing your reviewers, thus diminishing your chances for success.

You should divide your business plan into sections, not chapters. Here's the standard sequence and what each section contains:

- Table of Contents
- Executive Summary
- General Company Description
- Products and Services
- Marketing Plan
- Operational Plan
- Management and Organization
- Structure and Capitalization
- Financial Plan
- Attachments:
  - Résumés
  - Competitive Analyses
  - Confidentiality Agreements
  - Sales/Profit Analyses

Table of Contents. The table of contents serves the same function as a table of contents for a book. It doesn't need to be detailed or to show the exact page where each section of the plan begins. On the contrary, new pages or sections may be added in updates—thus numbering could be a problem.

Executive Summary. An executive summary captures and presents succinctly the essence of the report. It's essentially a capsule version of the entire plan.

General Company Description. The body of the business plan begins with a general description of the company. This description should take no more than a few pages and should present the fundamental activities and nature of the company. A high level of detail isn't appropriate in this section, since you'll have the opportunity to offer further detail in the rest of the proposal. You should, however, indicate:

- What sort of company you're proposing (manufacturer, retailer, or service business)
- What customer base you propose to serve
- What you'll provide to your customer base, and how you'll do it
- Where you're located
- Where you'll do business (locally, nationally, or internationally)
- What stage your company has reached
- What your business objectives are

Products and Services. You should express the nature of your products and services in a clear and simple fashion. The description generally includes:

- Physical description
- Use and appeal
- Stage of development

Marketing Plan. The marketing section is one of the most important parts of a business plan because it communicates most directly the nature of the intended business and the manner in which that business will be able to succeed. Specifically, the marketing section explains how you intend to manipulate and react to market conditions to generate sales. You must prepare a marketing plan that is both interesting and thought provoking. The plan can't simply explain a concept; it must sell a prospective business as an attractive investment opportunity, a good credit risk, or a valued vendor of a product or service.

Among the important issues that your marketing plan must address are:

- Market definition and opportunity
- Competition
- Marketing strategy

- Market research
- Sales forecasts
- Backup/support

Operational Plan. One set of fundamental issues that a business plan must address is how the business will create its products and services. Questions that this part of the plan must answer include:

- What is the stage of product development?
- What is the general approach to manufacturing?
- What are the sources of raw materials?
- What processes will be used in manufacturing?
- What are the labor requirements?
- How will suppliers and vendors be used?
- What external influences (e.g., govermental regulations) affect the company, and how will these issues be addressed?

Because the business plan has the objectives of both planning and raising capital, you may have some difficulty striking the proper balance between sophistication and simplicity in explaining the sometimes complicated manufacturing and process technologies. However, the operations of the business may constitute an important part of its appeal. This argues for a relatively detailed presentation. Your task, therefore, is to find a happy medium between an overly technical, complex presentation (which might make the reviewers' task difficult) and a presentation that's overly simplistic. As a sales tool for external review, the content of the operational plan may have to be relatively straightforward.

Management and Organization. It's not unusual for a business plan reviewer to read the personnel and organization section early in the review process. No matter how exciting the business concept, most reviewers are reluctant to make any kind of commitment to a venture unless they feel comfortable with the people involved. Venture capitalists have often commented that they invest in management teams, not in ideas or products. Your success in generating the interest of reviewers and the ultimate success of the business may well depend on the effectiveness of your staff and organization.

Many ventures ultimately fail because the proper talent hasn't been assembled. People with strong technical backgrounds might ignore the importance of including on a management team members with the appropriate business background, and vice versa.

To address this issue properly, you must begin with an objective assessment of your personal strengths and weaknesses, and with an assessment of the company's requirements. Based on these assessments, you may define the composition of the rest of the company. In turn, you will also define the company's personality. Among the questions you need to address are:

- Will management be participative or autocratic?
- Will personnel share in the company's financial success, or will they be treated more as a commodity?
- Will responsibilities and tasks be sharply defined, or will a more flexible approach prevail?

In answering these questions, you must treat the following issues:

Management Team/Principals. One of the most important parts of the business plan—and certainly the most important part of the personnel and organization section—is a presentation of the backgrounds of the people expected to play key roles in the initiation and operation of the venture. This group might include the entrepreneur, investors, members of the board of directors, key employees, or almost anyone who will have a significant impact on the company's ultimate success or failure.

Organizational Chart. After introducing the key participants in the venture, it's appropriate to provide an organizational chart that presents the relationships and divisions of responsibility within the organization. In some instances, a brief narrative instead of (or in addition to) a chart may be helpful in providing further detail.

Policy and Strategy. The business plan should include a statement regarding how employees will be selected, trained, and rewarded. Such background can be important for reviewers because it gives them a feeling for the company's style. A brief reference to the type of benefits and incentives planned may further help define the company's spirit.

A somewhat overused but nonetheless accurate statement often made by businesspeople is, "Our greatest asset is our people." This is especially true in the case of a startup or early-stage company, where errors in judgment and operations are often magnified because of a lack of stability and resources.

Structure and Capitalization. In the structure and capitalization section, your business plan allows you to tell a reviewer: "You've reviewed my business plan. If you're interested, here's what the business requires." This is where you identify what legal form you'll select and how you'll capitalize the venture. Typically, this section is concise and precise, although there are also occasions where you should deliberately omit some detail. This is one of the most critical parts of the proposal. Here you must convey what kind of financial resources you require for the venture to succeed during its early life.

See following sections for more detailed information on both structure and capitalization.

Financial Plan. The purpose of the financial section is to formulate a credible, comprehensive set of projections reflecting your company's anticipated financial performance. If these projections are carefully prepared and convincingly supported, they become one of the most critical yardsticks by which the business's attractiveness is measured. The rest of the business plan communicates a basic understanding of the nature of the enterprise; the projected financial performance addresses itself directly to the bottom-line interests and concerns of both you and the reviewer. It's here that the investor discovers what sort of return to anticipate and the lender learns about the borrower's capacity to service debt.

DECIDING WHICH BUSINESS STRUCTURE MAKES SENSE

Choosing the legal form under which your business will operate is one of the most complex and critical decisions to make when organizing a new business. This is a complex subject, however; our discussion here is merely a brief overview. You should study the question of legal form carefully in close consultation with a lawyer and tax accountant.

Major Variables

The three major variables you must deal with when choosing the legal form of a business are liability, control, and taxes. In responding to these variables, you should ask yourself the following questions:

- Will you be the sole owner? If not, how many other people—whether operators or investors—will have an ownership interest? How much control will each owner have? In what manner will the risks and rewards of the business be shared?
- How important is it for all owners to limit personal liability for debts or claims against the business?
- Which form of business organization affords the most advantageous tax treatment for both the business and the individual owner(s)?
- What legal form will be the simplest and least expensive to both establish and maintain?
- What are your long-term plans for the business?

Sometimes the answers to these questions will conflict with one another. If so, professional assistance from lawyers and accountants can help you sort through the issues.

However, be mindful of the following points:

Legal forms of business were established for legal reasons. Liability issues were paramount to those who wrote the earliest laws regarding business. Corporate taxation is a relatively recent phenomenon and has become an important and complex issue only over the past half century. Taxes should have an impact on, but not necessarily dictate, your decision about the legal form.

Don't underestimate the advantages of simplicity. A simple organizational form—one that often costs little or nothing to establish and maintain—can often save more than you'd gain in tax breaks by using a more complicated legal form. This is especially true for a small business.

The U.S. tax laws change constantly. After passage of the Tax Reform Act of 1986, members of Congress hinted that no significant tax law changes would occur for several years. Nevertheless, major tax bills were passed in 1987, 1988, 1990, 1993, 1996, 1997, and 1998. Congress continues to make tax law changes.

Forms of Organizing a Business

With this as background, let's review the alternative forms of organizing a business. Your main options are:

- Sole proprietorship
- Partnership
- Limited partnership
- Corporation
- S corporation
- Limited liability company

Sole Proprietorship. The sole proprietorship provides you with maximum simplicity and flexibility while trading off all protection against personal liability. It also affords you complete control. (Once other owners become involved, a sole proprietorship is no longer possible.)

If you wish to establish a sole proprietorship, you usually go through very few formalities on the state level, the most onerous being a simple registration of the business under the Fictitious Names Act. On the federal level, the sole proprietor needs only to keep accurate accounting records and file a Schedule C (Profit or Loss from a Business or Profession) as an attachment to IRS Form 1040 at the appropriate tax time. Sole proprietorships must operate on a calendar year but can use either the cash or accrual method of accounting (the accrual method may be mandatory if the business has inventories).

Under a sole proprietorship, you can't limit your personal liability against debt payment. Legal liability for defective products, professional malpractice, or any other claims are also a personal liability. However, you can guard your business against these liabilities by insurance, as with any business.

The tax advantages and disadvantages of sole proprietorships are becoming increasingly hard to discern. Until 1982, payroll taxes were an advantage, since the sole proprietor paid only 75% of the combined employer and employee share of the federal employment tax on his or her income. Since 1982, sole proprietors have gradually reached "parity" in Social Security payments, paying both the employer's and the employee's shares. Sole proprietors aren't required to pay Social Security taxes on salaries paid to their children who are under age 18 and employed in their trade business. In addition, owners are not subject to unemployment tax.

The implications for deductibility of life, medical, and disability insurance may be a disadvantage. However, self-employed individuals can take a deduction for a portion of the amount paid for health insurance to cover themselves and their spouses and dependents. The Tax and Trade Relief Extension Act of 1998 increases this deduction gradually until it reaches 100% in 2003.

Tax Year	Deductible Percentage of Health Insurance
1999-2001	60%
2002	70%
2003 and thereafter	100%

Unless you have a compelling business reason to incorporate, it's now usually advantageous from a tax standpoint to operate as a sole proprietor or a limited liability company. If incorporation serves other business interests, however, you may be able to achieve the tax benefits of sole proprietorship within corporate parameters by operating as an S corporation.

Partnership. Partnerships have many of the same advantages and disadvantages as those of sole proprietorships, except that there's more than one owner. A partnership can be relatively simple and informal and requires minimal paperwork for state and federal authorities in order to be established. However, it's always a good idea for partners to have some form of written agreement about how they will share in the partnership's obligations, profits or losses, and capital. Without a partnership agreement, state laws will generally dictate the allocation of such items.

Partnership agreements can include any items the partners think worthwhile to include. Some partnerships—especially limited partnerships set up for investment purposes—have a defined lifetime. How a partner joins or leaves the partnership, rights of interest purchase by other partners, terms of payment, and other such issues should be considered when drawing up partnership agreements.

Partnerships don't dissolve on the death of a partner. Because the estate or other successor beneficiary will continue to share in the partnership's profits, however, it's important to consider how the partnership can be least disrupted by this event. The right of surviving partners to buy out the deceased partner's spouse or other family members, often using the proceeds from "key person" insurance, is one way in which many partnerships cover themselves against this eventuality.

The big advantage of partnerships is the ease of getting assets into and out of a multiple-owner business without incurring taxes. This is important if investors are contributing more than money to a venture.

As with sole proprietorships, the tax advantages of incorporating were almost nullified by the Tax Reform Act of 1986; regardless, good business reasons shouldn't prevent a partnership from incorporating. However, an S corporation form of business (see next page) may offer most of a partnership's tax advantages with the legal advantages of a corporation. Limited liability companies or partnerships are attractive alternatives.

Limited Partnership. When partners need more money than they can put into a venture themselves and either can't or don't want to borrow, they turn to a method of organization known as a *limited partnership*. A limited partnership offers certain partners who agree to become general partners a chance to raise capital from others while keeping control over the venture. Investors—known as limited partners—have the opportunity to own an equity position while limiting their liability and involvement in the venture to a financial one. Limited partners have no say in how a business operates and are financially liable only up to the amount of their investment. The general partners manage the business and have full exposure to liability. Sometimes, the general partners will be special-purpose corporations so that the liability issue can be managed.

Corporation. Although most people think of corporations when they think of businesses, only a small percentage of American businesses are formally incorporated. Incorporating can be a costly and time-consuming process. State incorporation fees and legal fees for drawing up corporate documents can easily cost hundreds or thousands of dollars, and there are ongoing expenses to maintaining and operating a corporation.

Businesses are incorporated most often for the benefits of limited liability. In a corporation the owners, officers, and directors are not usually personally liable for the company's debts (although officers responsible for making employment-withholding tax payments to the federal government can be held personally liable if those payments aren't made). However, the "corporate veil" is often pierced by a bank asking for a personal signature on a corporate loan. This will most often be required of small, single-owner, or closely held corporations.

Corporations have unlimited lives and, in the event of the death of a shareholder, ownership is passed to the heirs designated by the shareholder. The corporate stock can always be sold to other investors. In this way, large blocks of voting stock or even controlling interest can pass from owners who have employment or entrepreneurial stakes in the business (or the heirs of these people) to new owners.

S Corporation. S corporations can offer entrepreneurs the best of both worlds in many ways. S corporations aren't different from corporations under federal law and under some states' corporate laws. They offer owners the benefits of limited liability. In addition, there are usually no federal income taxes at the corporate level for S corporations. Profits or losses from S corporations flow directly through the company to the shareholders, thereby avoiding double taxation. Investors are also able to use losses from S corporations as direct write-offs against other income, with limitations for those shareholders considered to be passive investors.

Because of this special tax treatment for federal tax purposes, an S corporation is treated much like a partnership. However, there are limits on S corporations with regard to their ownership structure. In many ways, S corporations provide the best of both worlds to entrepreneurs; however, the tax laws regarding S corporations are complex and the legal and accounting costs of starting and maintaining S status could override some of the tax advantages. State laws vary as to the taxability of an S corporation's income.

The owners' effective tax rate on income from an S corporation is as high as 39.6% (the maximum personal rate). However, for an individual operating in the form of a regular corporation, the effective tax depends on the level of that corporation's pretax income and the percentage of that corporation's net income paid out as cash dividends. Corporations are taxed at an effective rate of 34% on all pretax income if taxable income exceeds $335,000 but is less than $10,000,000. A corporation with taxable income in excess of $10,000,000 approaches a rate of 35%. Therefore, the old adage may no longer be true that there's rarely a point at which you are better off, taxwise, as a regular corporation. If the owner does not intend to pay much in the way of cash dividends, total taxes may be less than the 39.6% individual rate by doing business as a regular corporation.

Limited Liability Company (LLC). A limited liability company (LLC) is a business entity that has become accepted in most states. This entity has two major advantages over most other forms of doing business:

- In contrast to partnerships, all interest holders or "members" can enjoy limited personal liability for the debts of the organization.
- Unlike corporations, the entity can avoid the "double income tax" at the corporate and shareholder levels by being qualified for flow-through treatment of income.

In addition, LLCs aren't subject to the many restrictions imposed on S corporations, such as limits on the number of shareholders or the prohibition against corporate shareholders. Most states that accept the LLC will also recognize foreign LLCs, professional LLCs, and limited liability partnerships (LLPs). An LLC with one member is treated as a sole proprietorship for tax purposes

See the table on page 411 for a summary of the alternative forms of legal organization and their key characteristics.

USING ADVISORS

Although you should prepare the business plan yourself, you may benefit from professional input in the process. Formal sources of help include accountants, consultants, and lawyers. Informal sources of guidance—

mentors, advisors, and the like—may be valuable as well. These professionals will often ask you objective questions about your plan that you may not have explored yet, whether because you just didn't think of it or because the answer seemed too obvious. Professionals can often point out missing information or the magnitude of problems that somehow escaped you, they can tone down claims that may be overblown or misleading, and they can help you clarify specific points in the plan.

Reviewers go through a process known as *due diligence*—an in-depth evaluation—before lending or investing money in a project. In preparing your plan, you should go through the same process, and professionals can often be catalysts in this regard. They can help you identify gaps and flaws in the plan and address how to fix them. The questions that reviewers ask are worth asking early rather than late, and you should answer such questions in the business plan itself before the reviewers see it. If a question posed in the plan can't be answered immediately, you should say so directly in the plan.

E X A M P L E

■ Here's an instance of the give-and-take possible between entrepreneurs and professionals. About 10 years ago, James and Hallie owned a retail store that sold compact disks to music listeners. They decided to seek funding to expand to other locations. The first question asked by a consultant they hired to help them raise money was: "How do you know you can replicate your success in other locations?"

After Hallie and James convinced the consultant they could do it again, they told him they wanted to open 15 stores in 15 separate markets. They believed they'd spotted a window of opportunity in the then-new CD market; they wanted to be the first CD-only store in a number of markets. The consultant pointed out three major difficulties in having 15 stores in as many markets: The stores would be difficult to manage; it would be hard knowing the dynamics of 15 local markets; and there would be a loss of economy of scale with regard to advertising.

The consultant suggested trying to saturate a narrower regional market with five to eight stores at first. This would allow James and Hallie to gauge whether the CD-only idea would really work outside the immediate area. Hallie and James convinced the consultant that this wasn't a large enough market at that time to support so many stores. As a result, they compromised on a plan initially to put 10 stores in three areas—and then to expand into the other 12 cities over a few years. The entrepreneurs had realistic projections; their consultant helped them figure out how best to reach those numbers. ■

KEY CHARACTERISTICS OF ALTERNATIVE FORMS OF LEGAL ORGANIZATION

	Sole Proprietorship	Partnership	Limited Partnership	Corporation	S Corporation	LCC
Simplicity	Simplest and least expensive form to establish and maintain.	Relatively simple to establish and maintain. A written partnership agreement should be drawn up at the beginning.	More complex than simple partnership. Needs a formal written agreement. Many limited partnerships are marketable securities and must be registered, causing additional time and expense.	Generally requires the most formality in establishing and maintaining.	Same degree of formality and expense as a regular corporation to establish. Maintenance is more expensive because of the need for constant oversight.	Hybrid of Partnership and Corporation. Files articles of organization.
Liability	Owner has unlimited personal liability.	Each partner has unlimited personal liability.	General partners are personally liable, while limited partners are financially liable only to the extent of their investment.	Stockholders not generally liable. In many small, closely held corporations, the owner(s) must personally cosign and guarantee loans. Corporate officers may also be liable for payment of withholding taxes.	Same	Same
Federal tax of profits	Owner taxed at individual rate.	Each partner is taxed at individual rates.	Partners are taxed at individual rates.	Taxed to corporation at corporate rates.	Shareholders are taxed at individual rates.	Member taxed at individual rate.
Deduction of losses (for investors "materially participating" in the business)	Yes	Yes	In certain circumstances.	No. Corporations carry over (back) losses until they offset profits.	Yes	Yes
Double taxation	No	No	No	Yes	No	No

DETERMINING CAPITAL SOURCES

In general, there are two types of funding sources: *lenders* and *investors.*

The lenders are generally commercial banks, corporate finance companies, and investment bankers. When lenders consider a loan request, they concentrate on what are sometimes referred to as the "four C's" of credit: character, cash flow, collateral, and (equity) contribution. Lenders are looking for the company's ability to repay its debt. No matter how successful a company may be, a lender usually has only the promise of being rewarded with steady payments of principal and interest.

On the other hand, investors enjoy the possibility of a large rate of return since they have a "piece of the action" (an equity position) in a company in exchange for their investment. Consequently, they are willing to accept more risk.

To generalize further about the difference between lenders and investors: Lenders are more numbers-driven than investors are in their analyses of a business's potential, and more shortsighted in that they focus on the first couple of years of a business's life, when viability, rather than potential, is likely to be achieved. They will require that cash flow be sufficient to service the debt and will often concentrate on the downside more than the possible upside of the business. This is due to their reward structure. Unlike investors, lenders are not involved with a business for a piece of the action.

Lenders

When considering a company, lenders often look closely at the four C's:

- Character
- Cash flow
- Collateral
- Contribution

Character. Although this is a "soft" criterion, the issue of character definitely enters into a lender's decision-making process. The lender must have confidence in you in order to go forward with the venture. Among the traits considered are talent, reliability, and honesty. The more objective measure of your credit history also plays a significant role. However, the lender's final decision comes down to intuition. How capable are you? Will you run your business ethically, and will you keep the lender informed of the real status of the business? Will you repay your debt?

Cash Flow. Lenders need to feel satisfied that your cash flow will be adequate to cover debt service throughout the term of the obligation. To satisfy lenders your business must be strong enough to meet both the debt service and your operating obligations, yet you must also have enough available cash to provide a comfortable cushion for uncertainties.

Collateral. No good lender will make a decision to loan money based solely on strong collateral; however, every good lender will try to obtain the best collateral possible on a loan. This normally involves securing the lender's interest by liens and mortgages against tangible assets, such as real estate or equipment. In addition, most lenders will require your personal signature, both as additional security and as evidence of your real commitment to the venture.

Contribution. Lenders' requirements vary regarding the amount of personal equity contribution they want you to have in the business. However, almost all lenders require a significant commitment of both your time and money. This helps to ensure that you're closely tied to the company's success and therefore to the success of the financing. It also serves to reduce the lender's exposure relative to the deal's total size. This provides a cushion that allows the lender to come out "whole" in the event of a default.

Other important issues with lenders are:

- Ratios of debt
- Repayment period
- Rates

Ratios of Debt. In addition, different industries customarily have different ratios of debt to equity, commonly known as leverage. Some industries have traditionally been highly leveraged, with debt three to four times greater than equity, often because of high success rates and/or generally good-quality collateral. The real estate and apparel industries are good examples of highly leveraged businesses. An unusually high failure rate and/or poor-quality collateral may result in relatively low leverage in an industry, as exemplified by the restaurant business. Because of these vagaries, it's difficult to generalize as to how much you must personally contribute to a venture.

Repayment Period. The repayment period—the length of time over which the obligation is amortized (paid off)—usually depends on the useful life of the asset financed, although there can be some variance. If a lender really wants to make a deal, he or she can allow some latitude in structuring the debt so that the deal makes sense economically and cash flow is sufficient to amortize the debt. Working capital loans are usually paid off over the shortest periods of time and real estate loans over the longest. Remember, the longer the term is, the lower the monthly payment (principal and interest) will be; however, there will be more monthly payments, more interest accruing, and more money paid in total to meet the debt requirements.

Many lenders are willing to give initial moratoriums on principal payments—periods of time at the beginning of a loan when only interest is due. Often, these will be allowed during periods of startup or expansion, when a business is incurring expenses in excess of revenues. It's possible that an enlightened lender will extend such a moratorium up to 12 months.

Rates. Most business debt today is provided at a variable interest rate, usually fluctuating with the prime rate (the rate banks charge their "best" customers). This rate is usually quoted as "prime plus" x percentage points, often 0.5% to 2%, but it can be as much as 3% or even 4% above prime, depending on risk and other variables that motivate the lender. The effective rate changes as often as the prime rate changes; therefore, each monthly payment can be different.

Variable-rate debt has become prevalent since the late 1970s, when interest rates were volatile and commercial lenders decided that they would pass this volatility on to the borrower rather than absorbing it in their fixed-rate loan portfolio.

There will undoubtedly be a host of other covenants, rules, and restrictions to the loan, which restrict your freedom of management to such an extent that (for example) you may not give raises to senior management or obtain further financing without the lender's approval.

One of the major advantages of financing a business with debt instead of investment is that lenders often make decisions faster than investors. It's not outrageous to expect some decisions from lenders and even a closing on financing within 2 to 3 months of the time the lender first sees the business plan. With venture capitalists, this time is often doubled or even tripled. (These time frames assume an "arm's-length" relationship, where entrepreneurs and financing sources don't already know each other.)

Investors

There are a variety of important sources of equity financing. The most common are:

- Venture capital funds
- Yourself, your family, and friends
- "Angels"
- Vendors

- Corporate venture capitalists
- Ad hoc venture pools

Venture Capital Funds. When people think of venture capitalists, they normally are thinking about the professional venture capital fund managers who make the decisions about which companies a fund should invest in. Typically, these people are looking for young, high-growth "operating" companies—companies that are ongoing rather than "one-shot deals."

Venture capital funds are usually set up as limited partnerships, with the professional manager being the general or controlling partner. He or she (or the management company) usually puts up a very small amount of the fund's capital, often as little as 1%. The rest of the fund is financed by limited partners, who put their money at risk and can get great rewards but have no say in the fund's day-to-day management.

Many of the limited partners are financial institutions, pension funds, and corporations, which have contributed at least hundreds of thousands of dollars, and often millions. The venture capital fund (or individual) is looking for two key attributes:

- Rates of return of around 25% to 50%, compounded annually
- Investments that will become liquid within a short period of time

Some of the qualities that venture capitalists associate with companies having the potential to generate exciting returns are:

- *The quality of the individual entrepreneur.* They are most often looking for maturity and experience in the area of other businesses started, along with a track record of success. What defines a high-quality entrepreneur for a venture capitalist is subjective. The evaluation is often intuitive.
- *Functionally balanced teams.* More and more, venture capitalists are looking for entrepreneurial teams that meet the human resource needs of a new company. Venture capital managers have little time to devote to helping structure management teams and oversee day-to-day operations. Hence the one-man show is less attractive than the professional and aggressive team.
- *Proprietary characteristics.* Venture capitalists are always looking for businesses that have an edge on the competition that cannot easily be copied. Proprietary characteristics are often marked by patents, licenses, trademarks, or other legal protections. Venture capitalists are looking less for collateral than for commitment. They will want a seat on the company's board, and they may want an option to remove the entrepreneur or to change management, if necessary.

A smooth progression of a financing from a venture capitalist might look something like the following timetable, which would hold for a company that has a fully written business plan, a well-defined strategy, intact management team, and some easy-to-reach references.

For 4 to 6 weeks, an entrepreneur is developing a business plan, and, simultaneously, identifying the appropriate funding sources. Then:

- *Weeks 1–2.* Initial contact with potential financing sources by letter or phone
- *Week 3.* Mailing of executive summary or complete plan
- *Weeks 4–6.* Initial meeting with one or more potential financing sources
- *Weeks 7–18.* Follow-up with one or more financing sources; meetings, phone calls, additional information, or addenda to business plan
- *Week 18.* Offer from a financing source
- *Weeks 19–26.* Negotiation of the deal terms, drawing up of documents
- *Week 26.* Closing

Self, Family, and Friends. Despite the popular conception, most initial investment in new businesses isn't made by venture capitalists; rather, it's made by a number of investors who are at less than an arm's length from the entrepreneur. Friends and family often supplement the entrepreneur's own capital.

These investments can be profitable for the investors and can have the advantage to you of providing a faster closing. However, since these investors aren't professionals, they tend to use less due diligence in their analyses of potential investments. This may result in their not evaluating a potential business on its objective merit, and making investment decisions that could in turn have a negative impact on personal relationships. You must consider this potential result before pursuing such investments.

By far the most frequent investor in new businesses is the entrepreneur and immediate family. The investment may come from savings or other assets, such as marketable securities, or equity in a home, perhaps via a second mortgage. For many small entrepreneurs, these are the most likely sources of financing for a business initially, since it is very difficult to get a commercial loan of less than $10,000 or $20,000, and even more difficult to get venture capital funding of less than $500,000.

E
X
A
M
P
L
E

■ Some people find even more "creative" ways of finding liquid assets to invest in their own new business. One was a man who wanted to start a specialty butcher shop. He had $10,000 and needed another $10,000. His friend, a small-business consultant, told him that it would be a tough sum to raise. A few weeks later, the butcher called and invited his friend to his new shop. "Where did you raise the money?" the consultant asked. "I sold my wife's Corvette," his friend replied. This was not an exotic, high-finance source of funding, but it was inventive and effective (although one might wonder whether his wife would have agreed with this assessment). ■

"Angels." There's also a network of informal investors (sometimes called "angels") who are willing to put their money into new businesses. Some don't have enough funds to get into a venture capital fund but still like the risk of venture-type investments. Others like to take a more hands-on approach to their investment decisions. A few may even be gizmo-driven dilettantes looking for the next Rube Goldberg–type invention.

These people go through a review process, but it is often a limited review, and they usually make decisions much faster than do professional venture capitalists—often in 2 to 3 months or less. You may not have to show these people the opportunity for the company to be an enormous hit, but you must show the investor that the money will return more than the investor could get with other less risky types of investments. This often means showing the possibility of the business giving at least a 20% or more compounded annual return on investment.

Another nice thing about working with informal investors is that the deal can be structured in any way that the entrepreneur, the investor, and their respective lawyers wish to structure it. There can be a combination of debt and equity in such deals.

Vendors. One of the most overlooked sources for helping to finance a new venture is the vendors who do business with a company. If an entrepreneur can convince vendors to extend an extra 30 or 60 days' credit on accounts payable, this will greatly alleviate potential cash crunches and reduce capital requirements.

Corporate Venture Capitalists. A number of large companies have set up their own venture capital funds. Often, these funds are looking to help finance companies that can contribute technology to their company or are in some other way compatible. Sometimes the corporate venture company is even looking for entrepreneurs to spawn companies that the larger company will eventually acquire.

Ad Hoc Venture Pools. Some private investors have banded together to form informal investment groups or investment pools. Often, one private money source will turn to other private investors to get the money together to make an investment in a venture. Here are some possible sources:

- Small Business Investment Corporation (SBIC)
- Minority Enterprise Small Business Investment Corporation (MESBIC)
- Economic development groups (sometimes called "economic development corporations" or "business development corporations") administered on a federal, state, or local level
- Private foundations and universities that invest a small percentage of their endowment portfolios in small, risky ventures
- Mutual funds that invest in startup and small, growth-oriented companies

Using Your Home as Your Office

For many entrepreneurs, being self-employed starts at home. Some of the most successful U.S. companies start almost literally as cottage industries. (Steve Jobs built his first Apple computer in a garage.) Although many companies quickly outgrow this stage and move into bigger and more extravagant surroundings, you may find that running your business from home is ideal.

The Pros and Cons of Working at Home

The advantages of working at home are substantial for many people. Overhead is low. Flexibility is substantial. The morning commute is short. Working at home may be especially convenient if you have simultaneous work and family obligations, such as looking after children or elderly parents. A home office may be suitable for those professionals or tradespersons who need no other facility; typical in this regard would be some lawyers, artists or artisans, trade contractors (carpenters, electricians, plumbers, etc.), writers or editors, architects, and independent salespersons. Electronic equipment and home office supplies now make even a small family den into a powerful link in the information network.

However, working at home has significant drawbacks that you should consider carefully. In some cases a home-based business may not be feasible. Among the issues are:

- Legality
- Practicality
- Sanity

Legality. Local zoning laws may restrict what sort of work you can do at home. Restrictions affect not only work-related activities but use of signs, materials, and parking spaces. Before you proceed, check with the local zoning board about requirements. Even if you're able to run your business at home, you may need to apply for licenses, health department permits, and other documents.

Practicality. Many entrepreneurs underestimate what they can accomplish in a home setting. Although the earliest planning phases of a business may be possible at home, you may find your enterprise quickly outstripping available space. Here are some of the questions you should ask yourself before you assume you can work at home:

- Do you have enough space?
- Are your home's resources (electricity, water, ventilation, etc.) sufficient?
- Is the home safe enough, given potential hazards (presence of children, risk of fire, use of materials or chemicals, etc.)?
- Is your home presentable to customers and clients?

Sanity. Last, there's an issue that many people overlook: Can you stay sane working at home? Some people can; for others, it's a one-way ticket to Bedlam. Although you may imagine a home office as a blissful oasis in the business world, the reality may prove far different. You may resent the intrusion of customers or business associates into your private space. You may find yourself torn between work and family obligations. You may find that your business activities spill over into home life until distinguishing one from the other becomes impossible. To determine if you have the ability to filter out distractions and maintain some necessary barriers between personal and business-related activities, you should try working at home on a provisional basis before you commit yourself long-term. You may find that the potential problems are manageable or never even crop up at all. On the other hand, you may miss a clear-cut dividing line between home and workplace.

Tax Aspects of Working at Home

Another issue that some people misjudge is how much of their home office expenses can be deducted. Here again the reality is more complex than the common image. The costs of a home office can be deducted only if strict IRS guidelines are met—generally that the office is used exclusively for business purposes. The Taxpayer Relief Act of 1997 has eased the requirements for determining if the costs associated with a home office can be deducted. The new law states that a home office qualifies as the "principal place of business" if (1) the taxpayer uses the office to conduct administrative or management activities of a trade or business and (2) there is no other fixed location of the trade or business where the taxpayer conducts substantial administrative or management activities of the trade or business. Deductions will continue to be allowed for a home office meeting the above two-part test only if the taxpayer uses the office exclusively on a regular basis as a place of business and, in the case of an employee, only if such exclusive use is for the employer's convenience.

The home office deduction is limited to the gross income from the activity, reduced by expenses that would otherwise be deductible (such as mortgage interest or taxes) and all other expenses related to the activities that are not house-related. A deduction isn't allowed to the extent that it creates or increases a net loss from the activity. Any disallowed deduction may be carried over.

The percentage allowed is equal to the percentage of space you use to run your business. If your business requires using a 150-square-foot room in a 1,500-square-foot apartment, for instance, you can deduct 10% of your expenses.

In addition, you can also deduct depreciation on the portion of your home that you use for business purposes. Calculations for this purpose are more complex than those mentioned in the preceding percentage situation. Deducting depreciation requires calculating a percentage of the tax basis of your house—what you paid for the house, plus the cost of improvements, minus the value of the land your house is on.

Depreciating the business portion of your home may result in added taxes in the future if you sell the home at a profit. The reason? Business property doesn't benefit from some of the tax advantages that your personal residence does. And you can't exclude the gain on your residence which is attributable to depreciation after May 6, 1997. Consult your financial planner or accountant to assess the pros and cons of depreciation.

HIRING EMPLOYEES—AND DEALING WITH THEIR COSTS

Many businesses start small. The founder takes his or her idea, adds money, energy, and long hours, and makes a go of it alone. For some people, this is the key to success. They prefer to stay small-scale even given the work involved. And there's no question that modern technology—personal computers, fax machines, photocopiers, on-line data services, answering machines, and all the rest—allow a degree of autonomy that would have been unimaginable even 15 or 20 years ago. Entrepreneurs who wish to work independently now have a better chance of success than ever before.

On the other hand, just as many businesses start small and eventually expand, with employees joining the founder as opportunities arise. Starting small serves the entrepreneur well early on, but often as not, remaining small isn't a virtue in itself. There's profit, reputation, and pride in accomplishment to be gained by growing. In most cases, growing means hiring employees to share the load.

One of the decisions you'll face as an entrepreneur is whether to do everything (or almost everything) yourself or whether to hire someone to help you. There are several primary questions to ask yourself as you make this decision:

- How much help do you need?
- Are you willing to delegate tasks?
- Do you prefer a managerial role or hands-on running of the business?
- How much help can you afford?

If you decide to hire employees (and once you decide how many), here are some of the issues that will affect your costs.

Paying Your Employees

The most immediate cost will be paying your help. You have several options, the most common of which are:

- Hourly wages
- Flat fee per project
- Salary
- Base salary plus commission
- Commission only
- Bonuses based on profit

In addition to what you pay employees, however, you face the issue of other monetary costs you'll pay. It's crucial not to underestimate the effect of these costs to your business. The most significant (both from legal and financial standpoints) are:

- Social Security taxes
- Workers' compensation and unemployment taxes
- Employee benefits
- New overhead costs
- Using independent contractors

Social Security Taxes

Federal Insurance Contributions Act (FICA) taxes are an expense you'll share in equal amounts with your full- or part-time employees. In 1999 you and your employee will each pay 7.65% on the first $72,600 of wages and 1.45% on any excess.

Workers' Compensation and Unemployment Taxes

In addition, you'll have to pay federal and state unemployment taxes, as well as workers' compensation taxes, for your employees. Rates vary from state to state. You should consult with an accountant to determine the rates you'll pay.

Caveat: As an employer, you're liable for paying the payroll taxes on your employees. You withhold a portion of their salaries, which you then deposit in your business account for subsequent payment to the government. The payroll deduction funds may or may not be segregated from other funds in that account. If you don't pay those payroll taxes on time, and if you use the funds from your employees' deductions to keep the business going, you're liable for penalties. Even if you're not the proprietor of the business—if you're the chief accountant for the business, for example—your use of the payroll taxes to pay bills will leave you liable.

What's the solution to this problem? First, segregate the funds; make sure that they're deposited in separate accounts. Second—whatever else—make sure that you pay on time.

Employee Benefits

The amount of benefits you offer will influence the number and quality of employees you can hire. Generally speaking, established companies' benefits are worth approximately one-third of what the companies spend on salaries or wages; as a result, you should assume that benefits will be a significant portion of your expense in hiring employees. Among the benefits to consider are:

- Health insurance
- Paid vacation
- Sick days
- Group life insurance
- Group disability insurance
- Retirement plans

New Overhead Costs

As a one-person business, you may be able to operate out of your home or in limited workspace. Hiring employees probably changes that picture. (The exceptions involve situations like having a receptionist/secretary or a limited sales force out in the field.) Under most circumstances, employees will need office space, telephones, computer equipment, supplies, and whatever other kinds of equipment or supplies make it possible for them to do their work. Obviously, the requirements will vary. What's inevitable is that you'll now have new overhead costs—costs that you should project as early and as accurately as possible.

Using Independent Contractors

Depending on the nature of your business, using independent contractors may simplify your work, your personnel situation, or both. Independent contractors are nonemployees that you hire on an occasional basis to assist you in performing specific tasks. The costs of using contractors may seem higher at face value; however, the long-term costs may end up lower than hiring an employee. The IRS sets forth certain guidelines pertaining to use of contractors. Your main advantage in this regard is that you avoid having to pay employee-related costs, such as taxes, benefits, and so forth. In addition, using contractors may substantially simplify your task in keeping records.

22

DEALING WITH YOUR PARENTS

Another life event that hasn't received much attention from a financial planning standpoint isn't really one single event; rather, it's a series of events extending throughout several stages of life, each of which includes the task of dealing with your parents. As you and your parents enter different stages of your own lives and face new and different financial challenges, you'll find that the financial aspects of your relationship will change as well. Typically, these changes involve a shift from early financial dependence on parents toward greater independence. The changes often go beyond that shift, however; many people find that they are ultimately responsible for their parents' financial well-being.

Here's a sampling of typical questions that arise regarding finances and relationships with parents:

- At what age should you attain financial independence from your parents?
- Is there a way to arrange your finances to help your parents' income tax situation—or your own?
- Why don't your parents understand how tight your budget is?
- How can you communicate to your parents that they're lavishing too many gifts on your children?
- What are ways in which you can help your parents with estate planning?

- How can you ensure your parents' ability to fund their needs for medical costs such as nursing care during retirement?

To answer these and other questions, we should approach the issues involved from three different viewpoints: early adulthood, middle age, and the later years.

EARLY ADULTHOOD

In the immediate postcollege years, you're probably eager to disengage from your parents and start building your own life away from home. This is as it ought to be, and most young adults make the transition well. At the same time, there are challenges that you'll face in making this transition from a financial standpoint. The following are three issues we'll address in this regard:

- Financial self-reliance
- Good saving habits
- Income taxes

Financial Self-Reliance

The first issue concerns a situation that crops up more frequently than many families are willing to admit. Heading off to college, teenagers are usually dependent on their parents for financial support. What sometimes happens, though, is that as young adults finish school, they start building their own lives but don't necessarily take control of their own finances. They remain reliant on Mom and Dad for a full or partial subsidy of their activities. They may move back into the family home, receive help funding a home purchase or graduate education, or even expect a monthly stipend. There's nothing intrinsically wrong with these arrangements; however, each involves a degree of risk for both sides, since they postpone an event that's inevitable and necessary: financial emancipation.

A stage that many middle-class American families go through occurs when the children are in college and the parents are simultaneously at the peak of their careers. From a financial standpoint, the timing is perfect. The children's college costs coincide with a time when the parents' financial assets are most abundant. One result is that during the college and the immediate postcollege years, many young adults rely on their parents financially to a degree that was unheard of in the past. Some degree of financial dependence may continue through the now-grown children's early 20s into their middle- or late 20s, sometimes even into their 30s. Many parents grouse about this kind of dependency. Others go along with it uncomplaining.

If you're in your 20s and still dependent on your parents for support, the issue here is your need to take responsibility for your own financial life. You may, of course, have specific reasons for your dependency. If not, you should begin to phase out your reliance and take control of your finances. The change may be difficult, but it can be crucial for you as well as for your parents. The reason is that both generations need to attend to their own financial affairs in ways that won't constrict their future. The older generation needs to work toward building a financial nest egg that ensures they'll be able to live comfortably throughout their retirement years. The younger generation needs to have an incentive to earn enough money to support their current lifestyle and then start saving for the future.

Precisely *how* to address these issues is, of course, a complex and sensitive matter. The best way is to talk openly with one another about your own financial situation and identify why your parents are still helping you. Ask yourself the following kinds of questions:

Is the financial help fulfilling an emotional or a financial need? Sometimes parents (or, for that matter, their adult children) feel some sort of emotional satisfaction from the financial help that the younger generation receives. This isn't necessarily a problem—but you should be sure to clarify the nature of what's happening.

What is the impact of your financial need on your parents' financial situation? Make sure you look to the long term. Your parents may need more money for their later years than they realize. The extra money they have now may be important to save rather than give to you, since it may strengthen their ability to deal with negative cash flow years in the future.

What are your parents' financial goals? If possible, try to help your parents keep their own financial goals in mind—and even to clarify those goals when necessary. They may regard providing financial help to their children as important. But the more important long-term goal may be helping their children become financially independent.

What are your own financial goals and plans if your parents' help should cease? It's important to start looking ahead and imagine alternative financial scenarios even during your 20s. Your parents' support won't last indefinitely, so you may as well begin charting your own financial destiny.

Is this situation equitable? Perhaps you need some money and your parents have funds available. It's possible, however, that a gift from them will harm your parents' finances to a degree that's out of proportion compared to the benefits you gain.

What are the alternatives to direct support? If you need some degree of financial assistance from your parents, there may be better ways to obtain it than direct support. One possibility is to arrange a loan from them that's advantageous to both parties—a subject we discuss later in this chapter.

These questions can prompt your thinking on the general issues of financial dependence. To the degree possible, start talking with your parents about money matters now, since the subject will arise with increasing frequency as they reach retirement.

Good Savings Habits

Another issue that you should face in your 20s is the need to develop good savings habits. Saving money is just as appropriate for young adults as for people in middle age and later stages of life. Although many people will have relatively limited income and abundant expenses during the postcollege years, the truth remains that it's never too early to start a savings plan. Starting early gives you more than just a head start in time. It can also lead to highly advantageous compounding of your principal. Even relatively modest savings can become the foundation for eventual financial security. And you're never too young to begin identifying your financial goals and planning to achieve them.

As to how you save money during the early years of adulthood: The methods and component parts of a savings plan are fundamentally the same as at other stages of life. See Chapter 2 for an overview.

One caveat, however, is that you should be sure that you won't need the money you invest in retirement plans (such as IRAs), since early withdrawal of funds will undo much of what you'd accomplish through compounding. Consequently, part of your task at this stage of life isn't just assessing how much money you can realistically set aside; it's also what short- or midterm goals you may be funding. Young adults typically save money for major asset purchases such as a car, a house, and furniture. Although it can be very beneficial to put money into an IRA when you're in high school or college, you may actually hurt yourself financially under certain circumstances. Why? Because you can end up losing money if you withdraw funds to pay for major purchases at a time when your income tax bracket is higher as a result of increased compensation. In addition, your early withdrawal may be subject to a 10% penalty.

The Taxpayer Relief Act of 1997 has made investing in IRAs more attractive for younger individuals. After December 31, 1997, you may withdraw funds from your retirement IRA (including the new Roth IRA) and not be hit with the 10% early withdrawal penalty if the funds are withdrawn to cover the costs of a first-time home purchase or to pay for qualified education expenses (including graduate-level classes). The

Internal Revenue Service considers you a qualified first-time homebuyer if you have not had ownership interest in a residence during the past 2 years. You should also note that distributions taken to cover the costs of a first-time home purchase have a lifetime cap of $10,000.

The newly created Roth IRA is even more appealing to younger Americans. The Roth IRA allows for tax-free and penalty withdrawals if you do not start taking distributions until 5 years after your first contribution. The Roth IRA allows you to make nondeductible contributions of up to $2,000 per year. This amount is reduced by the aggregate contributions made during a taxable year to all other retirement IRAs. (For a more detailed information on IRAs, see Chapter 2.)

When you invest in an IRA during your teens, you may be in the lowest tax bracket—15%. When you withdraw the funds, you may be in the next tax bracket—28%. The rate differential between these two brackets (coupled with a possible 10% early withdrawal penalty) is so great that contributing money to an IRA may actually work against you if you take money out prematurely.

E X A M P L E

■ Let's suppose that you contribute $2,000 to your IRA at age 20 and receive a 15% tax benefit. Let's assume that the IRA earns 8% annual income until you withdraw the money to buy a car when you're 35. At that time you've reached the 28% tax bracket for the first time in your life. In this case you would have been better off if you hadn't contributed the $2,000 to your IRA 15 years earlier and had just saved the money. As the following table shows, you would have had $5,313 after-tax if you hadn't contributed to the IRA compared to the $4,730 you have available net of all taxes, including the 10% penalty for early withdrawal. This isn't to say that you shouldn't contribute to an IRA—just consider this choice carefully, and have a long-term plan. ■

IRA VERSUS TAXABLE SAVINGS ANALYSIS— WITHDRAWAL IN YEAR 15

ASSUME INVESTMENT RETURN 8%: TAX RATE 15% YEARS 1–14, 28% YEAR 15.

IRA account balance	$6,343	Investment account balance	$5,313
Less:		Less:	
Income taxes	(1,776)	Additional taxes or penalties	None
10% penalty	(634)		
Plus:			
Future value of tax deduction	797		
Net cash available	$4,730	Net cash available	$5,313

Referring to the previous example, if instead of withdrawing the money for a car you used the money for a qualified first-time home purchase, the IRA account balance would not be subject to the 10% early withdrawal penalty. If you then compare the net cash available from each account, you will notice the IRA account balance would be $6,506, and the investment account balance would be $5,313. Under these circumstances the IRA account would provide you with a higher after-tax value than the investment account. This point illustrates the importance of planning prior to deciding if you should open an IRA account and if so what type.

You also have the ability to convert an existing retirement IRA into a Roth IRA. Converting an existing IRA to a Roth IRA may be favorable, as long as the Roth IRA funds are not distributed for several years (i.e., to prevent the distribution from being included in gross income and possibly subject to the 10% early withdrawal penalty). The benefit of conversion also can be enhanced if the taxes due on the deemed distributions of the existing IRA can be paid with non-IRA funds—this maximizes the amount accumulating in a tax-favored environment. You should also note that rollovers can come from both deductible and nondeductible IRAs. Rollovers from nondeductible IRAs appear to be the most beneficial because only the earnings would be taxable when rolled over. This would be a small price to pay for tax-free withdrawals of all future earnings.

Income Taxes

Finally, here's an issue that won't affect you directly if you're a young adult—but may influence some of your decisions because of their effects on your parents. The *dependency rules* are important because they determine if someone can claim a tax exemption, which reduces taxable income by a specified amount. (For 1999, each exemption is worth $2,750.) According to the IRS, you are your parents' dependent only if you earn less than this exemption amount, receive more than half of your support from them, and don't file a joint income tax return with your spouse. There's an exception that may apply to you if you were in college during the year. A special rule will phase out the tax benefit of the exemption for taxpayers whose adjusted gross income exceeds specified amounts.

Whether your parents claim you as a dependent may or may not materially affect your or your parents' finances. Generally, you and your parents will pay less income tax overall if you qualify as their dependent. This is because your parents' tax bracket is probably higher than yours. The IRS will allow only you or your parents to reduce your or their income by your personal exemption amount. Thus if your tax bracket is 15% and your parents' bracket is 36%, Uncle Sam would get $578 less if your parents can claim you as a dependent. The important thing to note is that the timing of actions you may take could affect your parents' dependency claim and make at least some difference to their financial picture.

<table>
<tr><td>E
X
A
M
P
L
E</td><td>■ Suppose that you've been supported by your parents, who therefore claim you as a dependent on their income tax return. Now you've decided to get married. The relevant issue here is that the timing of your marriage may have financial consequences for your parents. The IRS rule states that if a grown child files a joint tax return with his or her spouse, the parents can't claim that child as a dependent for that year. This means that even if you lived with Mom and Dad while they supported you all year long, if you get married on December 31 and choose to file a joint return with your new spouse for that tax year, your parents would generally forfeit any claim to you as a dependent—at least for tax purposes. On the other hand, timing your wedding to occur even one day into the new year, or filing separate returns with your new spouse, may allow your parents to claim you as a dependent for the preceding year. ■</td></tr>
</table>

MIDDLE AGE

Perhaps the most complex phase of life for financial interactions with parents is middle age. The reasons are many and often emotionally charged. First, you may have attained a relationship of equals with your mother and father, yet even in the middle of your life you may still be financially reliant on them. Second, you may discover that a lack of open discussion of money matters causes problems between the generations. Third, you may find that starting your own family leaves you feeling conflicted over your parents' influence on your children, including their influence on money matters. As a result of these issues, middle age may be a stage of life that requires special attention as you deal both with your own and your parents' finances.

Here are three topics that may be useful as you consider this subject:

- Self-reliance
- The necessity of open discussion
- Children, money, and the older generation

Self-Reliance

In middle age, as during the early years of adulthood, there are important issues of self-reliance. Although you have a career and may be married and/or have children, it's still easy to expect your parents to be your safety net. This isn't necessarily inappropriate. Parents often are a safety net, and many of them accept or even embrace this role. Yet relying on them to help finance your purchases may or may not be in your best interests. Gifts of money—such as periodic infusions of cash to help you "get by"—may actually do both generations more harm than good. If you have a habit of expecting help, receiving it may delay or even inhibit your ability to manage your financial affairs effectively. If your parents habitually provide financial help, they may end up jeopardizing their own financial health.

Loans may be a better bet—one that can provide advantages to both you and your parents. Let's say that you need money to buy a car. Rather than arrange financing through the dealer or a bank, you borrow the funds from your parents. You agree to pay them interest on the loan. This interest rate can typically be set at a rate that's lower than what you'd pay to most other lenders; at the same time, it's higher than what your parents can receive on many investments. Everyone comes out ahead.

Here's a cause for concern, however: It's important to realize that the investment they've made isn't liquid. Moreover, they may end up unable to recoup their funds at all. What happens if your parents need the money right away—perhaps because of a health problem or financial shortfall—and you just don't have the cash and now can't get a loan collateralized by the car? Also, although you may have intended to pay them back when you took out the loan, your good intentions alone may not carry the day. Right or wrong, it's easier to default on Mom and Dad than on the bank.

Issues of this sort aren't at all far-fetched. They pop up with great frequency when you're establishing yourself professionally, especially if you're raising a family. The unpredictable expenses of raising children may tempt you to see Mom and Dad as a local bank. Family emergencies (such as losing a job or dealing with your own health care crises) can even prompt you to view them as a social service agency. Again, this isn't necesarily inappropriate. But the core issue is to think through what you're doing and try to anticipate the consequences for both parties.

The Necessity of Open Discussion

This brings us to another point: the necessity for open discussion between parents and grown children about their respective financial situations. (The importance of this subject applies to young adulthood and the later years as well.)

In many families, money is one of those subjects that everyone knows about but no one cares to discuss. Parents may feel that their personal finances are none of the younger generation's business, and they may hesitate to ask about their children's money matters because they don't want to intrude. Grown daughters and sons, meanwhile, may feel uneasy talking about either their own or their parents' finances. As a result, neither generation knows much about what the other faces from a financial standpoint, but both sides make assumptions about the other's finances when making decisions about everything from buying birthday presents to planning vacations. From this conspiracy of silence comes the potential for numerous and serious misconceptions.

Here are two examples of how both sides can express these misconceptions:

A father speaking about his daughter: "We helped put Margaret through college. Now she's got a job with a starting salary of $28,000 per year, yet somehow she still needs handouts to pay off her student loans. What on earth is she doing with all that money?"

A son speaking about his parents: "Mom and Dad have almost a million dollars socked away for retirement—and their expenses are only $50,000 a year. Yet when I ask them for a measly $10,000 to put toward a house, they act as if I'll bankrupt them."

The variations on these themes are almost infinite. Each generation figures that the other is well-heeled, while parents and grown children alike feel that they are the ones who are really strapped. The cause for both sets of misconceptions is a lack of information about the respective financial realities. Your parents may not understand how tight your money is—$28,000 went a lot further just 10 or 20 years ago. And you may not understand the rigors of retirement planning and other issues that affect the older generation. A middle-class couple nearing retirement isn't by any means awash in money if they've saved $1,000,000 to last them 30 years. (See the financial independence matrix below.) If this couple needs $50,000 per year now, inflation will cause their $1,000,000 nest egg to become entirely depleted within 30 years unless their after-tax rate of return is more than three percentage points above inflation. If their tax rate is 25% overall, they would need to achieve a rate of return of over 10.5% per year if inflation is

5%, or their assets will run out within 30 years. So not only might a $10,000 gift to their son obstruct their financial independence; the couple may also need to invest rather aggressively (or else reduce their living expenses) in order to be financially comfortable for their remaining years.

FINANCIAL INDEPENDENCE MATRIX

ASSUMPTIONS

Annual living expenses in first year of retirement	$50,000
Years of retirement	30

AMOUNT NEEDED AT RETIREMENT

Infla-tion	Annual After-Tax Rate of Return								
	4%	5%	6%	7%	8%	9%	10%	11%	12%
4%	$1,500,000	$1,310,143	$1,153,523	$1,023,498	$914,868	$823,540	$746,282	$680,525	$624,219
5%		1,500,000	1,311,782	1,156,239	1,026,894	918,666	827,547	750,365	684,594
6%			1,500,000	1,313,394	1,158,913	1,030,244	922,417	831,510	754,408
7%				1,500,000	1,314,978	1,161,547	1,033,547	926,122	835,429
8%					1,500,000	1,316,535	1,164,140	1,036,804	929,781
9%						1,500,000	1,318,067	1,166,694	1,040,018
10%							1,500,000	1,319,573	1,169,211
11%								1,500,000	1,321,055
12%									1,500,000

Without having a clearer sense of what each side is facing, it's easy to jump to conclusions about the other party's alleged stinginess or financial incompetence. Here are some suggestions to help you address this situation:

- Talk with one another about your respective financial situations. Keeping silent will probably create uncertainty (and perhaps resentment as well), while discussing your finances will start to dispel misconceptions.
- Try to share information that will encourage openmindedness in your parents. They may not understand your situation without a more detailed sense of your financial goals, strategies, and dilemmas.
- Stay openminded about what your parents are dealing with, financially speaking. The years immediately following retirement are a major financial transition and potentially a time of considerable anxiety. Your parents may have more than they need; then again, they may not. After they settle into their post-retirement lifestyle and investment strategy, they will be able to project accurately how much help they can give you—or, alternatively, how much help they may need to receive from *you*.

Children, Money, and the Older Generation

Another important issue during middle age concerns your parents' influence on how you discuss financial matters with your own children. In Chapter 15 we considered various ways of teaching your children about money. A related issue is the input that your parents (and parents-in-law) have in this process. As your children's grandparents, they will frequently influence your children's education pertaining to everything from socialization skills to understanding how money affects their lives. That influence may be positive and welcome, such as when your parents reinforce the financial values you want your children to absorb. On the other hand, you may discover that your parents are inadvertently undercutting your efforts. Either way, it's important to discuss the situation so that both sides know where you stand.

Here are some of the issues you should discuss:

- Discussing finances
- Indulging children's desires to spend money
- Holidays
- College funding

Discussing Finances. In some families, discussions with even very young children regarding finances are frequent, abundant, and specific. Children know how much things cost and what the limits are on spending money. In other families, the parents feel that their children shouldn't feel burdened by too much financial detail; the mother and father prefer that their children don't focus on cost. Whatever your approach, it's important for your parents to know what your wishes are and, ideally, to treat financial matters in a manner consistent with those wishes. The only way that your parents can handle this situation in the way you prefer is for you to make your wishes explicit.

Indulging Children's Desires to Spend Money. Some parents feel comfortable paying for any reasonable request their children make. Others prefer that their children prioritize their choices, learn to do without certain things, and pay for some purchases with their own money. As with so many other issues, there's a continuum of attitudes in this regard. Again, the salient point in this discussion is that your opinions may differ from your parents'. It's not uncommon for parents to feel that the grandparents are "spoiling the children," while the grandparents complain that the parents are too rigid in what they allow. The reverse scenario is also common. For most families, only frank discussions will map out the territory in this regard and create a zone of compromise.

■ Melissa, who is 6, asked her mother if she could take a gymnastics class at the local Y. Her mother, Sandra, didn't object to the notion itself; the problem was that as a single parent, Sandra simply couldn't afford the fee. She also felt that Melissa certainly got lots of exercise simply playing with her friends at school, in the backyard, and at a nearby park. Gymnastics seemed like a luxury. In addition, Sandra wanted her daughter to grow accustomed to the realities that their single income presented.

As it turned out, Melissa mentioned her interest in the gymnastics class to Sandra's parents, who immediately offered to foot the bill. Sandra was frustrated and angry when she heard the news. It wasn't just that her parents had upstaged her and perhaps had even made her look tightfisted in her daughter's eyes. What she really resented was that her parents, having not even consulted with her, had undercut Sandra's parental authority. ■

Holidays. One of the trickiest issues facing many families in this regard has to do with holiday times and birthdays. Holidays such as Christmas and Hanukkah may become an unhappy time instead of a joyous event if the parents and the grandparents disagree over what level of gift giving is appropriate for the children. One generation may prefer a more low-keyed celebration that stresses religious meanings; the other generation may want more opulent festivities. The same conflict can occur when a child has a birthday. This situation grows still more complex because there may be two sets of grandparents on the scene, so that the parents feel outnumbered and outmaneuvered. (To complicate things further, the grandparents may even disagree with *one another!*)

What's the solution? Again, there's no easy answer. But whatever answer you and your parents work out, it's likely to start with open—and open-minded—communication.

College Funding. Who will be funding your children's college educations? In Chapter 11 we discussed various ways in which the older generation can help the middle generation pay for the high cost of college. Your parents' utilization of one or more of these techniques can be the biggest boost that you'll ever have in paying for these expenses. However, your parents may not tell you what their plans are regarding assistance to fund college costs; as a result, you may make decisions (either funding or lack of funding) that turn out to be a mistake. Both you and your parents need to create an open dialogue on this matter that doesn't imply that you expect help from them.

■ Let's say you've assumed that virtually all of your son's or daughter's college fund will come from what you've set aside. You scrimp and save for years, giving up vacations and other family activities so that you can afford to send your child to college. Then, not long before your child heads off to school, your parents inform you that they've been saving money, too, and have accumulated a nice college fund themselves. Are you disappointed? Of course not. You need the money. However, you would have liked to learn about the situation with more than 5 seconds' warning since you might have made other decisions regarding your savings and spending patterns (including travel to visit your parents more often). Of course, it's not the end of the world to have accumulated more money than you need for funding your goals. Even so, a little advanced notice might have left you feeling even more grateful (and maybe less exasperated) than you do. ■

In affluent families, another aspect of the situation is that your own parents' contributions to your children's college fund may have advantages for the older as well as the younger and middle generations. As we noted in Chapter 11, the older generation may benefit from an estate planning standpoint by making gifts of assets now rather than waiting for these assets to be distributed after death.

PLANNER

A particularly beneficial tax rule is that a grandparent (or, for that matter, an uncle, aunt, or anyone else—the donor needn't be a relative) can fund your child's education by paying the tuition directly. There's no upper limit to the amount being paid. There are a few restrictions: (1) the money must be used only for tuition and books, and (2) the donor must pay the funds directly to the recipient's educational institution, not to the recipient or his or her parents. (Note: This rule also applies to the payment of medical bills.) You should also know that this form of payment is over and above the annual gift tax exclusion. After 1998, the current $10,000 annual exclusion will be indexed annually for inflation. Indexing of the annual exclusion is rounded to the lowest multiple of $1,000 and is likely to reach $11,000 in either 2001 or 2002.

Another vehicle to accumulate funds for a child's education is the new Education IRA created by the Taxpayer Relief Act of 1997. An Education IRA is a trust or custodial account that is created exclusively to pay qualified higher education expenses. A donor can make a nondeductible contribution of up to $500 per year per beneficiary into an Education IRA. It's also important to note that the contributor need not be related to the beneficiary, and there is no limit on the number of individual beneficiaries for whom one contributor can set up an education IRA (provided the contributor has modified AGI within the established limits, and that each contribution for each individual does not exceed $500 annually). You will not have to include distributions from an education IRA in your gross income to the extent that the distribution does not exceed qualified higher education expenses (i.e., post-secondary tuition, fees, books, supplies, equipment, and certain room and board expenses) incurred by you during the year the distribution is made. For more detailed information and income limitations related to the education IRA, please refer to Chapter 2.

The Later Years

One of the striking changes that you may experience during late middle age and the years that follow is a role reversal with your parents. During your childhood and youth, you depended on your mother and father for guidance and support; then you attained a relationship of equals; but now, as your parents age, they may end up more and more dependent on you for guidance and support. This can be a difficult transition for some families, while others find it relatively smooth. Either way, it's important to discuss as openly as possible whatever issues come up, since ignoring them will only complicate everyone's task.

The situations you're most likely to face are:

- Estate planning
- Health care issues
- Your parents' dependency

Estate Planning

How your parents decide to handle their estate is, of course, their own business. At the same time, they may not be aware of all their specific options—or may not have faced the general issues—and thus may need some guidance. You should therefore try to help them deal with the necessary estate planning issues and be willing to discuss these matters with them openly and objectively.

Wills. Your parents have probably arranged to have their wills made or revised. If not, you should urge them to proceed with at least this basic step in the estate planning process, given the potential for disruption otherwise on the entire family. If they've taken the necessary steps, you should nonetheless have them double-check to make sure that the wills are current and properly executed.

In addition, you should consider the degree to which you can coordinate your parents' wills with your own. This is a process that can save both generations money and hassle, and it may provide a financial advantage to your children or other family members in the younger generations.

E X A M P L E

■ Let's suppose that you and your spouse have saved a nest egg adequate to let you retire comfortably. You feel confident that you don't really need an inheritance from them at whatever point they die. In addition, you feel sure that your assets are substantial enough that your children will undoubtedly receive your assets as an inheritance when you pass away. Your concern, therefore, is that if you receive an inheritance from your own parents, estate taxes imposed at your death will cause your children to receive far less than they would have following your death *if your parents had simply transferred their estate directly to your children.* Currently, up to $1 million of such transfers can be made by your parents without fear of the generation-skipping transfer tax. After 1998, the $1,000,000 generation-skipping transfer tax exemption will be indexed annually for inflation. (Indexing of the exemption is rounded to the nearest lowest multiple of $10,000.) You may be able to achieve the same result by executing a written disclaimer of your inheritance even if your parents don't revise their wills to provide for a transfer to your children. ■

See Chapter 9 for more information about wills and Chapter 11 for information about the generation-skipping transfer tax.

Trusts

Normally, a transfer from your parents to your children would be accomplished by means of a *generation-skipping trust.* This arrangement involves transferring assets to a trust for your children's benefit during your parents' lifetime and/or upon death. If the trust is properly drafted, you could even be the trustee, enabling you to have management control over the trust without both the income tax and estate tax burden of the funds themselves. These types of trusts would typically permit you to use the funds for your children's health care costs, educational purposes, maintenance, or support. However, you should not be permitted to use the funds in this manner while your children are minors under state law. If you had such a power, you would be considered to have a power of appointment to satisfy your own legal support obligation, and the trust property would be included in your estate (if you died while your children were minors).

For a discussion of trusts, see Chapter 12.

Powers of Attorney. Although your parents may be competent in managing their money and health care decisions, the day may arrive when an accident or illness disrupts their abilities. The result may be great inconvenience—even hardship—for both you and them.

A simple solution to this problem is to arrange a *durable power of attorney, a health care power of attorney,* or both. These are legal arrangements granting someone the right to make financial, legal, and health care decisions if the person granting the power is incapacitated. What many couples do is to grant each other power of attorney; in the event that both are incapable of managing their affairs, however, a grown son or daughter or some other relative can assume the role. *Note:* The nature of these powers of attorney, as well as the specific powers that they grant, differ from state to state. Consult with a lawyer knowledgeable about the laws *of the state in which your parent is a resident* to determine the relevant issues.

There are generally three aspects to this arrangement:

- *Asset management.* This involves the power of attorney, and it designates who will look after income, expenses, investments, and so on, in cases of incapacity.
- *Health care decisions.* These require a health care power of attorney, which indicates who will consult with physicians and other providers about medical treatment.
- *Life support issues.* These involve a living will, which outlines personal preferences about when to cease medical treatment or avoid "life-sustaining measures" during terminal illness.

If your parents don't have durable powers of attorney, or if they've arranged powers of attorney that name each other as attorneys-in-fact, you should probably discuss the situation with them. The risk here is that given medical emergencies, neither of them may be capable of attending to the necessary decisions. One response to this potential problem is having your parents name you or one of your siblings as their attorney-in-fact. Factors influencing the particular choice will be the age, state of residence, and overall ability of your family members. In Chapter 13 we discussed each of these three issues in more detail.

Health Care Issues

Some of the most important discussions between you and your parents will focus on health care issues. On the one hand, Mom and Dad will have a significant portion of their medical needs covered through Medicare, and the so-called Medigap policies can take up most or all of the slack. On the other hand, these are complex topics, and your parents may need assistance sorting through their options and making the best choices. The same holds true for long-term care. Since these topics will affect you, too, as you approach retirement, we've covered them thoroughly in Chapter 25.

Medicare. Medicare is a federal health insurance program for people 65 and older, people of any age with permanent kidney failure, and certain disabled people under 65. Your parents can enroll in Medicare by contacting the Social Security Administration 3 months before their 65th birthdays. They are then eligible for benefits under both parts of the Medicare program: Part A, which helps pay for inpatient hospital care; and Part B, which helps pay for doctors' services, medical supplies, and other health care expenses. (Part A is available free; Part B is available for a monthly premium.) For an overview of Medicare, see Chapter 25.

Although many people have no problem dealing with Medicare, you should make sure that your parents understand the benefits they receive through the program as well as what they don't receive. There are significant gaps in Medicare coverage. For instance, even inpatient hospital coverage through Medicare has the following deductibles, coinsurance payments, and exclusions in 1999:

- A $768 deductible on the first admission to the hospital during each benefit period
- A $192 daily coinsurance payment for days 61 through 90
- A $384 coinsurance payment for each "lifetime reserve day" used
- A limitation on the number of lifetime reserve days available and used on coverage beyond 90 days
- No coverage for the first three units of whole blood or packed cells used each year in connection with covered services
- No coverage for a private hospital room (unless medically necessary) or for a private-duty nurse
- No coverage for personal convenience items (e.g., telephone or TV) in a hospital room

- No coverage for care that isn't medically necessary, or for nonemergency care in a hospital unless certified by Medicare
- No coverage for care received outside the United States and its territories, except under limited circumstances in Canada and Mexico

Although numerous, the items on this list are just the start in what Medicare doesn't provide. Other gaps exist in skilled nursing facility care, home health care, hospice care, and psychiatric care coverage. In short, your parents will be better off having Medicare than not having it, but their health care needs aren't adequately covered unless they have some other form of coverage to close the various gaps. For more about Medicare, see Chapter 25—Planning for Retirement: Health Care and Insurance Needs.

Medigap Insurance. The answer to this dilemma is private health insurance of the sort now colloquially called *Medigap*. This coverage takes the form of a policy that your parents (or you yourself) purchase to supplement their Medicare benefits. At present, there are 10 separate forms of Medigap insurance, each of which offers a different set of benefits. These forms are regulated by federal and state law, and they are uniform in attributes from one company to another. To determine specifically what sort of Medigap insurance your parents need, see the discussion of this subject in Chapter 25; then consult with your parents and their insurance agent to review the possibilities.

Long-Term Care. One issue that many people face is how to meet their elderly parents' needs if they require long-term care. (Long-term care is defined as unskilled nursing care in a nursing home or convalescent facility, or its equivalent in the recipient's own home.) This situation can be problematic because care of this sort is expensive, yet it isn't covered by Medicare. As a result, your parents may end up needing long-term care, yet be unable to afford it. This can leave you in a situation where you must either foot the bill or provide your parents with this sort of care yourself.

Because you may need to consider long-term care for yourself at some point, we discuss this subject in detail in Chapter 25. The issues that affect your parents are essentially the same; for this reason, you should refer to that chapter for an overview of the subject.

One other consideration, however: If your parents are likely to need long-term care but are unable to pay for it, you might consider funding this potential cost in advance. This is obviously an option that not all families can afford. In cases where it's a possibility, though, it can pay off well in the long run.

There are two main ways to accomplish this goal. One is purchasing long-term care insurance for your parent. The other is investing money that would pay for long-term care if it becomes necessary. Long-term care coverage isn't cheap, but it will pay for nursing home, convalescent facility, or in-home care when it's needed. Given the costs of such care, paying long-term care insurance premiums may involve a relatively modest investment. However, if your parents never need long-term care, the premium dollars invested in the policy are lost forever.

The other alternative—investing money to pay for long-term care out-of-pocket—has the advantage of offering you more flexibility. If your parent needs long-term care, you'll have some funds available for this purpose. You could use the funds to pay for institutional care if that's the family consensus; on the other hand, you could use the money instead to pay for modifying or adding onto your house so that Mom or Dad could move in with you. If the need never arises, then you can direct your investment to other goals. If the need does arise, it may cost you more than long-term care insurance premiums would have.

Your Parents' Dependency

Finally, there's the issue of what happens if your parents become financially dependent on you. This is a complex subject that rarely works out quite as people anticipate. The main issue here is how to fund your parents' support; the tax savings potential involved is almost always a secondary matter.

Here are two tax planning topics to consider:

• Claiming your parent as a dependent
• Paying medical expenses

Claiming Your Parent as a Dependent. The income tax benefits of claiming a dependent (discussed earlier in this chapter) apply to parents as well as to children. Your parent can be listed as a dependent on your tax return and thus potentially provide you with a significant annual deduction ($2,750 in 1999). To obtain this benefit, however, you must be sure that your parent meets the following requirements:

• His or her gross income must be less than the personal exemption amount for that year ($2,750 in 1999).
• More than one-half of his or her support for the year must be provided by you (however, see The Multiple Support Arrangement Exception on page 444).
• He or she does not file a joint income tax return.
• He or she is a U.S. citizen or resident of the United States, Canada, or Mexico.

The most difficult requirement to meet is usually the first one—income of less than the personal exemption amount. Although $2,750 isn't enough to provide more than half of many people's support, the fact remains that you won't get the deduction if your parent receives more than that small amount of income. To the extent that your parent's income can be reduced without adversely affecting his or her financial situation, planning to have his or her income be less than the personal exemption amount each year may be beneficial.

E X A M P L E

■ Let's say that your mother has $50,000 of investments, and they generate $3,000 of income per year. That amount of income means that you won't be able to claim her as a dependent. However, you might be able to have your mother use up her investment assets to fund her support instead of you paying her expenses for a while. Depleting her assets to pay her expenses should lower income in the future. Then, when you pay her expenses, you may be able to receive a tax break, because she'll qualify as your dependent. ■

The Multiple Support Arrangement Exception

In the discussion above, we mentioned the multiple support arrangement exception. This is a tax rule that may allow you to claim a dependency exemption for your parent under certain circumstances even if you share the burden of support with other persons, such as your brothers or sisters. Summarized briefly, this exception means that if more than half of your parent's support was furnished by two or more persons, each of whom would be entitled to the exemption except for the fact that he or she alone didn't furnish more than half of the support, a multiple support arrangement would entitle one of those persons to claim the dependency exemption. Other conditions apply, including the filing of Form 2120 by the other persons who contribute to the dependent's support.

Paying Medical Expenses. Even if you're unable to obtain a dependency exemption for your parent, paying his or her medical expenses may still allow you a tax benefit. As we mentioned earlier, there is no gift tax liability associated with paying medical expenses directly to the health care provider—even if the amount exceeds the $10,000 gift tax annual exclusion. After 1998, the current $10,000 annual exclusion will be indexed annually for inflation. Indexing of the annual exclusion is rounded to the lowest multiple of $1,000 and is likely to reach $11,000 in either 2001 or 2002.

In addition, if you qualify for an income tax benefit for medical deductions—that is, if your medical expenses in general exceed 7.5% of your adjusted gross income—you can go ahead and take a deduction for the medical expenses you pay on your parent's behalf even if your parent doesn't qualify for the dependency exemption because of the earnings limitation requirement. Your parent would need to meet the other dependency requirements discussed earlier, but his or her income does not need to be less than the personal exemption amount.

23

LOSING YOUR SPOUSE OR LIFE PARTNER

The death of a spouse, life partner, or any other close relation can be one of the most traumatic experiences you will ever face. The process of dealing with the personal and emotional loss often brought about by the death of a loved one, can be wrenching and often will leave the survivors confused, exhausted, and feeling alone. There have been many excellent books and articles written on the subject of handling the death of a close relation. In fact, more and more support groups are springing up around the country to bring together people that share these common issues and concerns to help each other through tough times and embark on the road to recovery. Unfortunately, as with many areas, a death in the family can also bring about many financial concerns that the survivors are either ill prepared or unable to handle. Few, if any, of the workshops or support groups that we have seen offer the kind of sound, unbiased, objective financial advice that survivors need during a critical time in their lives and in the lives of their family.

Should I pay off my mortgage? Will I need to sell our home? Can I afford to live the same lifestyle? Will I be able to afford education for my children? Can I retire or will I need to continue to work? What kinds of benefits am I eligible for? Can I collect Social Security benefits? Do I need a will? What about insurance? Who can I trust to help me with my investments?

These and other questions are the focus of this chapter. To encapsulate the various sources of information and potential issues that you may face, we have divided this chapter into several parts:

- Being a survivor
- Working with advisors
- Calculating total assets and liabilities
- Determining new living expenses
- Duties of an executor or executrix
- The decedent's estate
- Life insurance proceeds
- Employer benefits
- Retirement benefits
- Survivor long-term planning

BEING A SURVIVOR

Often the term *survivor* conjures up thoughts of someone who has endured a great ordeal. And in most cases, they have. Yet there are certainly instances where the death of a loved one has occurred suddenly, with no forewarning. Whether the road that you have traveled to your present survivorship status was a long one or a short one, one thing is clear: It has not been easy and it's likely that there are many pieces that you feel will need to be picked up. Recognize that many people have been through the same things you have experienced. In time people can, and do, heal and get on with their lives.

We do not mean to say that you should simply "flick a switch" and change the way you feel, but we do ask that you recognize that in time you will begin to feel more in control of your personal situation and probably more comfortable with your ability to manage your financial life. There will be many questions that are likely to arise as you adjust to your situation. Undoubtedly there will be many well-intentioned people—friends, relatives, co-workers, and others who will be happy to provide you with assistance, guidance, and even opinions on financial matters. While these people may be well-intentioned, you must try to distill those opinions that are knowledgeable from those that are not. There are some very critical decisions that you, as a survivor, will need to make that can have a far-reaching impact on you and your family for a long time to come.

In addition to friends and well wishers you will probably also begin to get solicitations from different kinds of financial advisors—stockbrokers, insurance salesmen, financial planners, and others. As a general rule of thumb, you should politely indicate to any unsolicited contact by anyone offering personal investment advice that you are currently interviewing several people and that if they will leave their name and number you will contact them when you are ready. Employing this approach accomplishes several things. First, it gives you an opportunity to check out the caller, his or her organization, and reputation. Second, it puts you in control of the situation—by affirmatively indicating that you are interviewing several people and taking their phone numbers, the callers are to some extent disarmed. Finally, it provides you with time to consult with some very close and trusted acquaintances so that you may get solid referrals for people that they know, trust, and feel confident enough in to make them want to give a referral. Finally, most of these callers will leave a name and number but few will pursue you too hard if you don't call them back.

WORKING WITH ADVISORS

The question of whether or not you need an attorney to help you with the estate's legal and tax issues is a difficult one to answer in objective terms. Generally, the law of the state that the decedent was "domiciled" in (that is, the state in which the individual made his or her permanent home) will determine the distribution of the assets, the process of that distribution, and who will control the distribution process. If the decedent left a will, you may need to determine whether the will needs to be "probated." These items are covered in greater detail in Chapters 9 through 13.

> **Probate:** Probate is a legal proceeding in which a decedent's will is processed by a special court. An executor or administrator is named to handle the decedent's affairs and administer the estate. Assets requiring probate will be subject to this special court's jurisdiction before they are transferred to the beneficiaries. Nonprobate assets, such as jointly owned property and life insurance, are transferred directly to beneficiaries without passing through the probate court's proceedings.

If you do decide you want or need an attorney, generally you will want to find one that specializes in estate settlements. An extensive knowledge of financial planning, including the tax aspects of the subject, is crucial. If you miss certain opportunities from a tax standpoint, you may end up paying for the consequences—literally—for years to come. (A brief example: If all of the assets in an estate are left outright to you, there is a possibility of losing significant tax and financial benefits that you or the estate are entitled to.) In trying to select an attorney, it is always a good idea to interview at least three people who have been referred to you by either a relative, friend, or business associate.

Your entire financial picture will have changed by the time the estate has been settled and closed. To take hold of your situation, you'll almost certainly need advice from an advisor who can help you plan for the long run. If you feel that you need to supplement your attorney's advice with information and recommendations from other advisors, then you should consider obtaining help from a financial planner, and perhaps from certain other professionals as well.

Financial Planners

If you decide to hire a financial planner, he or she should consult with you and your attorney to become familiar with the nature of the estate proceedings and relevant issues. After initial consultations, the planner should analyze and calculate your financial needs and resources. Among the considerations will be the total amount of your family's financial assets. This is especially important because maintaining your accustomed standard of living may be more difficult if the decedent was the family breadwinner.

To help you plan effectively, your financial planner will need all the data you have available regarding:

- Employment
- Recent wage and salary data, including raise notifications, W-2s, pay stubs, etc.
- Contracts
- Benefit statements
- Partnership or S-corporation K-1s
- Business tax returns
- Home ownership/rental
- Purchase documents
- Leases
- Insurance data

- Appraisals
- Income tax returns
- Life, health, and disability insurance policies
- Will and trust documents
- Investment portfolio information
- Data concerning income, expenses, and debts
- Other important information regarding assets, liabilities, income, and expenses

Using the kind of information listed above, your financial planner can perform a variety of tasks, including the following:

- Accumulating and analyzing data
- Expressing opinions to the courts on the value of property
- Projecting cash flow
- Preparing reports and financial analyses
- Projecting tax consequences
- Providing data and professional opinions on financial issues
- Helping you make financial decisions

Regarding this final point—help on financial decisions—the planner can help you make financial choices about a variety of issues. Some will be specific to survivorship, such as estimating the amount of income and cash flow you will need. Other choices will concern more generic financial planning tasks, such as determining how to fund children's education, dealing with debt, and doing various kinds of investment, insurance, and estate planning.

Once the estate process is complete, you may find your financial planner helpful in assisting with longer-term personal financial planning matters. Help of this sort will generally resemble financial planning services in a non-estate context.

Other Advisors

Your financial planner will probably provide the most comprehensive financial advice of the various advisors working with you. However, other professionals may be involved as well, such as bankers, insurance specialists, investment professionals, appraisers, and others. Consult with your financial planner if you feel that you need these advisors' services. The planner may be able to recommend specific persons to help you and may also coordinate interactions between them on your behalf.

CALCULATING TOTAL ASSETS AND LIABILITIES

One of the first financial tasks that you will need to perform is determining the total assets and liabilities of both the estate and yourself. This is usually required by the courts and, among other things, would be done pursuant to an estate settlement in which it would be decided who would take permanent possession of what assets, and when. What follows is a worksheet for making these calculations.

YOUR NET WORTH AS OF _____

ASSETS

Cash equivalents

Checking accounts	$_____
Savings accounts	_____
Money market accounts	_____
Money market fund accounts	_____
Certificates of deposit	_____
U.S. Treasury bills	_____
Cash value of life insurance	_____
Total	$_____

Investments

Stocks	_____
Bonds	_____
Mutual fund investments	_____
Partnership interests	_____
Other investments	_____
Total	$_____

Retirement funds

Pension (present lump-sum value)	_____
IRAs and Keogh accounts	_____
Employee savings plans (e.g., 401(k), SEP, ESOP)	_____
Total	$_____

Personal assets

Principal residence	_____
Second residence	_____

Collectibles/art/antiques	_____
Automobiles	_____
Home furnishings	_____
Furs and jewelry	_____
Other assets	_____
Total	$_____
Total Assets	$_____

LIABILITIES

Charge account balances	_____
Personal loans	_____
Student loans	_____
Auto loans	_____
401(k) loans	_____
Investment loans (margin, real estate, etc.)	_____
Home mortgages	_____
Home equity loans	_____
Alimony	_____
Child support	_____
Life insurance policy loans	_____
Projected income tax liability	_____
Other liabilities	_____
Total Liabilities	$(_____)
Net Worth (assets minus liabilities)	$_____

The difference between determining assets and liabilities in connection with an estate compared to that of financial planning calculations you may perform later is that you'll need to specify individual as well as joint ownership. This may mean three sets of worksheets: "Mine," "Yours," and "Ours." To complicate matters, the various state laws will influence how these assets and liabilities must be divided. For instance, the states that have community property laws divide property differently than do the non-community property states. This is just one of many issues for which an attorney or financial planner's advice may be useful.

Once you've set forth the total assets and liabilities, you'll also have to identify your items of income and expenditure. This analysis is an important component in ensuring that your current and long-term needs will be met. The following worksheet will be helpful in making these calculations:

PREPARING FOR SURVIVORSHIP: MONTHLY CASH FLOW ANALYSIS

INCOME WORKSHEET

GROSS MONTHLY INCOME FROM	SELF	PARTNER
a. Salary and wages (including commissions, allowance, and overtime)	$	$
b. Bonuses (annual, semiannual, or quarterly)		
c. Income from royalties, trusts, or estates		
d. Gains derived from dealing in property		
e. Business income from sources, such as self-employment, partnerships, etc.		
f. Pensions and retirement		
g. Social Security		
h. Disability and unemployment compensation		
i. Child support from any previous marriage		
j. Interest and dividends		
k. Rental income (net of expenses)		
l. All other sources (specify)		
_____		
_____		
_____		
Total Monthly Income	$	$

PREPARING FOR SURVIVORSHIP: MONTHLY CASH FLOW ANALYSIS *(continued)*

EXPENSE WORKSHEET

1. HOUSEHOLD EXPENSES

	SELF	PARTNER
a. Monthly rent/mortgage payment		$_____
b. Property taxes (monthly basis)		_____
c. Repairs and maintenance		_____
d. Groceries and household items		_____
e. Meals outside the home		_____
f. Services:		
Gardener/landscaping	$_____	
Housekeeper	_____	
Pool service	_____	
Trash collection	_____	
Security service	_____	
Other _____	_____	
Total		$_____
g. Utilities:		
Water and sewage	$_____	
Telephone	_____	
Gas/oil/electricity	_____	
Cable television	_____	
Other _____	_____	
Total		$_____
Total Household Expenses		$_____
2. AUTOMOBILE/TRANSPORTATION EXPENSES: (SPLIT SELF/PARTNER)		
a. Monthly payment/lease	$_____	$_____
b. Gasoline and oil	_____	_____
c. Repairs and maintenance	_____	_____
d. Auto tags and license	_____	_____
e. Public transportation	_____	_____
Total Automobile/ Transportation Expenses		$_____

PREPARING FOR SURVIVORSHIP: MONTHLY CASH FLOW ANALYSIS *(continued)*

	SELF	PARTNER
3. PERSONAL EXPENSES		
a. Toiletries/cosmetics	$ _____	$ _____
b. Nonprescription drugs	_____	_____
c. Dry cleaning/laundry	_____	_____
d. Clothing purchases	_____	_____
e. Grooming/hygiene	_____	_____
f. Gifts	_____	_____
g. Entertainment	_____	_____
h. Vacations/travel	_____	_____
i. Publications/records	_____	_____
j. Dues/club memberships	_____	_____
k. Charitable contributions	_____	_____
l. Other personal expenses	_____	_____
_____	_____	_____
_____	_____	_____
_____	_____	_____
Subtotals	$ _____	$ _____
Total Personal Expenses		$ _____
4. HEALTH CARE EXPENSES		
a. Medical	$ _____	$ _____
b. Dental	_____	_____
c. Prescription drugs	_____	_____
d. Vision	_____	_____
e. Nonprescription drugs	_____	_____
Subtotals	$ _____	$ _____
Total Health Care Expenses		$ _____

PREPARING FOR SURVIVORSHIP: MONTHLY CASH FLOW ANALYSIS *(continued)*

	SELF	PARTNER
5. CHILDREN'S EXPENSES		
a. Day care		$
b. School tuition/supplies		
c. Lunch money		
d. Allowance		
e. Clothing		
f. Grooming/hygiene		
g. Gifts		
h. Entertainment/activities/lessons		
i. Medical		
j. Dental		
k. Prescription drugs		
l. Vision		
Total Children's Expenses		
6. INSURANCE PREMIUMS		
a. Homeowner		$
b. Automobile		
c. Life		
d. Medical/hospital		
e. Disability		
f. Personal property		
g. Other _____		
Total Insurance Expenses (monthly)		$
7. OTHER MONTHLY EXPENSES		
a. Alimony to any previous spouse	$	$
b. Child support to any previous spouse		
_____		
_____		
_____		
Subtotals	$	$
Total Other Monthly Expenses		$

PREPARING FOR SURVIVORSHIP: MONTHLY CASH FLOW ANALYSIS (continued)

8. PAYMENTS TO CREDITORS

Creditor	Balance Owed	Monthly Payment
_____	$ _____	$ _____
_____	$ _____	$ _____
_____	$ _____	$ _____
_____	$ _____	$ _____
_____	$ _____	$ _____

**Total Monthly Payments
to Creditors**

Total Monthly Expenses

Net Worth

DETERMINING NEW LIVING EXPENSES

You will also need a second set of calculations to help you clarify your sources of income and living expenses. Many survivors don't realize how dramatically their financial picture is about to change; it's crucial that you look ahead and start to determine both what expenses you'll have and how you'll pay for them.

The issues involved in this regard are numerous and complex, and a single chapter in a book can only begin to address them. However, the issues that your attorney and financial planner should broach with you include:

- What will you need to receive in terms of monthly cash flow?
- What are the family's total current living expenses, and how will these change in the future?
- What modifications will be necessary in spending patterns given the probable reduction in income?

To answer these questions, you'll have to take the living expenses you've identified and scrutinize them more closely to determine which are core expenses, which are discretionary, and which may be altogether unnecessary. You'll also have to look ahead to how these expenses will change in the future. If you retain your residence, for instance, you will face expenses such as the mortgage, property taxes, homeowners' insurance and maintenance. The process of sizing up these expenses may well strike you as daunting, even depressing. However, it's important to keep in mind that the situation isn't permanent. Many survivors find that the initial increase in costs doesn't last indefinitely. Formerly dependent survivors start their own careers and earn an income of their own. Remember, the numbers you use for financial planning in the early years following a death aren't static. But you can't plan properly for the future unless you take some initial steps to size up your situation as accurately and thoughtfully as possible. Your attorney and financial planner can help you assess your specific situation and decide on the best response to it.

DUTIES OF AN EXECUTOR OR EXECUTRIX

The Estate

At the time of death, all of an individual's possessions and finances become part of his or her estate. The estate is the legal entity into which the deceased individual's separately owned assets are gathered, from which taxes—both estate and income—are paid for a period of time, and ultimately from which bequests are paid to beneficiaries of the estate.

In cases where there is a will, the estate is controlled by an executor (a man) or executrix (a woman), who is named in the deceased's will. Many widows or widowers are named as executor of a spouse's estate. Other times this task falls to one or more of the couple's grown children, one of the deceased's siblings, a close family relation, or a trusted friend. Another common executor could be the family attorney, or even a corporate executor, such as a bank. Finally, in some instances, a co-executor is named to act along with another executor to discharge their duties.

> *Executor, Executrix: Generally, an executor or executrix is the person named in a decedent's will to administer the estate property and debts left by the decedent and distribute property as the decedent has directed.*

When there is no will, an administrator is appointed by the local probate court and disbursements from the estate are governed by state law.

The executor's first tasks include:

1. Obtaining a number of copies of the death certificate (usually one for every item that the decedent had title to, such as bank or brokerage accounts, real estate, etc.)

2. Obtaining a tax identification number for the estate

3. Setting up a checking account for the estate, into which the cash holdings and any income due the deceased in the future can be deposited, and from which funeral expenses, attorney fees, taxes, and other expenses can be paid

4. Preparing an accounting of the estate's assets, as quickly as possible

5. Notifying insurance companies, banks, and brokerage firms of the death

File life insurance claims as soon as possible. Although the value of the death benefit is counted as part of the estate's value for tax purposes, life insurance payments pass to the beneficiary outside of probate. Life insurance companies also usually pay routine death benefits within weeks. This money provides a necessary financial cushion for the survivor.

Creating a full balance sheet for the estate as of the date of death is an important preliminary step. The gross estate includes all of the deceased's real property, as well as financial assets, to the extent they were owned by the deceased. A balance sheet for the estate includes a list of the fair market values of assets and the current balances of any liabilities.

In many instances, a couple will own many assets and maintain many financial assets jointly. See Chapter 9 on estate planning for more details.

The first statements to arrive after death from any bank, brokerage, mutual fund, or other account held jointly by the deceased and the widow or widower must be collected. Half of the proceeds of each of these joint accounts must be credited to the estate.

Valuations on real estate, cars, and other tangible assets must be obtained as soon as possible. Any ownership interest in partnerships or closely held businesses must be valued.

On the liabilities side, it is important to list all outstanding bills—from credit cards to the telephone and electricity, as liabilities. Proper accounting of these liabilities reduces the taxable estate.

If you are the named executor or executrix, be sure to get tax filing dates from your attorney, accountant, or other advisor. The estate will be responsible for both federal and state income taxes while it is open, and possibly for federal and state estate tax. Federal and state estate taxes must be paid within nine months of the time of death. Under current tax law, if the spouse is the sole beneficiary there will likely be no federal estate tax.

The Decedent's Estate

Federal estate tax is a levy on the transfer of property at death. The gross estate will include the fair market value of all property to the extent the decedent had an interest in it at the time of his or her death. The following items are the type normally included in your gross estate:

- Tangible personal property, real estate, and other assets
- Proportionate share of jointly owned property
- Life insurance benefits
- Employee benefits such as retirement plan balances
- Certain taxable gift/transfers made during lifetime
- Gift tax paid within three years of death

Jointly Owned Property

One area which often gives rise to confusion is the treatment of jointly owned property. As a general rule, only one-half of the value of property that a husband and wife own as joint tenants with right of survivorship (or tenants by the entirety) is included in the estate of the first spouse to die. The marital deduction prevents the property transfer from actually causing federal estate tax to be owed. Upon the survivor's death, however, the entire property will be subject to tax (assuming that it's still held at the time of death). If the joint tenants aren't married, the entire value of the property is included in the gross estate of the first to die unless the estate can prove that the other joint owner actually furnished all or part of the payment for acquiring the property. If you and another joint owner acquired property by gift or inheritance, only your fractional share of the property is included. Similarly, if you hold property as a tenant in common with someone else, your estate will include your fractional interest of the property's value.

For a more in-depth explanation of these topics, please refer to Chapter 10 on Estate Taxes.

Allowable Deductions

While the tax law requires an estate to include the value of all the decedent's assets in the gross estate, it also provides for certain deductions against the gross estate's value. For example, the gross estate may be reduced by items such as debts, mortgage liabilities, and administrative expenses (such as reasonable funeral costs, estate administration, executor's commissions, attorney's fees, accounting fees, appraisal fees, court costs, etc.).

VALUATION OF ESTATE PROPERTY

Property is included in an estate at its fair market value. Property that trades on an established market may be valued easily. For example, publicly traded stocks and bonds are valued based on the average of the high and low selling price on the date of death (or, if elected, the date 6 months after death). However, interests in closely held businesses or partnerships must generally be appraised to take the business's assets, earning capacity, and other factors into account. You're probably familiar with the process of getting a home appraised for purposes of obtaining a mortgage or home equity loan. It's especially important to have a certified appraiser with expertise in appraising the type of property that needs to be appraised. A CPA, attorney, or personal financial planner can assist in identifying an appropriate person to appraise business interests or other difficult-to-value property for estate or gift tax valuation purposes.

The gross estate is valued as of the date of death or 6 months later, whichever the personal representative elects. An election to value the estate 6 months after date of death will apply to all assets in the estate. The executor can make the election only if doing so results in a decrease in estate tax liability.

FEDERAL ESTATE TAX RATES

The federal estate tax is progressive in nature and ranges from the lowest rate of 18% up to a rate of 55% for estates larger than $3 million. There's an additional 5% tax on taxable estates between $10 million and $20 million.

Credits

In determining the net amount of federal estate tax due, the estate's personal representative can claim certain credits against your tentative tax:

- Unified estate and gift tax credit
- State death tax credit
- Foreign death tax credit
- Credit for tax on prior transfers

Unified Estate and Gift Tax Credit

In 1999 each person (or his or her estate) is entitled to a unified credit equivalent to the amount of tax generated by a transfer of $650,000. In other words, no estate or gift taxes will be assessed on the first $650,000 of combined taxable gifts and transfers at death. The unified credit is scheduled to increase from an effective exemption of $650,000 to an effective exemption of $1,000,000 in 2006. Estate tax is only owed once the aggregate amount of your taxable transfers during life and at death exceeds the unified credit. At that point, the tax rates start with a 37% bracket and range as high as 55%.

E X A M P L E

■ Here's a very basic example. Suppose that in 1999 your estate was $700,000. Your estate would owe no taxes on the first $650,000. For the remaining $50,000, your estate would owe tax at the 37% rate, or $18,500. ■

Please see Chapter 10 on estate taxes for an in-depth discussion of the federal estate tax process including strategies that can reduce the estate tax.

State Tax Considerations

All states impose some kind of estate and/or inheritance tax. As noted earlier, in many states the estate tax is simply a "soak-up tax"—the amount of the federal credit for state death taxes. In these states an estate that owes no federal estate tax because of the unified credit will generally owe no state death taxes, either. But remember: Many states impose an inheritance tax on the person that receives the property from the decedent. This tax falls heaviest on bequests outside the immediate family. Therefore, in states that have estate or inheritance taxes not tied to the federal credit or other federal rules, state death tax considerations should be considered.

LIFE INSURANCE

The gross estate will include life insurance proceeds that are receivable (1) by the estate or (2) by other beneficiaries if the decedent possessed any incidents of ownership in the policies at the time of his or her death.

 What do the incidents of ownership include?

- The power to change the beneficiary of the policy
- The right to cancel the policy and receive the cash value
- The right to borrow against the policy
- The right to assign the policy

If someone else owns the policy from its inception, the policy's proceeds aren't part of the estate. Also, if the policy is transferred to another party or to a trust and the decedent retained no incidents of ownership, the proceeds will generally be removed from the estate (assuming they survive for 3 years after the transfer).

Life Insurance Proceeds

Insurance policies offer a variety of options for paying the proceeds to the named beneficiaries. Having the proceeds paid in a lump sum is the most commonly used option. On the other hand, the beneficiary may elect to have the proceeds paid in an annuity over his or her life. An annuity is a contract issued by an insurance company that guarantees to pay back over a period of time a set amount. Annuities generally pay out a steady stream of money each month no matter how long the beneficiary, that is, the annuitant, lives.

If you are in a financial position where you do not need the insurance proceeds, some life insurance policies offer an "interest only" option, under which the survivor receives only interest on the principal for life. At death, the principal is paid to beneficiaries named by you. This arrangement will qualify for the marital deduction in your spouse's estate but the proceeds will be included in your estate.

Investing Life Insurance Proceeds

One question that often arises with survivors is how they should invest the proceeds from a life insurance policy. While there is no one answer that can address all of the varying situations survivors can find themselves in, chances are that the life insurance proceeds will provide a "nest egg" which can be used to generate cash flow to help you meet your cash flow needs. By referring to the cash flow worksheet earlier in this chapter you can start to gain insight into whether you will need to generate additional cash flow from the investment of life insurance proceeds. As a general rule of thumb, and assuming that cash flow generation is desired, survivors would be well-served to consider implementing a laddered bond portfolio. While this sounds complicated, in reality it is quite simple. Laddered portfolios are nothing more than a collection of bonds, each with maturity dates at pre-set intervals. For example, you may see a laddered portfolio that contains 10 bonds, each with an equal face value and each maturing exactly one year later than the predecessor bond. The benefit of a laddered portfolio is that you aren't locked into any one investment (and its related price/yield swings) because as the bonds mature you simply roll them over into new bonds that keep in synch with your overall bond ladder. In effect, think of it more as an escalator, constantly turning steps upon steps. Be sure to read the earlier sections on investments and fixed income securities to get a better overall understanding of the risks associated with investing.

EMPLOYER BENEFITS AND RETIREMENT BENEFITS

In many instances survivors will need to make decisions with respect to the continuation of benefits under the decedent's employer-provided benefit plans. Many plans allow for some automatic coverage continuation for a limited period and then allow for survivors to purchase additional coverage under the existing plan.

Normally, survivors should shop around for continued coverages, as the cost that the employer will charge will likely be higher than what the employee had been paying while in active service. Under a federal law called COBRA, employers are required to offer continued coverage to survivors for a period of time. For more about COBRA benefits, see Chapter 25.

In addition to health and welfare benefits, many employers also provide for pension payments to survivors or other beneficiaries. You should contact the survivor's employer in their Human Resources department to identify someone who can work with you to prepare the necessary forms and paperwork to process these types of payments. As with life insurance, pension plans often have payout options which you will need to choose before any distributions occur. As with anything else, before signing onto something, seek the advice of a knowledgeable financial professional to help you decide if the option you take is the right one for you.

The decedent may have had a defined benefit pension plan that continues to pay you a monthly pension after his or her death. For self-directed retirement plans—401(k), 403(b), Keogh, SEP, or IRA—you will need to either roll these over into your IRA, or a new IRA you set up for that purpose, or you may be able to leave the funds on deposit in the plan until a later date if the decedent had not been taking disbursements. In some cases, nothing needs to be done and you would be required to take minimum disbursements when the decedent would have reached age 70½. This becomes part of your retirement benefit, with any such plans you have in your name from your place of work or your personal business or practice. If the decedent had already begun taking disbursements from a retirement plan, you will generally continue receiving them.

You need to calculate the most advantageous time to begin withdrawals from your own retirement plans, and the payout schedule that fits you. You may want to plan your payout based on your life expectancy, or on the life expectancy of you and one of your beneficiaries. The latter will reduce the minimum benefit you are required to take from your retirement plan each year. Remember, this is only a minimum you are required to take; if at any time you find this does not provide you with enough current income, you may always increase the amount of your distribution.

SURVIVOR LONG-TERM PLANNING

Managing Assets for Yourself

One of the more difficult issues you may face is determining which assets should be liquidated and beginning to create a new financial plan—a plan that produces adequate current income while not sacrificing too much growth in principal.

Remember, just because you may not have managed the financial assets before does not mean that you are bound to continue managing those assets the way the decedent did. Whether you decide that you need assistance in managing these assets or not, you need to devise an investment strategy that is right for you.

For a while, you will need to manage both your assets and those of the estate. You will probably need two different strategies:

For the estate, you need a short-term time horizon—1 to 3 years—leaving adequate liquid reserves to pay annual income taxes on the income the estate earns, fees for attorneys and other professionals working on probating the estate, as well as federal and state estate taxes.

For your portion of any formerly jointly held bank, brokerage, or mutual fund accounts, it is time to begin looking at your more long-term planning requirements.

Getting a Financial Advisor

It may be tempting if the decedent had a long-term association with a broker or financial planner to simply continue that relationship. This may not be best for you. You need to develop your own relationship with your financial advisors. People that *you* are comfortable with. You may even decide to buy and sell based on your own research, or you may turn your assets over to a financial manager. In either case, your broker should be someone you choose, someone you feel comfortable with, not necessarily an old friend of the decedent.

Perhaps the most important thing to remember is that this is not the time to be making any rash financial decisions. This is the time to be educating yourself. You may want to take time to do a more detailed budget than you used in the past. You certainly need time to figure out how you're going to want to live in the future—the lifestyle you wish to maintain and can afford. If you were not involved in financial planning and investment management before, you'll need time to become familiar with the concepts and determine how rigorously you will want to plan and invest in the future.

You may be approached by a number of professionals, urging you to let them help you. Be cautious. Work with those you know—the family attorney, accountant, or financial planner, at first. Ask for referrals from them if you think you want professional financial management assistance.

Taking Care of (Tax) Business

While most survivors understand the necessity of moving forward with their financial planning and of maintaining an orderly estate, they often delay dealing with a few very emotional but necessary matters.

One is writing a new will. The other is dealing with the decedent's personal effects. Personal effects that are not part of particular bequests, and that you don't want or don't need, can be sold or donated to a charity. Clothing and books often make wonderful donations to local organizations, can make a difference in the life of a needy family, and can provide sizable tax deductions.

Another important tax consideration is to determine whether to claim a medical expense deduction on the current year's tax return or whether to elect to deduct any or all medical expenses of the illness or injury immediately preceding death in the prior year by amending your prior year's tax returns. This latter option may often lead to large savings, especially if you were in a higher tax bracket in the preceding year.

Survivor Planning After the Estate Is Closed

When the estate is closed and all of the appropriate assets have been distributed, it's time to reevaluate your financial situation and begin to create a long-term survivor plan. To do this, you need to go through a number of steps:

1. Define immediate and medium-term financial goals.
2. Define financial goals for retirement.
3. Reevaluate income tax strategy.

While you are thinking about taxes, please don't become overly anxious about the IRS. Despite the rhetoric, the Internal Revenue Code does take into account that grieving families aren't always thinking about their quarterly payments. As such, there is a section in the Code that waives the late-payment penalty for sickness or death, although interest will still be charged against late payments.

Immediate and Medium-Term Goals

The first questions to ask when redefining your financial goals is the same question you probably asked when originally defining your financial goals:

• What kind of cash flow does my lifestyle require?
• What is my risk tolerance for my investments?

In terms of lifestyle, you need to determine whether you will continue working, whether you want to increase or decrease your hours, or whether you want to, or must, go back to work after being out of the workforce for many years.

You must determine if you want to continue living in your present residence. Many survivors, especially those with grown children, find that the period immediately following the closing of an estate is a natural time to downsize from a large single-family house to a smaller house, condominium, cooperative apartment, or a rental unit. Older survivors are increasingly using a substantial portion of the proceeds of the estate to purchase a unit in a life-care facility. See the discussion of long-term care and life-care facilities in Chapter 25.

Your work status and your living status are the two primary variables in determining your lifestyle. Downsizing your residence, especially if you live in a part of the country where your home value has substantially increased, can provide you with a large cash infusion that can be invested for income rather than tied up in real estate.

As always, you should do a thorough cash flow analysis of both your income and expenses under current circumstances, and take income tax consequences into account for any transactions that you are thinking of undertaking.

Your decision to work should consider not only the current income you would earn, but also any health insurance or other benefits you could derive through work, and how working provides the wherewithal to continue saving more for retirement, either through a company's pension or 401(k) plan, or through your own tax-deductible IRA.

If your employment supplies the family's health insurance, and you no longer have any dependents to insure, remember to change your status as quickly as possible after a spouse's death from a family plan to a single plan. Even in plans that only have open enrollment once a year, there is usually a waiver for "change of life circumstances." Downsizing your health insurance can save you a significant amount of money. You may also want to increase the amount of life insurance you purchase through your employer to the maximum allowed if you have dependents, since these group policies are usually the least expensive form of life insurance you can have. It's also important to review the named beneficiaries of your life insurance policies and retirement funds.

Planning for Retirement

Planning for retirement is a little more complex for a survivor than for a couple because of the increased number of options for receiving Social Security. You may elect to begin receiving your early surviving spouse's benefits—based on your late spouse's earnings—at any time after age 60, or standard benefits at age 65. You may begin taking early Social Security benefits based on your own earnings at age 62, or standard benefits after age 65. You may shift from taking survivor benefits to taking your own benefits at any time after you become eligible. The Social Security office can help you calculate the various benefits and analyze which would be advantageous to you. For more information, call the Social Security Administration at (800) 772-1213, or visit www.ssa.gov.

Reevaluating Your Estate Plan

Now that your spouse's estate is closed, it's once again time to revisit your own estate plan. Depending on your degree of wealth and your family situation, you may need to update your will and to think about creating trusts. Since in some cases the spousal exemption may have been used to pass the estate to you, your estate could be heavily taxed when you die. Chapters 9 to 13 describe a number of possible mechanisms for reducing estate taxes.

Certainly younger widows or widowers with dependent children need to provide for guardianship of their children in the event of their death, and set up trusts under their wills for their financial benefit. As with every other estate planning issue, you need to create a plan that you are comfortable with; this includes determining if you wish the guardian of your children's physical well-being to also be the trustee for their financial well-being, and whether you want to name another individual as trustee, name an institution as trustee, or even name co-trustees, possibly a family member and an institution.

One thing you most likely will have to do in your estate is to be more specific in your instructions to your executor or executrix as you probably had certain unwritten assumptions about small bequests of personal items to family members or friends. Your new executor probably will not have that same degree of familiarity with your wishes. So you need to write them down, either as part of your will or in a separate letter to the executor.

Although losing a life partner, spouse, or close family member is certainly a personally tragic event, with proper planning before and immediately following the death, it does not have to be financially tragic.

10 Most Common and Most Costly Financial Mistakes in Dealing With the Death of Spouse, Life Partner, or Any Other Close Relation

1. **Selling assets too quickly.** Thought should go into the timing of the sale of securities and/or property, taking into account both market conditions and tax implications.

2. **Not filing, or not filing in a timely manner, appropriate federal and state estate tax forms.** Problems can crop up years later when assets are sold (especially real estate) and proof of estate tax payments are required for title transfer. Estate tax filings are required even when no tax is due. They also help to substantiate cost basis (fair market value at date of death) if assets are later sold.

3. **Failure to change beneficiary designation on retirement plans and insurance policies.** Assets in your qualified plans and your insurance policies will be subject to probate fees if you do not have a living beneficiary named on such plans. Your estate, as the beneficiary of your retirement plans, will be increased (as will your taxes).

10 MOST COMMON AND MOST COSTLY FINANCIAL MISTAKES IN DEALING WITH THE DEATH OF SPOUSE, LIFE PARTNER, OR ANY OTHER CLOSE RELATION *(continued)*

4. **Failure to segregate estate assets, liabilities, income, and expenses.** A new tax entity (the estate) is created at the date of death. This translates into tax savings, or at the very least a delay in the timing of required tax payments.

5. **Errors in calculating cost basis for assets inherited from the estate.** Even if the estate is not taxable, cost basis of property receives a step-up in basis so that there may be minimal or no capital gain tax due when sold by the beneficiary.

6. **Deceased spouse's will does not take advantage of the unified credit equivalent of $650,000.** A widow may disclaim part of an inheritance so that it may pass to other beneficiaries in order to take advantage of the unused portion of the deceased spouse's $650,000 unified credit equivalent. The unified credit is scheduled to increase from an effective exemption of $650,000 to an effective exemption of $1,000,000 in 2006. This formal disclaimer must take place within 9 months of the date of death.

7. **Not making a careful search for all assets.** Review prior year's income tax returns, all insurance policies, all decedent's papers, and so forth, for assets and pension plans (especially from former employers) and set up a meeting with the benefits department. Carefully review incoming mail.

8. **Making investments with insurance proceeds or retirement plan assets that are either too conservative or too risky.** Widows or widowers often have a distorted view of their finances once lump-sum investments suddenly appear and/or regular pay checks or pension checks stop appearing.

    Sit down with a financial professional to get a good handle on what your financial situation really is and which investments are appropriate to meet your needs.

9. **Taking distributions out of retirement plans.** IRA accounts, 401(k) or 403(b) plans, Keoghs, and SEP accounts contain pretax money, which will be taxable income to a beneficiary if he or she elects to take disbursement. As a general rule, tax-deferred status should be maintained as long as possible. Use other funds to pay expenses.

10. **Failure to contact Social Security Administration immediately if widow(er) or deceased is already retired.** A surviving spouse is entitled to decedent's higher social security benefit, if applicable. Widow(er)'s benefits can be collected as early as age 60, or even earlier if the widow(er) is disabled.

24

PLANNING FOR RETIREMENT

Having sufficient means to ensure an enjoyable and financially comfortable retirement depends on careful planning begun long before you retire. Unfortunately, planning for a goal that is years away often gets sidetracked by more immediate financial goals and demands, such as buying a home or paying college costs. There's also a constant temptation to avoid making the often tough decisions necessary to fund retirement. Recent statistics suggest that most Americans—especially those in the Baby Boom generation—aren't saving adequately for retirement, and many aren't saving at all. This is true even for affluent professionals at the height of their earning power. Unfortunately, the danger of following a "live for today" philosophy may be that you'll arrive at retirement with too few resources to meet your needs adequately.

To provide an overview of retirement planning issues, in this chapter we discuss the following subjects:

- Planning for a secure retirement
- Saving and investing for retirement
- Considering other retirement issues
- Dealing with Social Security

In Chapter 25 we then address a cluster of health- and insurance-related topics that will also affect your retirement planning.

For a more in-depth discussion on retirement plans, please refer to *Ernst & Young's Retirement Planning Guide.*

PLANNING FOR A SECURE RETIREMENT

When should you begin planning for retirement? Although it's never too soon or too late to plan for retirement, one possible guideline is the "20/20 Rule": *To plan for 20 years of retirement, start accumulating funds no later than 20 years before your retirement begins.* The earlier you start, the less money you'll have to put away over time and the less investment risk you'll have to take. Here's why.

Let's say that you've formulated a specific financial goal for retirement: You want to have $50,000 available after taxes to spend each year. Assuming that this sum stays constant, there are only three variables affecting how you accumulate the funds to generate your retirement income. Those variables are:

- The money you can invest to accumulate your retirement funds
- The time you have between now and retirement to "put your money to work"
- The rate of return that you can obtain on your money

The Importance of Starting Early

It's not difficult to discern how these three variables interact. To the extent that you start earlier rather than later, you need less money to invest and you don't need as high a rate of return. If you wait to start funding retirement until later, you'll need to invest more money to accumulate the same retirement fund, and you'll need a higher rate of return on your investment. A late start puts far more constraints on you—and heightens the level of risk you must take—compared to what you face by making an early start.

Concomitantly, an early start means having more time to:

- Realize appreciation in your investments.
- Evaluate alternative investment vehicles that can be used to fund your eventual retirement.
- Recoup a loss from a disappointing investment.

Given the realities of this situation, you would do well to start *earlier* than 20 years before you intend to retire. Starting in your late 20s or early 30s wouldn't be unreasonable, and getting an early start gives you a genuine advantage from the compounding of dividends and interest. Realistically speaking, however, you may not begin funding your retirement in earnest until your late 30s or early 40s. Launching a career, buying a house, or paying for the many expenses of raising a family may end up using all the discretionary income that you can generate. The result: You may not start serious retirement savings until middle age. That's not ideal, but midlife retirement planning doesn't necessarily mean that you won't be able to retire on your timetable. However, a midlife start may complicate the task of meeting your wealth accumulation goals.

To put the situation bluntly: *Don't assume that retirement is a stage of life that will simply take care of itself.* This is especially important given the increasing likelihood that Social Security will not pay the current benefit level to those who retire after 2020. Having a relatively comfortable retirement instead of one subject to substantial (even severe) financial constraints will almost certainly require careful planning, thoughtful choices among investment options, and constant vigilance over the long term. Consider the following issues and how they will affect your situation:

- Your retirement expenses may be far higher than you imagine.
- You may have to fund more of your retirement nest egg on your own (i.e., with less corporate or government help) than you assume.
- Investment returns may be lower—or at least less consistent—than you project.
- Inflation and taxes may take a more substantial toll on your investments than you anticipate.

These caveats aren't cause for panic. However, it's appropriate for you to see retirement planning as a significant, often challenging task that you should undertake energetically and with as much forethought as possible.

How to Plan for Retirement

Here are the steps you should take as you plan for retirement:

- *Step 1:* Establish your goals.
- *Step 2:* Estimate your retirement expenses.
- *Step 3:* Decide if you can afford to retire.
- *Step 4:* Choose where to live.
- *Step 5:* Address health care and other insurance issues.

STEP 1 ## ESTABLISH YOUR GOALS

Effective retirement planning begins with identifying and prioritizing reasonable and attainable goals. Typical retirement goals include:

- Generating enough income to maintain a desired lifestyle
- Resuming education

- Traveling
- Buying a retirement home
- Starting a second career

Keep in mind that unless you attain the first of the goals listed above, you're unlikely to attain the others. That is, *failure to meet your basic expenses will preclude accomplishing everything else you've set out to do.* Whatever your goals, commit them to writing and designate specifically *what* you intend to achieve and *when* you intend to achieve each goal. This should lead in turn to determining the amount of money you'll need to achieve your overall retirement goals.

STEP 2 ESTIMATE YOUR RETIREMENT EXPENSES

A general rule of thumb is that retirement income equal to 75% of your pre-retirement take-home pay should allow you to maintain your standard of living. However, many people retire quite comfortably on a lesser amount. A better way to measure your retirement income requirements is therefore to determine what you spend today; then, taking your current-year analysis and modifying these expenses—both upward and downward, as appropriate—you can anticipate, in today's dollars, the expenses during your first year of retirement.

You may end up adjusting your estimated expenses downward to reflect lower costs for children (i.e., as they leave home and start their own careers), reduced commuting, wardrobe, and other work-related costs, diminished disability or life insurance premiums, or even a paid-off mortgage. Another downward adjustment will come from no longer having to save for retirement. Try also to factor in costs based on where you plan to live during retirement. (For instance, there's a big difference between the cost of living in Manhattan and the cost of living in most parts of Florida.) On the other hand, you'll need to factor in any anticipated costs for a new or second home, increased travel and other leisure activities, and probable increases in health care expenses. The worksheet on page 475 will help you project your retirement expenses.

STEP 3 DECIDE IF YOU CAN AFFORD TO RETIRE

The next step is to determine whether you are presently on track to be able to pay these anticipated expenses. To make this determination, you should project the sources and amounts of the after-tax income that you'd have available if you retired today. In addition to Social Security, you need to estimate your other income, such as distributions from employer and personal retirement plan accounts and earnings from post-retirement employment.

PROJECTED ANNUAL RETIREMENT EXPENSES

	Current Year	During Retirement (in today's dollars)
Mortgage or rent	$_____	$_____
Other loan payments (e.g., car payments, bills, and credit cards)	_____	_____
Utilities, home maintenance, property taxes	_____	_____
Domestic help	_____	_____
Food and household supplies	_____	_____
Clothing, cleaning, personal supplies	_____	_____
Transportation costs, excluding car payments and insurance	_____	_____
Entertainment, clubs	_____	_____
Medical/dental expenses not covered by insurance	_____	_____
Travel	_____	_____
Hobby expenses	_____	_____
Charitable donations	_____	_____
Gifts to family/friends	_____	_____
Insurance premiums	_____	_____
Other: _____	_____	_____
Total Projected Expenses	$_____	$_____

The next worksheet lays out a step-by-step approach for estimating the gap, if any, between your projected retirement expenses and income. This is a means for calculating how much you'll need to put aside to fund any shortfall between now and your retirement date. Keep in mind that this computation assumes that you'll be using both income *and principal* during your retirement years. For this reason, you should be conservative when estimating the number of retirement years you'll need to fund, the rate of inflation you select, and the rate of return you can achieve. Under- or overestimating these factors may distort the outcome of your calculations, thus leading you to overly optimistic (or pessimistic) assumptions. If in doubt, assume that:

- You're funding a longer span of retirement rather than a shorter span.
- You're facing a higher rate of inflation rather than a lower rate.
- You're achieving a lower rate of return rather than a higher rate.

FUNDING YOUR FINANCIAL SHORTFALLS

	Example	You
1. Annual after-tax retirement expenses in today's dollars.	$42,000	$_____
2. Estimate in current dollars your annual after-tax retirement income from sources other than your present investments.	$27,000	$_____
3. Subtract (2) from (1). If the answer is greater than zero, you have a projected income shortfall.	$15,000	$_____
4. a. Figure the number of years until your anticipated retirement date.	15 Years	_____ Years
b. Estimate an anticipated average inflation rate.	5%	_____ %
c. Considering inflation, project how much would be needed at your expected retirement date to buy what *$15,000* (line 3) will buy today. Multiply the amount on line 3 by the inflation factor in Table 1. Using our estimate of 5% inflation (line 4b) over the next 15 years (line 4a) until retirement, the inflation factor from Table 1 is *2.079*.	$32,000	$_____
5. Determine the size of the fund you will need when you retire *15* years from now (line 4a) to pay estimated annual expenses of *$32,000* (line 4c) throughout your retirement years.		
a. Anticipated number of retirement years you expect to fund.	20 Years	_____ Years
b. Estimate an anticipated average inflation rate during your retirement years. We assumed that expenses will continue to increase annually at the same 5% inflation rate (line 4b) estimated for the preretirement years.	5%	_____ %
c. Estimate an anticipated average after-tax return on investments.	7%	_____ %
d. Figure the inflation-adjusted rate of return during retirement. Subtract line 5b from line 5c.	2%	_____ %
e. Multiply *$32,000* (line 4c) by the factor in Table 2 for *20* years (line 5a) at a 2% (line 5d) interest rate. For example: $32,000 × 16.351.	$523,232	$_____

FUNDING YOUR FINANCIAL SHORTFALLS (continued)

	Example	You

6. Figure the value in today's dollars of the fund needed on your retirement date. Multiply the amount on line 5e by the factor in Table 3 for *15* years (line 4a) at a 7% interest rate (line 5c).

Example: $189,410   You: $_____

7. a. How much of your investable assets can you put aside today for a retirement fund?

Example: $100,000   You: $_____

b. Subtract line 7a from line 6. This is the additional amount of money you would need to add to your retirement fund today to make up for the projected income shortfall.

Example: $ 89,410   You: $_____

8. To figure the annual amount you would have to put aside from now until retirement to build the fund needed, divide the amount on line 7b by the Table 2 factor. We determined the Table 2 factor by looking for *15* years (line 4a) at a 7% interest rate (line 5c).

Example: $ 9,817   You: $_____

TABLE 1: FUTURE VALUE OF $1 COMPOUNDED ANNUALLY

Years Hence	4%	5%	6%	7%	8%	9%	10%	Years Hence
1	1.040	1.050	1.060	1.070	1.080	1.090	1.100	1
2	1.082	1.102	1.124	1.145	1.166	1.188	1.210	2
3	1.125	1.158	1.191	1.225	1.260	1.295	1.331	3
4	1.170	1.215	1.262	1.311	1.360	1.412	1.464	4
5	1.217	1.276	1.338	1.403	1.469	1.539	1.610	5
6	1.265	1.340	1.418	1.501	1.587	1.677	1.772	6
7	1.316	1.407	1.504	1.606	1.714	1.828	1.949	7
8	1.369	1.477	1.594	1.718	1.851	1.993	2.144	8
9	1.423	1.551	1.689	1.838	1.999	2.172	2.358	9
10	1.480	1.629	1.791	1.967	2.159	2.367	2.594	10
11	1.539	1.710	1.898	2.105	2.332	2.580	2.853	11
12	1.601	1.796	2.012	2.252	2.518	2.813	3.138	12
13	1.665	1.886	2.133	2.410	2.720	3.066	3.452	13
14	1.732	1.980	2.261	2.578	2.937	3.342	3.797	14
15	1.801	2.079	2.397	2.759	3.172	3.642	4.177	15
16	1.873	2.183	2.540	2.952	3.426	3.970	4.595	16
17	1.948	2.292	2.693	3.159	3.700	4.328	5.054	17
18	2.026	2.407	2.854	3.380	3.996	4.717	5.560	18
19	2.107	2.527	3.026	3.616	4.316	5.142	6.116	19

TABLE 1: FUTURE VALUE OF $1 COMPOUNDED ANNUALLY (continued)

Years Hence	4%	5%	6%	7%	8%	9%	10%	Years Hence
20	2.191	2.653	3.207	3.870	4.661	5.604	6.727	20
21	2.279	2.786	3.400	4.141	5.034	6.109	7.400	21
22	2.370	2.925	3.603	4.430	5.436	6.659	8.140	22
23	2.465	3.071	3.820	4.740	5.872	7.258	8.954	23
24	2.563	3.225	4.049	5.072	6.341	7.911	9.850	24
25	2.666	3.386	4.292	5.427	6.848	8.623	10.835	25
26	2.772	3.556	4.549	5.807	7.396	9.599	11.918	26
27	2.883	3.733	4.822	6.214	7.988	10.245	13.110	27
28	2.999	3.920	5.112	6.649	8.627	11.167	14.421	28
29	3.119	4.116	5.418	7.114	9.317	12.172	15.864	29
30	3.243	4.322	5.743	7.612	10.063	13.268	17.449	30

TABLE 2: PRESENT VALUE OF AN ANNUITY OF $1
(Assuming that the $1 is received in a single payment on the last day of each year)

Years Hence	1%	2%	3%	4%	5%	6%	7%	8%	9%	10%	Years Hence
1	.990	.980	.971	.962	.952	.943	.935	.926	.917	.909	1
2	1.970	1.942	1.913	1.886	1.859	1.833	1.808	1.783	1.759	1.736	2
3	2.941	2.884	2.829	2.775	2.723	2.673	2.624	2.577	2.531	2.487	3
4	3.902	3.808	3.717	3.630	3.546	3.465	3.387	3.312	3.240	3.170	4
5	4.853	4.713	4.580	4.452	4.329	4.212	4.100	3.993	3.890	3.791	5
6	5.795	5.601	5.417	5.242	5.076	4.917	4.767	4.623	4.486	4.355	6
7	6.728	6.472	6.230	6.002	5.786	5.582	5.389	5.206	5.033	4.868	7
8	7.652	7.325	7.020	6.733	6.463	6.210	5.971	5.747	5.535	5.335	8
9	8.566	8.162	7.785	7.435	7.108	6.802	6.515	6.247	5.995	5.759	9
10	9.471	8.983	8.530	8.111	7.722	7.360	7.024	6.710	6.418	6.145	10
11	10.368	9.787	9.253	8.760	8.306	7.887	7.499	7.139	6.805	6.495	11
12	11.255	10.575	9.954	9.385	8.863	8.384	7.943	7.536	7.161	6.814	12
13	12.134	11.348	10.635	9.986	9.394	8.853	8.358	7.904	7.487	7.103	13
14	13.004	12.106	11.296	10.563	9.899	9.295	8.745	8.244	7.786	7.367	14
15	13.865	12.849	11.938	11.118	10.380	9.712	9.108	8.559	8.061	7.606	15
16	14.718	13.578	12.561	11.652	10.838	10.106	9.447	8.851	8.313	7.824	16
17	15.562	14.292	13.166	12.166	11.274	10.477	9.763	9.122	8.544	8.022	17
18	16.398	14.992	13.754	12.659	11.690	10.828	10.059	9.372	8.756	8.201	18
19	17.226	15.678	14.324	13.134	12.085	11.158	10.336	9.604	8.950	8.365	19
20	18.046	16.351	14.877	13.590	12.462	11.470	10.594	9.818	9.129	8.514	20
21	18.857	17.011	15.415	14.029	12.821	11.764	10.836	10.017	9.292	8.649	21
22	19.660	17.658	15.937	14.451	13.163	12.042	11.061	10.201	9.442	8.772	22
23	20.456	18.292	16.444	14.857	13.489	12.303	11.272	10.371	9.580	8.883	23
24	21.243	18.914	16.936	15.247	13.799	12.550	11.469	10.529	9.707	8.985	24
25	22.023	19.523	17.413	15.622	14.094	12.783	11.654	10.675	9.823	9.077	25

TABLE 3: PRESENT VALUE OF $1
(Assuming that the $1 is received in a single payment on the last day of each year)

Years Hence	4%	5%	6%	7%	8%	9%	10%	Years Hence
1	.962	.952	.943	.935	.926	.917	.909	1
2	.925	.907	.890	.873	.857	.842	.826	2
3	.889	.864	.840	.816	.794	.772	.751	3
4	.855	.823	.792	.763	.735	.708	.683	4
5	.822	.784	.747	.713	.681	.650	.621	5
6	.790	.746	.705	.666	.630	.596	.564	6
7	.760	.711	.665	.623	.583	.547	.513	7
8	.731	.677	.627	.582	.540	.502	.467	8
9	.703	.643	.592	.544	.500	.460	.424	9
10	.676	.614	.558	.508	.463	.422	.386	10
11	.650	.585	.527	.475	.429	.388	.350	11
12	.625	.557	.497	.444	.397	.356	.319	12
13	.601	.530	.469	.415	.368	.326	.290	13
14	.577	.505	.442	.388	.340	.299	.263	14
15	.555	.481	.417	.362	.315	.275	.239	15
16	.534	.458	.394	.339	.292	.252	.218	16
17	.513	.436	.371	.317	.270	.231	.198	17
18	.494	.416	.350	.296	.250	.212	.180	18
19	.475	.396	.331	.277	.232	.194	.164	19
20	.456	.377	.312	.258	.215	.178	.149	20
21	.439	.359	.294	.242	.199	.164	.135	21
22	.422	.342	.278	.226	.184	.150	.123	22
23	.406	.326	.262	.211	.170	.138	.112	23
24	.390	.310	.247	.197	.158	.126	.102	24
25	.375	.295	.233	.184	.146	.116	.092	25
30	.308	.231	.174	.131	.099	.075	.057	30

You can deal with a shortfall in anticipated retirement income by one or more of the following means:

- Planning to reduce or eliminate certain lower-priority expenditures
- Building a retirement fund large enough to close the gap
- Delaying the start of retirement

The sooner you perform this exercise, the more time you'll have to make any necessary adjustments both to the rate at which you're setting money aside and to the investment strategy you're using to build an adequate retirement fund. To consider these issues further, see later sections of this chapter.

In addition, Chapters 3 through 6 provide an overview of investment planning issues, many of which are applicable to retirement funding.

STEP 4   CHOOSE WHERE TO LIVE

On retiring, some people move from their long-standing state of residence to another state. A significant minority of retirees maintain residences in each of two states. Whether you take either of these courses of action or stay where you've been living, you should try to determine the consequences of your choice. Among the questions to ask yourself are how your choice of residence will affect your:

- Health (i.e., because of the climate, overall environment, etc.)
- Safety (given the nature of the immediate neighborhood, traffic conditions, distance from neighbors, etc.)
- Transportation costs (given the relative distance to family members, friends, stores, recreation sites, cultural sites, etc.)
- Tax picture (given state and local taxes)

In short, you should carefully assess where you should live as you grow older. Most people may experience a pattern of increasing dependence on other people late in life; it's easy to underestimate the consequences of these changes as you age.

You should carefully consider the issue of residence from a tax standpoint. The main issue is which state (or, worse yet, which states) will impose income tax on your earnings. To answer this question, you shouldn't look only at state income taxes, since there may be property and even gift or inheritance taxes to consider as well. Because the interrelationship of the rules is usually quite complex, you may want to obtain professional help in sorting through these issues. Planning wisely when selecting and establishing a new state of residence can help lower your overall state tax burden.

STEP 5   ADDRESS HEALTH CARE AND OTHER INSURANCE ISSUES

Among the most crucial issues to consider when planning for a secure retirement are various health care and insurance options. You should familiarize yourself with Medicare coverage rules so that you'll be equipped to obtain any needed supplemental or Medigap insurance. You may also want to look into long-term care insurance to protect yourself against the high cost of a lengthy stay in a nursing home. Because these issues are complex, however, we explore them in a separate chapter. See Chapters 8 and 22 for a detailed discussion of these subjects.

SAVING AND INVESTING FOR RETIREMENT

Many different types of investments are available to fund your retirement. Some investments can meet both your current life-event objectives and your retirement goals. For example, if you are thinking of buying a vacation home and have determined where you want to retire, you might consider purchasing a property that will serve as both a vacation home now and a retirement home in the future.

As retirement nears, it's natural for investment strategies to become more conservative. However, you shouldn't ignore the effects of inflation. Inflation robs your retirement dollars of their buying power; unless you anticipate it adequately and respond to it appropriately, inflation can undermine an otherwise well-laid-out retirement plan. As a result, you should invest some of your money in assets such as common stocks that have historically been good inflation hedges and that can provide a rising level of income. Since interest rates generally rise as the inflation rate rises, you should also make sure not to invest all of your assets in fixed-income securities that mature at the same time. Purchasing fixed-income investments of varying maturities, both short-term and long-term, can help you maintain the flexibility to deal with changing interest rates. This makes sense for your pre-retirement, as well as post-retirement, years.

In any case, you should minimize or eliminate excessively risky investments that could erode your retirement fund—particularly if you're nearing retirement and have already met your retirement accumulation goals. If risky investments fail while retirement is decades away, you have time to regroup. But if investments fall short of expectations when you're age 62, you may not have enough time to recoup the losses.

Investments should be matched to your need for cash flow to pay retirement expenses. Consider adopting a carefully planned strategy of converting illiquid assets that appreciate over time—which may have served you well during the years of building up a retirement fund—into more liquid assets that can be consumed during your retirement years. A classic example of this scenario is real estate. The real property you own may have appreciated substantially over the years, but it's often illiquid, which can cause you serious problems if you have to count on generating income through the sale of a home or other property. The idea is to avoid being forced to sell illiquid assets at inopportune times.

Finally, diversification of your investments remains paramount. Not putting all your eggs in one basket reduces the risk of having to absorb devastating losses in your retirement fund.

Here are some of the methods that you can use to invest for retirement:

- Using your home to fund retirement
- Saving through IRAs and Keoghs
- Saving through tax-deferred annuities

Using Your Home to Fund Retirement

If you have equity built up in your personal residence, you may be able to use it to generate retirement income. The decision to tap your equity involves both financial and nonfinancial decisions. Some people find that their long-time residence seems too large once their children have moved away, thus prompting them to question the wisdom of retaining the home. Others feel that the financial burdens and physical hassles of maintaining a large home become too much of a headache. In addition, it's not uncommon for the personal residence to represent the most substantial personal asset available, so that selling it and investing the proceeds in a more liquid asset is simply a necessity.

Fortunately, there's a tax break available that helps many people. A $250,000 exclusion for single filers ($500,000 for joint filers) is available to all taxpayers. This exclusion replaces the prior law rollover provisions and the one-time exclusion for taxpayers age 55 and over.

A taxpayer can claim the exclusion once every 2 years. To be eligible, a taxpayer must have owned the residence and occupied it as a principal residence for at least 2 of the 5 years before the sale or exchange. A taxpayer who fails to meet either of these requirements (the 2-out-of-5-years ownership rule or the once-every-2-years use of exclusion rule) by reason of a change of place of employment, health, or other unforeseen circumstances can exclude the fraction of the $250,000 ($500,000 if married filing a joint return) equal to the fraction of 2 years that these requirements are met.

Limiting the exclusion to only one sale every 2 years does not prevent a husband and wife filing a joint return from each excluding up to $250,000 of gain from the sale or exchange of each spouse's principal residence, provided that each spouse could exclude up to $250,000 of gain if they filed separate returns.

If a taxpayer acquired his or her current residence in a rollover transaction, periods of ownership and use of the prior residence would be taken into account in determining ownership and use of the current residence.

It's important to realize, however, that even a substantial capital gain from selling your home still leaves you with major questions to answer about where you'll be living afterward. Among the most important questions are:

- Do you plan to buy another property?
- If so, what kind—house, condo, coop?
- If not, will you rent a property instead?
- Either way, what will your new housing expenses be?
- How will your tax picture change following sale of the former residence?
- What new circumstances will the change of residence create (e.g., greater or lesser distance to family and friends, greater or lesser distance from shopping and social centers, etc.)?
- What will the move from one residence to another cost?

IRAs, SEPs, Keoghs, and SIMPLEs

As we discussed in Chapter 2, you can construct a personal retirement plan regardless of what your employer offers. For that matter, you can construct a retirement plan even if you have no employer at all. How? Through individual retirement accounts (IRAs) and Keoghs. The advantages for people who have these plans are numerous: flexibility, independence, tax savings, and portability. They require careful attention, but they can pay off nicely.

Here's a brief rundown of what they are and how they work.

Deductible Individual Retirement Account (IRA). A deductible individual retirement account (IRA) is a personal savings plan that lets you set aside funds for your retirement, using pretax dollars. Subject to the limitations discussed in Chapter 2, you may make a cash contribution to an IRA or for the purchase of an individual retirement annuity, and you can then deduct that contribution from gross income on your tax return. The basic difference between an *individual retirement account* and an *individual retirement annuity* is the type of investment and the method of funding. An individual retirement account is a type of trust or custodial account with various types of investments allowed. An individual retirement annuity is an investment in an insurance company's deferred annuity.

Contributing pretax earnings to an IRA can make a big difference in your retirement savings. For example, assume that you're in the 28% tax bracket and that you are earning 10% interest on your savings. You can earn approximately 1.6 times more money after tax (payable at the time of withdrawal) on a $2,000 IRA contribution held for 20 years than if you did not make that pretax contribution. If your tax rate drops after your retirement because you have less income, your savings could amount to an even bigger nest egg.

Nondeductible IRA Contributions. Even if you don't qualify for a tax-deductible contribution to your IRA, you can still contribute. The earnings on these contributions would be exempt from tax until you withdraw the money from your IRA. The maximum nondeductible contribution you can make to your IRA is figured as though the contribution were deductible, minus the amount of any deductible contribution you may make.

Roth IRA. A Roth IRA is a retirement IRA that was created by the Taxpayer Relief Act of 1997. The Roth IRA allows you to make nondeductible contributions of up to $2,000 per year and receive tax-free and penalty-free withdrawals if you don't start taking distributions for 5 years after the account is opened. The amount you can contribute is reduced by the aggregate contributions made during a taxable year to all other retirement IRAs. Because the income limitations for Roth IRAs are much higher than deductible IRAs you may qualify to contribute to a Roth IRA and not a deductible IRA.

When to Make Your IRA Contribution. Contributions to an IRA can be made starting from the first day of the tax year but no later than the due date (without extensions) of your tax return for that tax year. This means that IRA contributions can generally be made until April 15 of the year following the tax year.

You can maximize your savings by funding your IRA as early as possible for any given tax year. By contributing to your IRA at the beginning of a tax year instead of waiting until April 15 of the following year, your contribution can earn 15½ months' worth of interest. The earnings will not be taxed until the money is withdrawn from the account.

If you don't qualify for a deductible IRA you should determine if you can contribute to the new Roth IRA. If, on the other hand, you are eligible to contribute to either a deductible IRA or a Roth IRA you should determine whether it will be more beneficial to contribute pretax or receive tax-free distributions. If you are young and in a low tax bracket the Roth IRA could be more beneficial. The benefit of the current tax deduction may not outweigh tax-free distributions when you will most likely be in a higher tax bracket. In addition, if tax rates increase substantially, you are still going to receive tax-free distributions. These are things you will also want to consider in determining whether you should convert an existing IRA into a Roth IRA.

Penalties on Early Distributions. Distributions from an IRA that are made before you turn age 59½ are generally subject to a 10% penalty tax. However, a series of substantially equal (at least annual) periodic payments made for the life or life expectancy of the IRA owner or the joint lives or life expectancies of the IRA owner and his or her designated beneficiary, or distributions rolled over to another IRA, are not subject to the 10% penalty tax. See *The Ernst & Young Tax Guide* and *The Ernst & Young Retirement Planning Guide*, both published by John Wiley & Sons, Inc., for details on penalties and the substantially equal periodic payment rate.

■ **TIP:** If you need money for no longer than 60 days, consider withdrawing the money from your IRA *if you are sure you will have the cash to put into another IRA within 60 days.* You will not incur any tax or penalties, and you will have the cash for 60 days. You can do this only once in a 12-month period. ■

Distributions at retirement (other than your nondeductible contributions) are taxed as ordinary income when received. Distributions must begin by April 1 of the year following the year in which you reach age 70½. If you don't withdraw a minimum amount yearly, a 50% nondeductible tax is levied on the balance of the required minimum payment.

Simplified Employee Pensions. Whether you're completely self-employed or simply bring in some self-employment income from consultations or part-time work, you should consider setting up a simplified employee pension (SEP). A SEP allows an employer to make contributions toward an employee's retirement without becoming involved in more complex retirement plans. If you're self-employed, you can contribute to your own SEP.

The SEP rules permit an employer to make a deductible contribution each year to a participating employee's SEP of up to 15% of the employee's compensation or $24,000, whichever is less (this amount is indexed for inflation). If you're self-employed, special rules apply when figuring the maximum deduction for these contributions. In determining the percentage limit on contributions, compensation is net earnings from self-employment, taking into account the contributions to the SEP.

■ **TIP:** A self-employed person can claim a deduction to a SEP as long as the plan is set up and the contribution made by the due date of the return, including extensions. Even if you failed to set up a Keogh plan by December 31, you can still establish a SEP after the end of the year and make a timely payment. ■

Keoghs. Keogh plans (discussed in Chapter 2) are another form of retirement vehicle for the self-employed. Keogh plan contributions are deducted from your gross income, and the tax is deferred until you withdraw funds from the plan at a later date. You must establish your Keogh plan within the tax year for which you intend to make contributions. However, you don't have to make contributions to the plan until the due date for filing your return, including extensions.

There are four types of Keogh plans:

- Defined benefit
- Profit sharing
- Money purchase pension
- Combined profit sharing/money purchase plan

Defined Benefit Plan. This type of plan defines the benefit to be paid out of a plan. Under a defined benefit plan, you are promised a fixed benefit and the annual contributions are based on the amount that is actuarially needed to provide you that benefit at a normal retirement age.

Profit-Sharing Plan. You may contribute and deduct, at your discretion, up to the lesser of 15% of your self-employment income or $24,000 (indexed for inflation) into a profit-sharing plan. This type of plan is the simplest and most flexible. Typically, contributions to a profit-sharing plan are made out of a company's profits and therefore can vary from year to year.

Money Purchase Pension Plan. This plan enables you to contribute and deduct up to the lesser of $30,000 or 20% of your self-employment income each year. The money purchase pension plan enables you to contribute a higher annual amount than would be possible to a profit-sharing plan. However, you lose flexibility because the contribution is mandatory. Under a money purchase pension plan, the benefit you eventually receive is based solely on the contributions credited to your account and the earning attributable to those contributions.

Combined Profit Sharing/Money Purchase Plan. The combination of these two plans will allow you to make discretionary contributions of 12% (profit-sharing plan) and mandatory contributions of 8% (money purchase pension plan). If you maintain a combination of a profit-sharing Keogh plan and a money purchase Keogh plan, the maximum combined deductible contributions are limited to $30,000 or 20% of earned income per year.

SIMPLEs. SIMPLEs are another type of retirement plan available for small employers with little paperwork. They can be structured as IRAs or 401(k)s. If you have a small amount of self-employment income, a SIMPLE may be appropriate since you may be able to contribute up to 100% of your income.

Deferred Annuities

Annuities are, in a sense, the opposite of life insurance—an annuity insures you against the financial risk of living longer than your life expectancy, while life insurance protects your family against the financial risk of your dying sooner than actuarially expected.

Deferred annuities, available in fixed or variable formats, offer tax deferral on the savings attributable to your contributions. Two types of penalties can be imposed for early withdrawal of funds from an annuity. First, the company issuing the annuity will probably assess a contractual penalty for an early withdrawal. Second, the IRS will assess a 10% penalty for withdrawals prior to age 59½, unless certain exceptions are met.

ISSUES TO CONSIDER WHEN YOU RETIRE

At the time of your actual retirement, you must make a number of decisions concerning when and how to take your retirement distributions. Factors you must consider include:

- The form of your qualified retirement plan distributions
- Tax treatment of distributions

- Averaging versus rollover
- Other distribution considerations

The Form of Your Qualified Retirement Plan Distributions

You may be confronted with a big choice when you retire: Should you elect lifetime payments or a lump-sum distribution of your benefits? To pick the best payment scheme for you, consider the income tax ramifications of the proposed distribution, your personal objectives for the use of the funds, and your ability to handle the money. Generally, for financially sophisticated people, a lump-sum distribution is a better match with their financial objectives. Let's compare lifetime payments versus lump-sum distributions.

Lifetime Payments

- The employee or spouse can receive a fixed monthly amount no matter how long he or she lives.
- The employee is relieved of the investment burden.
- The family of an employee could lose unpaid amounts of a large plan balance if premature death(s) occurs.
- Unless the payments are indexed or variable, inflation erodes purchasing power.
- Access to assets is limited to monthly payments.

Lump-Sum Distribution

- The employee or spouse could outlive the fund.
- A large fund may present a temptation to overspend or make it difficult to plan a comfortable budget.
- The employee has the responsibility for investing a large sum of money.
- Lump-sum proceeds can be invested in assets that offer a hedge against inflation.
- There is full emergency access to proceeds at any time.
- The employee can roll all or part of the distribution into an IRA to extend the deferral.

Tax Treatment of Distributions

Lifetime payments will generally be taxable as ordinary income.

Rolling Over a Lump-Sum Distribution to an IRA. Instead of paying tax up front, a distribution of *any portion* of your account balance in a qualified plan—including, of course, a lump-sum distribution—may be "rolled over" to an IRA or another qualified plan. A rollover defers the tax on the distribution and allows income to accumulate "tax-free" until you withdraw it. Any part of your distribution that is not rolled over will be taxed as ordinary income. Moreover, any future payouts from your account will be ineligible for favorable averaging treatment. To qualify for rollover treatment, the distribution must be deposited in an IRA or other qualified plan within 60 days of receipt.

Other Distribution Considerations

Here are other issues to consider regarding distribution:

- 20% will be automatically withheld for federal taxes on any distribution you receive—other than an annuity payment—from a qualified plan. You can avoid withholding on the portion of the distribution you intend to roll over by having such an amount transferred directly from your old plan to the trustee of the IRA or new qualified plan. With certain exceptions, distributions not rolled over and received before age 59½ will be hit with a 10% penalty.
- There are rules governing the minimum amount that must be paid out annually from IRAs and other retirement plans—and when payments must begin.

DEALING WITH SOCIAL SECURITY

The subject of Social Security generates a disproportionate amount of confusion and anxiety when people start considering their retirement options. On the one hand, you probably know that Social Security will contribute a certain amount of money to your retirement funds; on the other hand, you may be unsure what that amount will be—and you may worry that the whole system will go belly-up before you have a chance to benefit from Social Security programs. There are, in fact, a number of uncertainties present in the system. Congress may well change the level of benefits that future Social Security recipients receive; alternatively, the benefits may remain the same while the taxation of those benefits changes. However, it seems unlikely that any of the more apocalyptic predictions will come true and the whole program will collapse into ruins. Modifications of the program are far more probable than catastrophe.

You should figure what you will need to save if Social Security continues to pay at 100% percent of today's benefits, with inflation taken into account, then recalculate using a figure of 70% of current benefits and a third calculation using a figure of 50% of current benefits, hopefully as a worst-case scenario.

The more immediate situation you face is simply making the usual decisions about Social Security and the benefits you'll derive from it. The aspects of the situation we discuss are:

- When should you start taking your Social Security benefits?
- Should you keep working?
- Checking your Social Security benefits.

When Should You Start Taking Your Social Security Benefits?

You are eligible for full Social Security benefits if you "retire" at age 65 or later. This "standard" retirement age is scheduled to increase gradually to age 67 by the year 2027. For each year you wait beyond age 65 to apply, your benefits will increase slightly. Currently, individuals retiring at age 62 can receive 80% of the benefits they would have received had they waited until age 65.

Does this mean that you should wait until age 65 to retire? Not necessarily. By starting benefits at age 62, you'll receive 35 additional months of benefits.

EXAMPLE

■ Assume that you're entitled to the maximum Social Security benefit and you elect to retire in 1999 at age 62. If you had been age 65, the monthly benefit would have been about $1,373. Since you're retiring at 62, the monthly benefit is reduced about 20%, to $1,098. Ignoring cost-of-living adjustments for simplicity, 35 months of benefits of $1,098 per month add up to $38,430. It will take nearly 12 years of the higher benefits at age 65 to make up the difference, and this doesn't even consider the time value of money. ■

Should You Keep Working?

You may be planning on working well beyond age 65. You may wish to start a second career. But remember: If you earn too much, your Social Security benefits will be cut. For 1999, retirees between ages 62 and 64 lose $1 in benefits for every $2 earned over $9,600. Recipients between ages 65 and 69 forfeit $1 of benefits for each $3 earned over $15,500. No earnings limit applies to retirees age 70 or older, or to unearned income, such as investment income or distributions from pensions. There is a reward for working past normal retirement age. For each month that you postpone collecting Social Security benefits past age 65 and before age 70, your retirement benefit is increased by a "delayed retirement credit." The maximum yearly credit increases to a ceiling of 8%.

Checking Your Social Security Benefits

It's a good idea to request a statement of your earnings history from the Social Security Administration every 2 or 3 years to check the accuracy of the administration's information. In addition to your earnings history, the Social Security Administration will provide you with a variety of benefits information. Simply file form SSA-7004-PC, which can be obtained free by calling (800) 772-1213 or visit www.ssa.gov. Within 3 to 6 weeks after submitting the form, you'll receive a Personal Earnings and Benefit Estimate Statement.

An enjoyable and comfortable retirement can be within your grasp. You owe it to yourself and your family to develop a financial strategy now that will enable you to realize your goals. Then, with the proper discipline to carry out your strategy, your retirement years can truly be golden.

25

Planning for Retirement: Health Care and Insurance Needs

In addition to the general retirement planning issues that we discussed in Chapter 24, there are several other specific issues that will affect you during retirement. These are certain health care and insurance needs. Addressing these issues carefully will help you retire with a minimum of anxiety for your future; on the other hand, ignoring these issues may cause you substantial worries—and perhaps big trouble—in your later years.

The issues we discuss in this chapter aren't a direct consequence of retirement; in fact, people can find themselves trying to answer the questions raised here well before (and well after) the typical age at which retirement begins. However, retirement is the event that causes most people to assess and plan for their long-term needs for health care, survivor income, and so forth.

To take control of these issues during retirement, here are the subjects you need to address:

- Risk management
- Life insurance

- Pension maximization
- Medicare
- Medigap insurance
- Private health insurance
- Long-term care (LTC)
- Accelerated death benefits

RISK MANAGEMENT

In Chapter 7 we discussed the importance of risk management as the start to determining most sorts of insurance needs. Risk management is just as important—if not more so—in assessing these needs at the time of retirement. In fact, any aspect of financial planning is likely to be more cogently and completely addressed by following a procedure designed to determine your current situation, objectives, and what, if anything, you must do to achieve those objectives.

In the area of risk management, the procedure typically includes:

- Understanding and quantifying your risks
- Evaluating your ability to retain risks (i.e., self-insure)
- Evaluating your ability to transfer risks (i.e., purchase insurance)
- Implementing appropriate product and nonproduct solutions

Our particular emphasis in this chapter is the life, health, and custodial care insurance aspects of retirement.

Data Gathering and Analysis

The first step you should take is to gather the information that will enable you to understand the nature and extent of the risks associated with your death, illness, or incapacity. Your data should include (but not be limited to):

- *Assets.* What do you own? How do you hold these assets? What are the tax liabilities associated with them? What is your liquidity position?
- *Liabilities.* Amount? Terms? Secured or unsecured?
- *Cash flow.* The key here is not just the result of a snapshot of today's income versus expenses. What is the trend of total income versus total outflow (expenses and taxes), taking into account the impact of inflation on your expenses? What are the sources of cash flow, and how vulnerable are they to inflation and investment risk?

- *Insurance.* What life and health insurance will you have during retirement? What are the types and amount of coverage, its duration, and its cost?
- *Estate plan.* Do you and your spouse have an up-to-date plan that provides for your possible incapacity as well as your death?
- *Health.* Are you and your spouse healthy? Are you insurable?
- *Special needs.* Do you have a disabled child? Is there a particular set of circumstances that might require special planning?
- *Estate conservation.* Do you want to preserve an estate for the next generation?

Identifying the Risks

Once we know about your financial position, we need to identify the risks and reduce them to dollar amounts, if possible. We'll actually cover this step of the process during the balance of this chapter. For now, let's note that we need to determine:

- *Survivor cash flow needs.* What would your spouse have for cash flow and capital in the event of your death? Are the numbers adjusted for inflation? Is survivor cash flow acceptable to you (not to mention your spouse)?
- *Your ability to withstand major medical or long-term care expenses.* How well could your finances withstand the expenses of a prolonged illness or a prolonged stay in a nursing home?

Retain Risks or Insure?

You simply can't fully retain the risk of dying (i.e., self-insure) without enough capital to maintain your spouse's security. You'll have to purchase insurance to bridge the gap between the capital your spouse needs and the capital that's available. Retaining the risks associated with a serious accident or illness isn't practical, either, or even necessary. Retaining risks for other than major medical costs is best done by electing to decline coverage, take higher deductibles, and so forth. Retaining the long-term care risk is also feasible. How much of the risk to retain, however, is another matter.

Insurance

To the extent that you've identified risks against which self-insurance is either not feasible or appropriate, you must purchase coverage. Most of the rest of this chapter considers the three primary types of coverage: life insurance, health insurance, and long-term care insurance.

LIFE INSURANCE DURING RETIREMENT

Life insurance can play one or more roles in your financial and estate planning. Life insurance may be needed to provide adequate income for your surviving spouse. Existing cash value policies may be valuable tax-deferred assets from which you can withdraw funds for income or medical care. An existing policy may also be exchanged for an annuity to supplement income.

Determining Your Need for Insurance

A good way to begin your task in sizing up your life insurance situation is to see what your surviving spouse's cash flow and capital would look like if you were to die tomorrow. Would your spouse have adequate cash flow through his or her life expectancy? This kind of analysis generally indicates either a surplus or a deficit in the amount of capital necessary to provide the level of cash flow you desire. It's not uncommon, however, for the result to be a deficit. As we noted in Chapter 7, what you then face—the capital gap—is almost always a shock to your system. However, running the numbers and discovering an unpleasant reality there can be helpful in the long run, as it helps you face the impact of your death on your spouse's finances. This analysis is particularly helpful in situations where:

- Your employer-provided insurance will phase out over a period of years.
- Your joint and survivor pension will be reduced at your death.
- Your pension has no cost-of-living adjustment.
- Social Security benefits will be reduced at your death.

You may benefit from seeing this analysis run at two or three different points: at a couple of years after your retirement; at the time when your employer's coverage is eliminated, and at your life expectancy. This analysis may end up offering a reassuring confirmation that your spouse will be adequately provided for in the event that she or he survives you. On the other hand, the analysis may be a sobering message that you'll have to be very careful about your money in the years ahead.

Acquiring the Coverage

In situations where post-retirement life insurance seems necessary or advisable, you'll have at least three options:

- Convert group term coverage to an individual permanent policy.
- Maintain or enhance existing cash value insurance.
- Acquire new coverage.

Convert Group Term Coverage to an Individual Permanent Policy.
Although converting group coverage may be an option, it typically isn't very attractive. You may have a limited choice of policies to which you can convert. What's more, conversion is generally not allowed at nonsmoker or preferred rates. Insurance professionals suggest that if you're healthy at retirement, you'll find a much better policy on the open market than you'll obtain through converting your group coverage.

Maintain or Enhance Existing Cash Value Insurance. You may have one or more cash value policies, such as an individual whole-life or universal life policy, or a group universal life policy. To size up your coverage, you should have your agent obtain and review these three items:

- A current statement
- An in-force ledger illustration
- The original sales illustration

These documents will help you and your agent determine the status of your policy and whether it's performing up to expectations. If those expectations aren't being met, the agent can tell how much additional premium may be necessary to put the policy back on track.

Where your cash flow, insurability, and policy terms permit, you may want to increase your premiums. There are several benefits to putting more money into the policy:

- The death benefit may grow.
- Since the insurance was priced in relation to your health at the time you took out the policy, additional insurance purchased through dividends will be a bargain for you if your health has deteriorated over the years.
- The policy is an income tax shelter; the cash value will grow tax deferred.
- The cash value will be available in subsequent years through partial surrenders or policy loans.

Acquire New Coverage. If you're insurable at a preferred (or reasonably standard) rate, you can consider buying new life coverage. Whole life, whole life/term insurance blends, and universal life are all possible options in this regard. Because of the intricacies involved, you should discuss the situation with your insurance agent.

Pension Maximization

If you'll be receiving a pension from your employer's defined benefit plan, you might want to consider the technique popularly known as "pension maximization." Here's how it works.

E X A M P L E

■ Let's say that you're a married man whose plan requires that you take a joint-and-survivor pension annuity unless your spouse consents to another form of annuity. The joint-and-survivor annuity will pay a certain amount to you each month and a certain amount (invariably lower) to your spouse if she survives you. For example, if you elect a 50% joint-and-survivor annuity in the amount of $4,000, you'll receive that $4,000 as long as you live. If your wife survives you when you die, she'll receive $2,000 (50% of $4,000) for the rest of her life. If you were to elect a single-life annuity (with your spouse's permission), the monthly benefit would be $4,400. You might be tempted to elect the higher pension, but the single-life annuity would be intolerably risky for your wife. ■

To respond to this dilemma, pension maximization is a strategy in which you elect the higher single-life annuity and insure your life to protect your spouse. Protecting your spouse adequately means that you must purchase enough insurance to enable him or her to buy an immediate annuity that will match the desired survivor benefit. Under the right circumstances, this strategy can be beneficial. Under the wrong circumstances, this same strategy can be a terrible mistake.

Here are some factors in considering pension maximization:

- Adequate amount of insurance
- The insurance premium for the necessary coverage
- The spouse's risks

Adequate Amount of Insurance

You'll need enough insurance to ensure your spouse's ability to purchase a lifetime annuity of whatever survivor benefit he or she considers appropriate. The insurance amount should be adequate from "day 1" of your retirement. Your agent can determine the necessary amount of insurance by referring to current annuity rates; however, the agent should use something closer to guaranteed annuity rates so that your spouse won't run the risk of the proceeds not buying the needed amount of income. If the pension annuity has a cost-of-living enhancement (COLA), the amount of insurance necessary to replace the survivor benefit will be much greater than if there is no COLA.

The Insurance Premium for the Necessary Coverage

Pension maximization won't work unless the insurance premium is less than the after-tax difference between the single-life annuity and the joint-and-survivor annuity. It's crucial to ensure that the premium hasn't been determined solely by reference to that difference. In other words, *the premium must be high enough to maintain the death benefit well beyond the insured's life expectancy.* Adequacy of the premium is less a concern with a whole life policy than a universal life policy because of the former's fixed premium. Often, however, the whole life premium won't fit within the cost parameters, in which case you must use a universal life policy.

The Spouse's Risks

What happens to the pension maximization plan if you and your spouse get divorced? What happens if you can't or won't pay the premiums after a while? What happens if the insurer fails? These are all difficult questions with complex answers. The point in raising them now is simply that your spouse's risks in the pension maximization plan have to be identified and managed.

MEDICARE

During retirement, your health insurance program is likely to consist of one of the following:

- Medicare and a Medicare supplement policy
- An employer's post-retirement coverage with Medicare as the primary provider

We'll discuss Medicare first; discussions of the other health care components will follow.

Medicare is a federal health insurance program for people 65 and older, people of any age with permanent kidney failure, and certain disabled people under 65. Medicare is administered by the Health Care Financing Administration (HCFA) of the U.S. Department of Health and Human Services. The Social Security Administration provides information about the program and handles enrollment.

Medicare has two parts:

- Hospital insurance (Part A)
- Medical insurance (Part B)

Medicare Part A: Hospital Insurance

Medicare Part A can help pay for inpatient hospital care, inpatient care in a skilled nursing facility, home health care, and hospice care. Part A is financed through the FICA tax; 1.45% of your compensation withheld and designated for this insurance.

If you plan to retire at age 65, you simply contact the Social Security Administration about 3 months prior to your 65th birthday. The Social Security Administration will enroll you in Medicare. If you're already receiving Social Security benefits when you turn 65, you'll be contacted by the Social Security Administration and automatically enrolled in Medicare Part A for your 65th birthday. There is no premium or fee for Part A.

Coverage under Medicare is described in terms of a "benefit period." A benefit period begins on the first day you receive service as an inpatient in a hospital and ends after you've been out of the hospital or skilled nursing facility for 60 days in a row or remain in a skilled nursing facility but do not receive skilled care there for 60 days in a row.

Medicare doesn't pay for custodial care (i.e., care that could be given by someone who isn't medically skilled: help with dressing, walking, or eating). If you're confined to your home and meet certain other conditions, Medicare Part A can pay the full approved cost of home health care visits from a Medicare-participating home health agency. No prior hospital stay is required, and there's no limit on the number of covered visits. Note, however, that coverage is for part-time or intermittent care only. Moreover, there's no coverage for services primarily of a home-maker sort.

Medicare Part B: Medical Insurance

Medicare medical insurance helps pay for doctor's services and many other medical services and supplies that aren't covered by Medicare Part A. Where you receive these services (i.e., hospital, clinic, or home) is irrelevant.

Part B is optional and is offered to all persons when they become entitled to Part A. You're enrolled in Part B automatically when you become entitled to Part A unless you elect otherwise. There's a monthly premium for Part B—$45.50 in 1999.

MEDICARE (PART A): HOSPITAL–INSURANCE-COVERED SERVICES PER BENEFIT PERIOD[a]

SERVICES	BENEFIT	MEDICARE PAYS[b]	YOU PAY[b]
HOSPITALIZATION Semiprivate room and board, general nursing, and miscellaneous hospital services and supplies.	First 60 days	All but $768	$768
	61st to 90th day	All but $192 a day	$192 a day
	91st to 150th day[c]	All but $384 a day	$384 a day
	Beyond 150 days	Nothing	All costs
POSTHOSPITAL SKILLED NURSING FACILITY CARE You must have been in a hospital for at least 3 days, enter a Medicare-approved facility generally within 30 days after hospital discharge, and meet other program requirements.[d]	First 20 days	100% of approved amount	Nothing
	Additional 80 days	All but $96 a day	Up to $96 a day
	Beyond 100 days	Nothing	All costs
HOME HEALTH CARE Medically necessary skilled care, home health aide services, medical supplies, etc.	Part-time or inter-mittent nursing care and other services for as long as you meet criteria for benefits.	100% of approved amount; 80% of approved amount for durable medical equipment.	Nothing for services; 20% of approved amount for durable medical equipment.
HOSPICE CARE Full scope of pain relief and support services available to the terminally ill.	As long as doctor certifies need.	All but limited costs for outpatient drugs and inpatient respite care.	Limited cost sharing for outpatient drugs and inpatient respite care.
BLOOD	Blood	All but first 3 pints per calendar year.	For first 3 pints.[e]

[a]Benefit period begins on the first day you receive service as an inpatient in a hospital and ends after you have been out of the hospital or skilled nursing facility for 60 days in a row or remain in a skilled nursing facility but do not receive skilled care there for 60 days in a row.
[b]These figures are for 1999 and are subject to change each year.
[c]60 reserve days may be used only once.
[d]Neither Medicare nor Medigap insurance will pay for most nursing home care.
[e]To the extent that the blood deductible is met under one part of Medicare during the calendar year, it does not have to be met under the other part.

Part B Covered Services per Calendar Year. There's a $100 annual deductible before Medicare Part B begins paying for covered services. The $100 deductible must represent services or supplies covered by Medicare. It must also be based on the Medicare-approved amounts, not the actual charges billed by the physician or medical supplier. Once you've spent $100 for covered services in 1999, the Part B deductible doesn't apply to further covered services received for the rest of the year.

In addition to Medicare coinsurance, you pay for charges higher than the amount approved by Medicare unless the doctor or supplier agrees to accept Medicare's approved amount as full payment for services rendered. The approved amount for physicians' services is determined by the HCFA and set forth in a national fee schedule. As noted in the chart on page 503, Medicare pays 80% of the approved amount.

MEDIGAP INSURANCE

Although Medicare will address many of your health insurance concerns after you turn 65, the truth remains that Medicare doesn't lack for limitations. It leaves you exposed in several ways, including deductibles, coinsurance amounts, and even some covered services themselves. For example, Medicare doesn't cover:

- Care in a skilled-nursing facility beyond 100 days per benefit period
- Care in a skilled facility not approved by Medicare
- Custodial care—probably the type of care most commonly required by those in a nursing home
- Out-of-pocket hospital prescription drugs
- Medical tests for (and cost of) eyeglasses or hearing aids
- Care received outside the United States

Given these and other gaps in Medicare coverage, how do you protect yourself during retirement? The answer: Close the gaps. The way to do so is to purchase *Medigap insurance*. Medigap insurance is private health insurance designed specifically to fill in the gaps between Medicare itself and the level of health insurance you desire.

Not long ago, *Medigap insurance* was exceedingly difficult for people to obtain in ways that suited their specific needs. The market offered such an array of plans and so many specific coverages and exclusions that consumers all too frequently ended up buying more (or less) than they needed. Many people ended up duplicating coverage, hence overpaying for what they received.

MEDICARE (PART B): MEDICAL INSURANCE–COVERED SERVICES PER CALENDAR YEAR

SERVICES	BENEFIT	MEDICARE PAYS	YOU PAY
MEDICAL EXPENSE Physician's services, inpatient and outpatient medical and surgical services and supplies, physical and speech therapy, diagnostic tests, durable medical equipment, etc.	Medicare pays for medical services in or out of the hospital.	80% of approved amount (after $100 deductible); 50% of approved charges for most outpatient mental health services.	$100 deductible,[a] plus 20% of approved amount and charges above approved amount.[b] 50% of approved charges for mental health services.
CLINICAL LABORATORY SERVICES	Blood tests, biopsies, urinalysis, etc.	Generally, 100% of approved amount.	Nothing for services.
HOME HEALTH CARE Medically necessary skilled care, home health aide services, medical supplies, etc.	Part-time or intermittent nursing care and other services for as long as you meet criteria for benefits.	100% of approved amount; 80% of approved amount for durable medical equipment.	Nothing for services; 20% of approved amount for durable medical equipment.
OUTPATIENT HOSPITAL TREATMENT Reasonable and necessary services for the diagnosis or treatment of an illness or injury.	Unlimited if medically necessary.	80% of approved amount (after $100 deductible).	Subject to deductible plus 20% of billed amount.
BLOOD	Blood	80% of approved amount (after $100 deductible and starting with fourth pint).	First 3 pints plus 20% of approved amount for additional pints (after $100 deductible).[c]

[a]Once you have had $100 of expense for covered services, the Part B deductible does not apply to other covered services you receive for the rest of the year.
[b]The amount by which a physician's charge can exceed the Medicare-approved amount is limited by law.
[c]To the extent that the blood deductible is met under one part of Medicare during the calendar year, it does not have to be met under the other part.

This situation is no longer inevitable. Medigap policies have now been standardized. As a result of standardization, benefits are consistent from one carrier to another, and overinsurance is much easier to prevent. In fact, you now need only one Medigap policy to close the gap between the coverage you need and what Medicare offers. Why is this so? Because federal law now requires that insurers offer no more than 10 standard Medigap policies. Each policy must provide at least a "core" of basic benefits. Built on top of that core are nine policies, each with a particular combination of additional benefits.

Here's how the standardization works:

The basic plan is designated *Plan A*. The other nine plans are designated *Plans B* through *J*. Each plan must provide a standard set of benefits. Insurers aren't permitted to change the designations, substitute titles, and so forth. An insurer isn't required to sell all 10 policies in a given state. However, if the insurer offers Plans B through J, they must offer Plan A as well.

The 10 Standard Medigap Plans

Here are the 10 standard Medigap plans. *Plan A* consists of these core benefits:

- Coverage for the Part A coinsurance amount ($192 per day in 1999) for days 61 through 90 of hospitalization in each Medicare benefit period.
- Coverage for the Part A coinsurance amount ($384 per day in 1999) for each of Medicare's nonrenewable lifetime hospital inpatient reserve days used.
- Coverage for 100% of the Medicare Part A eligible hospital expenses after all Medicare hospital benefits are exhausted. Coverage is limited to a maximum of 365 days of additional inpatient hospital care during the policyholder's lifetime.
- Coverage under Medicare Parts A and B for the reasonable cost of the first three pints of blood or equivalent quantities of packed red blood cells per calendar year unless replaced in accordance with federal regulations.
- Coverage for the 20% coinsurance amount for Part B services after the $100 annual deductible is met.

Plan B includes the core benefits plus coverage for:

- The Medicare Part A inpatient hospital deductible ($768 per benefit period in 1999).

Plan C includes the core benefits plus coverage for:

- The skilled nursing facility care coinsurance amount ($96 per day for days 21 through 100 per benefit period in 1999).
- The Medicare Part A deductible.
- The Medicare Part B deductible ($100 per calendar year in 1999).
- Medically necessary emergency care in a foreign country. This benefit is subject to a $250 deductible, but then pays 80% of emergency care in another country, up to a lifetime maximum of $50,000.

Plan D includes the core benefits plus coverage for:

- The skilled nursing facility care daily coinsurance amount.
- The Medicare Part A deductible.
- Medically necessary emergency care in a foreign country.
- At-home recovery. The at-home recovery benefit pays up to $1,600 per year for short-term, at-home assistance with activities of daily living (bathing, dressing, personal hygiene, etc.) for those recovering from an illness, injury, or surgery. There are various benefit requirements and limitations, but essentially this benefit covers the personal services needed for someone receiving skilled home health care under Medicare.

Plan E includes the core benefits plus coverage for:

- The skilled nursing facility care daily coinsurance amount.
- The Medicare Part A deductible.
- Medically necessary emergency care in a foreign country.
- Preventive medical care. The preventive medical care benefit pays up to $120 per year for such things as a physical examination, flu shot, serum cholesterol screening, hearing test, diabetes screenings, and thyroid function test.

Plan F includes the core benefits plus coverage for:

- The skilled nursing facility care daily coinsurance amount.
- The Medicare Part A deductible.
- The Medicare Part B deductible.
- 100% of Medicare Part B excess charges. This benefit covers the entire difference between the physician's charge and the Medicare-approved amount for a Medicare-approved service.
- Medically necessary emergency care in a foreign country.

Plan G includes the core benefits plus coverage for:

- The skilled nursing facility care daily coinsurance amount.
- The Medicare Part A deductible.
- 80% of the Medicare Part B excess coverage.
- Medically necessary emergency care in a foreign country.
- Coverage for at-home recovery.

Plan H includes the core benefits plus coverage for:

- The skilled nursing facility care daily coinsurance amount.
- The Medicare Part A deductible.
- Medically necessary emergency care in a foreign country.
- 50% of the cost of prescription drugs up to a maximum annual benefit of $1,250 after the policyholder meets a $250 per year deductible. This is called the "basic" prescription drug benefit.

Plan I includes the core benefits plus coverage for:

- The skilled nursing facility care daily coinsurance amount.
- The Medicare Part A deductible.
- 100% of Medicare Part B excess charges.
- Medically necessary emergency care in a foreign country.
- At-home recovery.
- 50% of the cost of prescription drugs up to a maximum annual benefit of $1,250 after the policyholder meets a $250 per year deductible (the "basic" prescription drug benefit).

Plan J includes the core benefits plus coverage for:

- The skilled nursing facility daily coinsurance amount.
- The Medicare Part A deductible.
- The Medicare Part B deductible.
- 100% of Medicare Part B excess charges.
- Medically necessary emergency care in a foreign country.
- At-home recovery.
- 50% of the cost of prescription drugs up to a maximum annual benefit of $3,000 after the policyholder meets a $250 per year deductible. This is called the "extended" drug benefit.
- Preventive medical care.

See the table on page 507 for an overview of how these Medigap policies compare.

10 STANDARD MEDICARE SUPPLEMENT BENEFIT PLANS

CORE BENEFITS	PLAN A	PLAN B	PLAN C	PLAN D	PLAN E	PLAN F	PLAN G	PLAN H	PLAN I	PLAN J
Part A hospital (days 61–90)	X	X	X	X	X	X	X	X	X	X
Lifetime reserve days (91–150)	X	X	X	X	X	X	X	X	X	X
365 Life hospital days, 100%	X	X	X	X	X	X	X	X	X	X
Parts A and B blood	X	X	X	X	X	X	X	X	X	X
Part B coinsurance, 20%	X	X	X	X	X	X	X	X	X	X
ADDITIONAL BENEFITS	**A**	**B**	**C**	**D**	**E**	**F**	**G**	**H**	**I**	**J**
Skilled nursing facility coinsurance (days 21–100)			X	X	X	X	X	X	X	X
Part A deductible		X	X	X	X	X	X	X	X	X
Part B deductible			X			X				X
Part B excess charges						100%	80%		100%	100%
Foreign travel emergency			X	X	X	X	X	X	X	X
At-home recovery				X			X		X	X
Prescription drugs								1	1	2
Preventive medical care					X					X

Core benefits pay the patient's share of Medicare's approved amount for physician services (generally 20%) after $100 annual deductible, the patient's cost of a long hospital stay ($192 day for days 61–90, $384 a day for days 91–150, approved costs not paid by Medicare after day 150 to a total of 365 days lifetime), and charges for the first 3 pints of blood not covered by Medicare.

Two prescription drug benefits are offered:

1. A "basic" benefit with $250 annual deductible, 50% coinsurance, and a $1,250 maximum annual benefit (plans H and I above)
2. An "extended" benefit (plan J above) containing a $250 annual deductible, 50% coinsurance, and a $3,000 maximum annual benefit

Each of the 10 plans has a letter designation ranging from A through J. Insurance companies are not permitted to change these designations or to substitute other names or titles. They may, however, add names or titles to these letter designations. While companies are not required to offer all the plans, they all must make plan A available if they sell any of the other nine in a state. Numbers are for 1999.

Selecting an Appropriate Plan

Shopping for a Medigap policy is much easier now than ever before. You should select your plan according to three criteria:

- The plan itself
- Service
- Price

Although these three criteria are obviously interrelated, we'll look at each criterion separately.

The Plan. You should study each benefit, then select a policy that includes the benefits you consider worthwhile and excludes the ones you don't need or want. On the one hand, you could just select the basic plan (Plan A) and self-insure for the additional benefits offered in policies B through J. This kind of "stop-loss" approach probably isn't advisable, however. Here are some general guidelines that may be more helpful. Benefits that insurance professionals generally recommend include:

- The skilled nursing home co-payment
- Part A hospital deductible
- Foreign travel emergency benefits

Benefits sometimes considered less worthwhile include:

- The Part B deductible benefit (which is likely to cost as much as the benefit itself)
- Preventive care
- At-home recovery benefits

This may be true as well for Part B excess doctor expenses. First, this coverage comes into play only if the physician doesn't accept the assignment from Medicare. Second, the law restricts the amount that the physician can charge over and above the Medicare-approved payment. Therefore, you should carefully consider the cost of this benefit.

You should also consider the prescription drug benefits in the context of their pricing and their utility to you. If you're healthy today, a long time may pass before you reap any benefit from the prescription drug benefits. Even then (given the 50% basic prescription drug benefit), you won't reach the maximum benefit until you spent $2,750 per year on medicine ($250 deductible plus 50% of $2,500). The 100% benefit is maximized at an expenditure of $6,250 per year.

Service. It seems to make sense that price is the next immediate criterion. However, you're probably better off long-term by identifying an insurer that has distinguished itself for policyholder service. Here are some relevant questions to ask:

- How does the insurer manage claims?
- How does the insurer coordinate Medicare claims with its Medigap policy?
- Is coordination done electronically, or are forms necessary?
- Is there an "800" telephone number for customer service?

These are examples of things that can distinguish one insurer's policyholder service from another.

Price. Once you've identified the Medigap plan (or plans) that interest you, and once you've identified one or more companies worthy of your business, you should compare prices. As always, the price differential between two providers is probably something you can attribute to some value added from the higher-priced provider.

PRIVATE HEALTH INSURANCE AFTER RETIREMENT

You may be fortunate enough to be able to maintain post-retirement health coverage under your employer's plan. If this is true, Medicare becomes the primary insurer (payer) and your plan becomes the secondary payer. Circumstances such as these generally mean that you don't need a Medigap policy.

It's just as likely, however, that you won't have post-retirement health coverage from your employer. In this case, you'll be entitled to Medicare at age 65, and your health insurance program following retirement will therefore consist of Medicare Parts A and B, supplemented by a Medigap policy. Yet even this arrangement may not solve your health care insurance problems. The reason: Although you yourself may be eligible for Medicare, your spouse will not be eligible if younger than 65. Fortunately, the law may offer some protection in these circumstances.

Continuing Your Health Care Coverage Under COBRA

In Chapter 8 we discussed how the Consolidated Omnibus Budget Reconciliation Act of 1985 (COBRA) assists employees and their qualified beneficiaries to extend health coverage under certain circumstances. COBRA requires employers of 20 or more people maintaining group health coverage to extend that coverage for the employee or certain dependents after one or more of several specified events occur. These qualifying events include:

- The employee's death
- The employee's termination or reduction in hours (e.g., retirement)
- The employee's entitlement to Medicare benefits

The continuing coverage must be the same as the coverage provided to other similarly situated employees covered under the plan for whom a qualifying event has not occurred. The continuing coverage cannot be subject to insurability. Here are some issues to consider:

- How long will continuing coverage last?
- Who is eligible?

- What will you pay?
- Entitlement to Medicare as a qualifying event
- Planning where COBRA is of inadequate duration

How Long Will Continuing Coverage Last? The required length of time for which you may receive continuing coverage depends on which qualifying event triggers the option for continuation. When you retire, you have the option of continuing coverage for at least 18 months. With respect to all other qualifying events, the continuation must be at least 36 months. Your employer's obligation to provide continuing coverage ceases when you become entitled to Medicare.

Who Is Eligible? The employee and your qualified beneficiaries are eligible for continuation of coverage under COBRA. In general, qualified beneficiaries will include the employee's spouse and dependent children.

What Will You Pay?
If you're eligible for continuing coverage, you (or qualified beneficiary) may be required to pay for the coverage. The premium cannot exceed 102% of what people pay in similar situations.

Entitlement to Medicare as a Qualifying Event. Let's suppose that you've retired at age 65. You have no post-retirement coverage under your employer's plan, but you're eligible for Medicare. Your spouse is 62—3 years shy of Medicare eligibility. The law requires that your spouse be offered continuing coverage for 36 months from the date on which you become entitled to Medicare.

Planning Where COBRA Is of Inadequate Duration. If your spouse is younger than 62 when you retire at age 65, the 36-month continuation period leaves your spouse vulnerable during the "window" between the end of the continuation period and age 65. Assume, for example, that your spouse is age 59 when you retire. Even if your spouse has 36 months of coverage, he or she will still not be entitled to Medicare at the end of the continuing coverage. In a situation of this sort, your spouse might do well to purchase an individual health policy now. Once insured individually, the spouse wouldn't choose to purchase continuation coverage once eligibility for that coverage had been triggered by a qualifying event.

If your spouse isn't insurable, he or she would choose the continuation coverage and would maintain it for as long as possible. At the end of the continuation period, it might be possible to convert from the employer's plan to an individual policy under the plan's conversion option. If there's no conversion option, your spouse might have to seek coverage in the state's assigned risk pool or a similar insurance vehicle. As soon as your spouse turns 65, he or she will be entitled to Medicare.

The complexities of this situation suggest that you might do well to work with an agent who specializes in this area. The agent can help you compare available individual coverage with continuing coverage under COBRA followed by conversion. This advice will be particularly valuable if your spouse has a medical problem.

LONG-TERM CARE

Perhaps no other aspect of risk management for retirees causes as much concern as long-term care (LTC). You may be aware of the statistics on this subject, such as the relatively high probability that you'll spend some span of time in a nursing home if you're age 65 or older. You may also have heard stories about how expensive this kind of care can be. You probably know that Medicare and Medigap policies are unlikely to cover the expenses associated with LTC. You may even have heard that LTC policies tend to be expensive, not very good, or both. So now you're wondering if you should buy an LTC policy.

To address this issue, let's consider (1) whether you should purchase an LTC policy, and (2) how you should evaluate an LTC policy.

We'll approach the discussion through these topics:

- What do we mean by LTC?
- Deciding whether you need LTC
- How you pay for LTC
- Group LTC policies
- Should you purchase an LTC policy?

Long-Term Care (LTC) Insurance

The Health Insurance Portability and Accountability Act of 1996 contained several provisions that address the income taxation of LTC insurance policies.

1. Exclusion of Benefits from LTC Policies
   Amounts received under qualified LTC policies are generally excludable from gross income. This exclusion is subject to daily and annual maximums of $190 and $69,350 (for 1999), respectively, on per diem contracts only. These limits are indexed by the medical care cost component of the Consumer Price Index. Payments in excess of these limits will be excludable only to the extent the individual has incurred actual costs for LTC services.

2. Exclusion for Employer-Provided LTC Coverage
   An employer-sponsored plan providing coverage under an LTC insurance contract will generally be treated as an accident and health plan. Thus, employees will not be subject to income tax on the employer-provided benefits. However, coverage will not be excludable by an employee if provided through a cafeteria plan.

3. Deduction for LTC Insurance Premiums
   Subject to the following limits, in 1999 premiums for qualified LTC policies will be treated as deductible medical expenses:

Attained Age Before the Close of the Taxable Year	Deductible Premium Limit
Not more than 40	$ 210
More than 40 but not more than 50	400
More than 50 but not more than 60	800
More than 60 but not more than 70	2,120
More than 70	2,660

What Do We Mean by LTC?

LTC is the kind of help you need if you're unable to care for yourself because of a prolonged illness or disability. LTC encompasses services ranging from skilled nursing care in a nursing home to assistance in daily activities at home. While typically associated with skilled nursing care provided in a nursing home, LTC more properly includes services at several levels of care, including:

- *Skilled nursing care:* acute nursing and rehabilitative care given by a registered nurse or therapist, usually daily (i.e., around the clock) and supervised by a physician.
- *Intermediate nursing care:* occasional nursing and rehabilitative care under supervision of skilled medical personnel. This level of care differs from skilled care in that it is not on a 24-hour basis.
- *Custodial care:* assistance in performing activities of daily living. This level of care is often given by nonmedical personnel, whether in nursing homes, adult day-care centers, or in your home.
- *Home care:* can include part-time skilled care, therapy, homemakers' assistance, home health aides' care, and other forms of assistance in your own home.

Deciding Whether You Need LTC

Although the general need for LTC is statistically significant, your own individual need is harder to predict. Bear in mind that LTC may be necessary for a variety of reasons that range from arthritis to Alzheimer's to accidents. Whether you yourself (or your spouse) will need LTC depends on your current state of health, your family health history, and a variety of other factors, many of them unpredictable. These are issues you should discuss with your physician as well as with your insurance agent.

From a cost standpoint, the situation is somewhat more predictable. The cost of a nursing home stay varies by geographical location but will range from $30,000 to $70,000 a year.

How You Pay for LTC

Medicare LTC benefits are highly restricted and not particularly substantial. For example, Medicare Part A covers only skilled nursing and rehabilitative care in a Medicare-approved facility. The care must be needed on a daily basis. The care must be preceded by at least 3 days of hospitalization, and must commence within 30 days of the patient's discharge from the hospital. Even then, Medicare pays benefits for only 100 days in a Medicare-approved facility. During the first 20 days, Medicare pays 100% of the cost of care. For days 21 to 100, Medicare pays for costs in excess of $96 per day. Medicare Part A provides home health benefits for people who are confined to their home and need intermittent skilled nursing care (or therapy) under a physician's care. The key criterion here is that the need must be for *skilled* nursing care. However, there's no requirement of prior hospitalization, and Medicare pays the full cost without a deductible.

In short, Medicare isn't a reliable form of insurance for your overall LTC risk. In fact, Medicare pays only about 2% of the costs of LTC. In any event, Medicare doesn't pay for a prolonged nursing home stay, meaning a stay of more than 100 days. Medicare covers skilled care, not intermediate or custodial care, which are the levels of care typically needed. Home care benefits under Medicare are restrictive.

Given this situation, what are your options? You can self-insure, transfer the risk to an LTC insurer, or do both.

An LTC policy will help you pay the costs of one or more levels of LTC. The better policies available today typically cover all levels of LTC described above, although the terms of coverage and the benefits payable vary widely among these policies. Let's look now at these policies' more important features and points of comparison.

Coverage. At least at the start, you should look for a policy offering the most expansive coverage. That is, you should find a policy that covers all levels of care: skilled, intermediate, custodial, and home health care. The better policies today offer such expansive coverage. However, we want to look at the definitions of the care provided at each level. Here are some questions you should ask:

- What level of care will you receive in particular types of facilities?
- Is custodial care (the type of care actually required by most people) provided by licensed or certified professionals?
- Is home care (the type desired by so many people) provided by licensed or certified professionals?
- Does the policy offer the benefits mandated by your state of residence?

It's fair to say that the more expansive the coverage and the more flexible the provisions, the more expensive the policy will be.

Benefit Periods. You're able to select the duration of benefits under the policy. Choices typically include periods of 2 to 6 years or a lifetime benefit for nursing home care. The home health care benefit period can either be integrated with the nursing home benefit or stated (and determined) separately. Some policies set the maximum limits in terms of days, some in years, and some in dollars. The way the benefit period is measured (or "capped") can be meaningful. For instance, you might pay for a benefit of $150 per day but actually incur lower costs of care. A policy maximum measured in dollars would extend the benefit period. A policy may also provide that if the benefits available for one type of coverage (e.g., home health care) are exhausted, remaining nursing home benefits will be available.

Here again, the longer the benefit period, the more expensive the policy. The duration of the health care benefit is likely to be commensurate with the nursing home benefit.

Benefits. Most LTC policies are indemnity policies; that is, they pay a certain fixed dollar amount for each day (or month) of care. You can select from a range of benefit amounts between perhaps $30 and $250 for nursing home care. The home health care benefit can be equal to the nursing home benefit or, quite commonly, about one-half of the nursing home benefit. For each benefit you must determine whether the policy pays the full benefit amount, 100% of the actual expenses up to the benefit amount, or a lesser percentage of those expenses, up to the benefit amount.

One way to select a benefit amount is to find out the cost of care in your geographic area. From there you can determine how much of that cost you wish to pay for.

Elimination Period. The elimination period refers to the *deductible*— meaning the number of days of care in a facility (or visits at home) you must receive before the policy pays its benefits. The longer the elimination period, the lower the cost of the policy. Of course, there's more to selecting an elimination period than meets the eye. You need to know if the elimination period is the same for all levels of care. You should also know if the policy counts calendar days or days when you actually receive care (e.g., a home visit).

Selection of an elimination period is obviously a function of the premium and, once again, the extent to which you wish to retain the LTC risk or transfer it to the insurer. Bear in mind that you may require several short-term stays in a nursing home (e.g., for postoperative care), so a policy with an extended elimination period may not prove to be particularly worthwhile.

Benefit Eligibility. A key provision in any LTC policy is the set of conditions under which you'll be eligible for benefits.

Gatekeepers. Unlike policies of several years ago, competitive policies today require no hospitalization before you enter a nursing home. (Such prior hospitalizations were called *gatekeepers*.) Typically, you don't need prior hospitalization for home health care benefits, either. In fact, the better policy won't impose a requirement of receiving a higher level of care before receiving the care for which benefits are sought.

Benefit Triggers. Lacking these sorts of gatekeepers, what condition or conditions will trigger payment of benefits? It's now common for an LTC policy to condition eligibility for benefits on such criteria as the following:

- Your doctor certifies that you require substantial supervision to protect yourself from threats to health and safety due to severe cognitive impairment.
- Your doctor certifies that you are unable to perform, without substantial assistance from another individual, at least two activities of daily living (ADLs: bathing, dressing, transferring, eating, toileting, continence, etc.) for at least 90 days, due to a loss of functional capacity. Policies typically require that you need assistance with at least two out of five or six ADLs.

A policy that follows the disability model of design will pay benefits once you've met the applicable conditions. You don't actually have to receive LTC services as a condition for benefits. A policy that follows the reimbursement model will not only require you to meet the applicable conditions, but also incur expense for the applicable care.

Nonforfeiture Benefits. Much like a term life or disability policy, most LTC policies provide no residual value. Once the policy lapses, the coverage ceases. Some policies now offer some form of nonforfeiture benefit: Under certain conditions, there will be some residual benefit when the LTC policy lapses or you die. The nonforfeiture benefit can take at least two forms:

- The insurer will return a certain percentage of the premiums you've paid (minus any benefits you've received) when you either terminate the policy or die.
- You may be entitled to a smaller benefit amount if the policy lapses after being in force for a minimum number of years.

Guaranteed Renewable. This provision is fundamentally important. It guarantees you that the policy can't be canceled as long as you pay the premium.

Premium Increases. Even though the LTC policy may be guaranteed renewable, the insurer has the right to increase the premium for that class of policies. This provision clearly brings all elements of uncertainty (and risk) into the acquisition, particularly because insurers simply don't have the indemnity experience in LTC that they have in more traditional forms of insurance.

Waiver of Premiums. Policies generally provide that premiums are waived (i.e., excused) during periods when LTC benefits are being paid. Waiver provisions vary significantly among LTC policies.

Inflation Riders. You should be concerned about the impact of inflation on your benefits' purchasing power. Policies generally offer two or three options (riders) that address the inflation concern. Typical options include:

- *Simple increases.* The policy's benefit amounts will automatically increase each year by 5% of the original benefit amounts.
- *Compounded increases.* The policy's benefit amounts will automatically increase each year by 5% of the previous year's benefit amounts. These riders call for additional premiums, but the premiums are level.
- *Future purchase options.* You'll be offered the option to buy more benefits at certain intervals (e.g., 3 years) based on the changes in the Consumer Price Index (CPI). Premiums under this option increase when the benefits increase.

Many insurance professionals tend to recommend the compound option over the simple option. However, the inflation rider is expensive, so you should be young enough to have a significant probability of getting your money's worth from the rider.

Group LTC Policies

Some employers are now starting to offer group LTC policies. These policies are typically employee-paid and offer coverage, limits, and exclusions that are similar to those for individual policies. Premiums can be highly competitive; you may be able to cover not only yourself but also your spouse (and often your parents and in-laws as well) under the policy. Your coverage is also portable—you can keep the coverage even if you leave your employer.

Should You Purchase an LTC Policy?

If you feel that your circumstances might warrant purchase of an LTC policy, here are the main factors that should enter into your decision:

Affordability. Premiums for someone in his or her early to mid-60s are likely to range from $2,000 to $4,000 each, depending on the age, benefit amount, benefit period, elimination period, and so forth. You should ask your insurance agent to show you the relative costs of various policy structures.

Attitudes Toward Receiving Public Assistance. What are your sentiments on this subject? If you end up needing long-term care but lack the funds to pay for private caregivers, are you comfortable with the notion of receiving care through Medicaid? Or do you prefer to pay for insurance that would allow you to maintain your independence and the sense of control that goes with it?

Family History. If your parents required long-term care during their late years, you're statistically more likely to need LTC yourself, thus making the case for LTC insurance more compelling.

Availability, Reliability, and Desirability of Care by Family Members. Do you have relatives who can give you long-term care at your home? Do you want to be cared for by (and be dependent on) a family member? Some people may find this an acceptable option; others may find it unappealing. Even if you're comfortable with the possibility, are your relatives sufficiently skilled, patient, and generous enough to provide you with the care you might need?

Attitude Toward Leaving an Estate for the Children. An LTC policy can be a "stop-loss" mechanism that could preserve at least some portion of your estate for the children. Given the costs associated with LTC, insurance coverage could limit the drain on your assets if you required long-term care.

Flexibility for Later Years. You may have a notion of moving into a congregate care facility in a few years. The facility may or may not provide LTC as a part of its program. For this reason, you may want your own policy to cover you in the interim.

Broader (and Better) Choices for Care. You may find that because of your assets, income level, and LTC policy, you'll have greater choice of LTC facilities than some people of comparable or more limited assets who have no LTC insurance.

It's difficult to determine a precise combination of benefit amounts, elimination period, inflation riders, and so forth. One way to deal with this decision is to determine how much of the LTC risk you can reasonably retain and then transfer the balance of the risk to the insurer. For example, you might decide to retain the risks of a brief period of care but insure for some portion of the risk of extended care. Thus a longer elimination period and a benefit amount that's a reasonable percentage of today's daily costs would be appropriate. A benefit period of at least 3 years would also serve you well, for it will give your assets time to compound and allow you and your family time to plan for possible asset transfers.

LIFE-CARE FACILITIES

An increasing number of older Americans are choosing to cover their possible need for long-term care by purchasing or renting a residence in a life-care facility. Life-care facilities usually are condominium-style residences that offer an individual living unit. You must meet the age, health, and financial criteria set by the facility. Generally, you pay an entrance fee by making a one-time lump sum payment which entitles you to lifetime exclusive occupancy of a residence as long as you are capable of independent living. A monthly fee pays not only for upkeep of the common space, but also for meals in a communal dining room. And a portion of the monthly fee may also serve as "insurance," in the event the individual needs to move from independent living into long-term skilled nursing home care.

Some life-care facilities have skilled nursing homes on site, while others contract with such a facility. Some have assisted-living capabilities such as aides and nurses who will make visits to the individual's apartment. Some have space in their nursing facilities for people rehabilitating after hospitalization who will then return to their individual living units.

Tax treatment of such living arrangements is somewhat complex and involves tax issues relating to whether any part of the payments you make qualify as deductible medical expenses. We suggest you discuss these issues with your tax advisor. To learn more about these matters, see *The Ernst & Young Tax Guide.*

ACCELERATED DEATH BENEFITS

A relatively new (and still evolving) aspect of managing some portion of the LTC risk is what's called the *accelerated benefits rider*. This is an enhancement of a life insurance policy designed to allow you access to the death benefit under certain conditions. That is, you yourself may be able to use some of the benefit that your beneficiaries would receive following your death. It's important to emphasize that *these riders are not a comprehensive approach to LTC insurance, nor are they intended as substitutes for LTC insurance policies.* However, these riders can be extremely helpful in certain situations.

Here are some aspects of accelerated benefits riders to consider:

- Availability
- Benefit triggers
- Benefit limits

- Payment method
- Impact of the advance on the policy itself
- Tax issues
- The role of the accelerated benefit rider in LTC risk management

Availability

Accelerated benefits riders are increasingly available to you under individual or group policies. Well over 125 insurers offer these riders.

Benefit Triggers

Insurers may offer these benefit triggers on an "either/or" basis:

- *Terminal illness.* You may receive early payment when your doctor certifies that you're not expected to live more than a certain number of months.
- *Confinement to a nursing home.* You may receive the benefit if you've spent a certain period of time in a nursing home and aren't expected to leave.
- *Diagnosis of certain illnesses or conditions.* You may be paid benefits if you suffer a heart attack or are diagnosed with cancer or Alzheimer's disease.
- *Other events.* You may receive benefits if you have an organ transplant.

From a planning standpoint, the principal distinction among these riders is whether they are designed to advance a death benefit to a terminally ill person or serve as a form of nursing home insurance.

Benefit Limits

Significant variations exist regarding (1) the percentage of the death benefit that you can obtain, and (2) the maximum dollar amount available. Where the rider can be triggered by more than one situation, the benefit available may also differ under each triggering event. Here's an example: One insurer will advance up to approximately 75% of the death benefit for the nursing home aspect of the rider, and 90% if the insured is terminally ill.

Payment Method

Key differences include the availability of a lump sum versus regular periodic payments, ability to take more than one advance, and so forth. Riders having a nursing home or other LTC orientation may restrict payments to a certain method (e.g., monthly) for a certain benefit trigger and type of care.

You can generally obtain these living benefit riders without additional premium cost. However, some insurers do charge for their riders. Here are some of the possible charges:

- A "cost" for accessing the benefit early
- A discount for the advance
- An administrative fee
- Interest charge on the advance (assessed against policy values and/or death benefit)

Impact of the Advance on the Policy Itself

An advance under an accelerated death benefit rider will affect the policy in one way or another. The death benefit will be reduced by at least the amount of the advance and perhaps by any interest charge in addition. Check with your insurance agent to clarify the impact of the advance on death benefit, cash value, dividends, credited interest, and so forth.

Tax Treatment of Accelerated Benefits

Benefits actually paid at the insured person's death are generally free of income tax. The tax law expands that exclusion to include amounts received by the insured during life under a life insurance policy if the insured is either terminally ill or chronically ill. The exclusion is complete for an insured who is terminally ill. If the insured is chronically ill, then the exclusion is the same as that for benefits under a long-term care policy.

The Role of the Accelerated Benefit Rider in LTC Risk Management

These riders clearly serve a useful purpose. Early access to the death benefit can make a significant difference to you and your family. An important question remains, however: Assuming that the rider triggers when you enter a nursing home, to what extent is that rider an adequate substitute for a true LTC insurance policy? The answer seems to be that unless the policy itself is substantial, and unless the rider covers such services as custodial care, the rider is *not* adequate as an LTC insurance policy. It is, however, a respectable *complement* for such a policy.

26

A FEW WORDS IN PARTING

Our introduction noted that in this book we would take a targeted approach to financial planning. Rather than perceive financial planning as a massive, comprehensive subject, we prefer to view it from the vantage point of specific life events. This approach is why we present our treatment partly as a "cafeteria" of topics—a compendium of discussions from which you can pick and choose according to your personal needs. Perhaps you've read the book straight through. Perhaps you've read only specific sections that apply to your own stage of life. Either way, however, we at Ernst & Young wish to end the book with a few final recommendations on financial planning that should apply to all readers, regardless of their ages and backgrounds.

First and foremost, *take action on your plan.* Perhaps your plan is a formal document that you've received following consultations with a professional financial planner; on the other hand, perhaps you've created your own plan by reading this book. Either way, you need to take the specific steps that your plan recommends. Make a budget. Pay off your debts. Start saving money. Begin investing to fund your goals. Purchase the insurance policies that will adequately protect your family. Write your will and attend to any other necessary estate planning tasks. In short, do what needs to be done. If you simply go through the motions of financial planning but don't act on what you've planned, you may as well not have bothered in the first place. The best financial plan in the world is useless if it's merely sitting on a shelf or in a file cabinet.

Second, *review your plan frequently.* Financial planning isn't a one-shot deal. By definition it's a process. You must alter your objectives, tactics, and actions as circumstances change. The changes in circumstances may be either general (such as the stock market's ups and downs) or personal (such as switching jobs or getting married). Either way, you need to see financial planning as dynamic, not static. Reviewing your plan once a year seems a safe minimum. Some people will have to do so more often. In addition, you should review your plan whenever a major life event occurs. Typical of such events would be:

- Changing jobs
- Getting married
- Having a new baby
- Receiving an inheritance
- Sending a child off to college
- Getting divorced
- Retiring

Although you may have used this book to focus on just one or two financial life events, consider reading about other such events as your life progresses.

Third, *maintain a long time horizon.* By its very nature, financial planning takes the long view. You should try to keep an eye on upcoming events as a way of controlling their effects on you. For instance, it's appropriate to start funding retirement 20 or 30 years before the event itself occurs. Many people find planning of this sort difficult precisely because the goal is distant and hard to imagine. Yet taking a short-term view may ultimately leave you in a bind. The same holds true for investment planning, which must respond to changes not only in investment vehicles but also to overall changes in the markets. Moreover, the long span of years required to reach some goals means that you must respond carefully to economic changes—interest rates, inflation rates, changes in investment vehicles, and so forth—to avoid negative consequences. What works well for you now may not work well later. Your own personal situation may change. Looking ahead can keep you a few steps ahead of circumstances that could cause trouble otherwise.

Fourth, *keep a close watch on your insurance position.* One of the most common mistakes that people make is being underinsured. You may have a splendid investment portfolio, but illness, disability, or death could leave your family strapped for liquid assets or even at the brink of financial disaster. Similarly, a car accident or a serious mishap on your property could leave you vulnerable to ruinous litigation. You must be properly insured. And your financial plan should take into account your changing insurance needs over the years, since the policies that serve you well at 50 or 65 will differ greatly from those that served you well at 30. Other factors will be decisions about distribution options late in life—for instance, whether to take the cash value from a life insurance policy as an annuity.

Fifth, *be wary of shortcuts and get-rich-quick schemes.* Financial planning isn't a path to painless wealth. Neither is it a process that you can simply delegate to someone else and forget about. Whether you seek professional help or go it alone, you'll have to educate yourself on the issues, size up your options thoughtfully, and make your own decisions. Anyone who promises instant riches may well have his or her own riches, not yours, in mind.

Finally, *consider obtaining professional assistance on your financial planning tasks.* Many financial planners are responsive to the variety of needs that their clients present. It's not necessary that you commit to a comprehensive planning program; you may be able to find someone who can assist you in certain ways initially and in other ways in the future. For instance, you may wish to gain an overview of the financial process at first; later, you'll focus on insurance issues or investment planning; still later, you'll zero in on estate planning. Alternatively, you may prefer to do most of your planning independently, then seek a professional assessment of your plan. Some people like the idea of establishing a long-term relationship with a financial planner, just as they have long-term relationships with a lawyer, a physician, and other professionals.

Whatever route to financial planning you take, we at Ernst & Young wish you happiness, health, and financial security throughout all of life's many stages and events.

INDEX

A Public Service of Ernst & Young's Financial Education Program

www.moneyopolis.org

ERNST & YOUNG LLP

SPECIAL CONSUMER OFFERS!

**Get a one dollar rebate on your purchase of each
of the following tax and financial planning books:**

For Year-Round Tax Planning:
$1.00 Rebate for *The Ernst & Young Tax Saver's Guide 2000*

For Preparing Federal Tax Returns:
$1.00 Rebate for *The Ernst & Young Tax Guide 2000*

For Financial Planning:
$1.00 Rebate for *Ernst & Young's Personal Financial Planning Guide, Third Edition*

OFFICIAL REFUND CERTIFICATE

I have purchased the Ernst & Young books checked below and have enclosed
the purchase receipt with the books' prices circled. Please send me the appropriate refund.

❑ (1 book) $1 Refund   ❑ (2 books) $2 Refund   ❑ (3 books) $3 Refund

Mail to: The E&Y Rebate Offer '00, P.O. Box 1357, Grand Rapids, MN 55745-1357.

Name (Please Print)

Address

City   State   Zip

Signature

Store Where Purchased